KB241878

HOW TO TOEFL® *i*BT
120
SPEAKING

넥서스

The Best Solution for TOEFL iBT

HOW TO TOEFL® iBT 120 SPEAKING

지은이 찰스 정
펴낸이 안용백
펴낸곳 (주) 넥서스

초판 1쇄 2008년 1월 5일
초판 3쇄 2008년 8월 30일

2판 1쇄 2011년 6월 20일
2판 2쇄 2011년 9월 10일

출판신고 1992년 4월 3일 제311-2002-2호
121-840 서울시 마포구 서교동 394-2
Tel (02)330-5500 Fax (02)330-5555

ISBN 978-89-5797-653-1 18740
     978-89-5797-651-7 (세트)

가격은 뒤표지에 있습니다.
잘못 만들어진 책은 구입처에서 바꾸어 드립니다.
본 책은 〈TOEFL iBT Final 120 speaking〉의 개정판입니다.

www.nexusbook.com

The Best Solution for TOEFL iBT

HOW
TO
TOEFL®

120

SPEAKING

찰스 정 지음

머리말

영어권 국가에서 공부하려는 학생들에게 필요한 영어 실력을 평가하는 것을 목적으로 만들어진 TOEFL 시험이 PBT와 CBT를 거쳐 TOEFL iBT라는 형태로 거듭나게 되었다. TOEFL 점수는 높지만 충분히 의사 표시를 하지 못하고 의사 소통을 하는 데 어려움을 겪는 학생들이 많았기에 TOEFL iBT는 영어의 네 가지 기본 영역인 listening, reading, speaking, writing을 충실하게 평가한다는 면에서 실질적인 영어 실력을 가늠하는 새로운 평가의 장을 열었다고 할 수 있다.

TOEFL iBT에서는 기존 TOEFL에 포함되어 있던 Structure 섹션이 제외되고 Speaking 섹션이 추가되었다. Speaking 섹션은 단순한 의사 소통이 아니라 주어진 주제에 대한 자신의 의견을 논리적으로 전개해야 한다는 점에서 많은 학생들에게 크나큰 도전이 아닐 수 없다. 또한 통합적인 평가를 지향하는 TOEFL iBT의 특성을 반영하는 Integrated Task는 Reading과 Listening을 Speaking과 접목시킨 새로운 형태의 문제로, 통합적인 영어 실력이 뒷받침되지 않으면 높은 점수를 얻기가 매우 어렵다. 지금까지의 TSE 강의 경험 및 TOEFL iBT 강의 경험을 고려해 볼 때 미국적 사고에 따라 논리적으로 자신의 생각을 전개하고, 중요한 정보를 효과적으로 요약 정리하고, 설득력 있게 이를 전개하는 연습을 꾸준히 하는 것이 TOEFL iBT Speaking 섹션에서의 고득점을 결정하는 중요한 요소임이 분명하다.

본 실전서는 지난 12년간 TSE를 강의한 노하우와 TOEFL iBT 강의 경력을 토대로 Speaking 섹션에 등장하는 문제를 Task별로 구성하였으며, 각 Task에 필요한 구체적인 학습 전략을 제시하였다. 또한 그동안 실제 TOEFL iBT에 출제되었던 문제를 구현한 다량의 실전형 문제를 수록하여, 철저하게 실전에 대비할 수 있도록 하였으며, 각 Task별로 자주 사용되는 유용한 표현 목록 및 연습 문제를 부록으로 수록하여 speaking 섹션에 출제되는 Task를 보다 효과적으로 대비하도록 하였다.

이 책이 TOEFL iBT Speaking이라는 낯선 산을 정복하는 든든한 길잡이가 되었으면 하는 바람이다.

찰스 정

교재의 구성

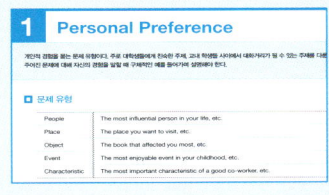

Strategy

각 task에서 요구되는 구체적인 전략을 소개하였으며, 고득점을 위해 적용해야 할 중요한 tip을 수록했다.

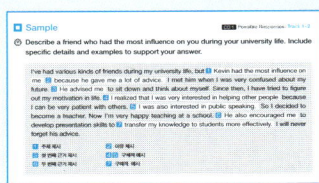

Sample

각 task별 문제를 소개함으로써 문제 유형을 정확하고 빠르게 이해할 수 있도록 했다.

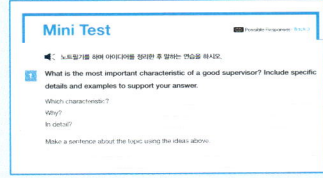

Mini Test

짧고 간단하게 구현된 문제를 통해 앞서 설명한 다양한 전략을 적용해 볼 수 있도록 했다.

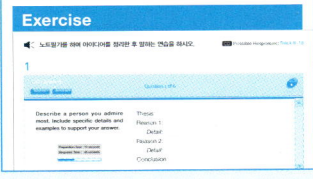

Exercise

iBT TOEFL에 실제로 출제된 문제를 구현하여 현실감 있는 연습을 유도하고 보다 난이도 높은 연습을 통해 실전 감각을 익힐 수 있도록 했다.

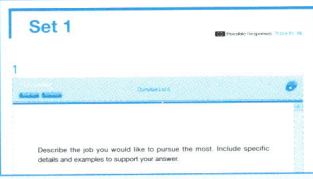

Actual Test

실전에 철저히 대비할 수 있도록 구현된 실전형 모의고사를 수록했다.

교재의 특징

High Quality of Contents

ETS의 문제 유형을 완벽히 분석하였으며, 이를 토대로 구현한 고난이도 실전 대비형 문제들을 풍부하게 수록했다.

Task-based Organization

Speaking 섹션에 출제되는 task별로 구성을 하여 문제 유형을 논리적으로 분석할 수 있도록 했으며, 쉽고 빠르게 해당 문제 유형에 익숙해 질 수 있도록 했다.

Building Strategies

각 task별로 꼭 주목해야 할 특징과 답을 전개하는 구체적인 전략들을 소개하고 이를 적용 연습하여 실전에 응용할 수 있는 능력을 함양하도록 했다.

Diversity

캠퍼스에서 발생하는 여러 가지 소재의 대화 지문 및 다양한 학문 분야의 학술적 강의를 통하여 주어진 문제에 대해 능동적으로 대처할 수 있는 능력을 키울 수 있도록 했다.

Effectiveness

스피킹 학습의 효율성을 도모하기 위해 Speaking Skill Workbook을 별도로 제공하여 각 task별로 유용한 표현을 익히고 문장을 통해 활용하는 연습을 충분히 할 수 있도록 했다.

목차

Part 1

Independent Task

Task 1

Personal Preference

1 Personal Preference

개인적 경험을 묻는 문제 유형이다. 주로 대학생들에게 친숙한 주제, 교내 학생들 사이에서 대화거리가 될 수 있는 주제를 다룬다. 주어진 문제에 대해 자신의 경험을 말할 때 구체적인 예를 들어가며 설명해야 한다.

◼ 문제 유형

People	The most influential person in your life, etc.
Place	The place you want to visit, etc.
Object	The book that affected you most, etc.
Event	The most enjoyable event in your childhood, etc.
Characteristic	The most important characteristic of a good co-worker, etc.

◼ 화면 구성

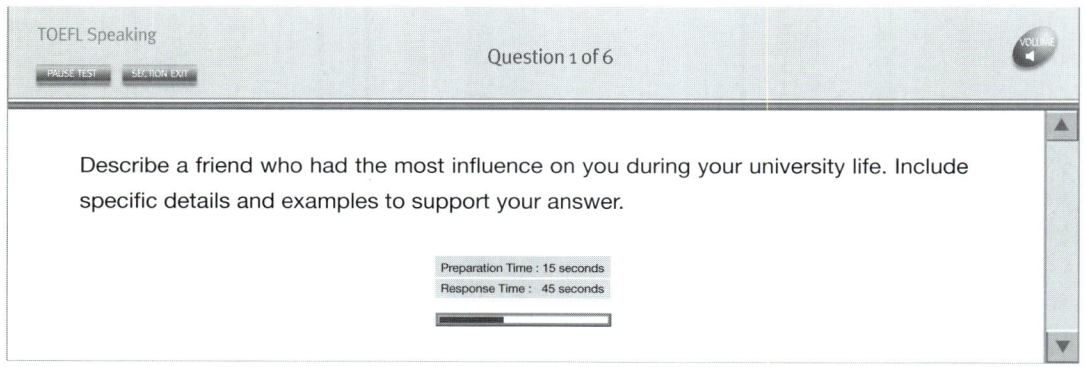

나레이션과 스크린으로 문제가 주어지는데, 15초간 준비한 후 45초 동안 대답한다.
주어진 문제를 스크린으로 보면서 답을 준비한다.

◼ Strategy

1단계 : 주제 이해 및 의사 표시하기

반드시 사실적인 경험에 근거해서 말할 필요는 없다. 답을 전개하기 쉬운 아이디어를 선택하면 효과적으로 답할 수 있다. 또한, 문제에서 주어진 keyword를 이용하면 답을 하는데 유용하다.

2단계 : 이유 설명하기

이유를 말할 때 일반 상식에 의존하여 답할 필요는 없다. 즉, 그 이유를 자신만의 관점에서 말할 수도 있고, 가상적으로 만들어서 답할 수도 있다. 또한, 특별한 이유를 말하기 위해 너무 시간을 소비할 필요는 없다. 이 문제는 아이디어를 시험하는 것이 아니라 논리적으로 이야기를 전개하는 능력을 평가하는 것이 목적임을 기억해야 한다. 참고로 너무 한국적이거나 외국인이 이해하기 힘든 문화에 대한 언급은 피하는 것이 좋다. 예) 개고기 문화

3단계 : 구체적인 이유 제시하기

예를 들어 "그녀는 친절하다"라는 사실을 설명하고자 할 때 "kind"라는 단어를 직접 언급하지 않고 구체적인 예시를 들어 그녀가 친절하다는 것을 느끼도록 한다.

4단계 : 요약 정리하기

앞서 말한 내용을 마무리하기 위해 끝에서 요점을 한 문장으로 간단히 요약하면 효과적이며, 이때 새로운 사실을 첨부해서는 안 된다. 주제문을 고쳐 말하면 요약하는데 도움이 된다.

Tip
1 이유와 예를 위주로 하는 간단한 틀을 짜고 이를 이용하여 답을 전개하는 것이 좋다
2 자신감 있게 답을 전개하라. 약간 오버해서 발음하고 억양을 주어 말하는 것이 좋다
3 평소 잘 사용하는 단어를 이용하여 답하라
4 지나치게 문법에 연연하지 마라
5 45초 동안에 말할 분량을 잘 조절하여 답하라

▣ Sample

CD Possible Response: Track 1

Q **Describe a friend who had the most influence on you during your university life. Include specific details and examples to support your answer.**

I've had various kinds of friends during my university life, but **1** Kevin had the most influence on me **2** because he gave me a lot of advice. I met him when I was very confused about my future. **3** He advised me to sit down and think about myself. Since then, I have tried to figure out my motivation in life. **4** I realized that I was very interested in helping other people because I can be very patient with others. **5** I was also interested in public speaking. So I decided to become a teacher. Now I'm very happy teaching at a school. **6** He also encouraged me to develop presentation skills to **7** transfer my knowledge to students more effectively. I will never forget his advice.

1 주제 제시
2 이유 제시
3 첫 번째 근거 제시
4 5 구체적 예시
6 두 번째 근거 제시
7 구체적 예시

Mini Test

🔊 노트필기를 하며 아이디어를 정리한 후 말하는 연습을 하시오.

1 **What is the most important characteristic of a good supervisor? Include specific details and examples to support your answer.**

Which characteristic?

Why?

In detail?

Make a sentence about the topic using the ideas above.

2 **What do you consider to be the most important room in a house? Why is this room more important to you than any other room? Include specific details and examples to support your answer.**

Which room?

Why?

In detail?

Make a sentence about the topic using the ideas above.

3 **What do you want to accomplish in the future? Include specific details and examples to support your answer.**

What?

Why?

In detail?

Make a sentence about the topic using the ideas above.

4 Describe the most enjoyable event in your childhood. Include specific details and examples to support your answer.

Which event?

Why?

In detail?

Make a sentence about the topic using the ideas above.

5 What is the most important characteristic of a good co-worker? Include specific details and examples to support your answer.

Which characteristic?

Why?

In detail?

Make a sentence about the topic using the ideas above.

6 Describe a book that affected you the most. Include specific details and examples to support your answer.

Which book?

Why?

In detail?

Make a sentence about the topic using the ideas above.

7 Describe the most memorable event from the schools you attended. Include specific details and examples to support your answer.

Which event?

Why?

In detail?

Make a sentence about the topic using the ideas above.

_____

_____

_____

8 Choose a city that you wish to visit that you've never been to. Include specific details and examples to support your answer.

Which city?

Why?

In detail?

Make a sentence about the topic using the ideas above.

_____

_____

_____

9 What was the most important decision in your life? Include specific details and examples to support your answer.

Which decision?

Why?

In detail?

Make a sentence about the topic using the ideas above.

_____

_____

_____

10 **Describe the most disappointing moment in your life. Include specific details and examples to support your answer.**

Which moment?

Why?

In detail?

Make a sentence about the topic using the ideas above.

11 **Describe a challenge that you overcame. Include specific details and examples to support your answer.**

What?

Why?

In detail?

Make a sentence about the topic using the ideas above.

12 **Describe the best time of the year. Include specific details and examples to support your answer.**

Which season?

Why?

In detail?

Make a sentence about the topic using the ideas above.

13 What do you consider most when you choose a restaurant or a cafe? Include specific details and examples to support your answer.

Which feature? _____

Why? _____

In detail? _____

Make a sentence about the topic using the ideas above.

_____

_____

_____

14 What sport do you think will become more popular in your country in ten years? Include specific details and examples to support your answer.

Which sports? _____

Why? _____

In detail? _____

Make a sentence about the topic using the ideas above.

_____

_____

_____

15 Every country has its own traditional drinks. Which traditional drink is famous in your country? Include specific details and examples to support your answer.

Which drink? _____

Why? _____

In detail? _____

Make a sentence about the topic using the ideas above.

_____

_____

_____

16 Describe a tourist attraction in your city. Include specific details and examples to support your answer.

Which place? _____

Why? _____

In detail? _____

Make a sentence about the topic using the ideas above.

_____

_____

_____

17 Choose a skill that is necessary to be successful in the world today. Include specific details and examples to support your answer.

Which skill? _____

Why? _____

In detail? _____

Make a sentence about the topic using the ideas above.

_____

_____

_____

18 Describe a poem, a song, or a painting that is impressive to you. Include specific details and examples to support your answer.

What? _____

Why? _____

In detail? _____

Make a sentence about the topic using the ideas above.

_____

_____

_____

19 Describe one of your goals in life. Include specific details and examples to support your answer.

What?

Why?

In detail?

Make a sentence about the topic using the ideas above.

20 Describe a special opportunity that was given to you. Include specific details and examples to support your answer.

What?

Why?

In detail?

Make a sentence about the topic using the ideas above.

21 Describe a job you would like to have. Include specific details and examples to support your answer.

What?

Why?

In detail?

Make a sentence about the topic using the ideas above.

22 Describe a skill or something that you are good at. Include specific details and examples to support your answer.

What?

Why?

In detail?

Make a sentence about the topic using the ideas above.

23 What is the most important characteristic of a good leader? Include specific details and examples to support your answer.

Which characteristic?

Why?

In detail?

Make a sentence about the topic using the ideas above.

24 When do you miss your family or country the most? Include specific details and examples to support your answer.

When?

Why?

In detail?

Make a sentence about the topic using the ideas above.

Exercise

🔊 노트필기를 하며 아이디어를 정리한 후 말하는 연습을 하시오.　　🔲 CD Possible Responses: Track 8~15

1

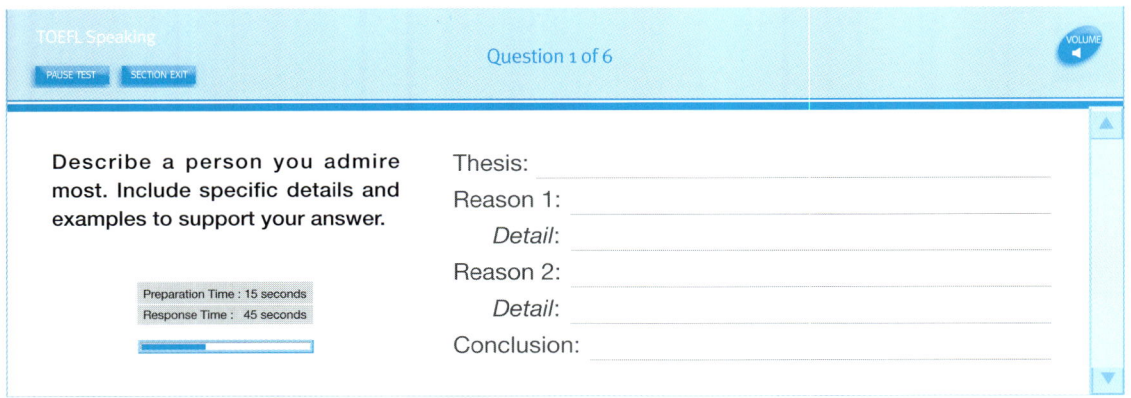

▶ 자신이 녹음한 답변을 듣고 받아쓰기 하시오.

2

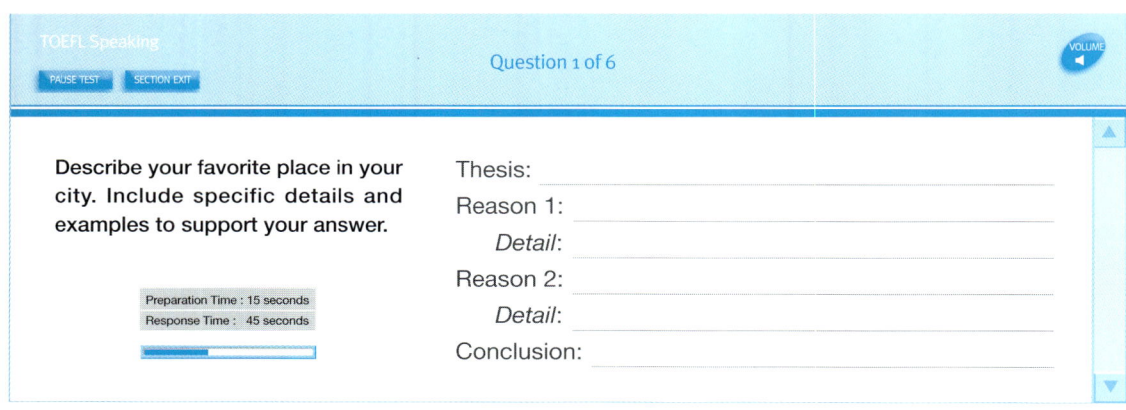

▶ 자신이 녹음한 답변을 듣고 받아쓰기 하시오.

3

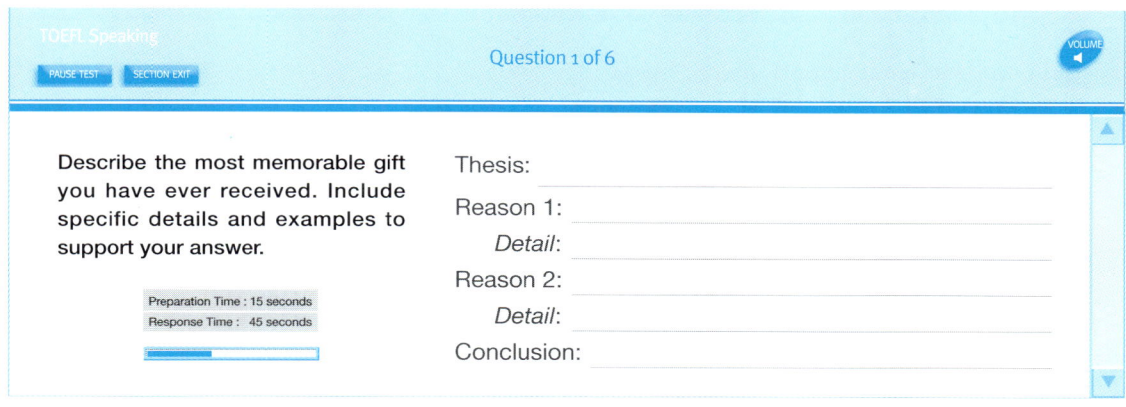

Describe the most memorable gift you have ever received. Include specific details and examples to support your answer.

Preparation Time : 15 seconds
Response Time : 45 seconds

Thesis:
Reason 1:
   Detail:
Reason 2:
   Detail:
Conclusion:

▶ 자신이 녹음한 답변을 듣고 받아쓰기 하시오.

4

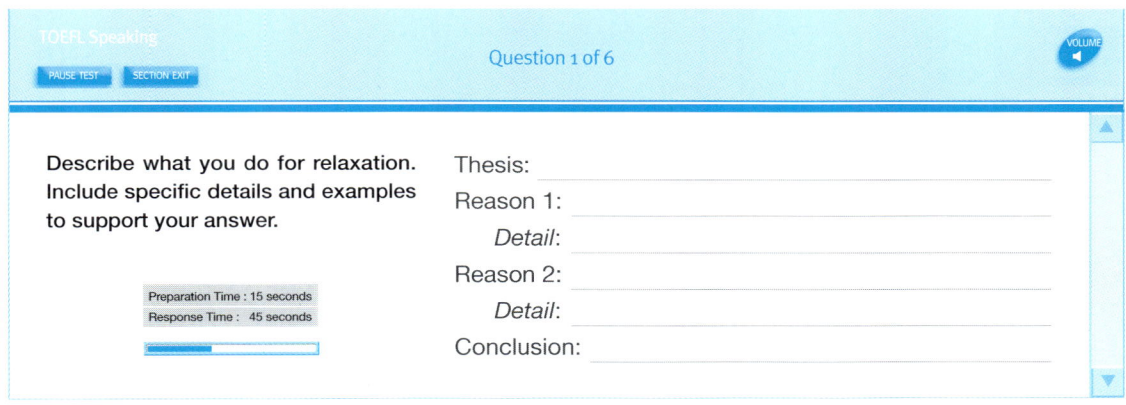

Describe what you do for relaxation. Include specific details and examples to support your answer.

Preparation Time : 15 seconds
Response Time : 45 seconds

Thesis:
Reason 1:
   Detail:
Reason 2:
   Detail:
Conclusion:

▶ 자신이 녹음한 답변을 듣고 받아쓰기 하시오.

Exercise

5

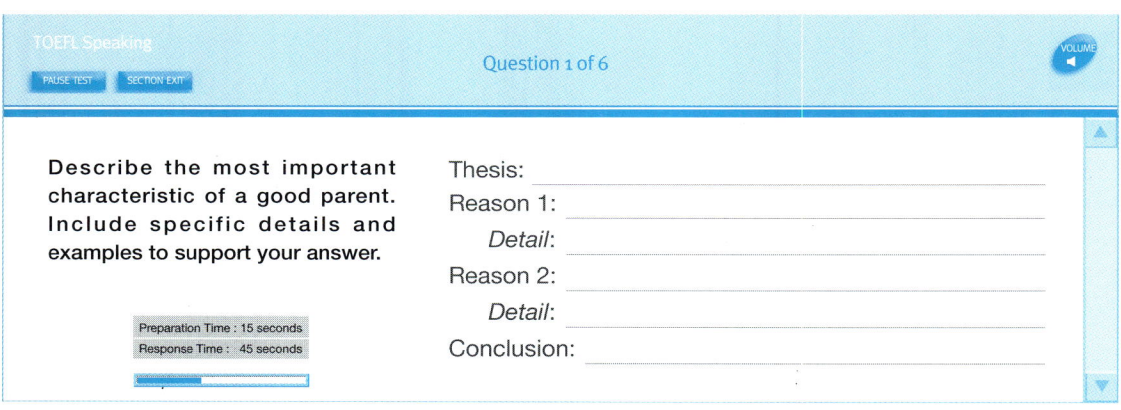

Describe the most important characteristic of a good parent. Include specific details and examples to support your answer.

Preparation Time : 15 seconds
Response Time : 45 seconds

Thesis:
Reason 1:
   Detail:
Reason 2:
   Detail:
Conclusion:

▶ 자신이 녹음한 답변을 듣고 받아쓰기 하시오.

6

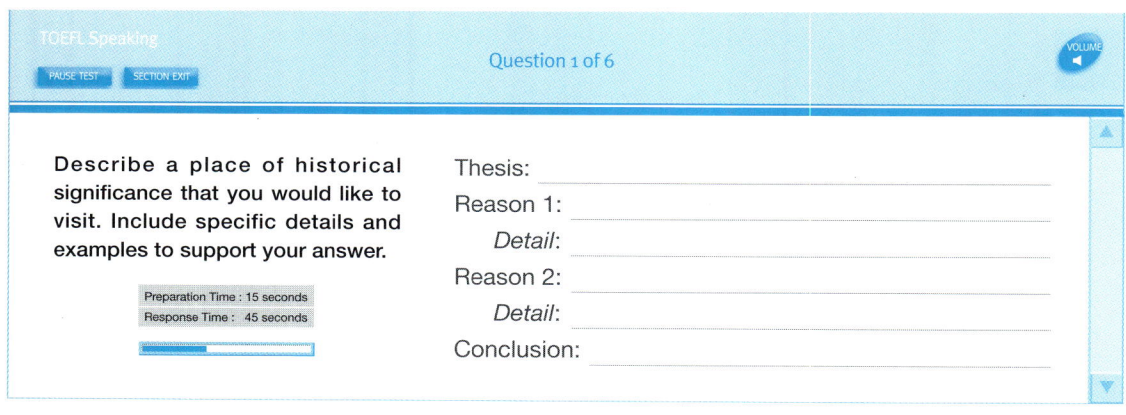

Describe a place of historical significance that you would like to visit. Include specific details and examples to support your answer.

Preparation Time : 15 seconds
Response Time : 45 seconds

Thesis:
Reason 1:
   Detail:
Reason 2:
   Detail:
Conclusion:

▶ 자신이 녹음한 답변을 듣고 받아쓰기 하시오.

7

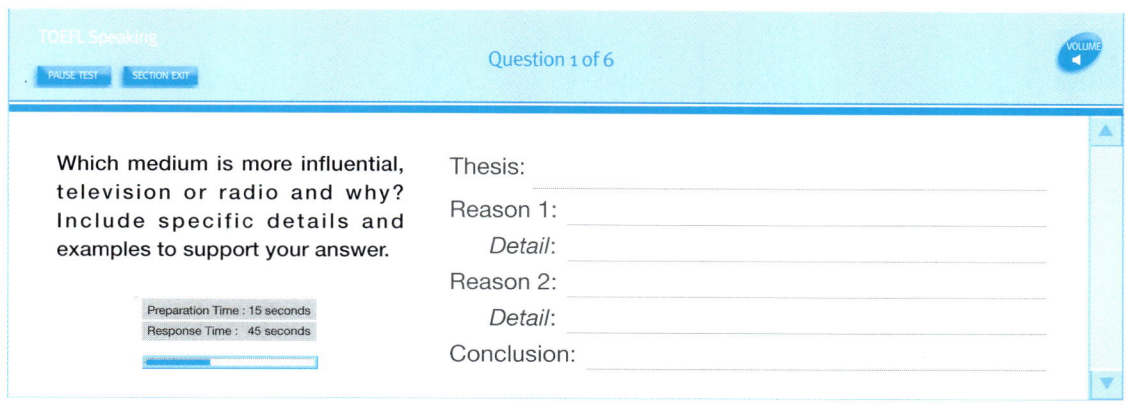

Which medium is more influential, television or radio and why? Include specific details and examples to support your answer.

Preparation Time : 15 seconds
Response Time :   45 seconds

Thesis: ....
Reason 1: ....
　　Detail: ....
Reason 2: ....
　　Detail: ....
Conclusion: ....

▶ 자신이 녹음한 답변을 듣고 받아쓰기 하시오.

8

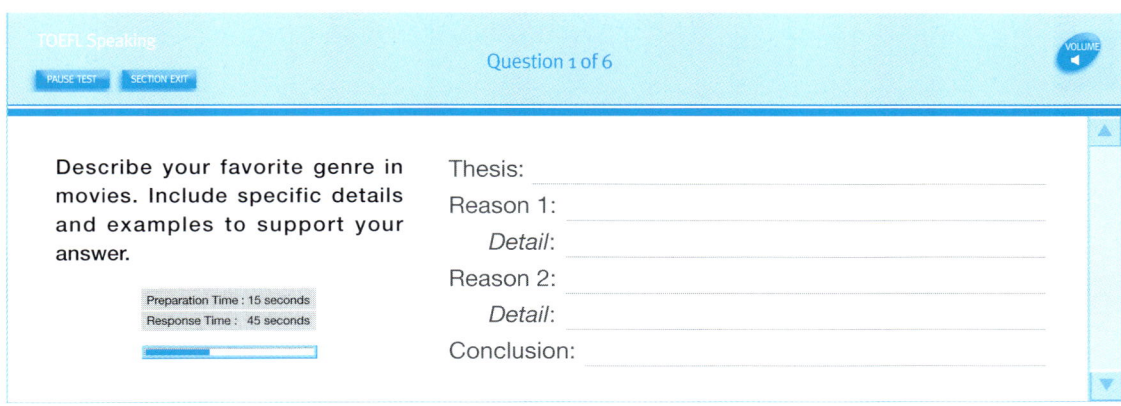

Describe your favorite genre in movies. Include specific details and examples to support your answer.

Preparation Time : 15 seconds
Response Time :   45 seconds

Thesis: ....
Reason 1: ....
　　Detail: ....
Reason 2: ....
　　Detail: ....
Conclusion: ....

▶ 자신이 녹음한 답변을 듣고 받아쓰기 하시오.

Task 2

Paired Choice

2 Paired Choice

두 가지 상반되는 상황을 주고 그 중 하나를 선택해 주장을 전개하거나, 주어진 의견에 대한 찬반을 논하는 문제이다. 주제와 관련된 생각을 논리적으로, 자연스럽고 유창하게 전개하는 능력을 평가한다. 주어진 두 가지 대상에서 하나를 선택하고, 그 대상을 선택한 이유를 설명하고 구체적인 예시를 제공해야 한다.

■ 문제 유형

Type 1	하나의 주제가 주어지고, 두 가지 선택 중 어느 쪽을 선택할지 묻는 유형
	- Some people think it is better to eat at home, while others think it is better to eat at restaurants. Which do you think is the better?
Type 2	- Some people take a long time to make a decision and others make it immediately. Which do you prefer and why? 대립되는 두 주제가 주어지고, 어느 의견에 동의하는지 묻는 유형
	- Do you agree that television is harmful to children? - Do you agree or disagree with the following statement? Telling the truth is always the best choice.

■ 화면 구성

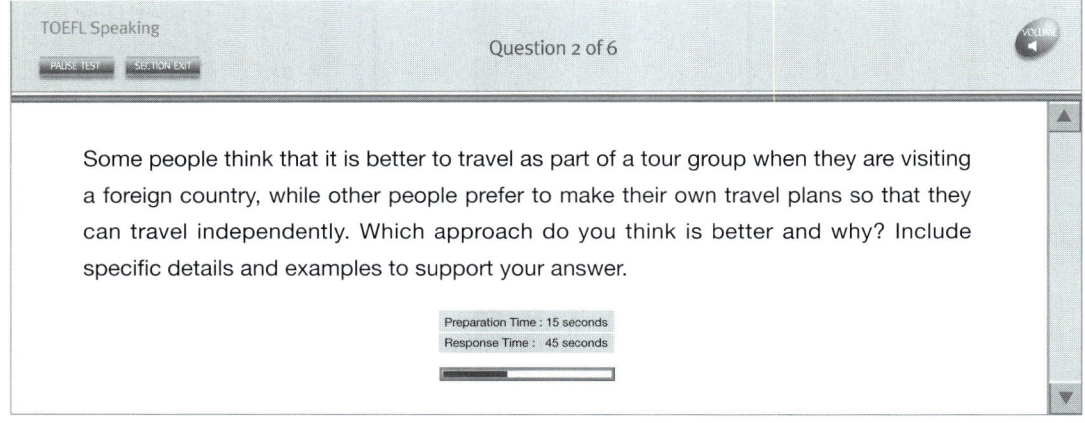

나레이션과 스크린으로 문제가 주어지는데, 15초간 준비한 후 45초간 설명한다.
주어진 문제를 스크린으로 보면서 답을 준비한다.

■ Strategy

※ 논리를 전개하는 방식은 TASK 1과 동일하지만 TASK 2 고유의 비법들이 있다.

답변이 용이한 선택하기

짧은 시간에 풍부한 내용의 답변을 만들어 낼 수 있는 것으로 고른다. 도입 부분에 반대의 의견을 언급하면서 시작하는 것도 효과적인 방법 중 하나이다. 한 대상의 단점은 다른 한쪽의 장점이 될 수 있음을 기억하자.

비교/대조 사용하기

선택한 것의 장점과 선택하지 않은 것의 단점을 적절히 섞어가며 말한다. 선택한 것의 장점을 주로 말하고 선택하지 않은 것의 단점을 첨가하여 말하면 비교 후 나은 것을 선택했다는 신뢰감을 줄 수 있다. 분명하고 명확한 장점을 선택하는 것이 훨씬 설득력이 있다.

선택한 것의 장점 부각하기

45초는 짧다. 선택하지 않은 것의 단점보다는 선택한 것의 장점을 부각시켜 말하는 것이 더 효과적인 전략이다.

중립적인 답변 피하기

45초 안에 두 가지 대상에 대한 완벽한 논리를 세우는 것은 쉬운 일이 아니다. 둘 다 좋다거나 둘 다 싫다는 말을 할 수 있다면 가능하지만, 말하기에 능숙한 사람이 아니라면 추천할 만한 방법은 아니다. 예시를 충분히 들 수 있는 쪽으로 선택하여 말하는 것이 유리하다.

■ Sample

CD Possible Response: **Track 16**

Q Some people think that it is better to travel as part of a tour group when they are visiting a foreign country, while other people prefer to make their own travel plans so that they can travel independently. Which approach do you think is better and why? Include specific details and examples to support your answer.

> I have taken various tours, but **1** I would rather make my own travel plans for a couple of reasons. **2** First of all , people in a group tend to miss out on the exotic culture of the country they are visiting. **3** For example, they usually stay in large hotels where they are served basic meals and do not get a chance to taste the exotic food of that particular country. **4** Secondly, another reason that I like to travel by myself is that I am an adventurous person, so I like to explore places that not many people have been to. **5** These are the reasons why I like traveling alone.

1 주제 제시
2 첫 번째 근거 제시
3 구체적 예시
4 두 번째 근거 제시
5 요약 정리

Mini Test

CD Possible Responses: Track 18

🔊 노트필기를 하며 아이디어를 정리한 후 말하는 연습을 하시오.

1 Some students like to study at school, while others like to study at home. Which do you prefer and why? Include specific details and examples to support your answer.

Your preference? _____

Why? _____

In detail? _____

Make a sentence about the topic using the ideas above.

_____

_____

2 When trying to find a job, some people think money is the most important factor, while others think their aptitude is more important. Which do you agree with and why? Include specific details and examples to support your answer.

Your opinion? _____

Why? _____

In detail? _____

Make a sentence about the topic using the ideas above.

_____

_____

3 Some people like to participate in indoor activities while others like to participate in outdoor activities. Which do you prefer and why? Include specific details and examples to support your answer.

Your preference? _____

Why? _____

In detail? _____

Make a sentence about the topic using the ideas above.

_____

_____

4 Do you agree or disagree with the following statement? Telling the truth is always the best choice. Include specific details and examples to support your answer.

Your opinion? _____
Why? _____
In detail? _____

Make a sentence about the topic using the ideas above.

_____
_____

5 Some people think most of what they learn happens outside of the classroom, while others think it happens in the classroom. Which do you agree with and why? Include specific details and examples to support your answer.

Your opinion? _____
Why? _____
In detail? _____

Make a sentence about the topic using the ideas above.

_____
_____

6 Some people like to learn by listening to people around them such as friends and family, while others like to learn from their own experience. Which do you prefer and why? Include specific details and examples to support your answer.

Your preference? _____
Why? _____
In detail? _____

Make a sentence about the topic using the ideas above.

_____
_____

7 Some people like to watch movies during their free time, while others like to read books. Which do you prefer and why? Include specific details and examples to support your answer.

Your preference? _____
Why? _____
In detail? _____

Make a sentence about the topic using the ideas above.

_____

_____

8 Some people prefer to study for their assignments in groups, while others like to study individually. Which do you prefer and why? Include specific details and examples to support your answer.

Your preference? _____
Why? _____
In detail? _____

Make a sentence about the topic using the ideas above.

_____

_____

9 Some students like to live in a dormitory on campus, while other students like to live in their own apartment. Which do you prefer and why? Include specific details and examples to support your answer.

Your preference? _____
Why? _____
In detail? _____

Make a sentence about the topic using the ideas above.

_____

10 Some people are always in a hurry to go to places and get things done. Other people prefer to take their time and live life at a slower pace. Which do you prefer and why? Include specific details and examples to support your answer.

Your preference? _____

Why? _____

In detail? _____

Make a sentence about the topic using the ideas above.

_____

_____

11 While traveling, some people like to get to their destinations quickly and others take their time to explore places here and there. Which do you prefer and why? Include specific details and examples to support your answer.

Your preference? _____

Why? _____

In detail? _____

Make a sentence about the topic using the ideas above.

_____

_____

12 Some people take a long time to make a decision and others make it immediately. Which do you prefer and why? Include specific details and examples to support your answer.

Your preference? _____

Why? _____

In detail? _____

Make a sentence about the topic using the ideas above.

_____

_____

13 Some people like to work for themselves or own a business. Others prefer to work for an employer. Would you rather be self-employed or work for someone else? Include specific details and examples to support your answer.

Your preference? _____

Why? _____

In detail? _____

Make a sentence about the topic using the ideas above.

_____

_____

14 Some people prefer to talk to their friends on the telephone. Other people write a letter or send an e-mail. Which means of communication do you like and why? Include specific details and examples to support your answer.

Your preference? _____

Why? _____

In detail? _____

Make a sentence about the topic using the ideas above.

_____

_____

15 Some students like to take large classes, while others like to attend small classes. Which do you prefer and why? Include specific details and examples to support your answer.

Your preference? _____

Why? _____

In detail? _____

Make a sentence about the topic using the ideas above.

_____

_____

16 Some people believe that parents should limit their children's TV hours, while others believe that they should let them watch TV without limitations. Which view do you agree with and why? Include specific details and examples to support your answer.

Your preference? _____

Why? _____

In detail? _____

Make a sentence about the topic using the ideas above.

_____

_____

17 Do you agree or disagree with the following statement? Students should not be allowed to bring their cell phones to class. Include specific details and examples to support your answer.

Your preference? _____

Why? _____

In detail? _____

Make a sentence about the topic using the ideas above.

_____

_____

18 Some people think business success is more important than friendship. What do you think is more important and why? Include specific details and examples to support your answer.

Your preference? _____

Why? _____

In detail? _____

Make a sentence about the topic using the ideas above.

_____

_____

19 Some people like to work on many things at the same time. Others like to do one thing at a time. Which do you prefer and why? Include specific details and examples to support your answer.

Your preference? _____

Why? _____

In detail? _____

Make a sentence about the topic using the ideas above.

_____

_____

20 Some students like to enroll as full-time students, while others prefer going to school part-time. Which do you prefer and why? Include specific details and examples to support your answer.

Your preference? _____

Why? _____

In detail? _____

Make a sentence about the topic using the ideas above.

_____

_____

21 Do you agree or disagree with the following statement? The best way to learn about a new city is visiting its landmarks or historical monuments. Include specific details and examples to support your answer.

Your preference? _____

Why? _____

In detail? _____

Make a sentence about the topic using the ideas above.

_____

_____

22 Some people say that conserving old buildings is more important than constructing new buildings, while others believe constructing new buildings is more important. Which view do you agree with and why? Include specific details and examples to support your answer.

Your preference? _____

Why? _____

In detail? _____

Make a sentence about the topic using the ideas above.

_____

_____

23 Some people like to plan out their trips while others like to play it by ear. Which do you prefer and why? Include specific details and examples to support your answer.

Your preference? _____

Why? _____

In detail? _____

Make a sentence about the topic using the ideas above.

_____

_____

24 Some people like to read a book until they finish it, while others like to start new books without finishing them. Which do you prefer and why? Include specific details and examples to support your answer.

Your preference? _____

Why? _____

In detail? _____

Make a sentence about the topic using the ideas above.

_____

_____

25 Some individuals believe that people need to learn how to play a musical instrument from childhood. Do you agree or disagree with this idea? Include specific details and examples to support your answer.

Your opinion?

Why?

In detail?

Make a sentence about the topic using the ideas above.

26 Some people trust their first impressions about a person's character because they believe these judgments are generally correct, while others do not judge a person's character quickly because they believe first impressions are often wrong. Which do you agree with and why? Include specific details and examples to support your answer.

Your opinion?

Why?

In detail?

Make a sentence about the topic using the ideas above.

27 Some people say that childhood is the best time of one's life. Do you agree or disagree with this idea? Include specific details and examples to support your answer.

Your opinion?

Why?

In detail?

Make a sentence about the topic using the ideas above.

28 Some people think trying new food is better than trying familiar foods all the time. Do you agree or disagree with this idea? Include specific details and examples to support your answer.

Your opinion? _____

Why? _____

In detail? _____

Make a sentence about the topic using the ideas above.

_____

_____

29 Do you agree or disagree with the following statement? Some people think high school students should wear school uniforms. Include specific details and examples to support your answer.

Your opinion? _____

Why? _____

In detail? _____

Make a sentence about the topic using the ideas above.

_____

_____

30 Some people like to read newspapers or magazines to get information, while others watch TV or other media to get it. Which do you prefer and why? Include specific details and examples to support your answer.

Your preference? _____

Why? _____

In detail? _____

Make a sentence about the topic using the ideas above.

_____

_____

Exercise

🔊 노트필기를 하며 아이디어를 정리한 후 말하는 연습을 하시오. 　　　**CD** Possible Responses: Track 24~31

1

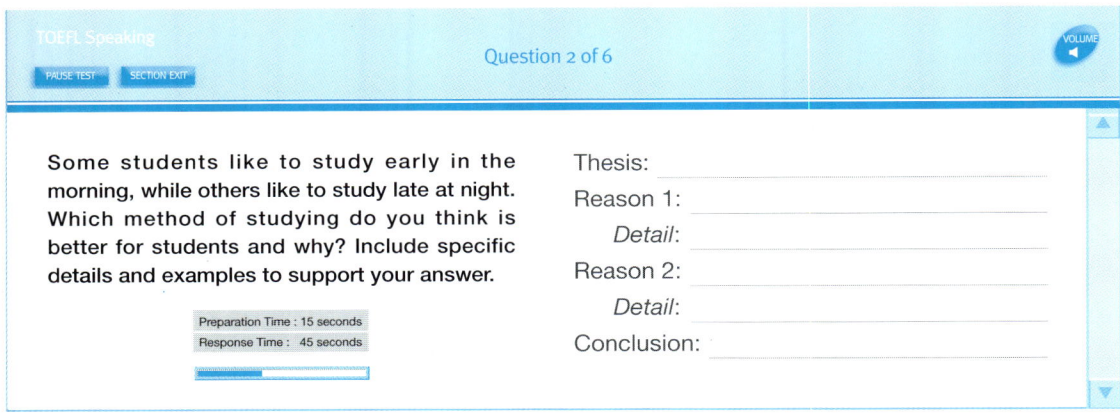

TOEFL Speaking　　　　　　　Question 2 of 6　　　　　　　VOLUME ◀
[PAUSE TEST] [SECTION EXIT]

Some students like to study early in the morning, while others like to study late at night. Which method of studying do you think is better for students and why? Include specific details and examples to support your answer.

Preparation Time : 15 seconds
Response Time :   45 seconds

Thesis:
Reason 1: _____
　　Detail: _____
Reason 2: _____
　　Detail: _____
Conclusion: _____

▶ 자신이 녹음한 답변을 듣고 받아쓰기 하시오.

_____

_____

_____

2

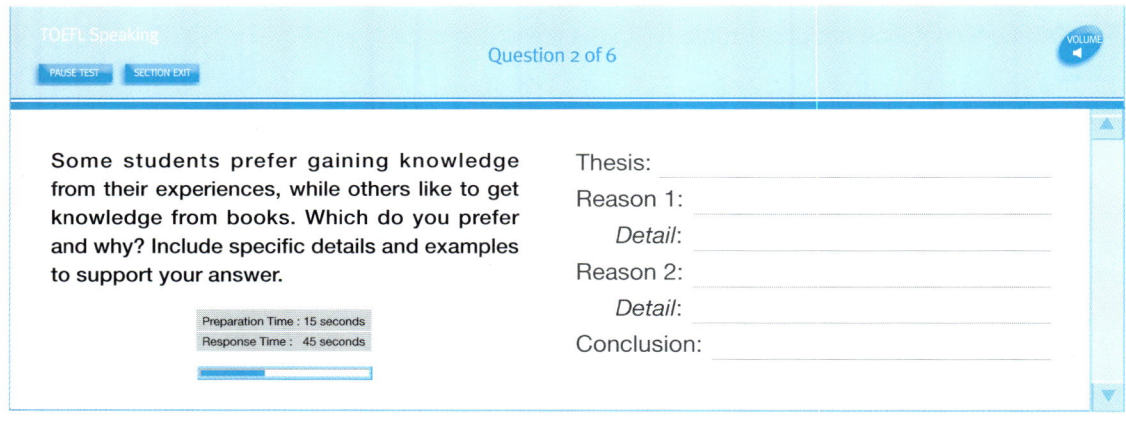

TOEFL Speaking　　　　　　　Question 2 of 6　　　　　　　VOLUME ◀
[PAUSE TEST] [SECTION EXIT]

Some students prefer gaining knowledge from their experiences, while others like to get knowledge from books. Which do you prefer and why? Include specific details and examples to support your answer.

Preparation Time : 15 seconds
Response Time :   45 seconds

Thesis:
Reason 1: _____
　　Detail: _____
Reason 2: _____
　　Detail: _____
Conclusion: _____

▶ 자신이 녹음한 답변을 듣고 받아쓰기 하시오.

_____

_____

_____

3

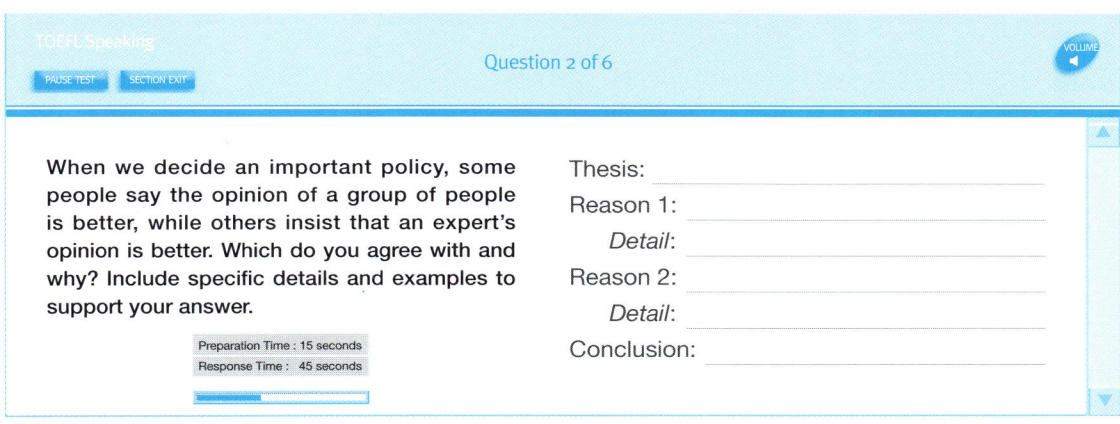

When we decide an important policy, some people say the opinion of a group of people is better, while others insist that an expert's opinion is better. Which do you agree with and why? Include specific details and examples to support your answer.

Preparation Time : 15 seconds
Response Time :   45 seconds

Thesis: _____
Reason 1: _____
   Detail: _____
Reason 2: _____
   Detail: _____
Conclusion: _____

▶ 자신이 녹음한 답변을 듣고 받아쓰기 하시오.

_____

_____

_____

4

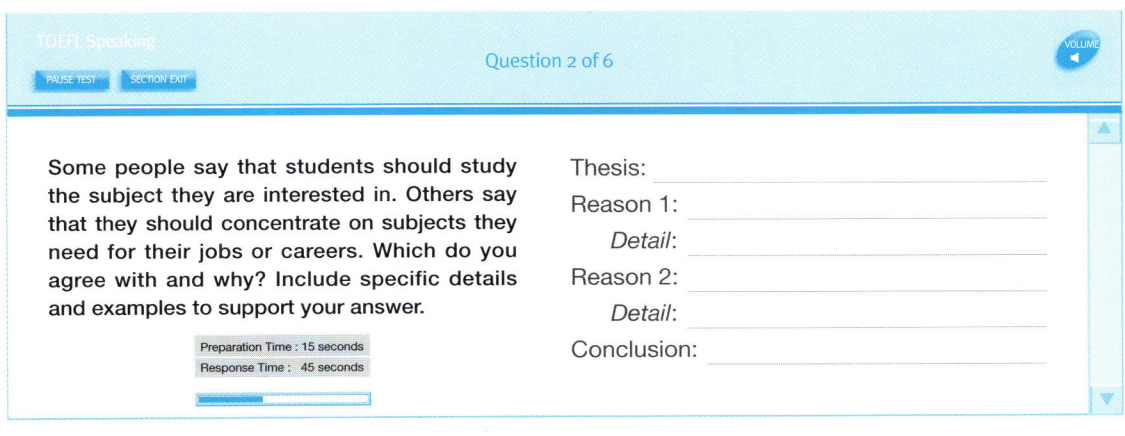

Some people say that students should study the subject they are interested in. Others say that they should concentrate on subjects they need for their jobs or careers. Which do you agree with and why? Include specific details and examples to support your answer.

Preparation Time : 15 seconds
Response Time :   45 seconds

Thesis: _____
Reason 1: _____
   Detail: _____
Reason 2: _____
   Detail: _____
Conclusion: _____

▶ 자신이 녹음한 답변을 듣고 받아쓰기 하시오.

_____

_____

_____

Exercise

5

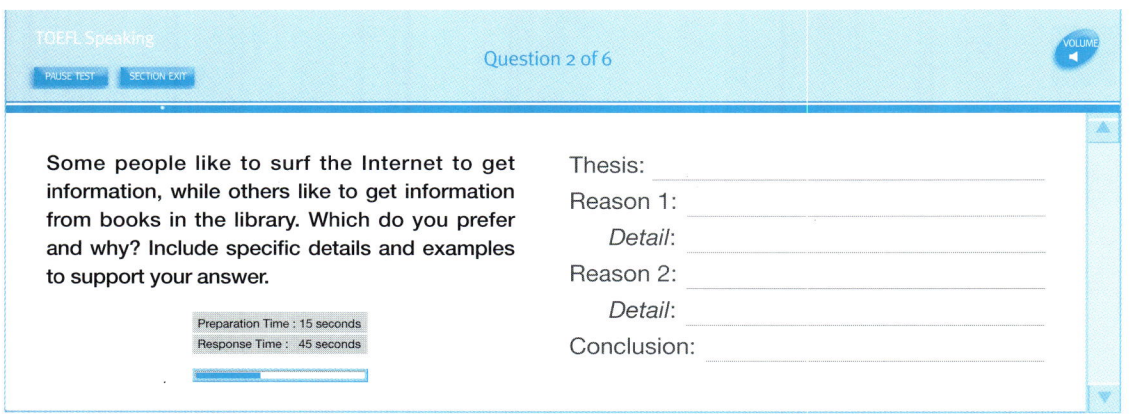

PAUSE TEST   SECTION EXIT   VOLUME

Some people like to surf the Internet to get information, while others like to get information from books in the library. Which do you prefer and why? Include specific details and examples to support your answer.

Preparation Time : 15 seconds
Response Time :   45 seconds

Thesis: _____
Reason 1: _____
    Detail: _____
Reason 2: _____
    Detail: _____
Conclusion: _____

▶ 자신이 녹음한 답변을 듣고 받아쓰기 하시오.

_____

_____

_____

6

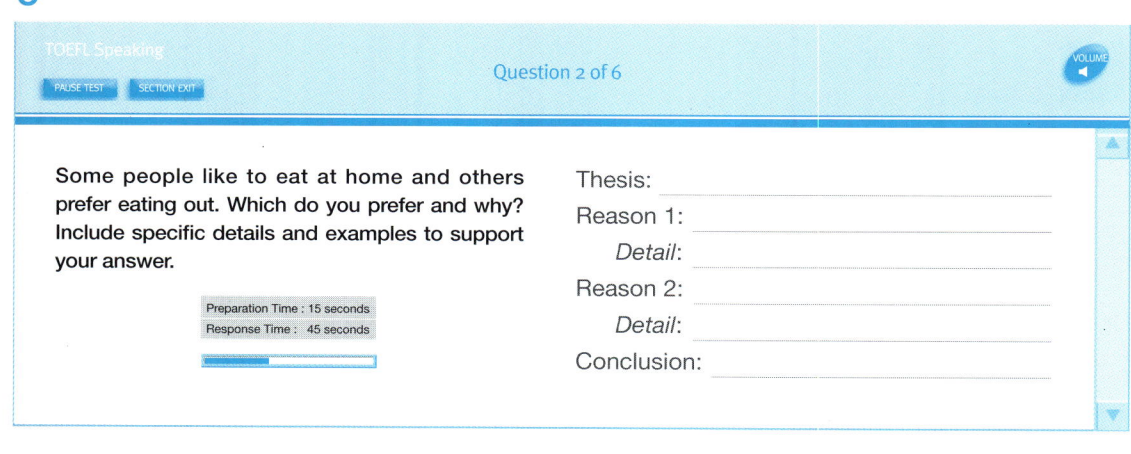

PAUSE TEST   SECTION EXIT   VOLUME

Some people like to eat at home and others prefer eating out. Which do you prefer and why? Include specific details and examples to support your answer.

Preparation Time : 15 seconds
Response Time :   45 seconds

Thesis: _____
Reason 1: _____
    Detail: _____
Reason 2: _____
    Detail: _____
Conclusion: _____

▶ 자신이 녹음한 답변을 듣고 받아쓰기 하시오.

_____

_____

_____

7

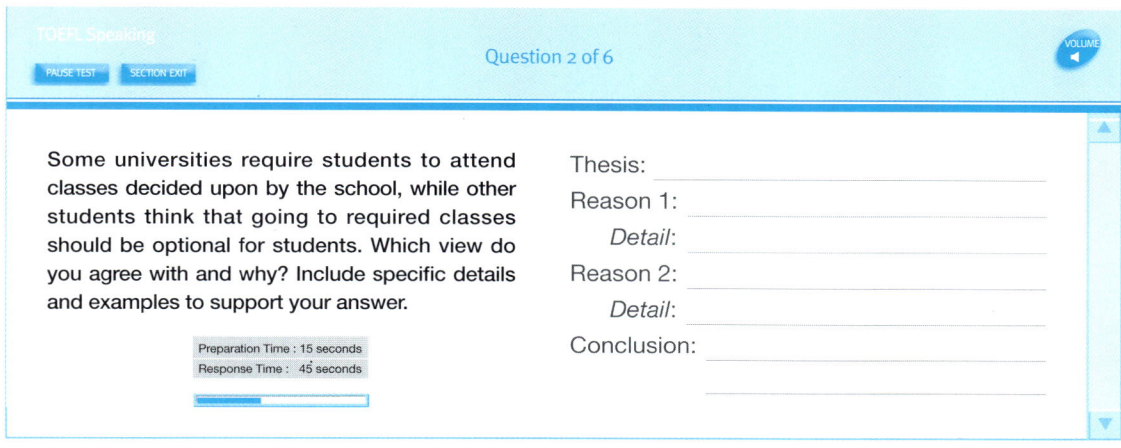

Some universities require students to attend classes decided upon by the school, while other students think that going to required classes should be optional for students. Which view do you agree with and why? Include specific details and examples to support your answer.

Preparation Time : 15 seconds
Response Time : 45 seconds

Thesis: _____
Reason 1: _____
    Detail: _____
Reason 2: _____
    Detail: _____
Conclusion: _____

▶ 자신이 녹음한 답변을 듣고 받아쓰기 하시오.

_____
_____
_____

8

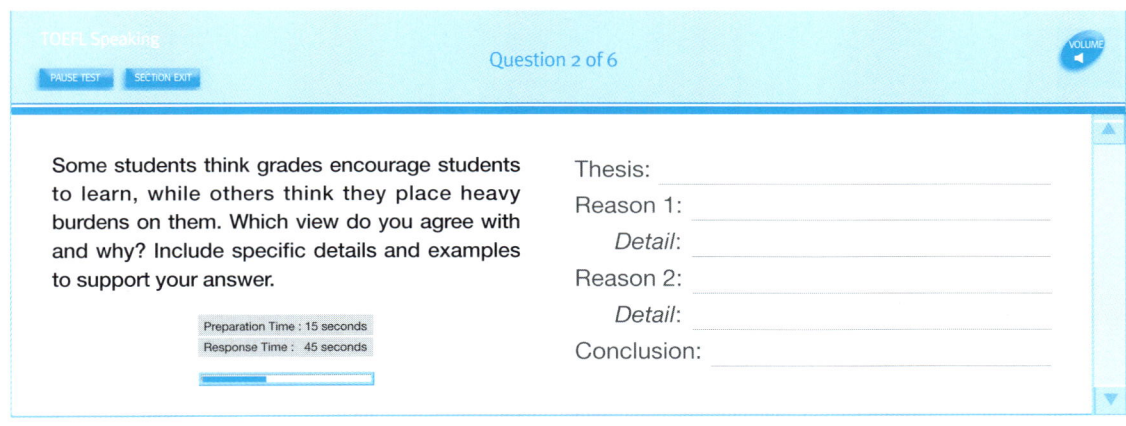

Some students think grades encourage students to learn, while others think they place heavy burdens on them. Which view do you agree with and why? Include specific details and examples to support your answer.

Preparation Time : 15 seconds
Response Time : 45 seconds

Thesis: _____
Reason 1: _____
    Detail: _____
Reason 2: _____
    Detail: _____
Conclusion: _____

▶ 자신이 녹음한 답변을 듣고 받아쓰기 하시오.

_____
_____
_____

Part 2

Integrated Task

Task 3

Fit and Explain

3 | Fit and Explain

읽기, 듣기, 말하기가 결합된 문제 유형이다. 45초 동안 짧은 지문을 읽은 후 그 주제에 관련된 두 학생의 대화를 듣고, 둘 중 한 학생의 의견을 요약한다. 답을 전개할 때는 읽고 들은 정보와 의견을 이해하고 선별하는 능력과 이를 정확하고 완성도 있게, 그리고 논리적으로 요약하는 능력을 보여주어야 한다.

■ 문제 유형

읽기	길이	45초 (75–100단어)
	종류	announcement from the dean, article from the campus newspaper, letter to a campus newspaper editor, etc.
	소재	campus-related issues (new facilities on campus, changed parking policy on campus, dining service, etc.)
듣기	길이	60–80초 (150–180단어)
	내용	남, 여학생이 방금 읽은 지문에 대해 찬/반을 표시하고 그 이유를 두 가지로 밝힌다
말하기	내용	한 명의 의견과 그에 대한 근거를 읽기 지문을 사용하여 요약하시오

■ 기출 주제

- Announcement from the President
- Statue for the School
- Removal of Evening Classes
- Now Hiring: Computer Lab Assistant
- Health Center
- Building a New Dorm Off Campus
- Library Expansion

- Changing the Computer Lab Policy
- Change in the Final Exam
- New Dean of the Humanities Department
- Dining service
- Writing Requirements for Science Majors
- University Parking Policy

■ 화면 구성

1 읽기 : 대학 생활에 관련된 내용을 45초간 독해한다.

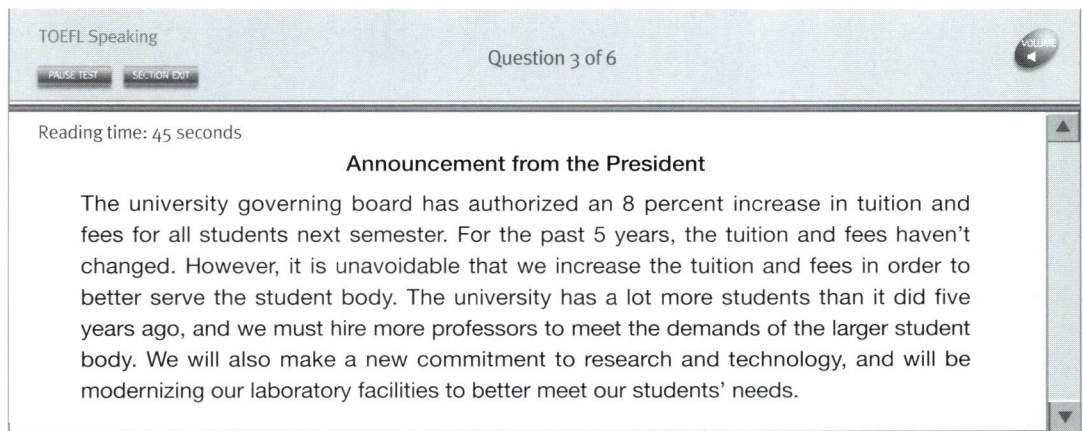

2 듣기: 읽기 지문의 내용에 찬성 / 반대하는 두 학생의 대화를 60~80초간 청취한다.

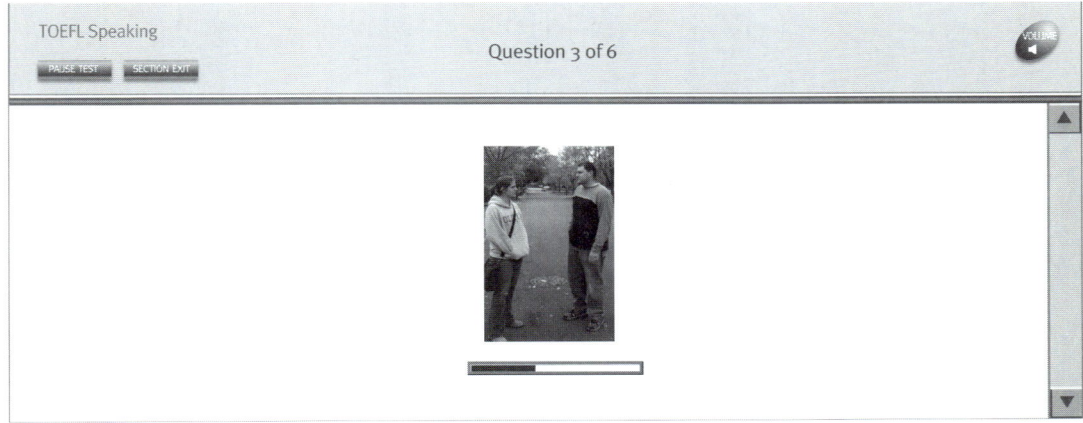

3 말하기: 남 / 여학생 중 한 명을 지정하여 그 / 그녀의 의견과 그 이유를 30초간 준비한 후, 60초간 말한다.

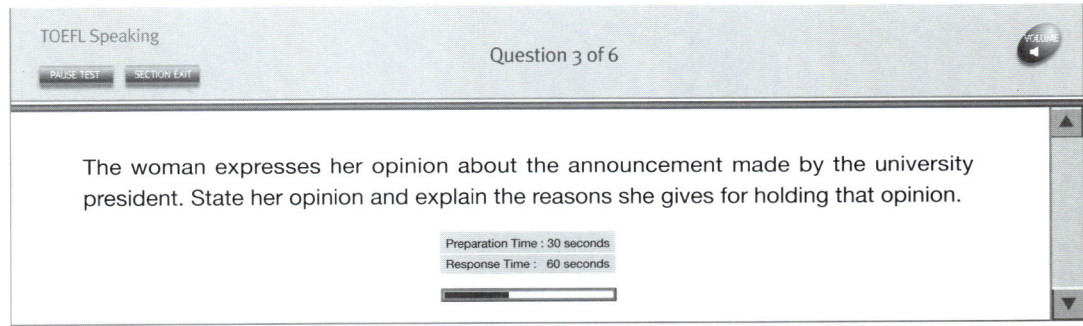

◼ Strategy

읽으면서 대화 내용 예측하기

대화에서는 주로 읽기 지문에서 어떤 주제가 언급된 이유나 그 장단점이 토론된다. 따라서 읽기 지문을 읽으면서 청취할 내용을 예측하는 연습을 하는 것이 효과적이다.

※ 문제에서 지정된 학생이 발표문에 찬성하면 발표문에서 언급된 이유나 장점에 대해 긍정적으로 토론을 하고 발표문에 반대하면 발표문에서 언급된 이유나 장점에 대해 부정적으로 토론을 한다.

주제에 대한 이해 보여주기

두 학생 중에 질문에서 지정한 학생이 동의한 의견을 분명하게 언급함으로써 답을 시작하면 되는데 동의하지 않은 의견을 언급하면서 시작하는 것도 좋다. 즉, 한 학생은 학교 당국이 발표한 기획이나 내용에 동의하지만 다른 학생은 그 계획에 반대한다는 것을 언급하며 시작하면 효과적이다. 양쪽 견해를 다 언급해 줌으로써 주제에 대한 이해를 더 잘 보여줄 수 있고 신뢰도를 높일 수 있다.

진부한 요약 피하기

등장한 모든 내용을 다 말하려고 해서는 안 된다. First, she said .... Then she said .... Then she answered .... And then she said ....라는 식의 진부한 요약은 피하는 것이 좋다.

자신의 의견 제시하지 않기

이 문제는 요약하는 문제이므로 대화에서 주어진 정보를 이용하여 답해야 한다. 자신의 의견을 첨가하는 것은 금물이다. 문제에서 지정된 사람에 따라서 the man 또는 the woman으로 시작되어야 하며, I는 주어로 쓰일 수 없다. 또한 인칭대명사 he, she보다는 명사 the man 또는 the woman으로 시작하는 것이 좋다.

> **Tip**
> 1 독립형 문제에서와 마찬가지로 요약을 할 때에도 general를 먼저 요약하고 specific을 나중에 요약해야 한다. 따라서 주어진 대화에서 general이 무엇이고 specific이 무엇인지 잘 이해해서 노트필기해야 한다
> 2 답을 전개할 때는 주어진 문장을 자기 말로 바꾸어 말해야 하는데 이것 역시 general에서 specific으로 해야 한다. 예를 들어 rose를 바꾸어 말할 때는 상위 개념인 flower로 해야 한다. Yellow rose나 red rose로 바꾸어서는 안 된다
> 3 광고나 공지의 내용을 부분적으로 답에 사용할 수는 있지만 인위적으로 요약해서는 안 된다
> 4 답을 다 마쳤는데도 시간이 남으면 앞에서 언급했던 자신의 의견을 다시 한번 간단히 요약하여 정리하는 것이 효과적이다

☐ Sample

▌Reading

Reading time: 45 seconds

Announcement from the President

1 The university governing board has authorized an 8 percent increase in tuition and fees for all students next semester. For the past 5 years, the tuition and fees haven't changed. However, it is unavoidable that we increase the tuition and fees **2** in order to better serve the student body. The university has a lot more students than it did five years ago, and we must hire more professors to meet the demands of the larger student body. **3** We will also make a new commitment to research and technology, and **4** will be modernizing our laboratory facilities to better meet our students' needs.

1 주제 제시   **2** 이유 제시   **3** 첫 번째 근거 제시   **4** 두 번째 근거 제시

▌Listening

M: Oh, great! Now we have to pay more for our tuition next semester.

W: Yeah, I know, but **1** I can understand why. When I was a freshman, classes were a lot smaller than they are now. There are so many new students now and it's hard to get any personal attention from the professors.

M: Yeah, I guess you're right. You know, in some classes, it's even difficult to find a seat. And I couldn't take the biology course I wanted because it was already full when I tried to sign up.

W: **2** Another thing that I'm really worried about is whether I'll be able to find a job after I graduate.

M: Why? You're one of the top students in your class, aren't you?

W: I'm doing pretty well, but the facilities here are so old-fashioned. There are so many important experiments in biology that are being developed, but we don't have the facilities to try them here. Also, there isn't enough equipment in the laboratories. How can we compete for jobs with people who study in modern facilities? **3** I think the extra tuition will be a great help.

1 첫 번째 근거 제시   **2** 두 번째 근거 제시   **3** 요약 정리

Q The woman expresses her opinion about the announcement made by the university president. State her opinion and explain the reasons she gives for holding that opinion.

▌Speaking

The woman is concerned that the increase in tuition might be a burden on students, but she believes that the increase in tuition and fees will bring a lot of benefits to students. For example, students will be able to **1** get more personal care from the professors. She also points out that the school needs to **2** improve school facilities because most of the facilities in the school are out-of-date, especially the biology laboratory. More modern facilities will enable students to compete for better jobs. **3** In the end, the woman feels that increasing tuition and fees is a good idea for the students on campus.

1 첫 번째 근거 제시   **2** 두 번째 근거 제시   **3** 요약 정리

Mini Test

읽기 지문을 읽은 후, 듣기 지문을 들으며 노트필기 공간에 주요 내용을 필기하시오.
필기 내용을 토대로 말하는 연습을 하시오.

1

Elimination of Evening Classes

The university has decided to eliminate evening classes. These days, the numbers of students who enroll in the classes are decreasing. Therefore, it would be a huge burden for the school to maintain evening classes. In order to better serve students, extra morning classes will be provided.

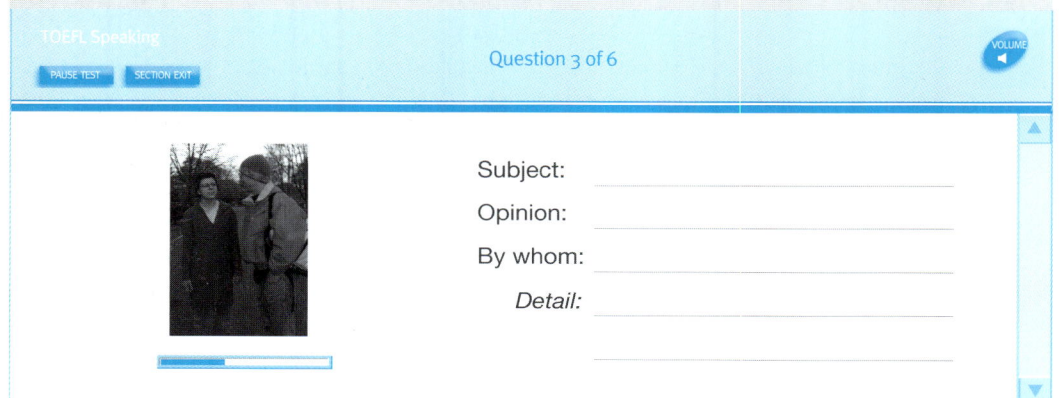

TOEFL Speaking

PAUSE TEST   SECTION EXIT

Question 3 of 6

VOLUME

Subject: _____
Opinion: _____
By whom: _____
Detail: _____

Q The man expresses his opinion of the university's plan to eliminate the evening classes. State his opinion and explain the reasons he gives for holding that opinion.

_____
_____
_____
_____

Useful Expressions

찬성할 때 (◯)	반대할 때 (✕)
■ S + agree(s) with ~ ■ S + consent(s) to ~	■ S + disagree(s) with ~ ■ S + oppose(s) ~

2

Library Expansion

The university has decided to increase the size of the library. The school has been around for a long time, and therefore, has a lot of books to stack. Because there is not enough space in the library, school authorities have decided to build an additional wing to make more space for the books. With the construction of the additional wing, students will also benefit from more study space.

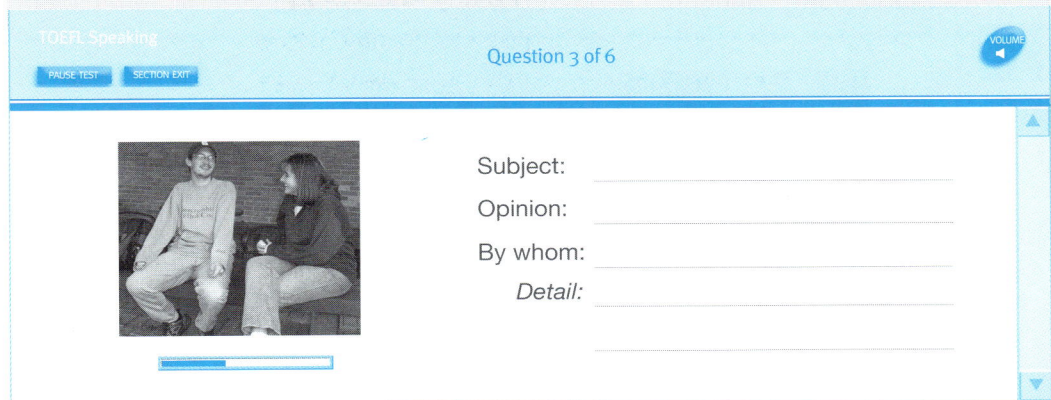

Subject:

Opinion:

By whom:

Detail:

Q The man expresses his opinion of the library expansion. State his opinion and explain the reasons he gives for holding that opinion.

Useful Expressions

찬성할 때 (○)

■ S + be fond of ~

■ S + favor(s) ~

반대할 때 (✗)

■ S + object(s) to ~

■ S + V + against ~

3

Changing the Computer Lab Policy

I think it is a good idea to change the computer lab policy. These days, the school lab is so crowded that we have to wait for a long time to use it. It is quite time-consuming. The school should have students make reservations to use the lab. Also, students waiting outside the lab make a lot of noise and create disturbances in the halls. In my opinion, the school should consider all these situations.

TOEFL Speaking

PAUSE TEST   SECTION EXIT

Question 3 of 6

VOLUME

Subject:
Opinion:
By whom:
Detail:

Q The woman expresses her opinion of the article. State her opinion and explain the reasons she gives for holding that opinion.

Useful Expressions

찬성할 때 (◯)
- S + concede(s) ~
- S + support(s) ~
- S + accept(s) ~

반대할 때 (✗)
- S + do(does) not concede ~
- S + do(does) not support ~
- S + do(does) not accept ~

4

University Parking Policy

The university has decided to limit the central parking lot for non-resident students only. Non-resident students have trouble finding parking spaces in the lot, and are often late for their classes. The main reason for this is that many resident students park their cars in the central parking lot. Considering regular complaints from non-resident students on this matter, the school authorities have decided to limit the central parking lot to non-resident students only. Resident students must park their cars off campus.

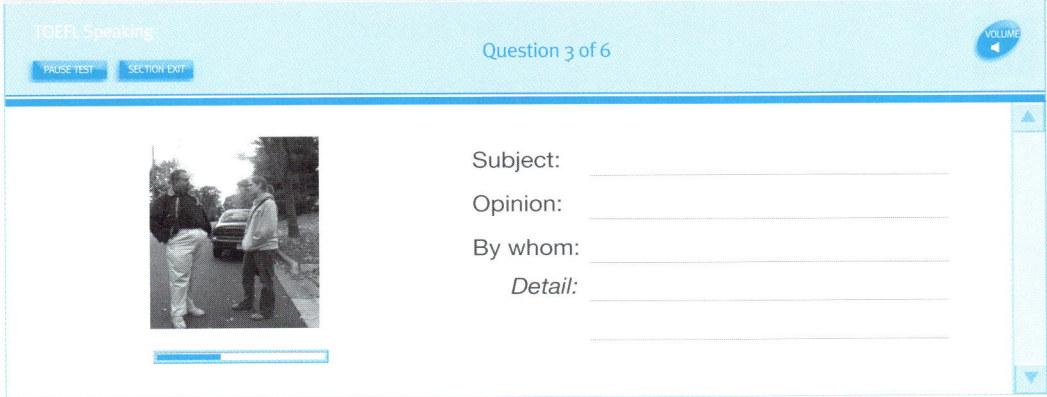

Subject:
Opinion:
By whom:
Detail:

Q The man expresses his opinion of the announcement. State his opinion and explain the reasons he gives for holding that opinion.

Useful Expressions

찬성할 때 (○)
- S + think(s) that it is better to ~
- S + believe(s) that it is much better ~

반대할 때 (✗)
- S + do(does) not think that it is better to ~
- S + do(does) not believe that it is much better ~

Exercise

🔊 읽기 지문을 읽은 후, 듣기 지문을 들으며 노트필기 공간에 주요 내용을 필기하시오.
필기 내용을 토대로 말하는 연습을 하시오.

CD Possible Responses: Track 36~43

1

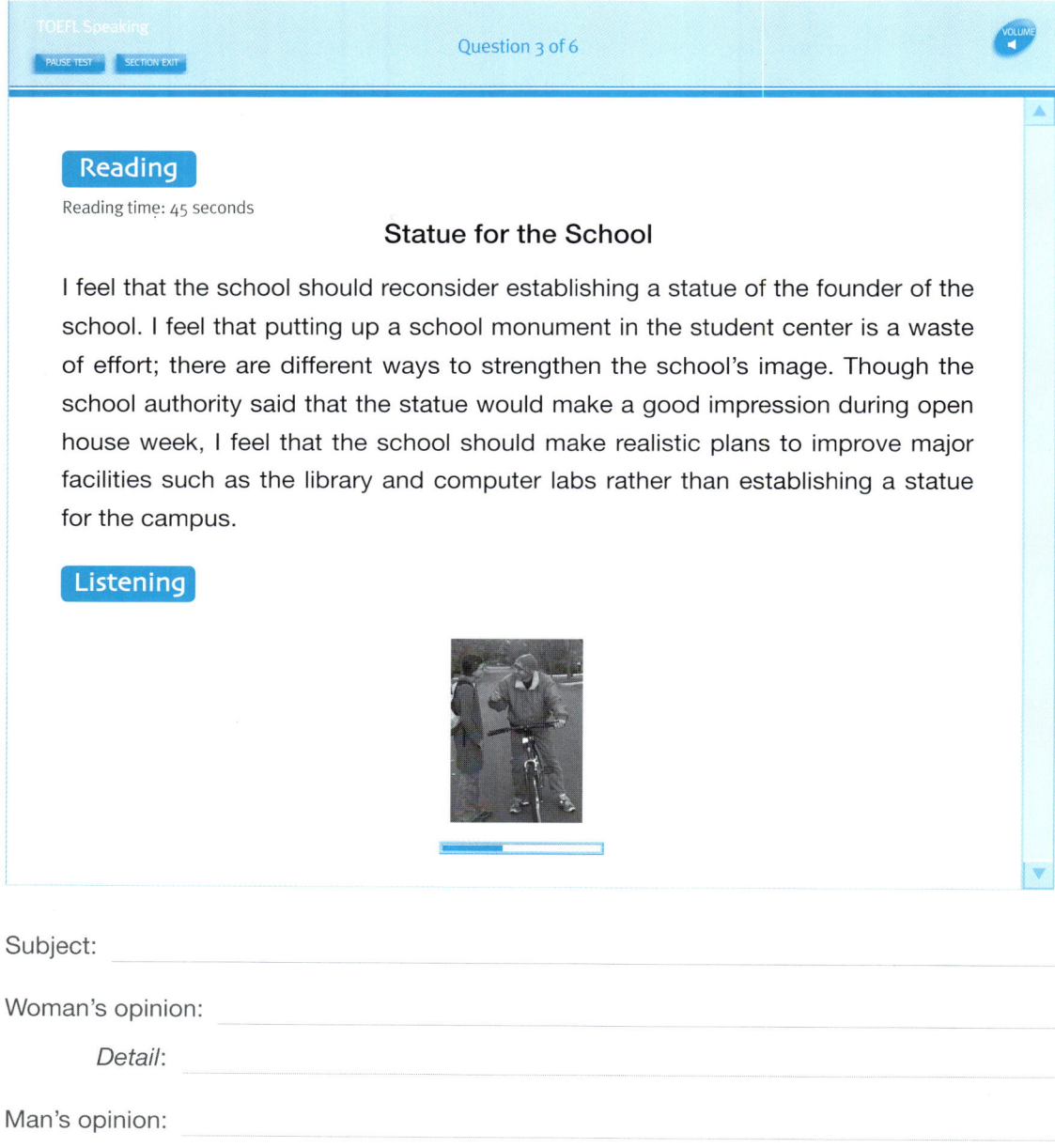

Reading

Reading time: 45 seconds

Statue for the School

I feel that the school should reconsider establishing a statue of the founder of the school. I feel that putting up a school monument in the student center is a waste of effort; there are different ways to strengthen the school's image. Though the school authority said that the statue would make a good impression during open house week, I feel that the school should make realistic plans to improve major facilities such as the library and computer labs rather than establishing a statue for the campus.

Listening

Subject: _____

Woman's opinion: _____

    Detail: _____

Man's opinion: _____

    Detail: _____

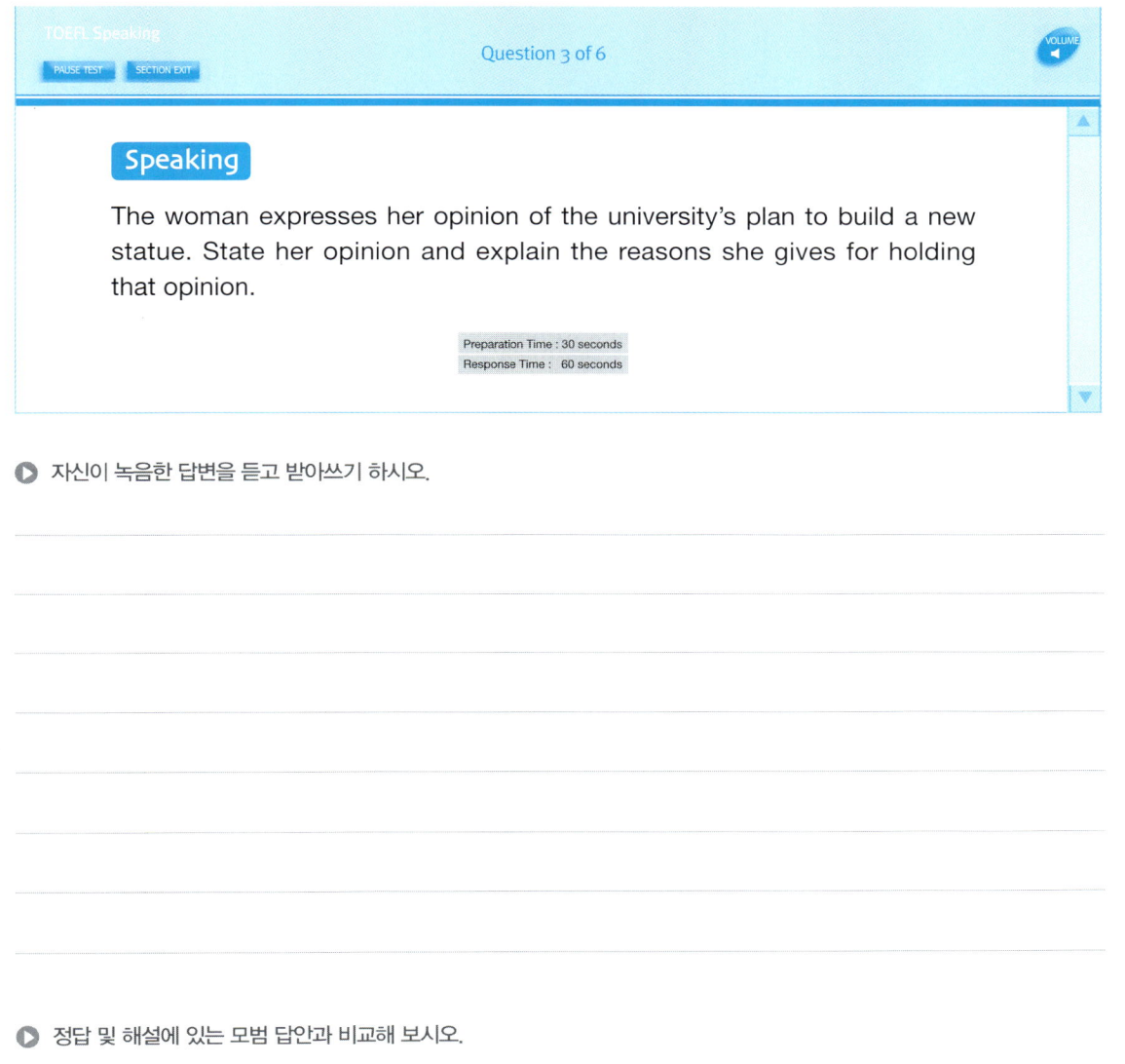

Speaking

The woman expresses her opinion of the university's plan to build a new statue. State her opinion and explain the reasons she gives for holding that opinion.

Preparation Time : 30 seconds
Response Time : 60 seconds

▶ 자신이 녹음한 답변을 듣고 받아쓰기 하시오.

▶ 정답 및 해설에 있는 모범 답안과 비교해 보시오.

Exercise

2

PAUSE TEST   SECTION EXIT

VOLUME

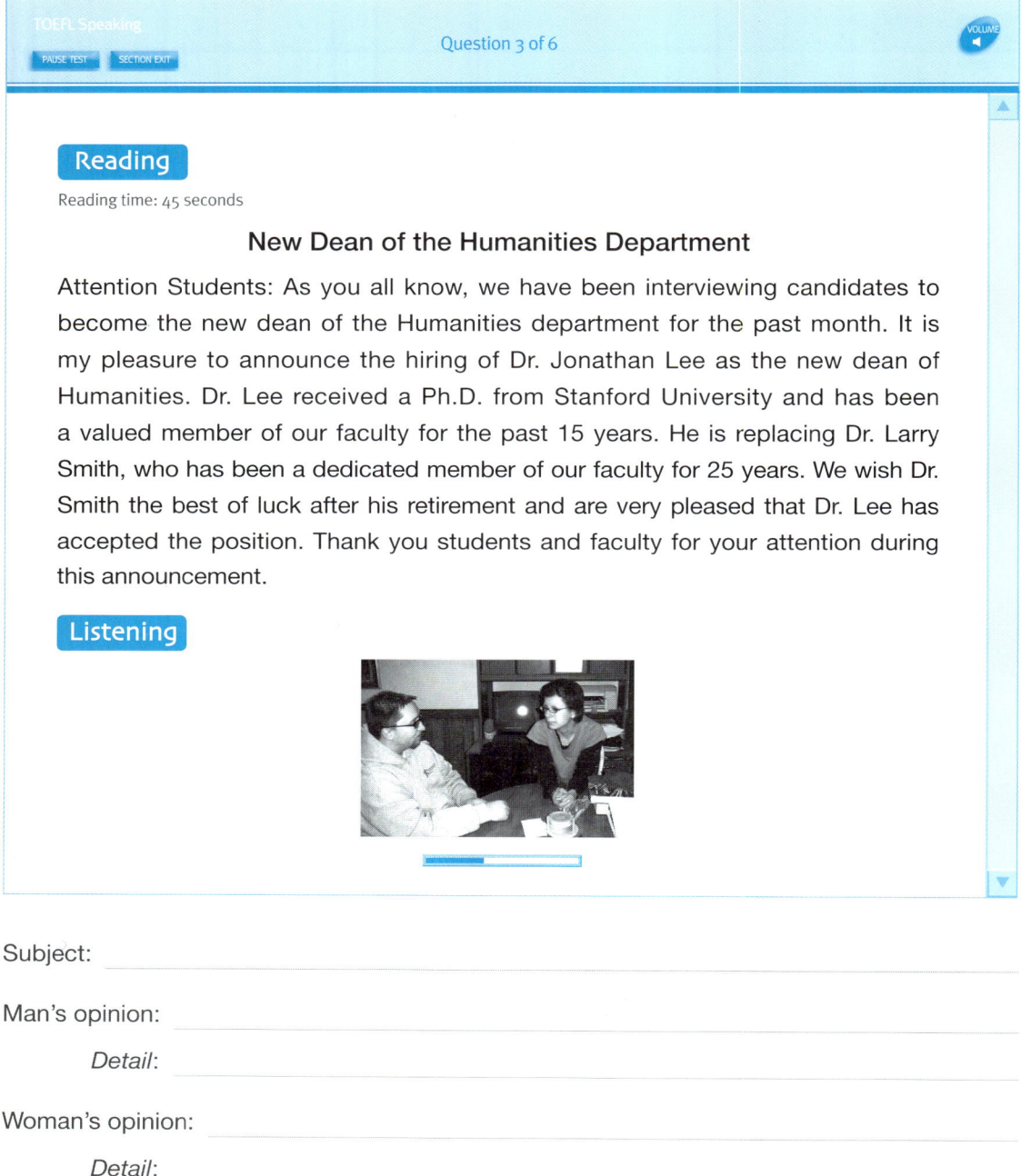

Reading

Reading time: 45 seconds

New Dean of the Humanities Department

Attention Students: As you all know, we have been interviewing candidates to become the new dean of the Humanities department for the past month. It is my pleasure to announce the hiring of Dr. Jonathan Lee as the new dean of Humanities. Dr. Lee received a Ph.D. from Stanford University and has been a valued member of our faculty for the past 15 years. He is replacing Dr. Larry Smith, who has been a dedicated member of our faculty for 25 years. We wish Dr. Smith the best of luck after his retirement and are very pleased that Dr. Lee has accepted the position. Thank you students and faculty for your attention during this announcement.

Listening

Subject: _____

Man's opinion: _____

     Detail: _____

Woman's opinion: _____

     Detail: _____

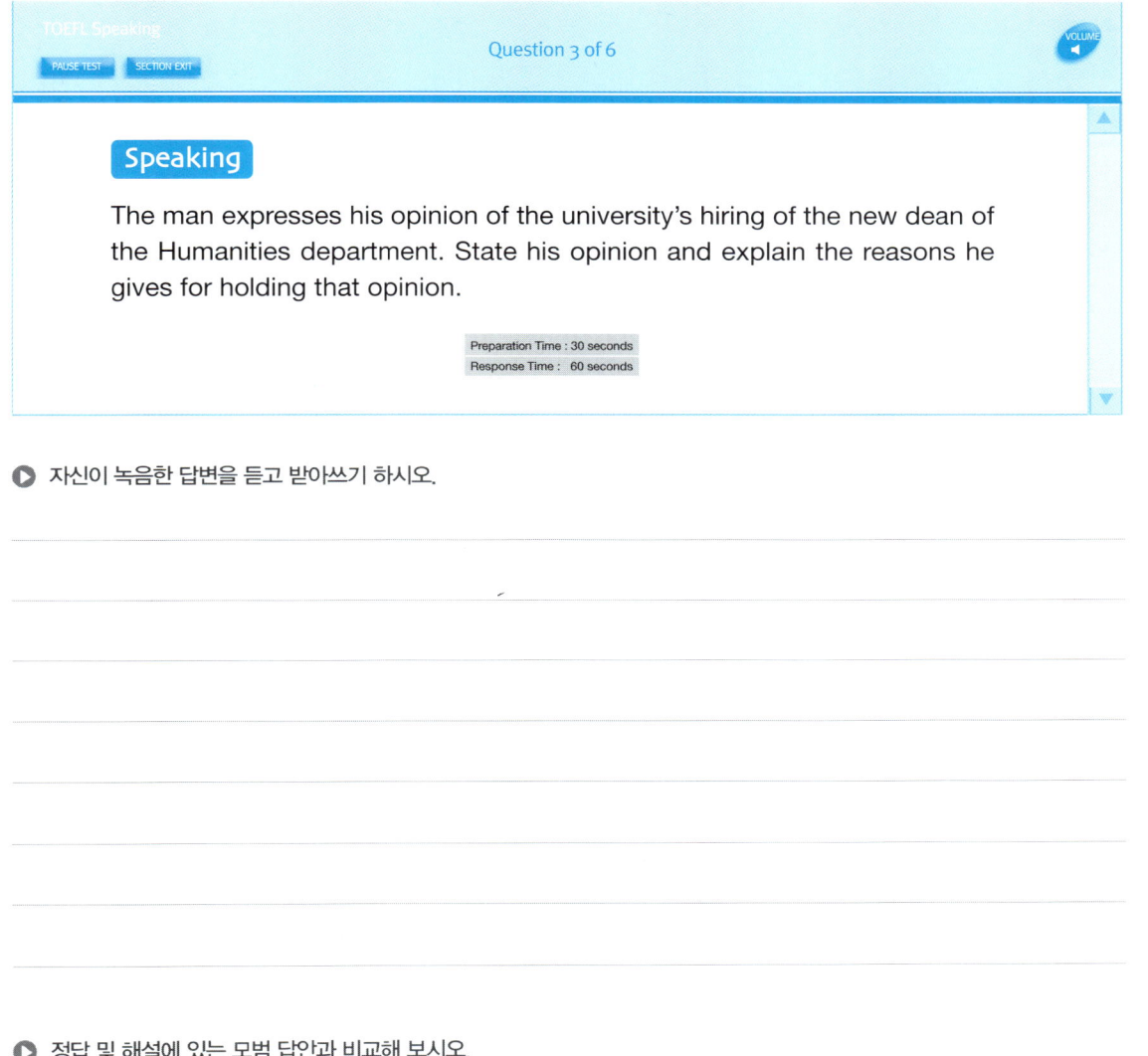

Speaking

The man expresses his opinion of the university's hiring of the new dean of the Humanities department. State his opinion and explain the reasons he gives for holding that opinion.

Preparation Time : 30 seconds
Response Time :   60 seconds

▶ 자신이 녹음한 답변을 듣고 받아쓰기 하시오.

▶ 정답 및 해설에 있는 모범 답안과 비교해 보시오.

Exercise

3

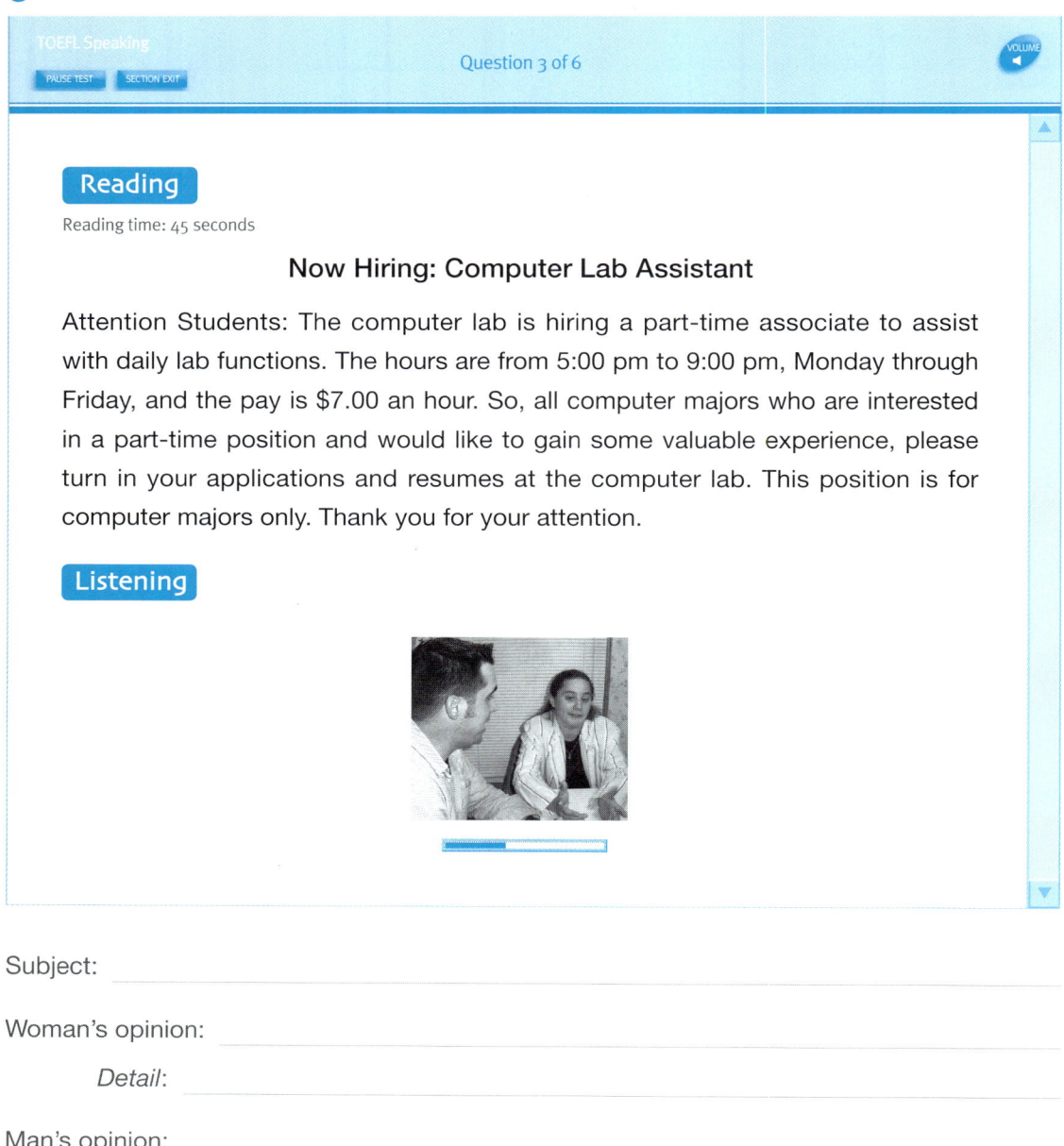

Reading

Reading time: 45 seconds

Now Hiring: Computer Lab Assistant

Attention Students: The computer lab is hiring a part-time associate to assist with daily lab functions. The hours are from 5:00 pm to 9:00 pm, Monday through Friday, and the pay is $7.00 an hour. So, all computer majors who are interested in a part-time position and would like to gain some valuable experience, please turn in your applications and resumes at the computer lab. This position is for computer majors only. Thank you for your attention.

Listening

Subject: _____

Woman's opinion: _____

    Detail: _____

Man's opinion: _____

    Detail: _____

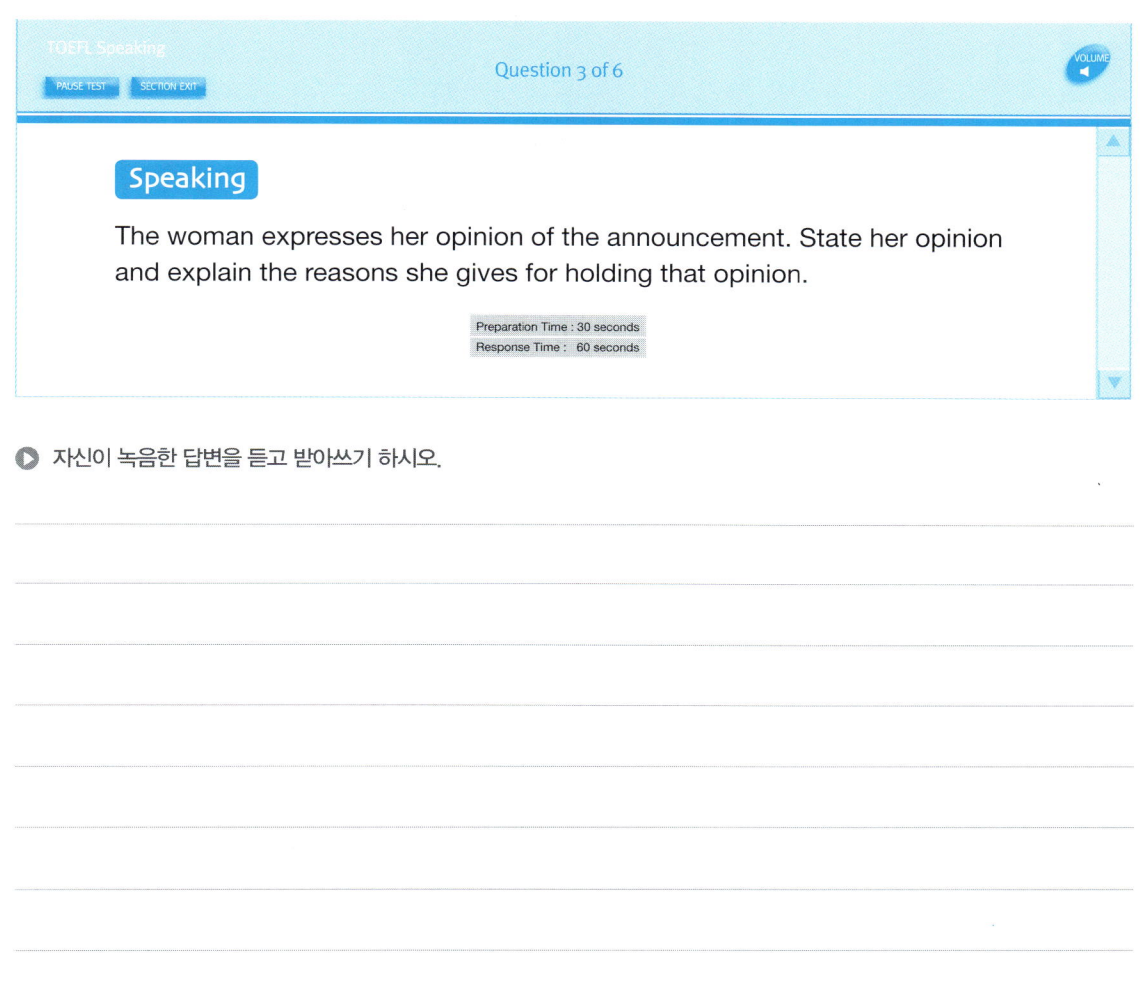

TOEFL Speaking

PAUSE TEST   SECTION EXIT

VOLUME

Speaking

The woman expresses her opinion of the announcement. State her opinion and explain the reasons she gives for holding that opinion.

Preparation Time : 30 seconds
Response Time : 60 seconds

▶ 자신이 녹음한 답변을 듣고 받아쓰기 하시오.

_____

_____

_____

_____

_____

_____

_____

▶ 정답 및 해설에 있는 모범 답안과 비교해 보시오.

Exercise

4

TOEFL Speaking

PAUSE TEST SECTION EXIT

Question 3 of 6

VOLUME

Reading

Reading time: 45 seconds

Change in the Final Exam

The history professor has announced that the final exam will be an oral presentation. However, it is mandatory that all students prepare for their presentations with an assigned partner. The reason is that students can learn a lot by working together. Students can learn how to cooperate and can share their ideas and knowledge. It will be very beneficial for the class.

Listening

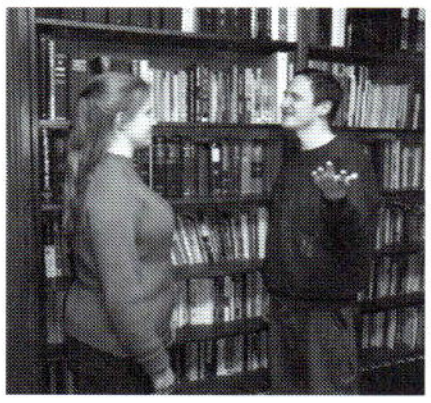

Subject: ____________________

Woman's opinion: ____________________

Detail: ____________________

Man's opinion: ____________________

Detail: ____________________

Speaking

The woman expresses her opinion of the change in the final exam. State her opinion and explain the reasons she gives for holding that opinion.

Preparation Time : 30 seconds
Response Time :   60 seconds

▶ 자신이 녹음한 답변을 듣고 받아쓰기 하시오.

_____

_____

_____

_____

_____

_____

_____

_____

▶ 정답 및 해설에 있는 모범 답안과 비교해 보시오.

Exercise

5

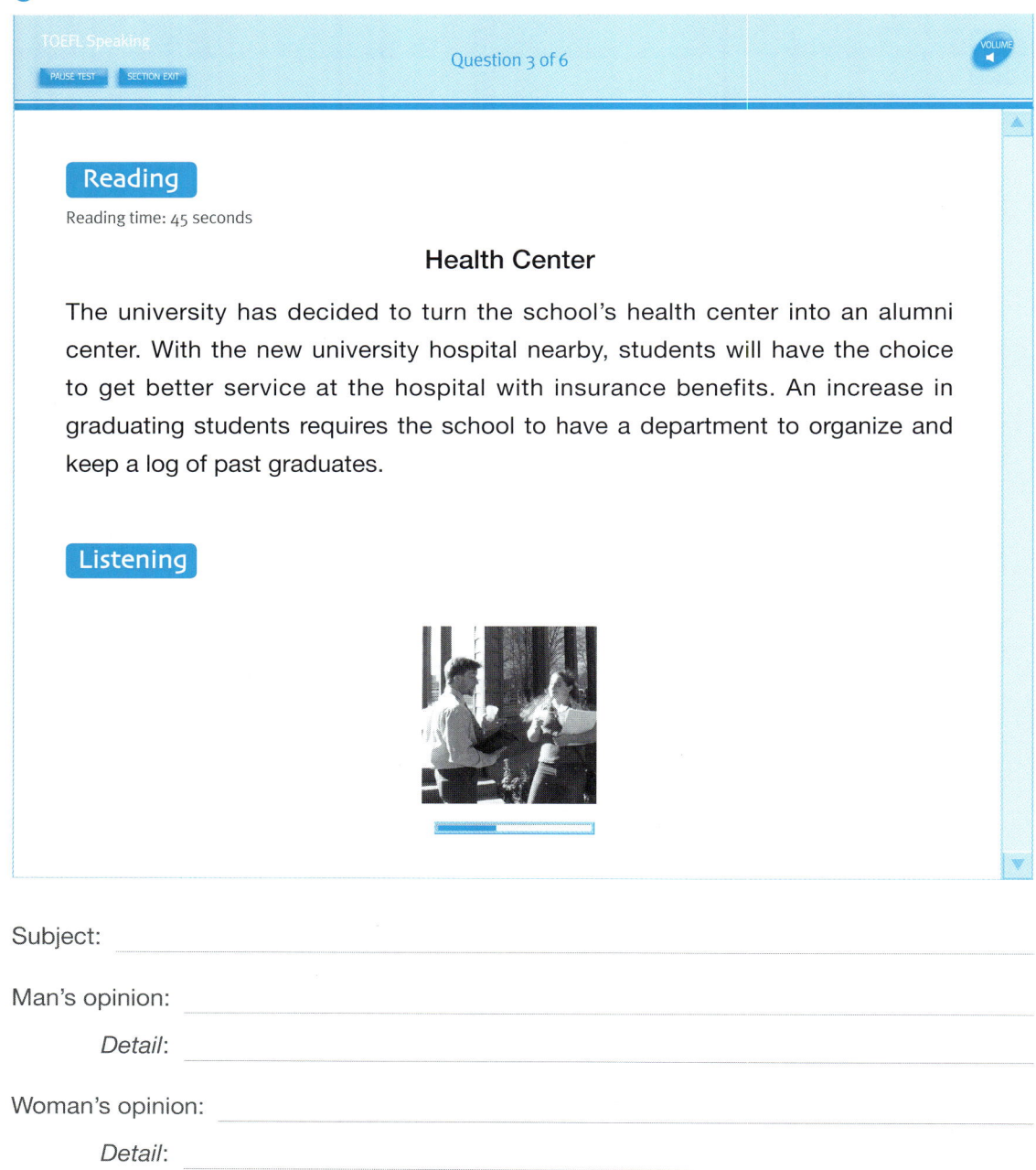

Reading

Reading time: 45 seconds

Health Center

The university has decided to turn the school's health center into an alumni center. With the new university hospital nearby, students will have the choice to get better service at the hospital with insurance benefits. An increase in graduating students requires the school to have a department to organize and keep a log of past graduates.

Listening

Subject: _____

Man's opinion: _____

    Detail: _____

Woman's opinion: _____

    Detail: _____

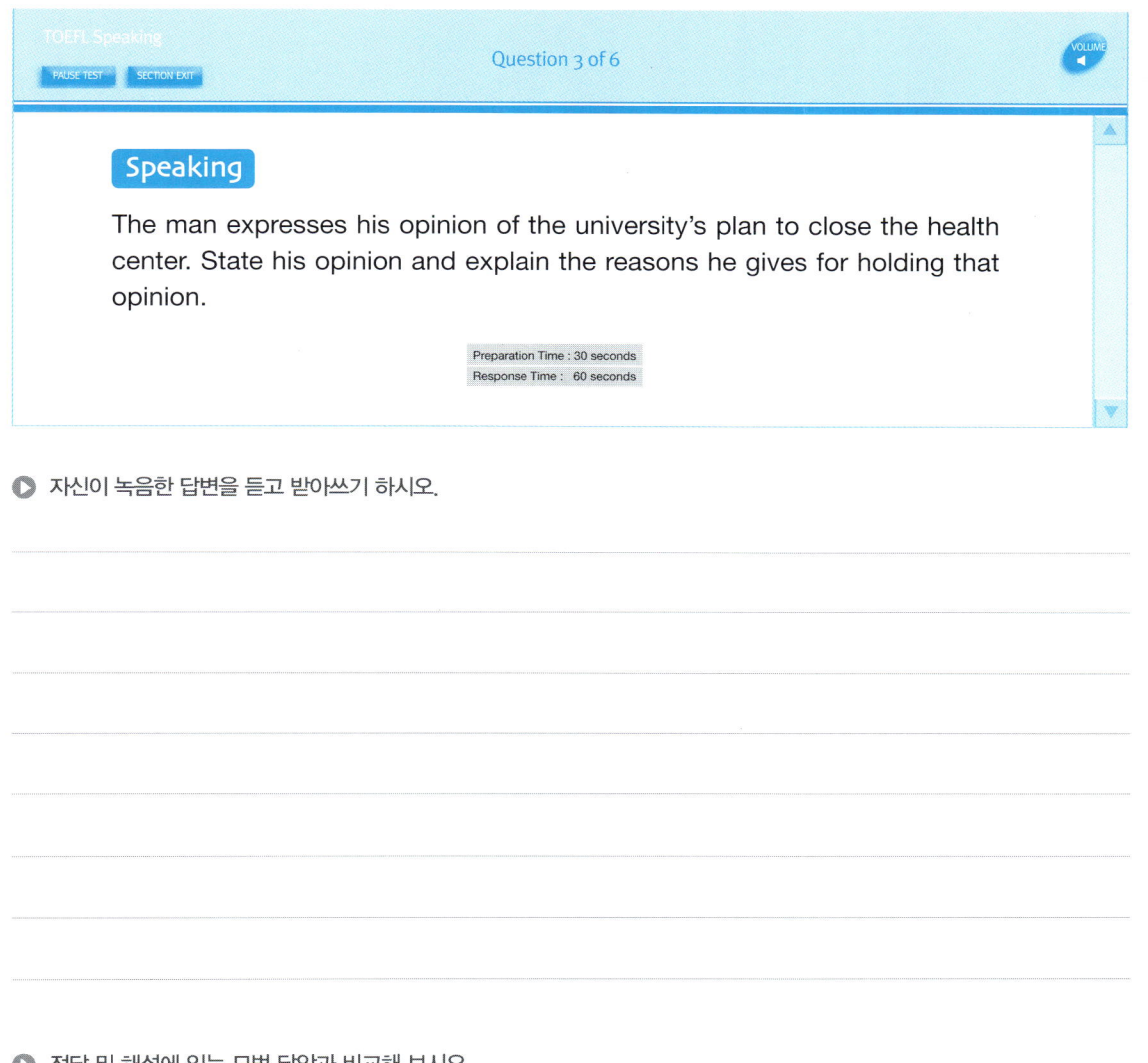

Speaking

The man expresses his opinion of the university's plan to close the health center. State his opinion and explain the reasons he gives for holding that opinion.

Preparation Time : 30 seconds
Response Time : 60 seconds

▶ 자신이 녹음한 답변을 듣고 받아쓰기 하시오.

▶ 정답 및 해설에 있는 모범 답안과 비교해 보시오.

Exercise

6

TOEFL Speaking

PAUSE TEST SECTION EXIT

Question 3 of 6

VOLUME

Reading

Reading time: 45 seconds

Dining Service

The university dining services are planning to change the menu for the upcoming semester. The plan consists of changing all hot foods in the cafeterias and dorm meal serving areas to cold foods in the mornings. The cold foods will be healthier and cheaper than the hot foods. This plan is due to the increase in health concerns for our fellow students at the university.

Listening

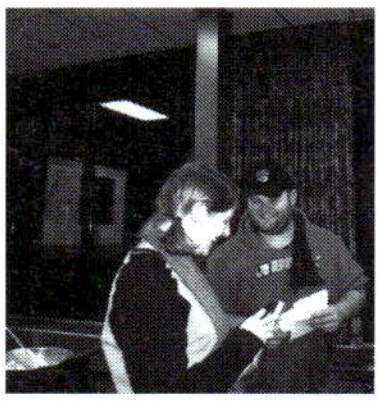

Subject: ______________________________

Woman's opinion: ______________________________

Detail: ______________________________

Man's opinion: ______________________________

Detail: ______________________________

Speaking

The woman expresses her opinion of the university's plan to change the dining service. State her opinion and explain the reasons she gives for holding that opinion.

Preparation Time : 30 seconds
Response Time : 60 seconds

▶ 자신이 녹음한 답변을 듣고 받아쓰기 하시오.

▶ 정답 및 해설에 있는 모범 답안과 비교해 보시오.

Exercise

7

Reading

Reading time: 45 seconds

Writing Requirements for Science Majors

For science majors, there were no writing requirements after the first semester of the freshman year. However, the school board has decided to add twelve more intensive writing requirements for graduation. The reason is that students who are enrolled in science have poor essay writing skills, and the department of science has decided to increase the credit hours to help students graduate easier.

Listening

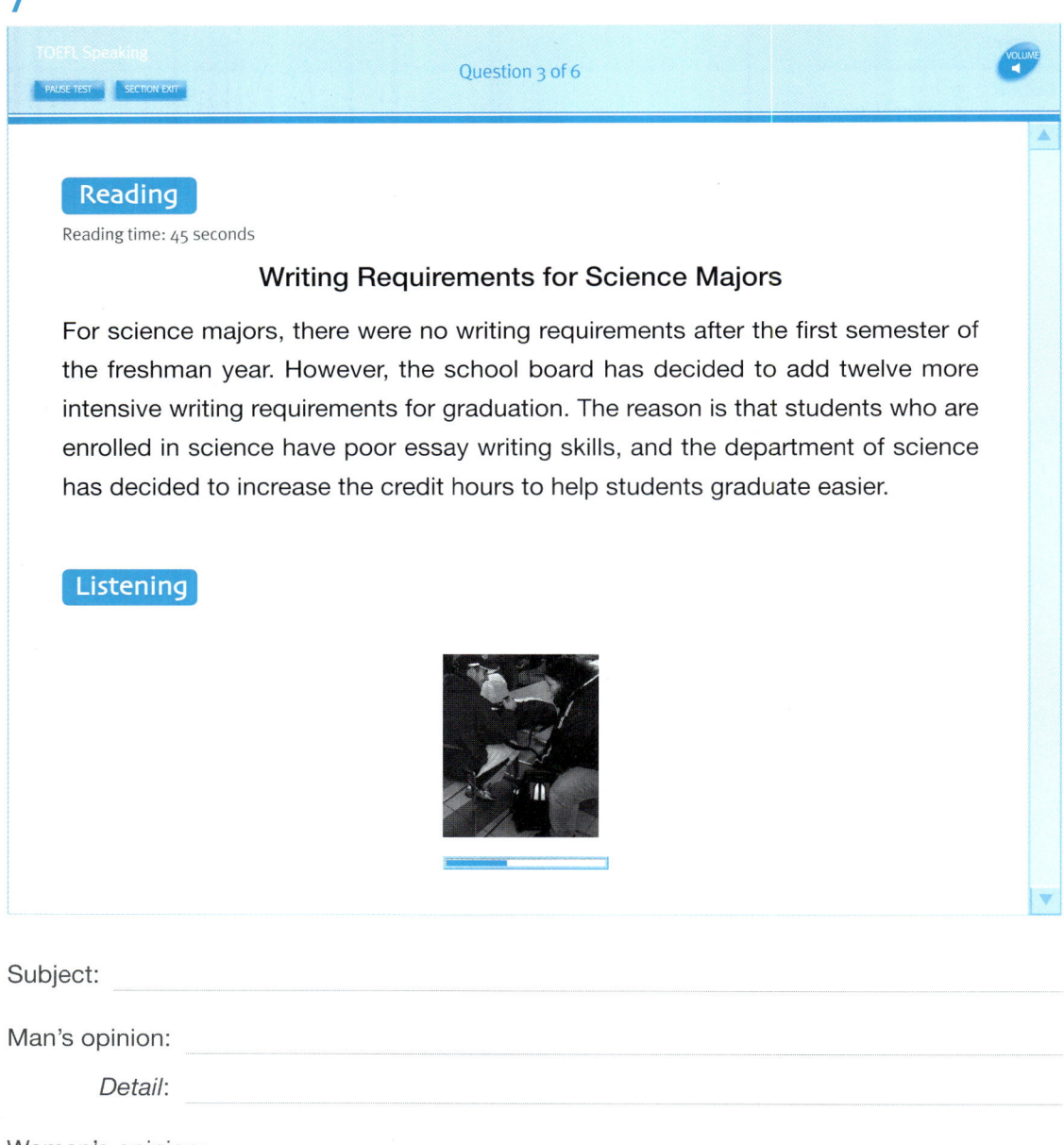

Subject: _____

Man's opinion: _____

    Detail: _____

Woman's opinion: _____

    Detail: _____

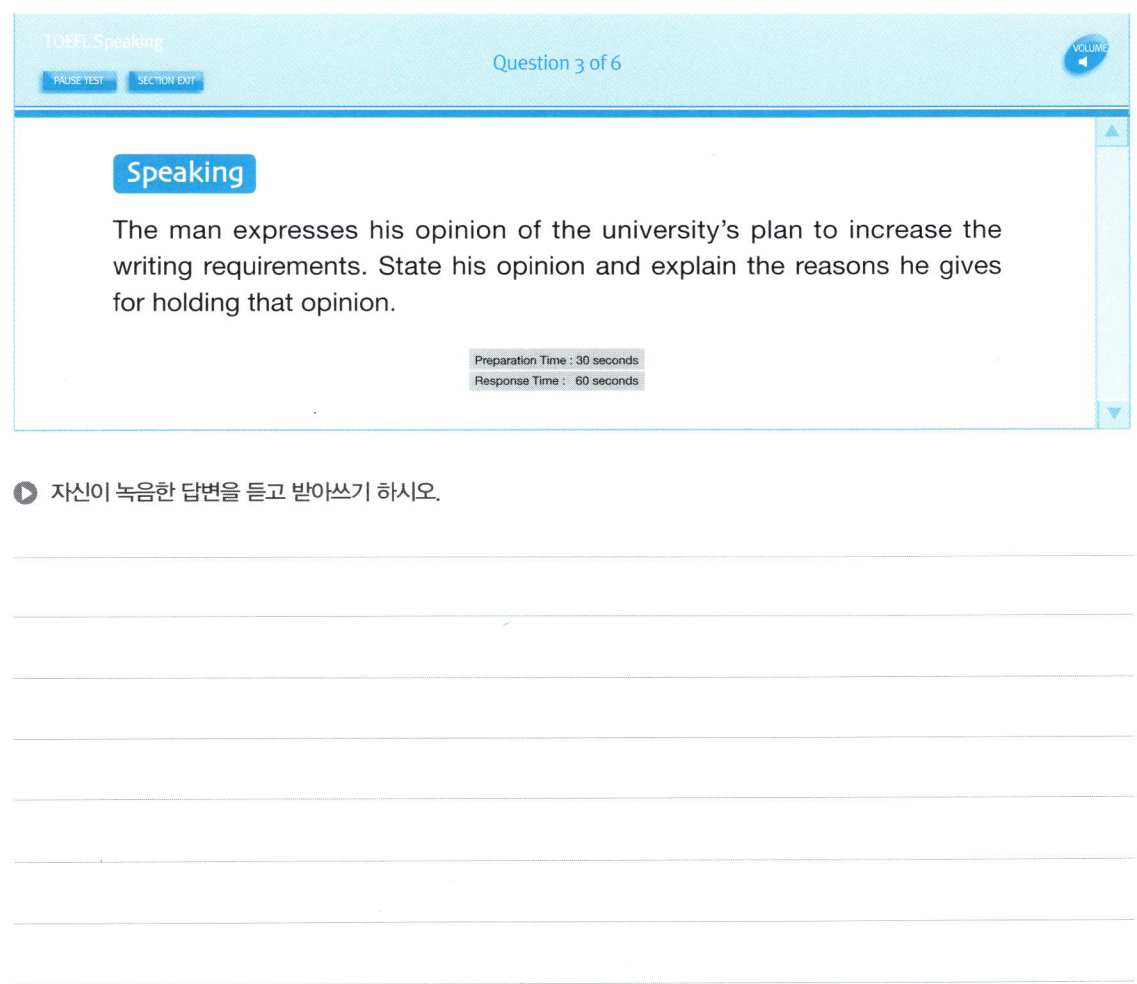

Speaking

The man expresses his opinion of the university's plan to increase the writing requirements. State his opinion and explain the reasons he gives for holding that opinion.

Preparation Time : 30 seconds
Response Time : 60 seconds

▶ 자신이 녹음한 답변을 듣고 받아쓰기 하시오.

▶ 정답 및 해설에 있는 모범 답안과 비교해 보시오.

Exercise

8

Reading

Reading time: 45 seconds

Building a New Dorm Off Campus

The university has decided to build the school dormitory outside of campus due to limited space on campus. The dormitory will be located away from campus 10 minutes by bus in the local community. A network of campus police and community police will monitor students' security. There will be shuttle bus services for students without cars during the weekday.

Listening

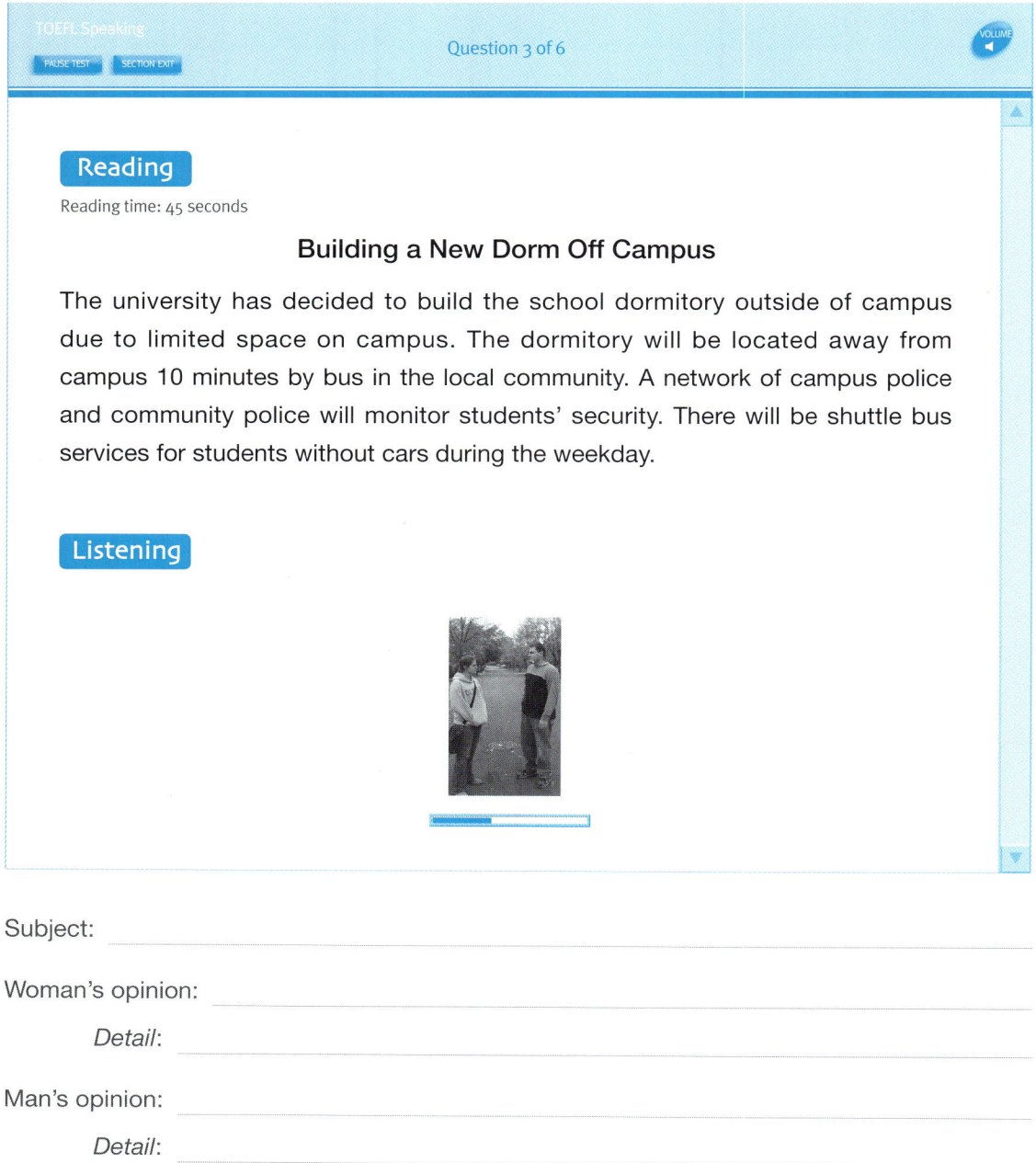

Subject: _____

Woman's opinion: _____

    Detail: _____

Man's opinion: _____

    Detail: _____

Speaking

The woman expresses her opinion of the university's plan to build the dormitory off campus. State her opinion and explain the reasons she gives for holding that opinion.

Preparation Time : 30 seconds
Response Time : 60 seconds

▶ 자신이 녹음한 답변을 듣고 받아쓰기 하시오.

_____

_____

_____

_____

_____

_____

_____

▶ 정답 및 해설에 있는 모범 답안과 비교해 보시오.

Task 4

General and Specific

4 General and Specific

읽기, 듣기, 말하기가 결합된 문제 유형이다. 학술적인 주제에 대한 짧은 지문을 읽은 후, 그 주제에 관련된 교수의 강의를 듣고, 강의에서 주어진 주제와 예를 요약한다. 답을 전개할 때는 읽고 들은 정보를 이용하여 문제에서 요구한 정보를 선별하는 능력과 그 정보를 정확하고 논리적으로 요약하는 능력이 필요하다.

■ 문제 유형

읽기	길이	45초 (75–100단어)
	종류	학술적인 내용을 담고 있다. 이어지는 강의에 대한 일반적 사실이나 배경 지식을 제공하고 주제를 highlight 해준다. 강의의 이해를 돕는 것이 주된 목적이다 1) 배경 지식을 제공한 후 주제를 환기시켜준다 2) 특정 학문 분야(특히 심리학, 생물학)의 전문 용어와 정의가 주어진다
듣기	길이	60–80초 (150–180단어)
	내용	학술적인 내용에 대한 두 가지의 구체적 예시가 주어진다. 읽기 지문에서 주어진 일반적 사실과 대립되는 예(extended examples, counterexample)가 주어지는 경우도 있다
말하기	내용	읽기와 듣기에서 제공된 정보를 종합하여 전달하시오 (강의의 정보를 사용하여 주제를 설명하시오)

■ 기출 주제

- Moral Persuasion
- Instinctive Behavior
- Supranational Organizations
- Animal Coloration
- Secondary Ecological Succession
- Buyer's Remorse
- Role Conflicts

- Diffusion of Responsibility
- Assumption
- Cognitive Dissonance
- The Positive Effect
- Short-term Memory
- Mental Script

■ 화면 구성

1 읽기: 학술적인 내용에 대한 지문을 45초간 독해한다.

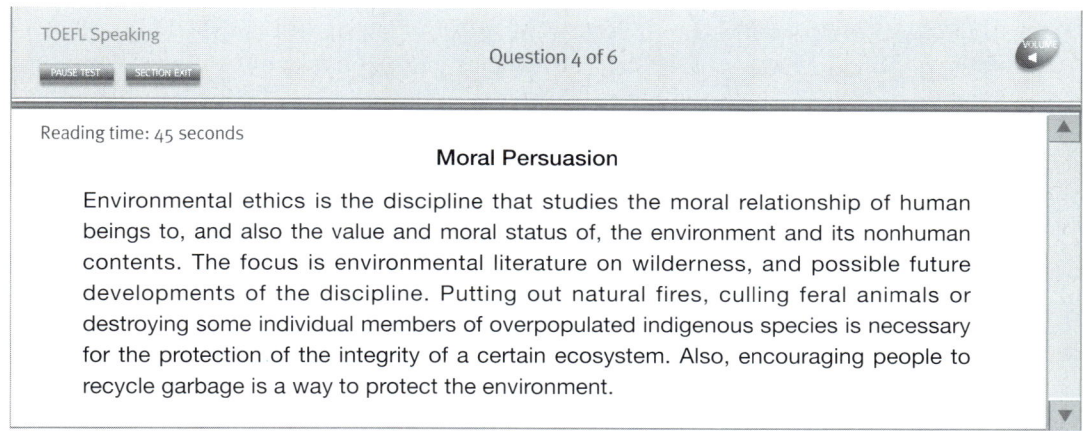

2 듣기: 읽기 지문에서 언급된 주제에 대한 구체적 근거나 그 반대의 관점을 60~90초간 청취한다.

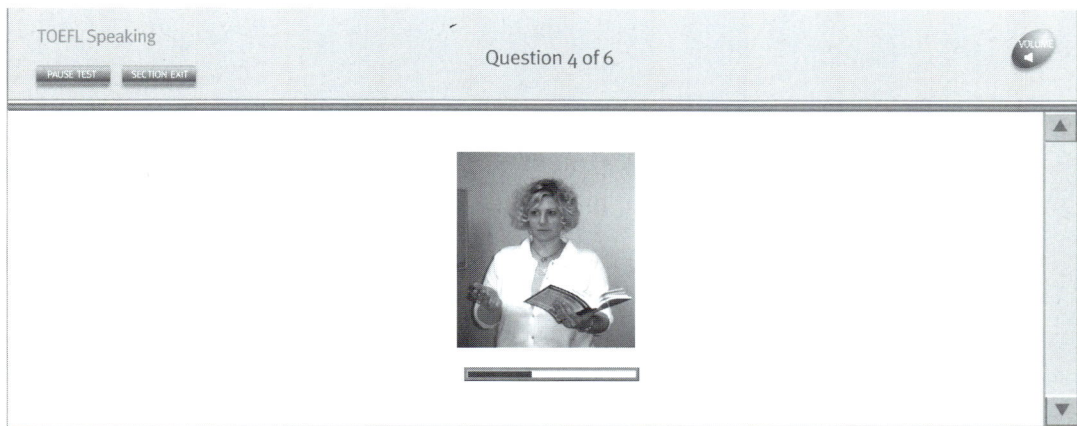

3 말하기: 읽기 지문과 듣기를 통해 얻은 구체적 정보를 종합하여 주제의 원리나 과정에 대해 30초간 준비한 후, 60초간 설명한다.

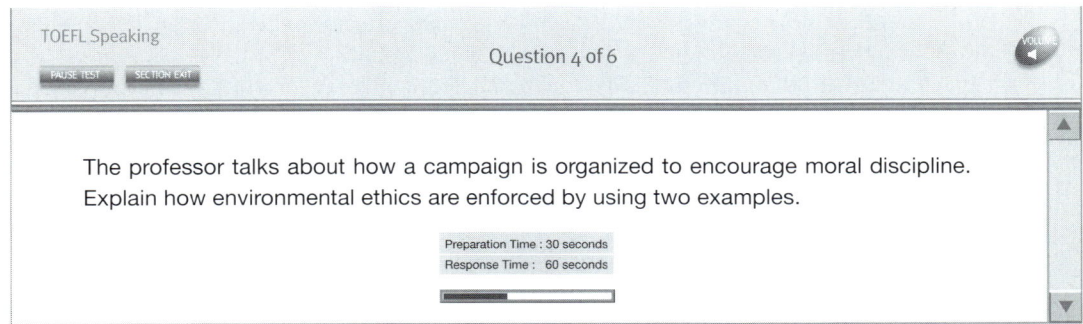

■ Strategy

강의 주제 및 목적 이해하기

강의의 주제와 목적을 이해하는 것은 답을 전개할 때 필수적이다. Task 4의 강의에서는 심리학, 생물학 및 경제학과 관련된 내용이 자주 출제된다. 심리학은 주로 부정적인 측면과 긍정적인 측면에서 실시된 실험의 결과들을 다룬다. 생물학에서는 유전, 환경, 생존 등과 관련된 내용이 자주 출제되며, 경제학에서는 주로 심리학과 관련되어 주어지는데 광고를 통한 판매증진으로 인한 이윤창출이 가장 보편적 주제이다.

청취의 포인트 파악하기

주제는 읽기 지문의 제목일 확률이 매우 높으며 주로 강의의 도입이나 결말 부분에서 언급될 확률이 높다. 따라서 이 부분을 주의 깊게 들으면 주제를 파악하는데 유용하다.

예측하며 청취하기

강의는 읽기 지문에서 주어진 주제에 대한 예를 설명하는 형식이므로 예측이 가능하다. 제시된 내용을 예측하여 들으면 이해하는데 큰 도움이 된다. 또한 강의의 모든 부분을 이해할 필요는 없다. 주어진 예시를 요약하여 말하라는 문제가 주어지므로 특히 예시 부분을 주목하여 듣고 필기해 두는 것이 효과적이다. 예는 일반적으로 두 가지가 주어지지만 때때로 한 가지가 주어지기도 하고 두 가지를 주고 하나만 요약하라고 주어지기도 한다.

자신의 말로 요약하기

읽기 지문에서 주어진 내용을 요약해서는 안 된다. 답에 필요한 모든 정보는 듣기 지문에서 주어진 정보를 이용해야 하며 강의에서 등장한 문장을 똑같이 사용하는 것보다는 자신의 말로 바꾸어 요약하는 것이 바람직하다. 1단계에서는 강의에 초점을 맞추고 (The lecture is mainly about ~) 2단계에서는 화자에 초점을 맞춘다. (The professor explains ~)
※ 바꾸어 쓰는 방법(paraphrase)은 Task 3 **Tip** 참고

주어진 정보만을 사용하기

자신의 의견을 더하거나 임의적으로 정보를 해석하면 안 된다. 강의에서 주어진 정보만을 요약하여 문제에서 요구하는 것을 제시해야 하며 general에서 specific으로 요약하는 것을 잊어서는 안 된다. 또한 결론은 반드시 필요한 것은 아니다.

> **Tip** 생물학의 주제 이해
> 1 생물학은 크게 두 가지, 즉 위장과 개체수의 증감이 가장 보편적인 주제이다. 위장에 관한 경우 하나의 예는 일정한 지역에 알맞도록 맞춤형 유전인자를 갖는 동물의 예가 (예: horned frog, cuttlefish, black pander, polar bear 등) 주어지고 또 다른 예는 (lizard, octopus 등) 변화는 환경에 적응할 수 있는 유전인자를 갖는 예가 주어진다. 이에 대한 강의의 목적은 생존이다.
> 2 개체수의 증감에 대한 주제는 식물과 식물 사이, 동물과 식물 사이, 동물과 동물 사이에서 어떻게 서로의 개체수에 영향을 미치는지에 대한 문제가 출제되는데 강의의 주제는 사람이 개입하지 않는다면 서로의 개체수를 조절하여 생태계를 잘 조절할 수 있다는 것이다.
>
> 경제학의 주제 이해
>   광고는 일반적으로 두 가지 관점에서 주어지는데 하나는 광고하는 제품 그 자체의 quality에 초점을 맞춰 광고하는 기법이 주어지고 나머지 하나는 image광고로 광고하는 제품과 관련된 유명인이나 image를 통해서 광고하는 기법이 주어진다. 예) 광고하는 차가 빠르다는 것을 image기법을 이용하여 광고할 때 유명한 자동차 경주 선수를 고용하여 차 안에 앉아 있는 모습을 보여준다.

❚ Reading

Reading time: 45 seconds

Moral Persuasion

1 Environmental ethics is the study of the moral relationship of human beings to the environment. The focus is environmental literature on wilderness, and possible future developments of the discipline. **2** Putting out natural fires, culling feral animals or destroying some individual members of overpopulated indigenous species is necessary for the protection of the integrity of a certain ecosystem. **3** Also, encouraging people to recycle garbage is a way to protect the environment.

1 주제 제시   **2** 첫 번째 근거 제시   **3** 두 번째 근거 제시

❚ Listening

P: **1** Today, we'll talk about measures the Environmental Protection Agency is taking to educate the public about environmental ethics. Conserving the environment is a very important issue that the EPA is focusing on in a number of ways.
Alright, so to start the campaign, the Environmental Protection Agency has begun two approaches to enforce environmental ethics. **2** First they introduced a friendly bear and named it "Smokey the Bear" to remind all citizens about forest fires and safety in the woods. Smokey the Bear received its name from the great American Brown Bear cub which acts as the mascot to represent the forests of the USA. The campaign chose this character to teach about saving animals by watching out for forest fires and the safety of the animals. **3** Another approach the EPA used was encouraging recycling by putting up signs and placing trash bins in convenient locations. This sparked the beginning of teaching the public about the ethics and discipline of our environment. This started with putting recycling bins in front of each house. **4** With these two campaigns, the EPA will enforce moral persuasion on all citizens by enforcing ethics and discipline towards the environment.

1 주제 제시   **2** 첫 번째 근거 제시   **3** 두 번째 근거 제시   **4** 요약 정리

Q The professor talks about how a campaign is organized to encourage moral discipline. Explain how environmental ethics are enforced by using two examples.

❚ Speaking

The professor talks about two campaigns to enforce environmental ethics on the public. According to this lecture, Smokey the Bear is used to encourage people to be careful about forest fires which can endanger wildlife. **1** For example, the American Brown Bear cub is used as the mascot of the forests in the USA because this campaign teaches how we can save the animals by watching out for forest fires. **2** He also points out that recycling should be enforced by placing recycling containers near homes. **3** The professor thinks by taking these two actions, the ecosystem will become more balanced.

1 첫 번째 근거 제시   **2** 두 번째 근거 제시   **3** 요약 정리

Mini Test

CD Possible Responses: Track 46

🔊 읽기 지문을 읽은 후, 듣기 지문을 들으며 노트필기 공간에 주요 내용을 필기하시오.
필기 내용을 토대로 말하는 연습을 하시오.

1

Supranational Organization

Many studies have shown that it is more effective and practical to work together in groups than by oneself. It is much easier to solve problems and achieve goals when you work with others. The reason for supranational organizations is based on this principle. Supranational organizations work together globally to efficiently achieve.

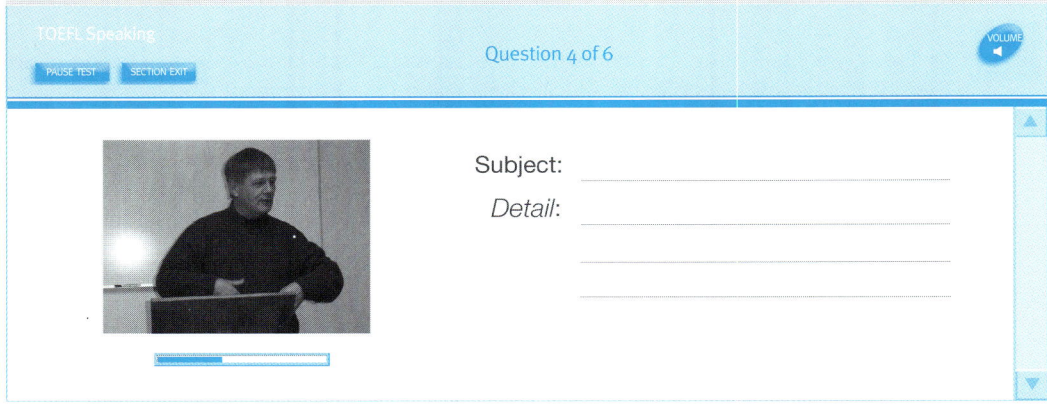

TOEFL Speaking

PAUSE TEST   SECTION EXIT

Question 4 of 6

VOLUME

Subject: _____

Detail: _____
_____
_____

Q The professor talks about a supranational organization and their main goals. Explain the idea of a supranational organization.

_____
_____
_____
_____

Useful Expressions

주제를 말할 때

* The professor talks about ~
* The lecture discusses ~
* The main topic of the lecture is ~

예를 말할 때

* For example, ~
* In this example, ~

2

Diffusion of Responsibility

The diffusion of responsibility says that the more people that are around, the less chance someone will help another person. A common explanation of this phenomenon is that, with others present, observers all assume that someone else is going to intervene; thus, they each refrain from doing so. People may also assume that other bystanders may be more qualified to help, such as a doctor or police officer, and their intervention would thus be unneeded.

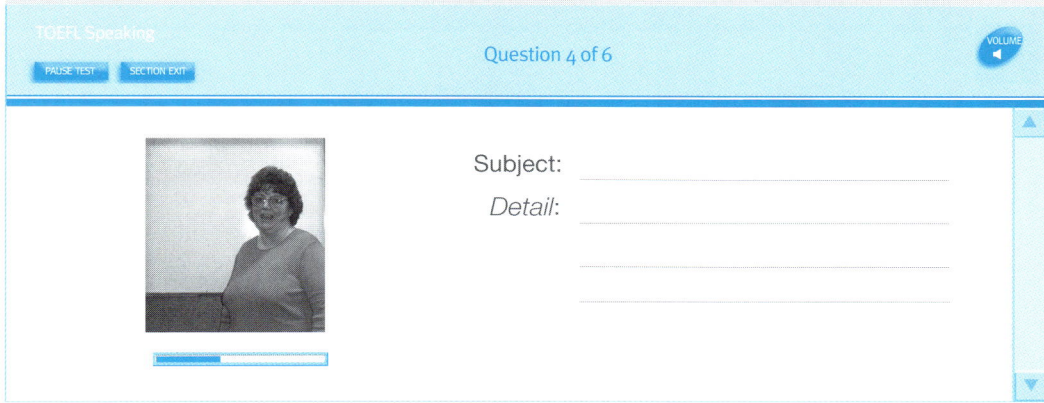

Subject:
Detail:

Q The professor discusses the diffusion of responsibility. Explain the idea of diffusion of responsibility.

Useful Expressions	
주제를 말할 때	예를 말할 때
■ The professor introduces ~	■ For instance ~
■ The professor explains ~	■ Such as ~
■ The lecture is mostly about ~	

3

The Positive Effect

In psychology and cognitive science, the positive effect is the tendency of people, when they evaluate the causes of the behaviors of a person they like. The term positive effect also refers to how people's emotional attention is different. Studies have found that people are more likely to pay attention to positive rather than negative connotations.

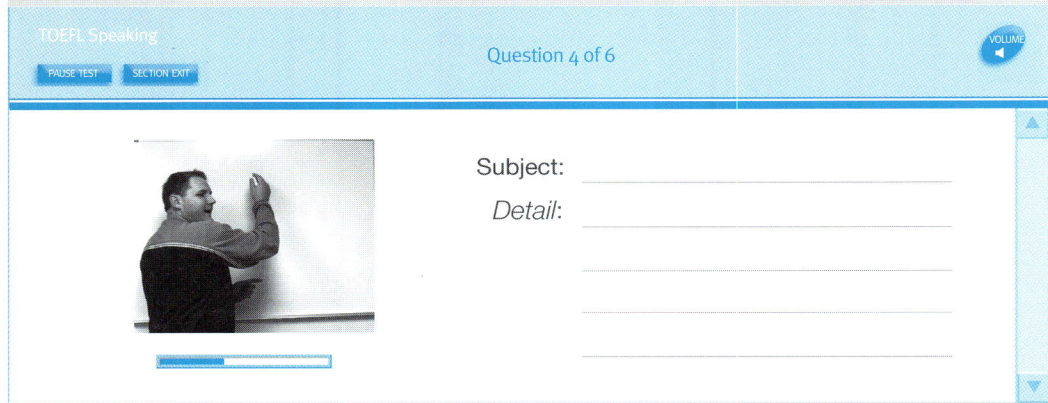

Subject: _____

Detail: _____

_____

_____

_____

Q The professor discusses positive effect. Explain how people show their interest in positive effect.

Useful Expressions

주제를 말할 때

- The professor is discussing ~
- The lecture describes ~
- The speaker points out ~

예를 말할 때

- The professor provides an example of ~

4

Short-term Memory

Short-term memory is that part of memory which stores a limited amount of information for a few seconds. This can be contrasted to long-term memory, in which a seemingly unlimited amount of information is stored indefinitely. Short-term memory can be described as the capacity for holding in mind, in an active, highly available state, a small amount of information. The information held in short-term memory may be recently processed sensory input, items recently retrieved from long-term memory, or the results of recent mental processing, although that is more generally related to the concept of working memory. In general, when new information comes in, old information goes out.

TOEFL Speaking

PAUSE TEST   SECTION EXIT

Question 4 of 6

VOLUME

Subject: _____

Detail: _____

_____

_____

_____

Q The professor discusses short-term memory. Explain the example of short-term memory.

Useful Expressions

주제를 말할 때	예를 말할 때
▪ The lecture is about ~ ▪ The professor made a point that ~ ▪ The professor's main point is ~	▪ This extended example ~

Exercise

🔊 읽기 지문을 읽은 후, 듣기 지문을 들으며 노트필기 공간에 주요 내용을 필기하시오.
필기 내용을 토대로 말하는 연습을 하시오.

CD Possible Responses: Track 48~55

1

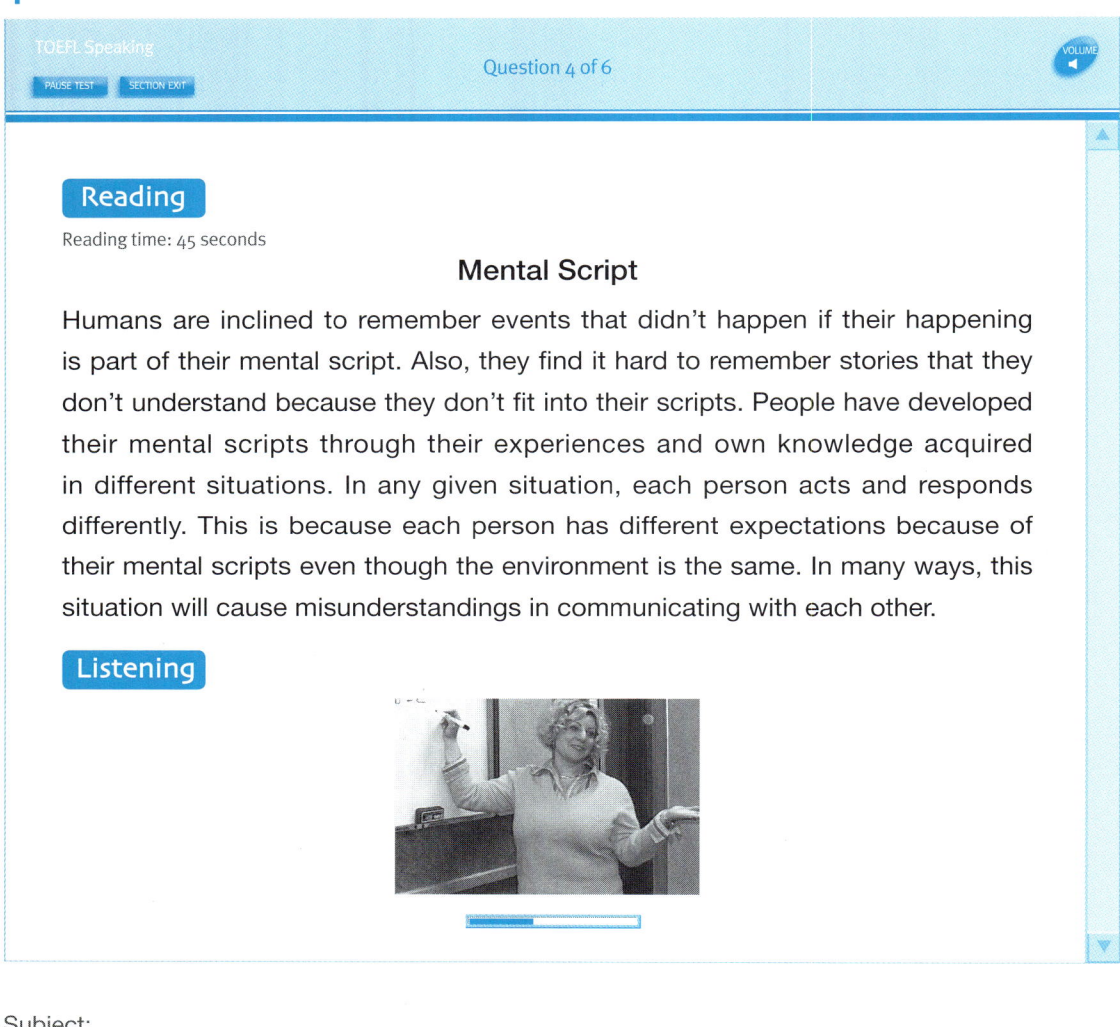

Reading

Reading time: 45 seconds

Mental Script

Humans are inclined to remember events that didn't happen if their happening is part of their mental script. Also, they find it hard to remember stories that they don't understand because they don't fit into their scripts. People have developed their mental scripts through their experiences and own knowledge acquired in different situations. In any given situation, each person acts and responds differently. This is because each person has different expectations because of their mental scripts even though the environment is the same. In many ways, this situation will cause misunderstandings in communicating with each other.

Listening

Subject:

Detail:

Speaking

The professor talks about mental script. Explain how the professor explains mental script through her own personal experiences.

Preparation Time : 30 seconds
Response Time : 60 seconds

▶ 자신이 녹음한 답변을 듣고 받아쓰기 하시오.

_____

_____

_____

_____

_____

_____

_____

▶ 정답 및 해설에 있는 모범 답안과 비교해 보시오.

Exercise

2

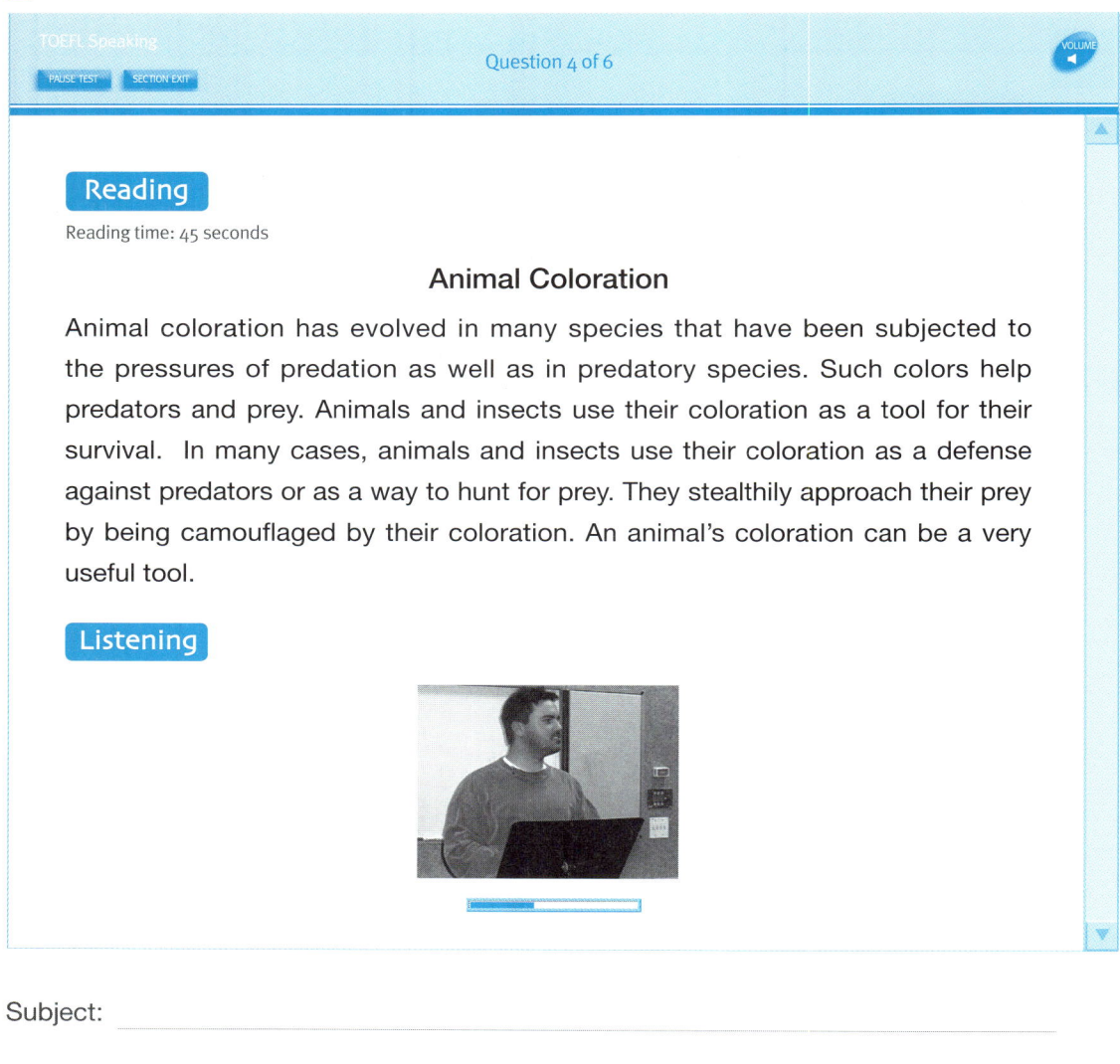

Reading

Reading time: 45 seconds

Animal Coloration

Animal coloration has evolved in many species that have been subjected to the pressures of predation as well as in predatory species. Such colors help predators and prey. Animals and insects use their coloration as a tool for their survival. In many cases, animals and insects use their coloration as a defense against predators or as a way to hunt for prey. They stealthily approach their prey by being camouflaged by their coloration. An animal's coloration can be a very useful tool.

Listening

Subject: ....

Detail: ....

....

....

....

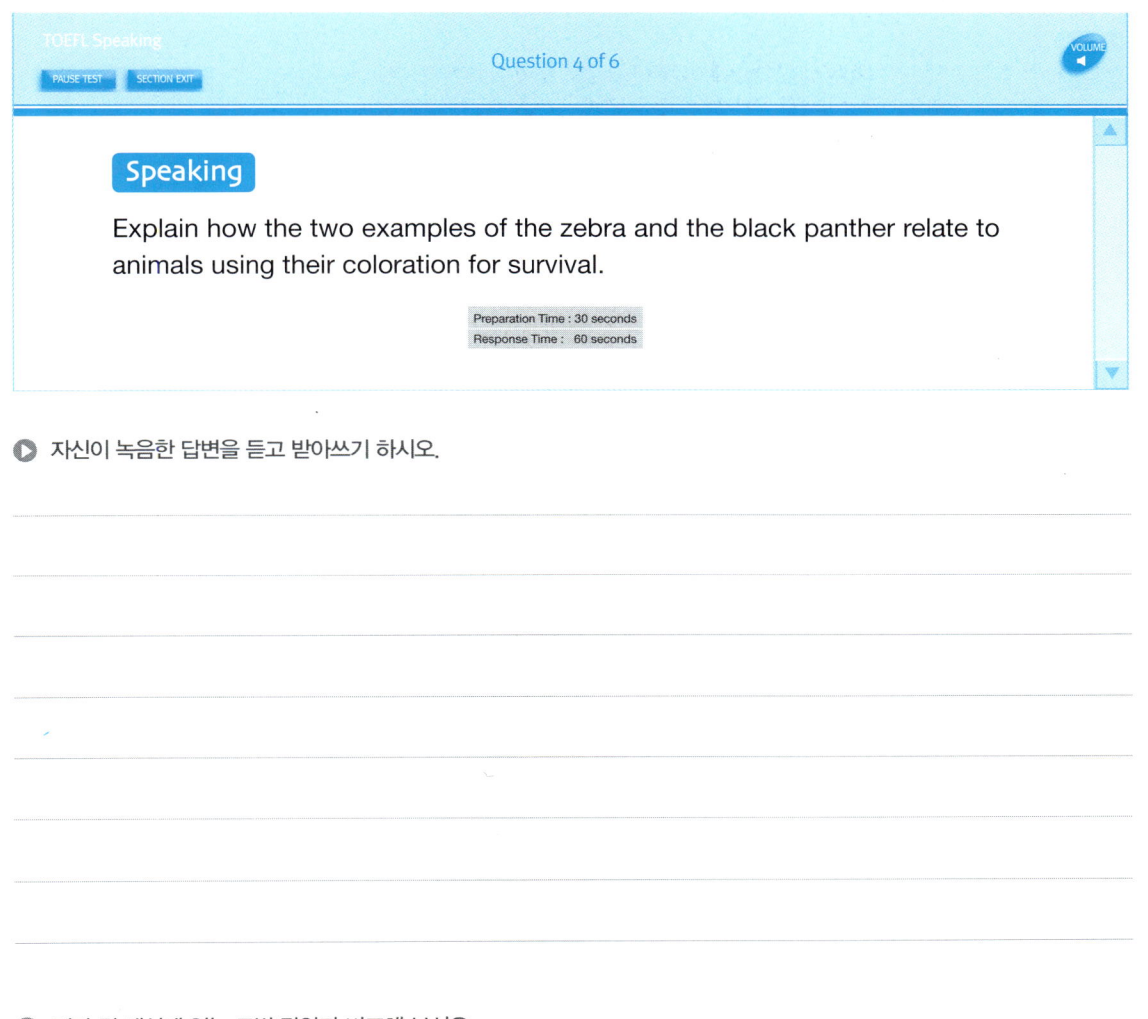

Speaking

Explain how the two examples of the zebra and the black panther relate to animals using their coloration for survival.

Preparation Time : 30 seconds
Response Time :   60 seconds

▶ 자신이 녹음한 답변을 듣고 받아쓰기 하시오.

▶ 정답 및 해설에 있는 모범 답안과 비교해 보시오.

Exercise

3

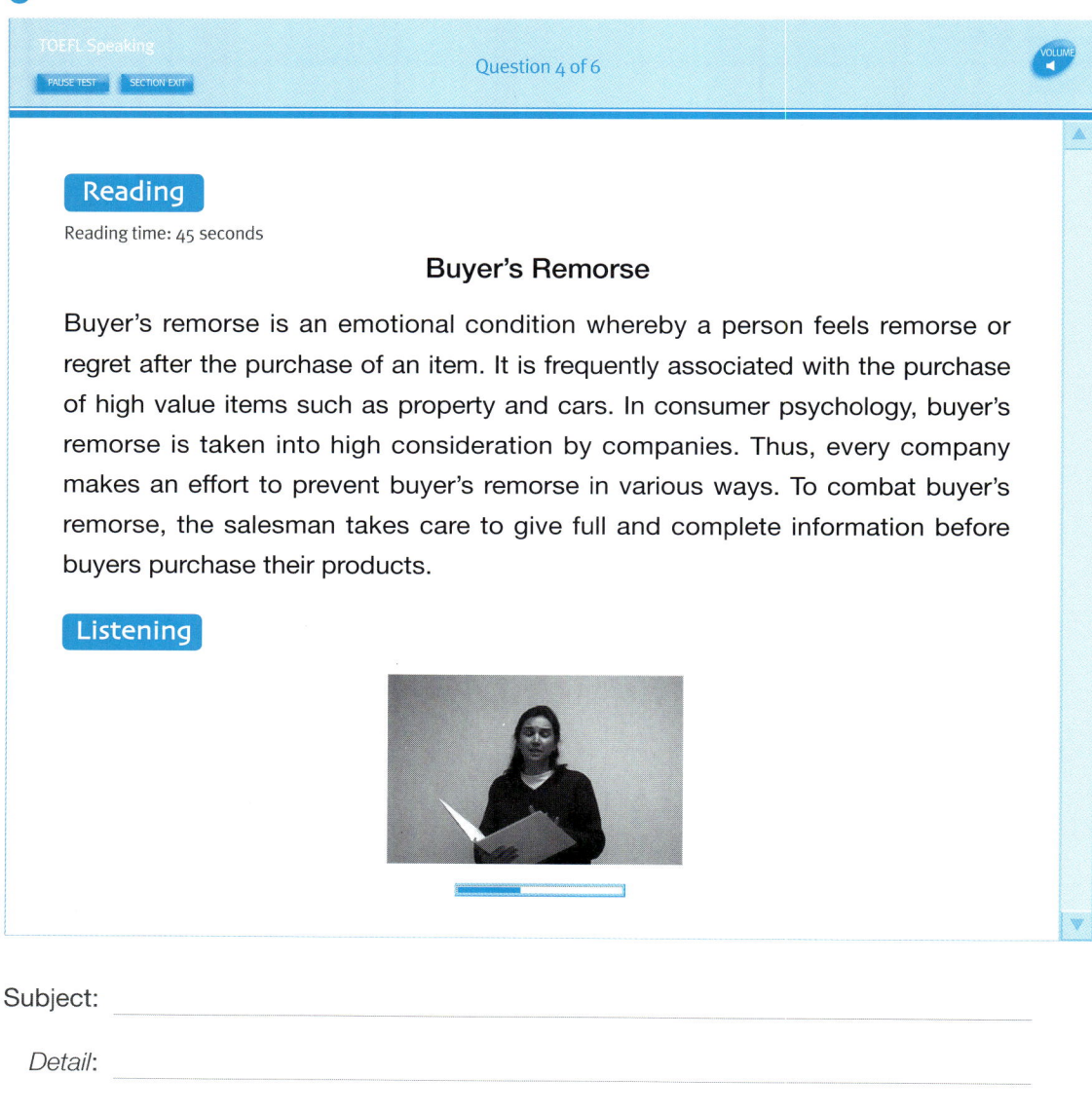

Reading

Reading time: 45 seconds

Buyer's Remorse

Buyer's remorse is an emotional condition whereby a person feels remorse or regret after the purchase of an item. It is frequently associated with the purchase of high value items such as property and cars. In consumer psychology, buyer's remorse is taken into high consideration by companies. Thus, every company makes an effort to prevent buyer's remorse in various ways. To combat buyer's remorse, the salesman takes care to give full and complete information before buyers purchase their products.

Listening

Subject: _____

Detail: _____

_____

_____

_____

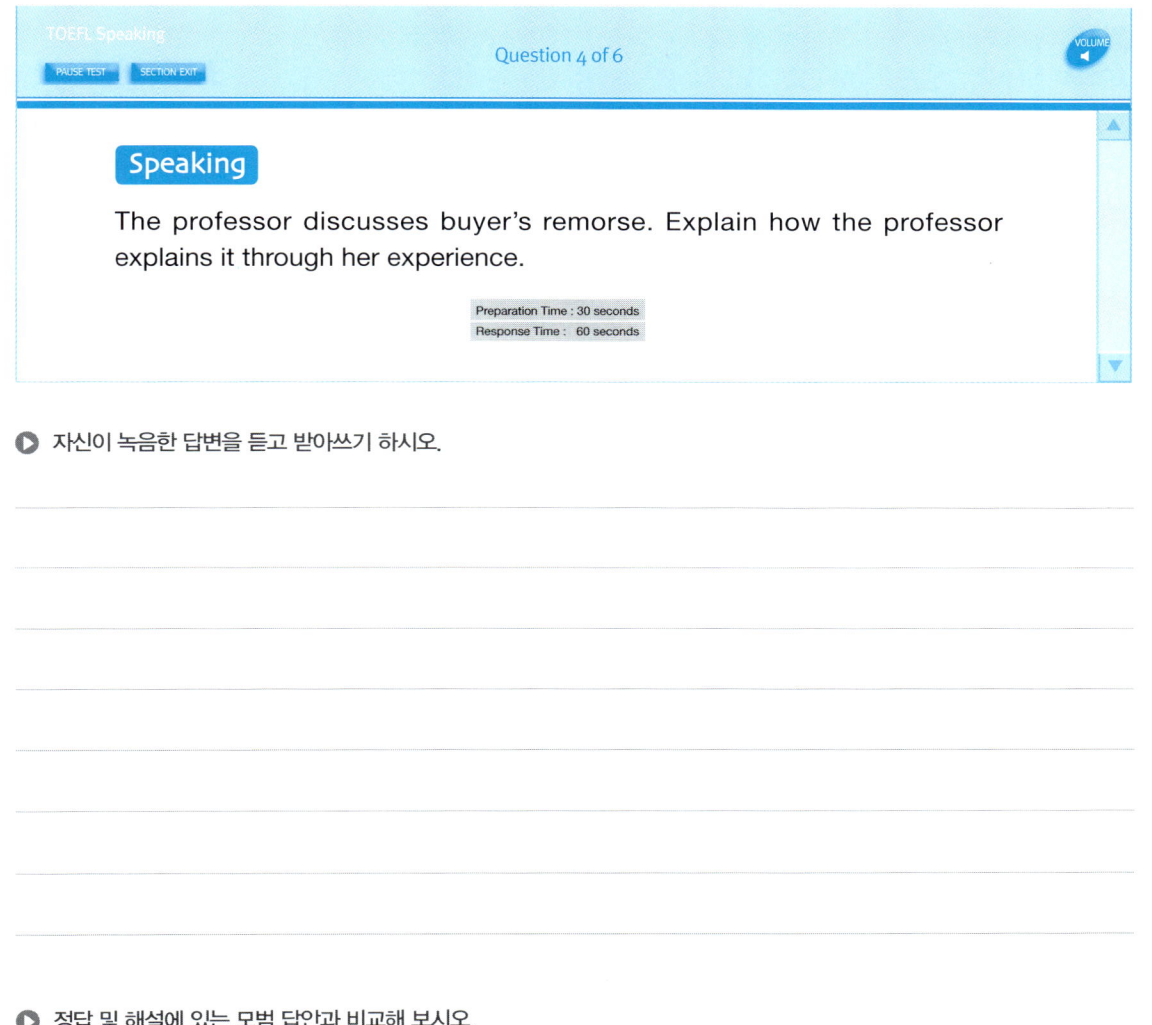

TOEFL Speaking

PAUSE TEST   SECTION EXIT

VOLUME

Speaking

The professor discusses buyer's remorse. Explain how the professor explains it through her experience.

Preparation Time : 30 seconds
Response Time : 60 seconds

▶ 자신이 녹음한 답변을 듣고 받아쓰기 하시오.

▶ 정답 및 해설에 있는 모범 답안과 비교해 보시오.

Exercise

4

TOEFL Speaking

PAUSE TEST SECTION EXIT

Question 4 of 6

VOLUME

Reading

Reading time: 45 seconds

Secondary Ecological Succession

Nature has a way of fixing its own problems in a natural setting. Without human intervention, nature has the ability to solve problems. The important thing here is that trees coexist to give each plant a chance to grow and to allow enough time for a budding seed to grow into another tree. Nature fixes the problem where different types of trees both need sunlight and water. Nature only allows for one type of tree to grow or reproduce per season. The change in seasons kills one type of tree and then the other type of tree starts to grow.

Listening

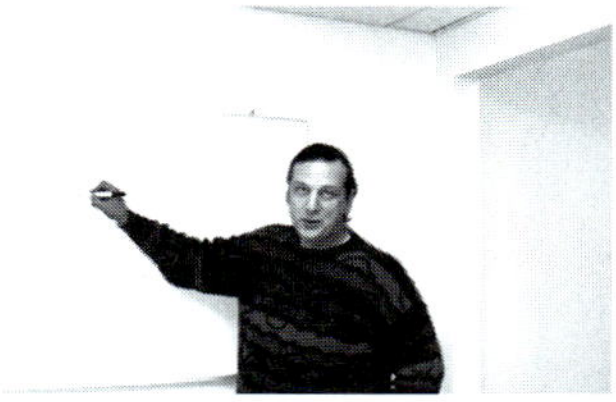

Subject:

Detail:

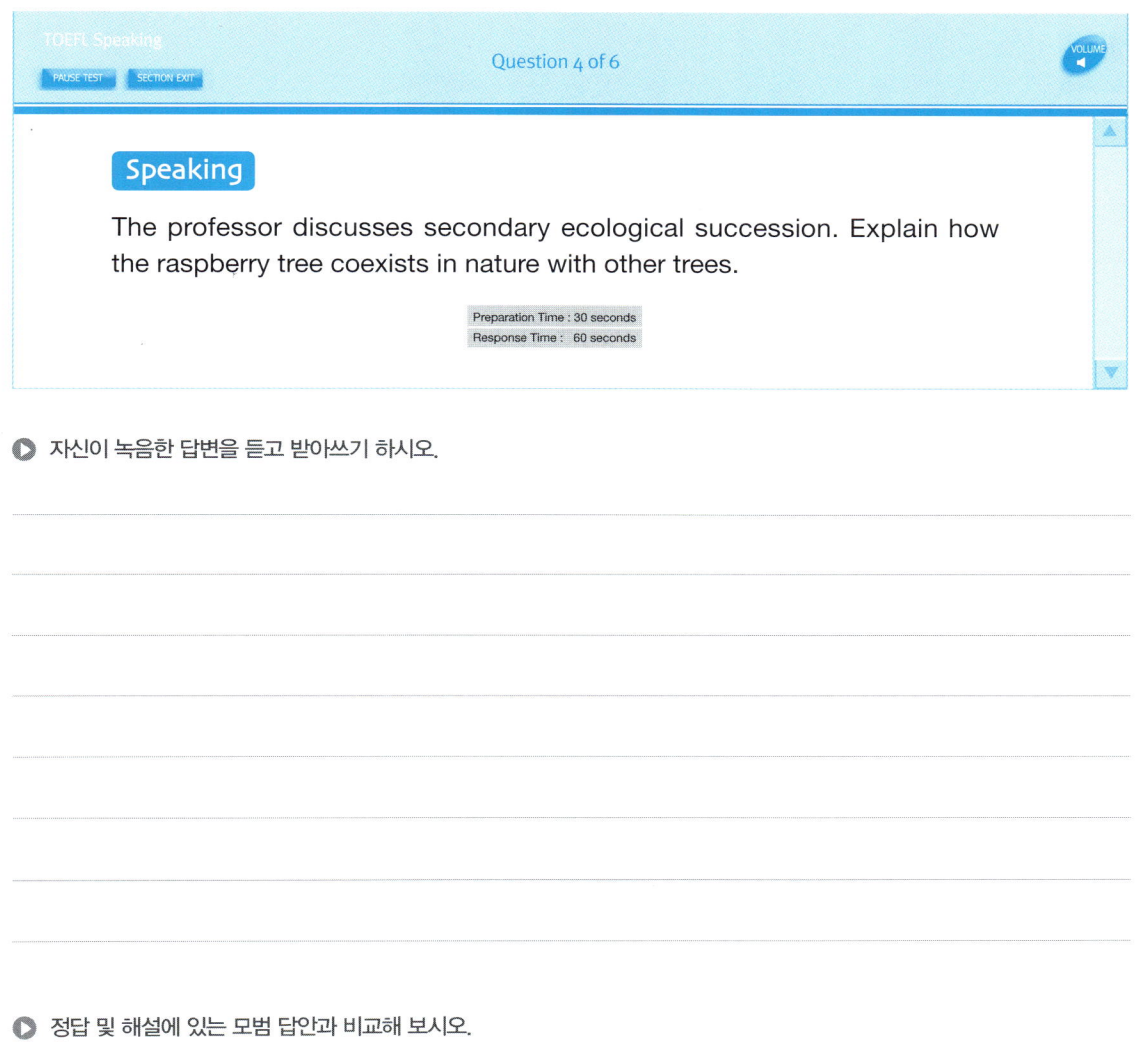

Speaking

The professor discusses secondary ecological succession. Explain how the raspberry tree coexists in nature with other trees.

Preparation Time : 30 seconds
Response Time : 60 seconds

▶ 자신이 녹음한 답변을 듣고 받아쓰기 하시오.

▶ 정답 및 해설에 있는 모범 답안과 비교해 보시오.

Exercise

5

Reading

Reading time: 45 seconds

Instinctive Behavior

Animals have specific instinctive behavior when around their habitation. Animals act instinctively to warn or send different messages to their fellow animals that an intruder is near. But in some animals, instinctive behavior is often modified by the outside world. When they feel they are in danger they behave wildly, but when they feel they are not threatened, they behave gently. These instinctive behaviors are indigenous in the area that the animals live. These animals are very territorial and guard their territory from any friend or foe.

Listening

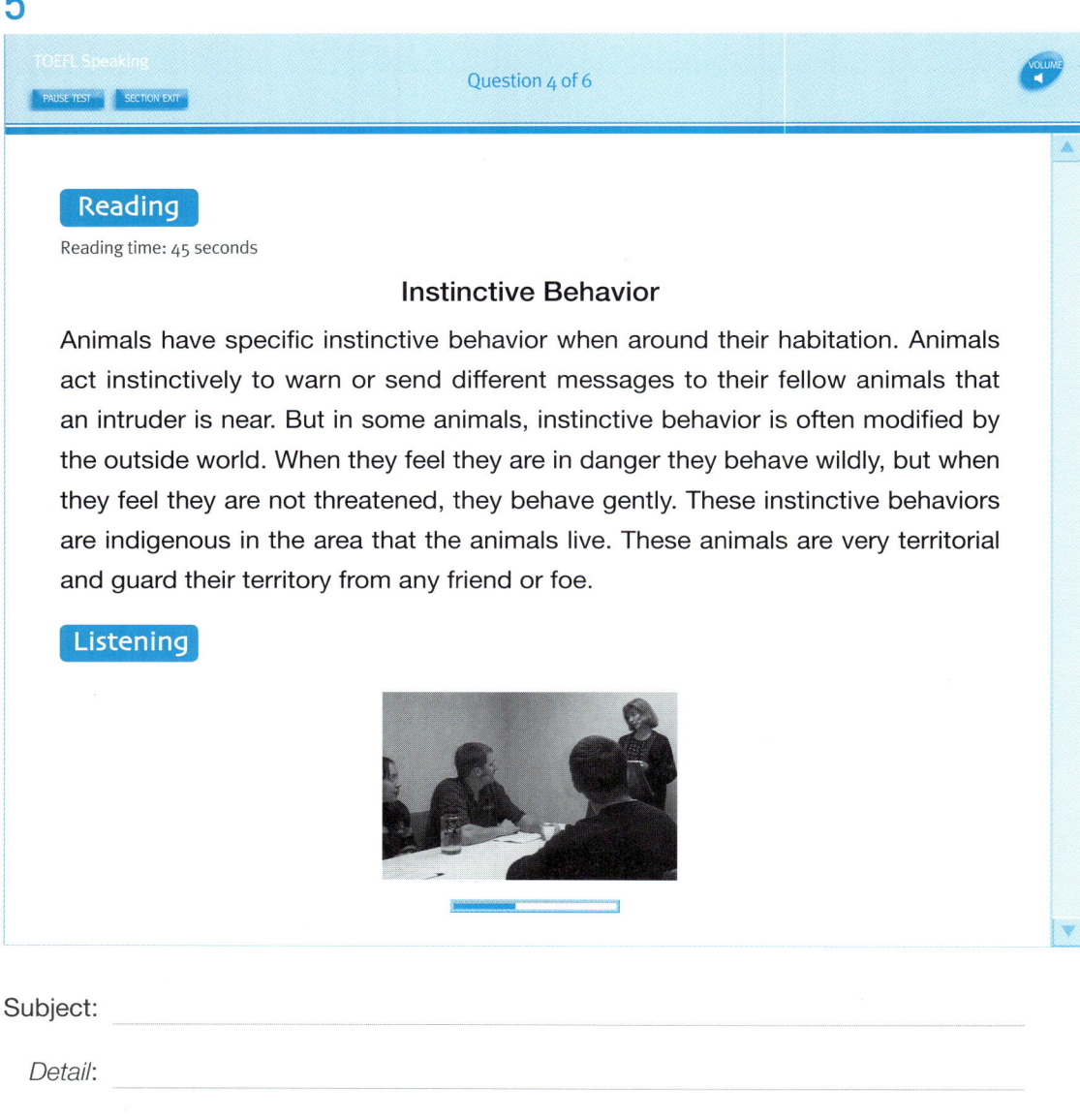

Subject: ....

Detail: ....

....

....

....

TOEFL Speaking

PAUSE TEST   SECTION EXIT

VOLUME

Speaking

The professor talks about the instinctive behavior of animals. Explain how prairie dogs behave.

Preparation Time : 30 seconds
Response Time :   60 seconds

▶ 자신이 녹음한 답변을 듣고 받아쓰기 하시오.

▶ 정답 및 해설에 있는 모범 답안과 비교해 보시오.

Exercise

6

TOEFL Speaking

PAUSE TEST SECTION EXIT

Question 4 of 6

VOLUME

Reading

Reading time: 45 seconds

Assumption

An assumption is something taken for granted or accepted as the truth without proof. Assumptions are made constantly when most individuals believe that other people act upon their assumptions. Ordinary people generally believe that most others act upon their assumptions.

Listening

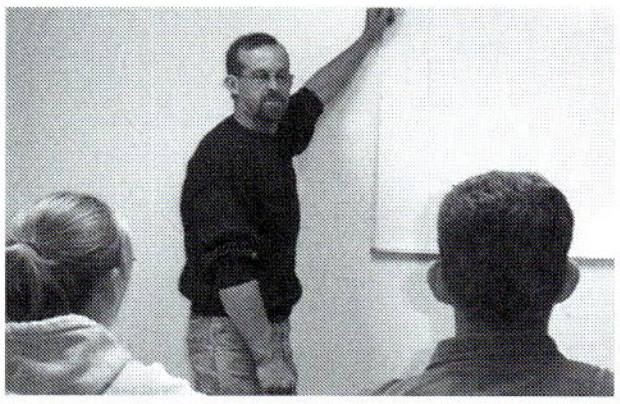

Subject:

Detail:

TOEFL Speaking

PAUSE TEST　SECTION EXIT

VOLUME

Speaking

The professor talks about assumption. Explain how the experiment explains people's assumption.

Preparation Time : 30 seconds
Response Time :　60 seconds

▶ 자신이 녹음한 답변을 듣고 받아쓰기 하시오.

▶ 정답 및 해설에 있는 모범 답안과 비교해 보시오.

Exercise

7

Reading

Reading time: 45 seconds

Cognitive Dissonance

In psychology, cognitive dissonance is the perception of incompatibility between two cognitions. A cognition is any element of knowledge, including attitude, emotion, belief, or behavior. People don't want to change their behavior when they are acting according to their beliefs. To reduce the amount of dissonance (conflict) between thoughts, people have the consciousness to acquire or invent new thoughts or beliefs, or to modify their existing beliefs.

Listening

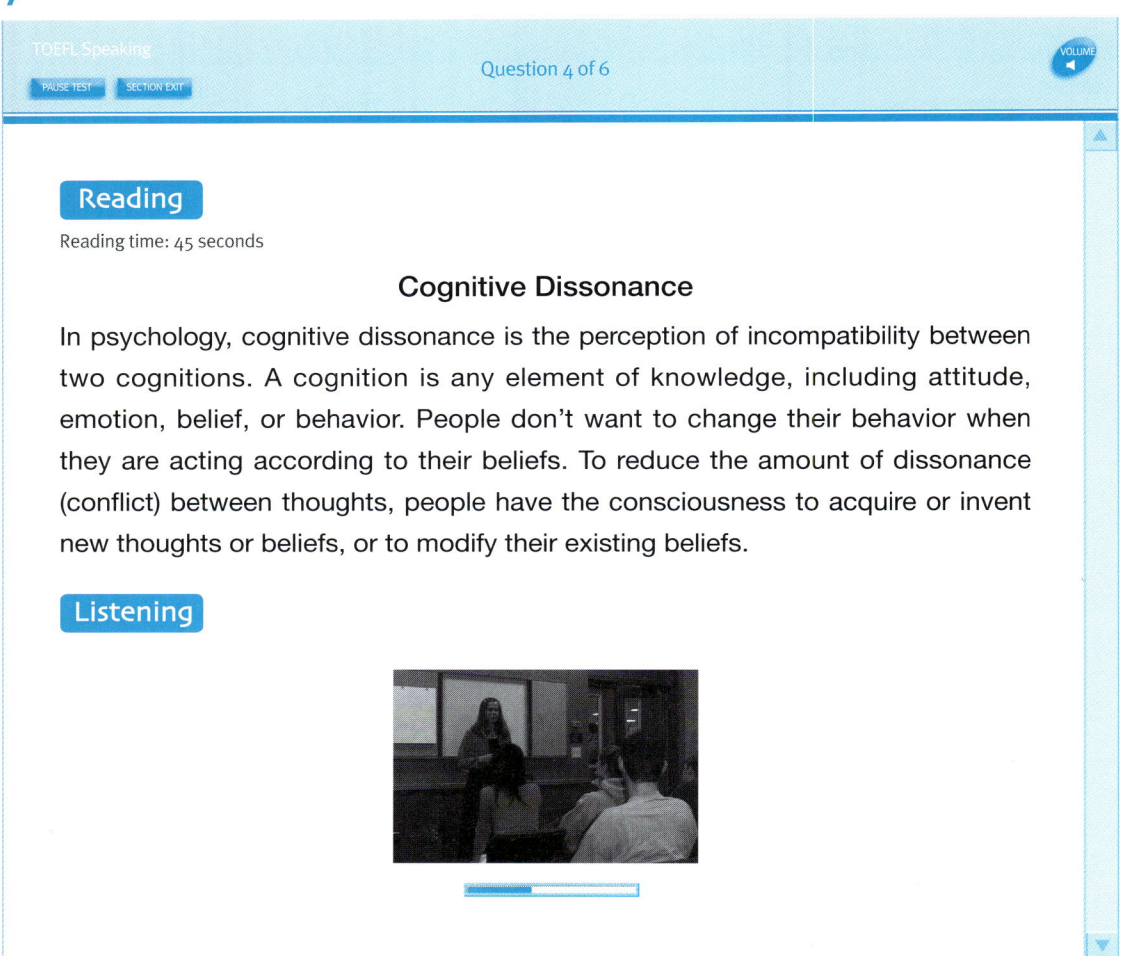

Subject:

Detail:

Speaking

The professor talks about cognitive dissonance. Explain how the professor explains it through her personal experience.

Preparation Time : 30 seconds
Response Time : 60 seconds

▶ 자신이 녹음한 답변을 듣고 받아쓰기 하시오.

▶ 정답 및 해설에 있는 모범 답안과 비교해 보시오.

Exercise

8

Reading

Reading time: 45 seconds

Role Conflict

Role conflict is a conflict among the roles corresponding to two or more statuses. Today, people juggle many responsibilities created by their various statuses and roles in an attempt to create a more peaceful environment. But people often fail to carry out their various roles, so they cannot satisfy everyone who is involved in the situation. The main reason for this is that while they are choosing their roles, they cannot carry out their other roles. This happens because as time goes by, modern society gets more complicated. This problem is getting more serious in society among people both inside and outside of the home.

Listening

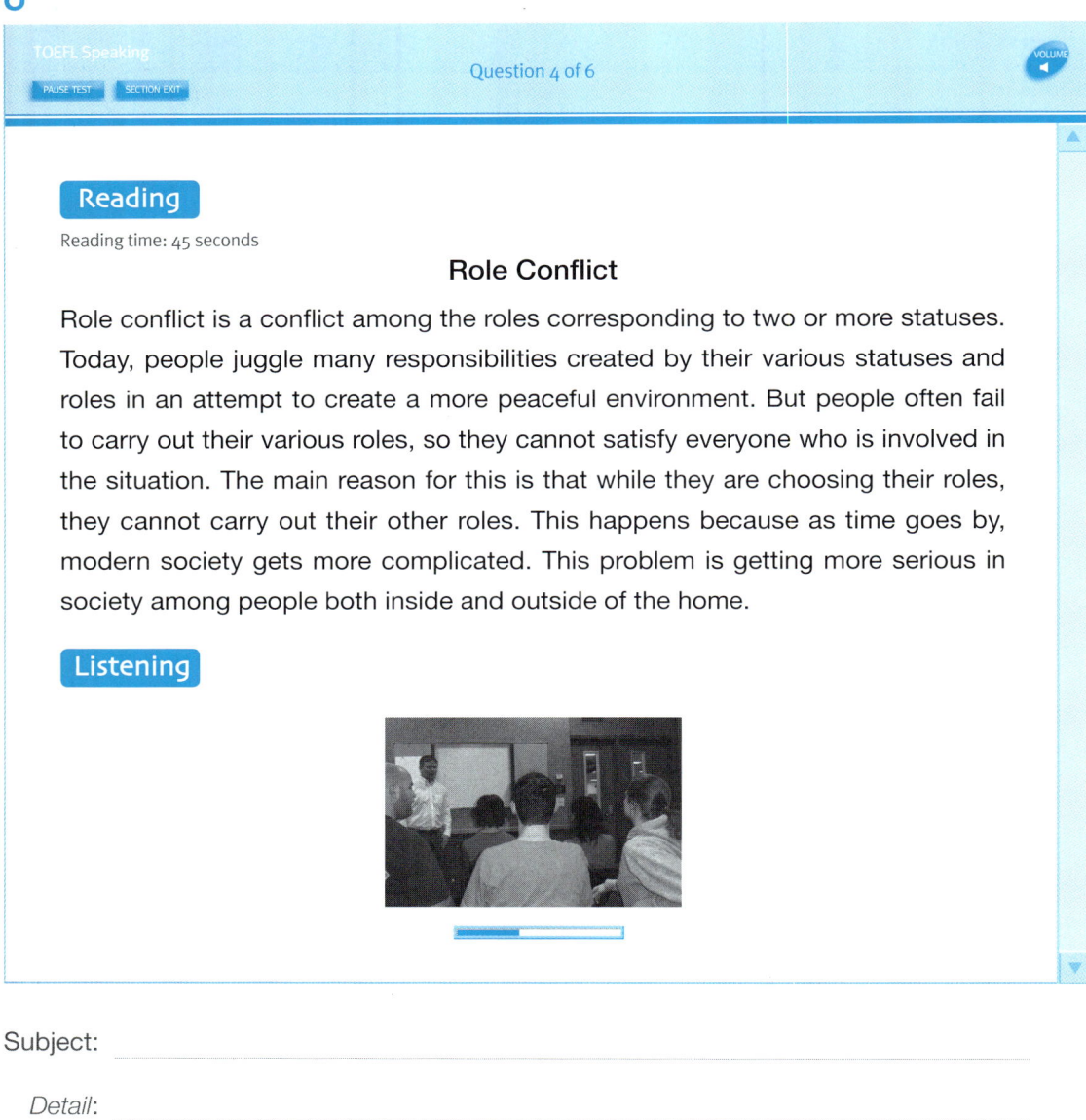

Subject: _____

Detail: _____

_____

_____

_____

Speaking

The professor talks about role conflict. Explain how role conflict is illustrated by using the given examples.

Preparation Time : 30 seconds
Response Time : 60 seconds

▶ 자신이 녹음한 답변을 듣고 받아쓰기 하시오.

▶ 정답 및 해설에 있는 모범 답안과 비교해 보시오.

Task 5

Problem and Solution

5 | Problem and Solution

요약과 의견 제시가 결합된 문제 유형으로 대학 생활에서 발생할 수 있는 문제와 그 해결책에 관한 두 학생의 대화를 듣고 그와 관련된 질문에 답해야 한다. 문제를 이해하고 해결 방안을 요약하는 능력이 필요하며 선호하는 해결 방법을 선택해 그 이유를 개인적인 경험이나 주어진 정보를 토대로 주어진 시간 안에 분명하고 논리적으로 제시해야 한다.

◘ 문제 유형

듣기	길이	60–90초 (180–220 단어)
	화자	1) 두 학생 2) 학생과 교수 3) 학생과 대학 교직원
	주제	1) 학교 수업이나 대학 생활의 문제점을 제시 2) 문제 해결을 위한 두 가지 해결 방안 제시
말하기	내용	1) 제시된 학생의 문제점은 무엇인가? 2) 다른 학생이 제안한 두 가지 해결 방안은 무엇인가? 3) 둘 중 선호하는 해결 방안을 선택하고 그 이유를 밝히시오

◘ 기출 주제

- Schoolwork
- Conflict in schedule
- Finding the classroom
- Inviting a speaker for a lecture
- Directing a school play
- Problem with enrolling
- Taking children on a field trip

- Disagreement with grade
- Publishing a photo magazine
- Transportation problem
- Housing problem
- Conflict with taking a class
- Problem with two meetings

■ 화면 구성

1 듣기: 문제점 및 그에 대한 두 가지 해결 방안에 대해 나누는 대화를 60~90초간 청취한다.

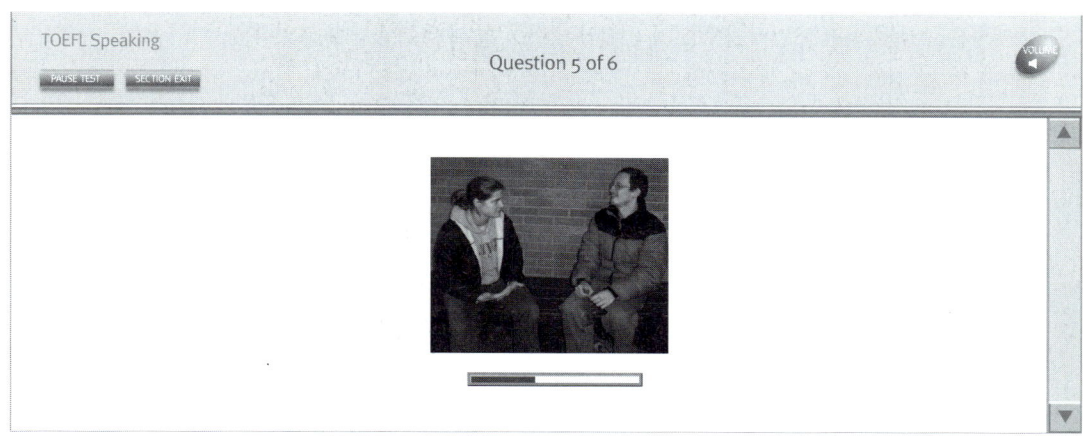

2 말하기: 청취 내용에서 언급된 학생의 문제점 및 제시된 해결책을 밝히고 선호하는 해결책 및 근거를 20초간 준비한 후 60초간 말한다.

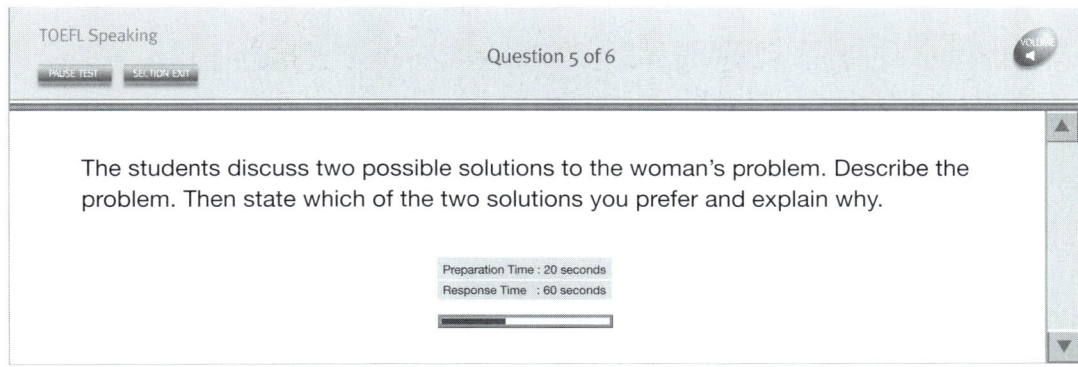

■ Strategy

문제점 파악하기
문제점은 주로 대화의 초반에 주어지며 주제와 연관이 있기 때문에 대화 도입부에 주목하여 들어야 한다.

선호하는 해결 방안 선택하기
두 가지의 해결 방안이 제안되는데 이 중 자신이 선호하는 해결 방안을 선택해야 한다. 따라서 각각의 장단점을 파악하고 해결 방안을 제안 받은 사람의 반응과 자신의 의견을 고려하여 말하기 쉬운 쪽을 선택하는 것이 효과적이다. 두 개의 제안을 받기 위해서는 첫 번째 제안에 대하여 부정적인 반응을 보이는 것이 보편적이다. 따라서 두 번째 제안을 자신이 선호하는 것으로 선택하면 답하는 것이 보다 수월하다.

화자의 반응에 주목하기
해결책에 대한 화자의 반응에 주목하자. 제시된 해결 방안의 장단점이 이 부분에서 언급되는 경우가 있으므로 자신이 선호하는 해결책에 대한 답을 할 때 유용한 정보가 될 수 있다. 예를 들어, 전공 필수 과목이 이번 학기에 개설되지 않아서 들을 수 없다고 말하는 학생에게 커뮤니티 칼리지에서 수업을 들으라고 제안했을 때, 같은 대학에서 수업을 듣는 것이 더 편하다고 반응한다면, 커뮤니티 칼리지에서 수업을 듣는 것이 불편하다는 것을 알 수 있으므로, 이것을 선택하지 않는 이유로 활용할 수 있다.

자신의 경험 활용하기
대화에서 언급된 이유를 자신의 이유인 것처럼 답할 수도 있고 비슷한 경험이 있다면 자신의 경험을 이용하여 답할 수도 있다.

의견 제시 강조하기
이 문제는 요약과 의견 제시가 결합된 유일한 문제이다. 이처럼 요약과 의견 제시가 결합된 문제는 요약의 비중을 1/3 정도로 유지하고 의견 제시에 2/3 정도의 비중을 두어 말하는 것이 바람직하다. 선택하지 않는 해결 방안에 대해서는 그에 대한 문제점이 언급된 경우, 이것을 언급하는 것이 더욱 설득력 있다.

– 이렇게 답을 전개하지 말라.
  남자의 문제는 ~이다. 여자가 두 가지의 제안을 했는데 첫 번째는 ~이고 두 번째는 ~인데 나는 ~이 좋다. 그 이유는 ~이다.

– 이렇게 답을 전개하라
  남자의 문제는 ~이다. 여자는 첫 번째로 ~을 제안했는데 이것의 문제는 ~이다. 그래서 나는 두 번째 제안 ~이 더 좋다고 생각한다. 그 이유는 ~과 ~이다. The woman으로 시작하는 것이 좋다.

> **Tip** 1 문제는 항상 똑같다. 따라서 문제를 읽어주는 동안 답을 준비하라
> 2 두 번째 제안에 대하여 부정적인 반응을 보일 때는 그 부정적인 반응을 희석한 후 장점을 말하라. 예) 비록 ~한 단점이 있지만 ~한 장점이 더욱 이익이 된다

▌ Listening

M: Hey, Linda! How's it going?

W: Hi, Mike. I'm fine, I guess, but my schoolwork is really stressing me out.

M: Yeah? What's the matter?

W: **1** Well, I have to write a paper, prepare for two exams, and finish my math homework. It's just too much to handle. One minute I'm trying to concentrate on studying for one of my exams, and the next minute I'm wondering when I can finish that math homework.

M: Wow, sounds like you have much more work than you can handle. **2** Look, have you met some of your professors... I mean, have you tried to explain your situation? You might be able to get an extension on your paper or your math homework...

W: But I'm worried whether I'll be able to get the same grade as other students if I get an extension.

M: Well, **3** another thing that you might do is to make a schedule for yourself. That's what I do when I feel overwhelmed.

W: What do you mean?

M: Well, I mean, try to make your own schedule for the next few days on how much time to spend on each assignment...

W: Oh! That's a good idea. I'll try it.

1 문제 제시   **2** 첫 번째 제안   **3** 두 번째 제안

Q The students discuss two possible solutions to the woman's problem. Describe the problem. Then state which of the two solutions you prefer and explain why.

▌ Speaking

1 The woman's problem is that she can't handle her school workload. She has to write her term paper, prepare for two exams, and finish her math homework. **2** The man suggests meeting her professors to get an extension on her term paper. **3** But the problem is that even though her professors might be willing to give her an extension, they might somehow penalize her for it by grading her assignments more severely. **4** The other idea like preparing a schedule seems better **5** because she can carry out her tasks one at a time and **6** if she learns how to organize a schedule now, it will help her throughout her academic career. **7** So, I support her making a schedule that she can handle.

1 문제 제시   **2** 첫 번째 제안   **3** 첫 번째 제안에 대한 문제점   **4** 내가 선택한 두 번째 제안
5 선택한 제안에 대한 첫 번째 이유   **6** 선택한 제안에 대한 두 번째 이유   **7** 요약 정리

Mini Test

CD Possible Responses: Track 58

🔊 듣기 지문을 들으며 노트필기 공간에 주요 내용을 필기하시오.
필기 내용을 토대로 말하는 연습을 하시오.

1

TOEFL Speaking		VOLUME
PAUSE TEST SECTION EXIT	Question 5 of 6	

Problem : _____

Solution 1 : _____

    Response → _____

Solution 2 : _____

    Response → _____

Q The students discuss two possible solutions to the man's problem. Describe the problem. Then state which of the two solutions you prefer and explain why.

_____

_____

_____

_____

Useful Expressions

문제점을 말할 때

- The man's problem is ~
- The woman's problem is ~
- The problem he(she) has is ~

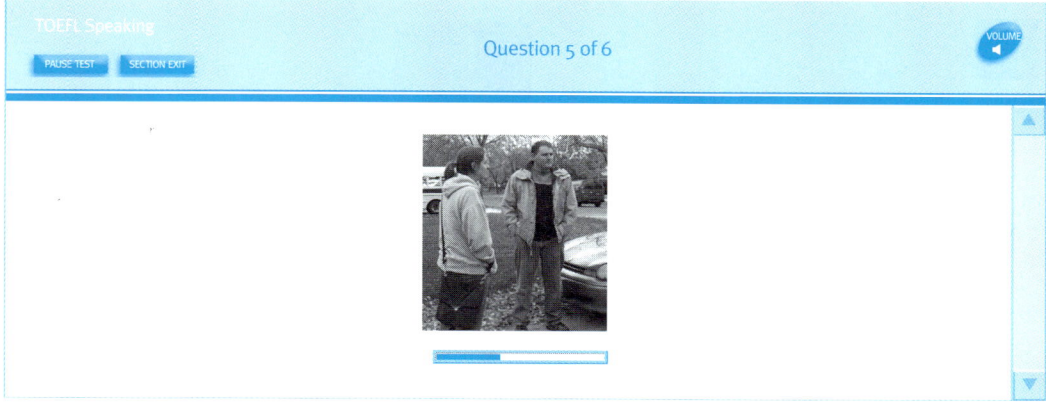

Problem :

Solution 1 :

     Response →

Solution 2 :

     Response →

Q The students discuss two possible solutions to the woman's problem. Describe the problem. Then state which of the two solutions you prefer and explain why.

Useful Expressions

제안을 말할 때

- The man suggests ~
- The woman suggests ~
- The man(woman) proposes ~

3

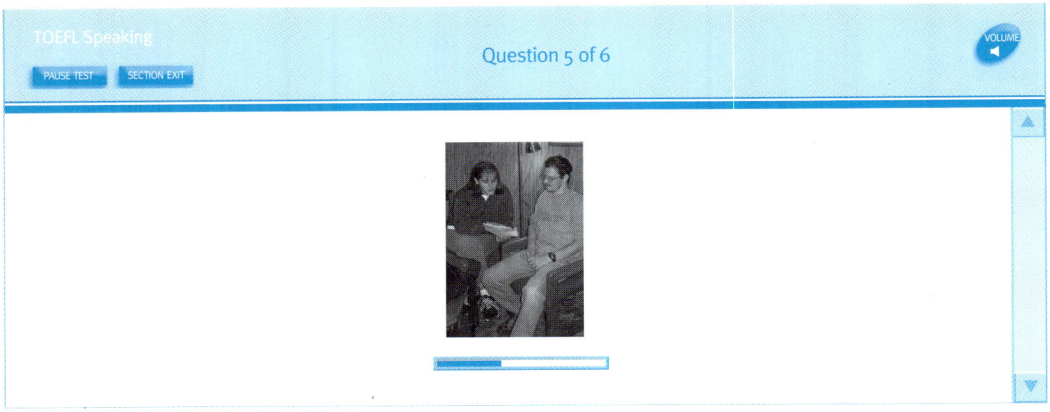

Problem : _____

Solution 1 : _____

    Response → _____

Solution 2 : _____

    Response → _____

Q The students discuss two possible solutions to the man's problem. Describe the problem. Then state which of the two solutions you prefer and explain why.

_____

_____

_____

_____

Useful Expressions

선호를 말할 때

- I think that the other idea, like, ~ is better
- I prefer ~
- I would rather ~

4

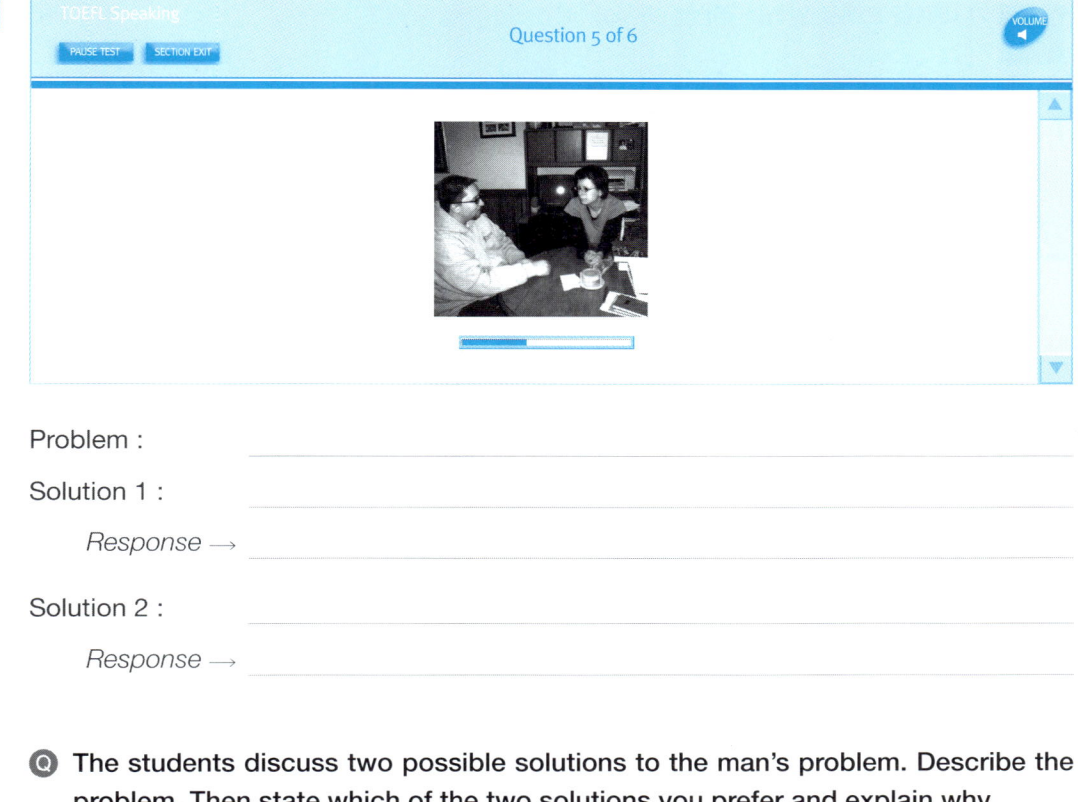

Problem : _____

Solution 1 : _____

    Response → _____

Solution 2 : _____

    Response → _____

Q The students discuss two possible solutions to the man's problem. Describe the problem. Then state which of the two solutions you prefer and explain why.

_____

_____

_____

_____

Useful Expressions

이유를 말할 때

- because (of) ~
- due to ~
- owing to ~

Exercise

🔊 듣기 지문을 들으며 노트필기 공간에 주요 내용을 필기하시오.
필기 내용을 토대로 말하는 연습을 하시오.

CD Possible Responses: Track 60~67

1

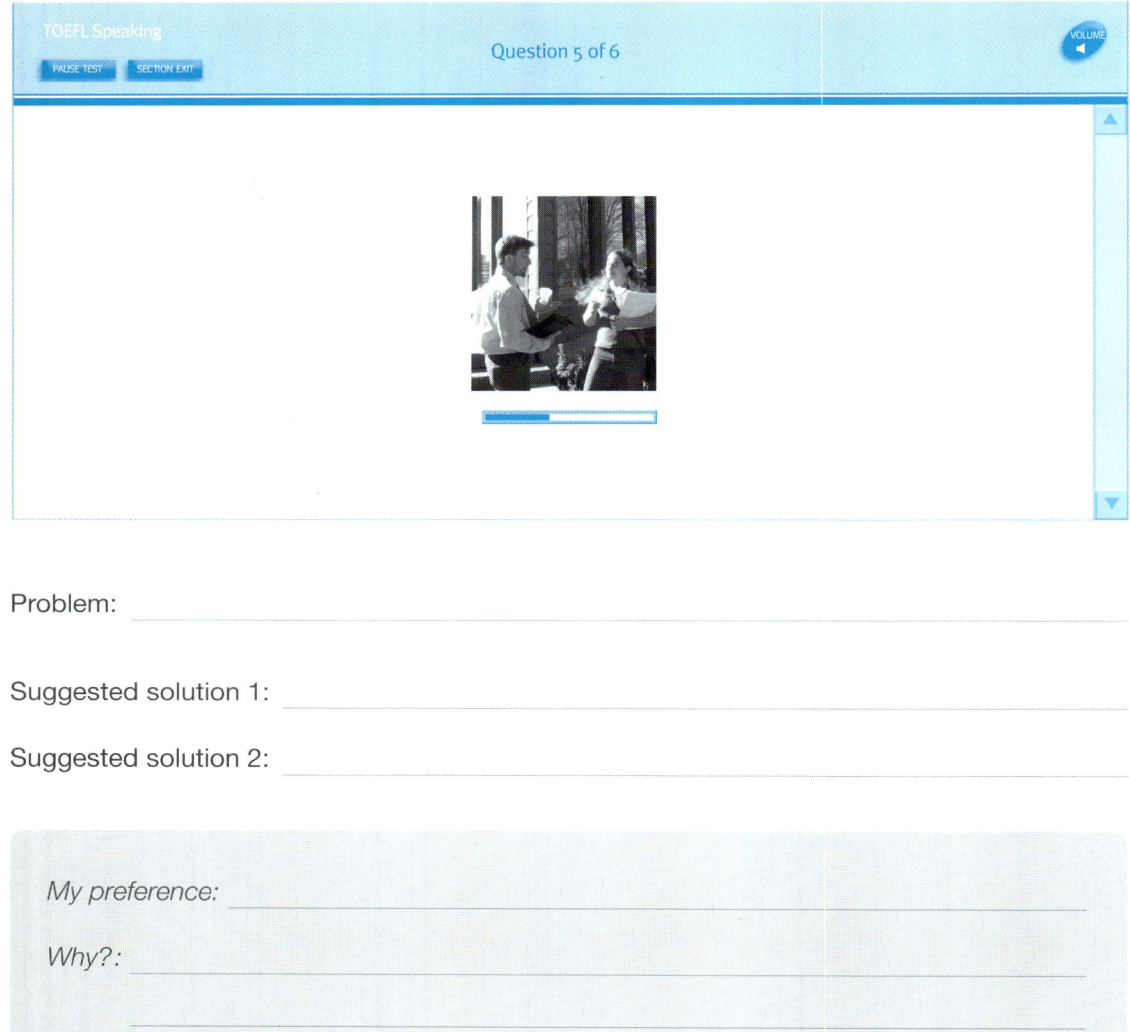

Problem: _____

Suggested solution 1: _____

Suggested solution 2: _____

My preference: _____

Why?: _____
_____

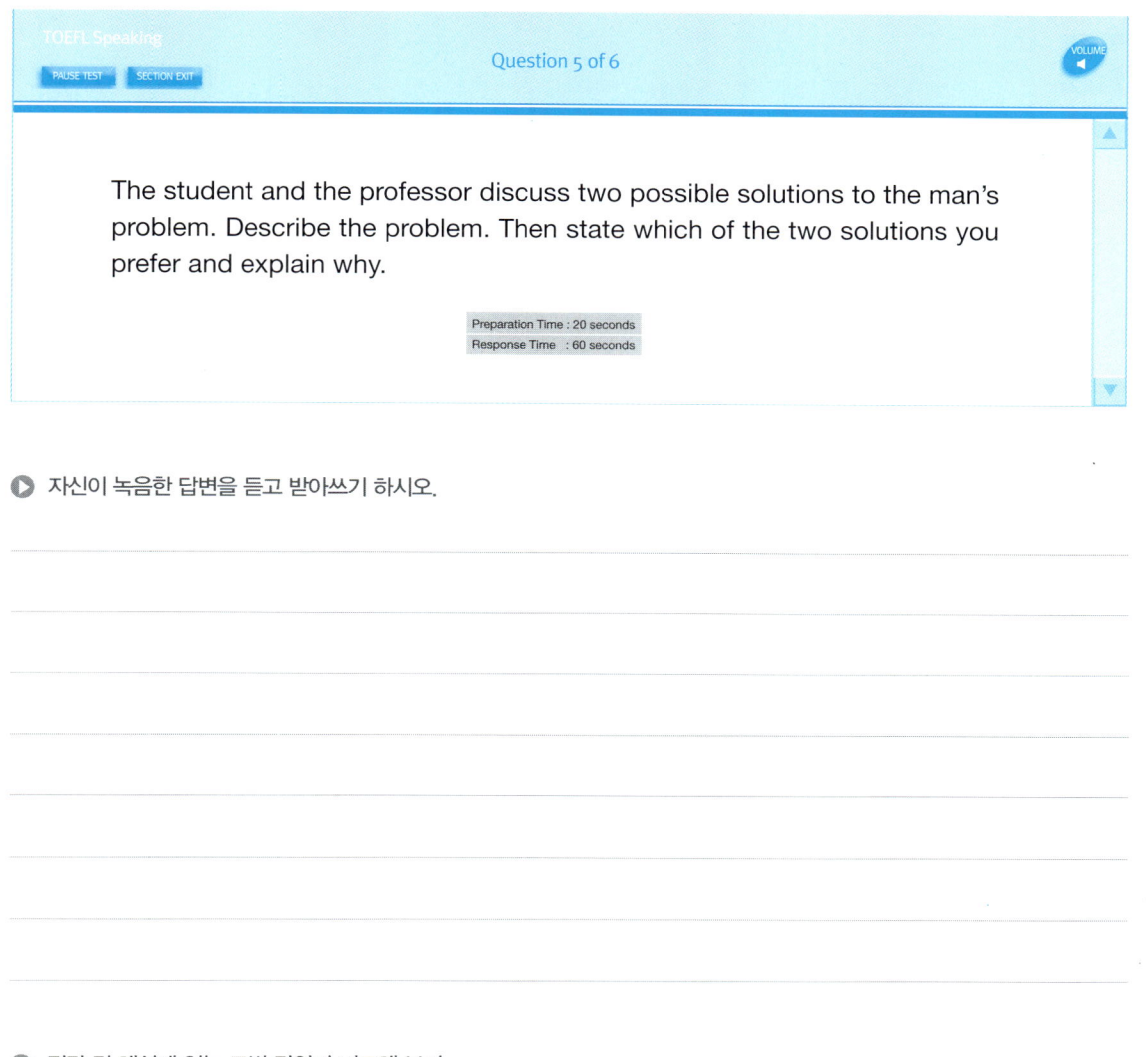

The student and the professor discuss two possible solutions to the man's problem. Describe the problem. Then state which of the two solutions you prefer and explain why.

Preparation Time : 20 seconds
Response Time   : 60 seconds

▶ 자신이 녹음한 답변을 듣고 받아쓰기 하시오.

▶ 정답 및 해설에 있는 모범 답안과 비교해 보자.

Exercise

2

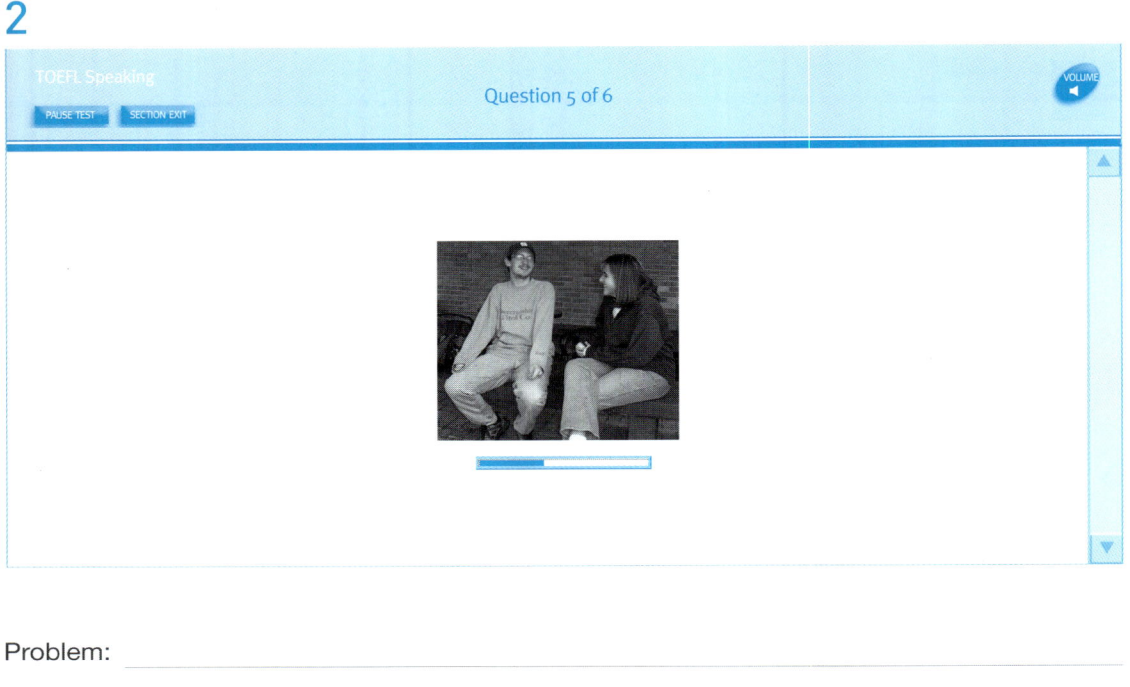

Problem: _____

Suggested solution 1: _____

Suggested solution 2: _____

My preference: _____

Why?: _____
_____

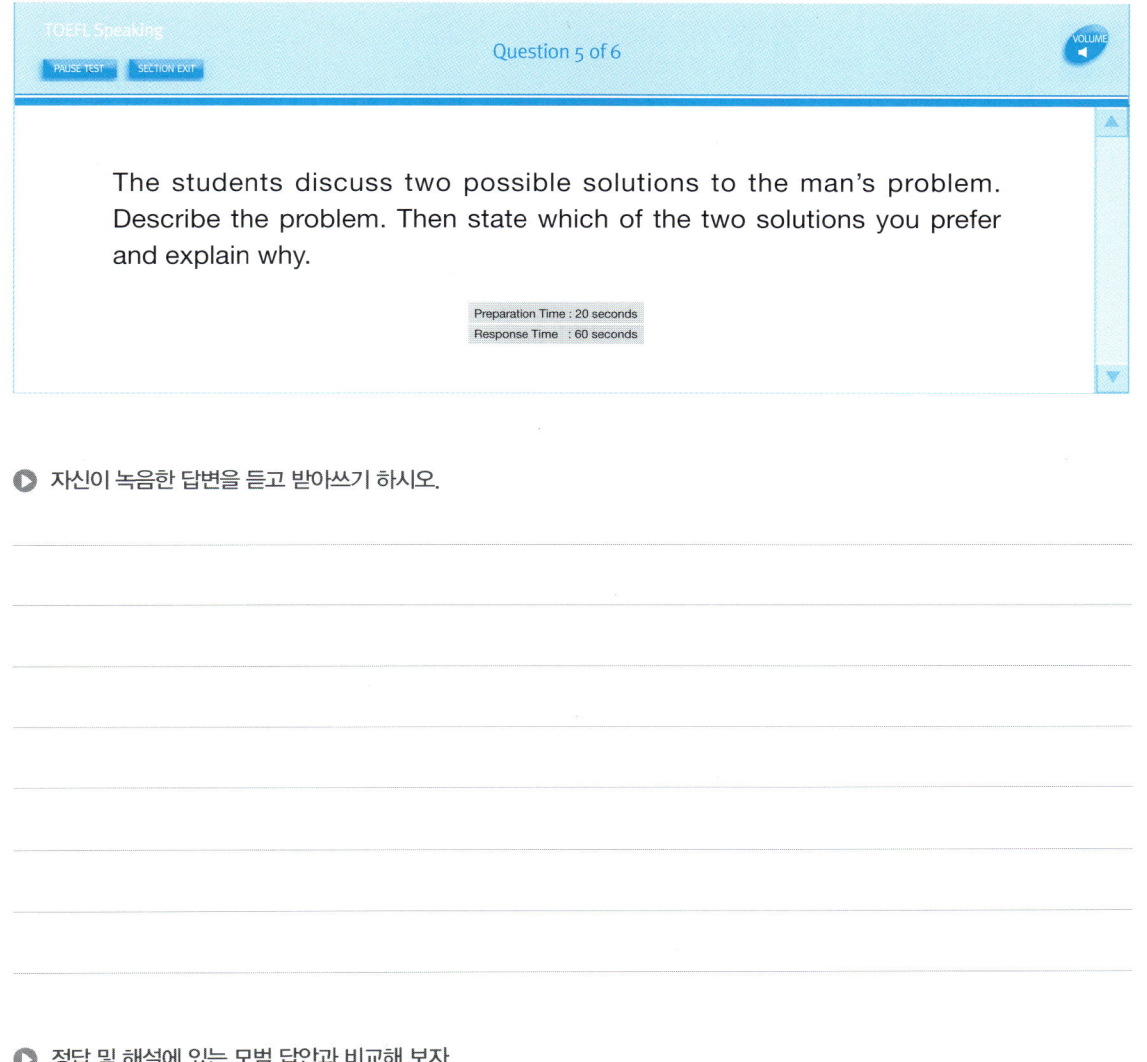

The students discuss two possible solutions to the man's problem. Describe the problem. Then state which of the two solutions you prefer and explain why.

Preparation Time : 20 seconds
Response Time   : 60 seconds

▶ 자신이 녹음한 답변을 듣고 받아쓰기 하시오.

▶ 정답 및 해설에 있는 모범 답안과 비교해 보자.

Exercise

3

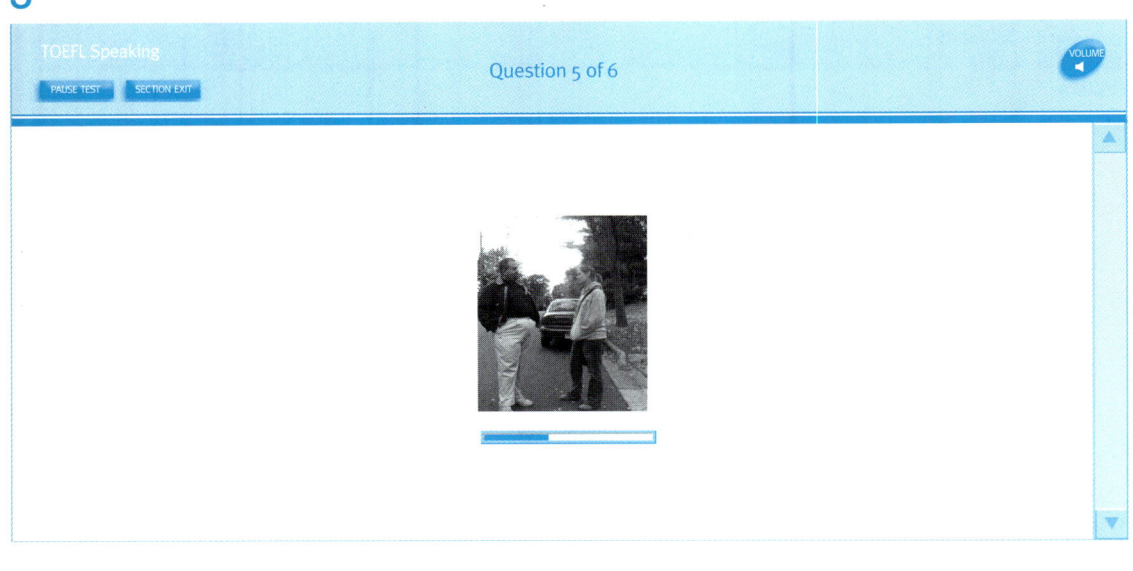

Problem: _____

Suggested solution 1: _____

Suggested solution 2: _____

My preference: _____

Why?: _____

_____

TOEFL Speaking

PAUSE TEST   SECTION EXIT

VOLUME

The students discuss two solutions the woman's problem. Describe the problem. Then state which of the two solutions you prefer and explain why.

Preparation Time : 20 seconds
Response Time   : 60 seconds

▶ 자신이 녹음한 답변을 듣고 받아쓰기 하시오.

▶ 정답 및 해설에 있는 모범 답안과 비교해 보자.

Exercise

4

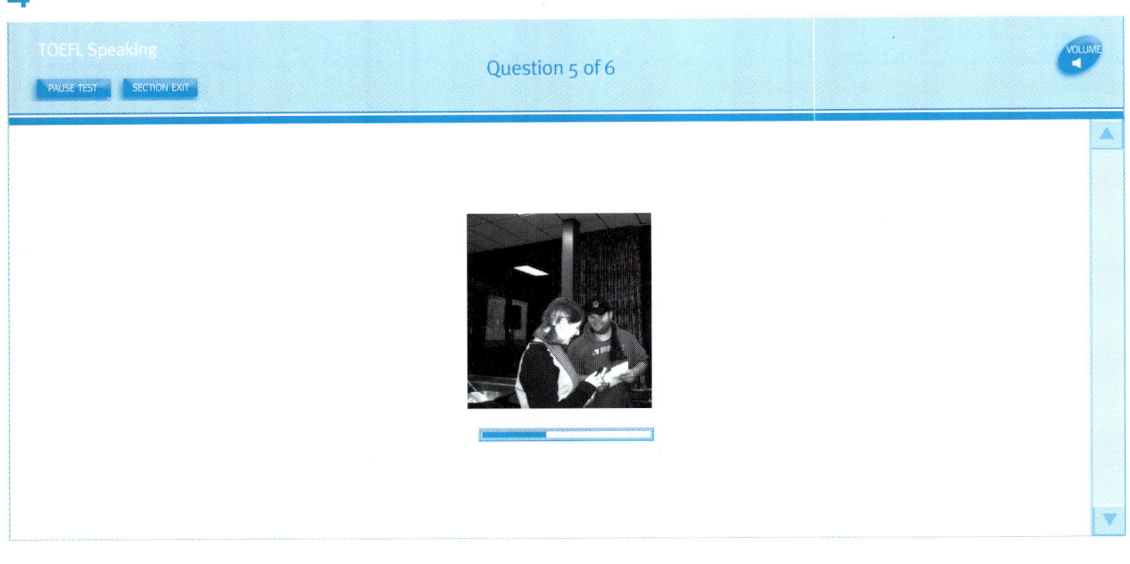

Problem: _____

Suggested solution 1: _____

Suggested solution 2: _____

My preference: _____

Why?: _____

_____

The students discuss two possible solutions to the woman's problem. Describe the problem. Then state which of the two solutions you prefer and explain why.

Preparation Time : 20 seconds
Response Time   : 60 seconds

▶ 자신이 녹음한 답변을 듣고 받아쓰기 하시오.

_____

_____

_____

_____

_____

_____

_____

_____

▶ 정답 및 해설에 있는 모범 답안과 비교해 보자.

Exercise

5

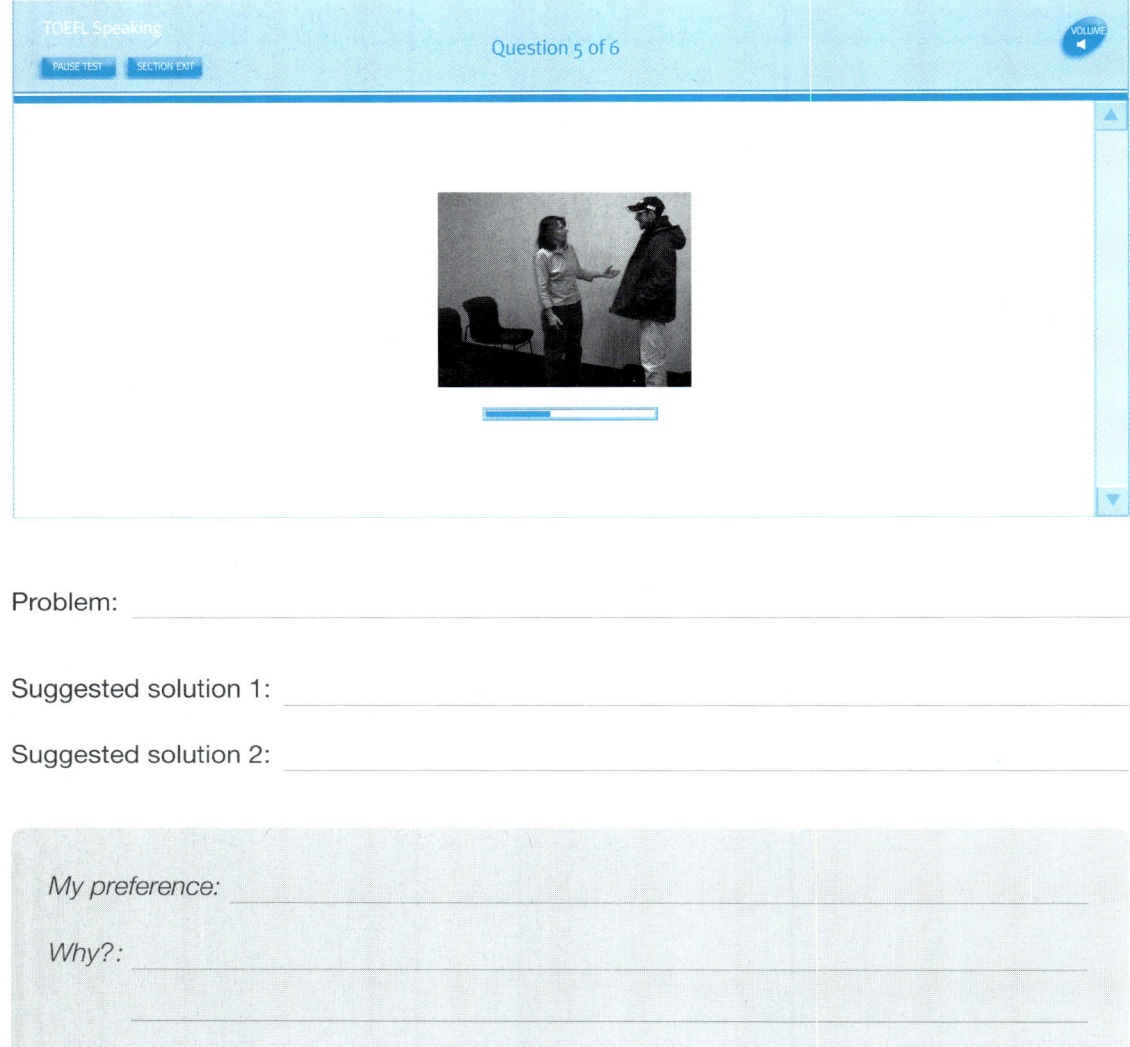

Problem: _____

Suggested solution 1: _____

Suggested solution 2: _____

My preference: _____

Why?: _____

_____

The students discuss two possible solutions to the woman's problem. Describe the problem. Then state which of the two solutions you prefer and explain why.

Preparation Time : 20 seconds
Response Time   : 60 seconds

▶ 자신이 녹음한 답변을 듣고 받아쓰기 하시오.

▶ 정답 및 해설에 있는 모범 답안과 비교해 보자.

Exercise

6

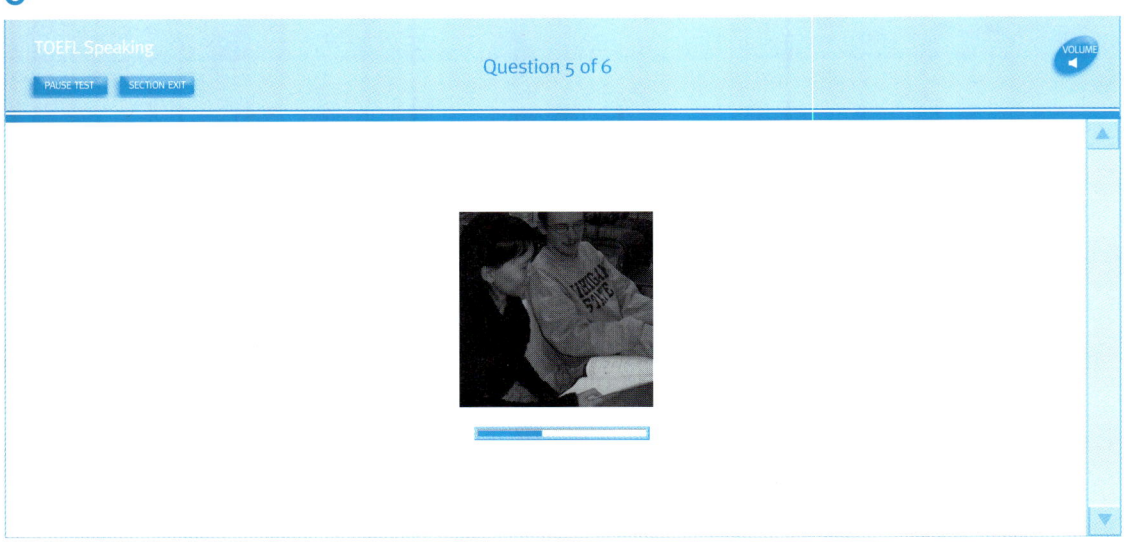

Problem: _____

Suggested solution 1: _____

Suggested solution 2: _____

My preference: _____

Why?: _____

_____

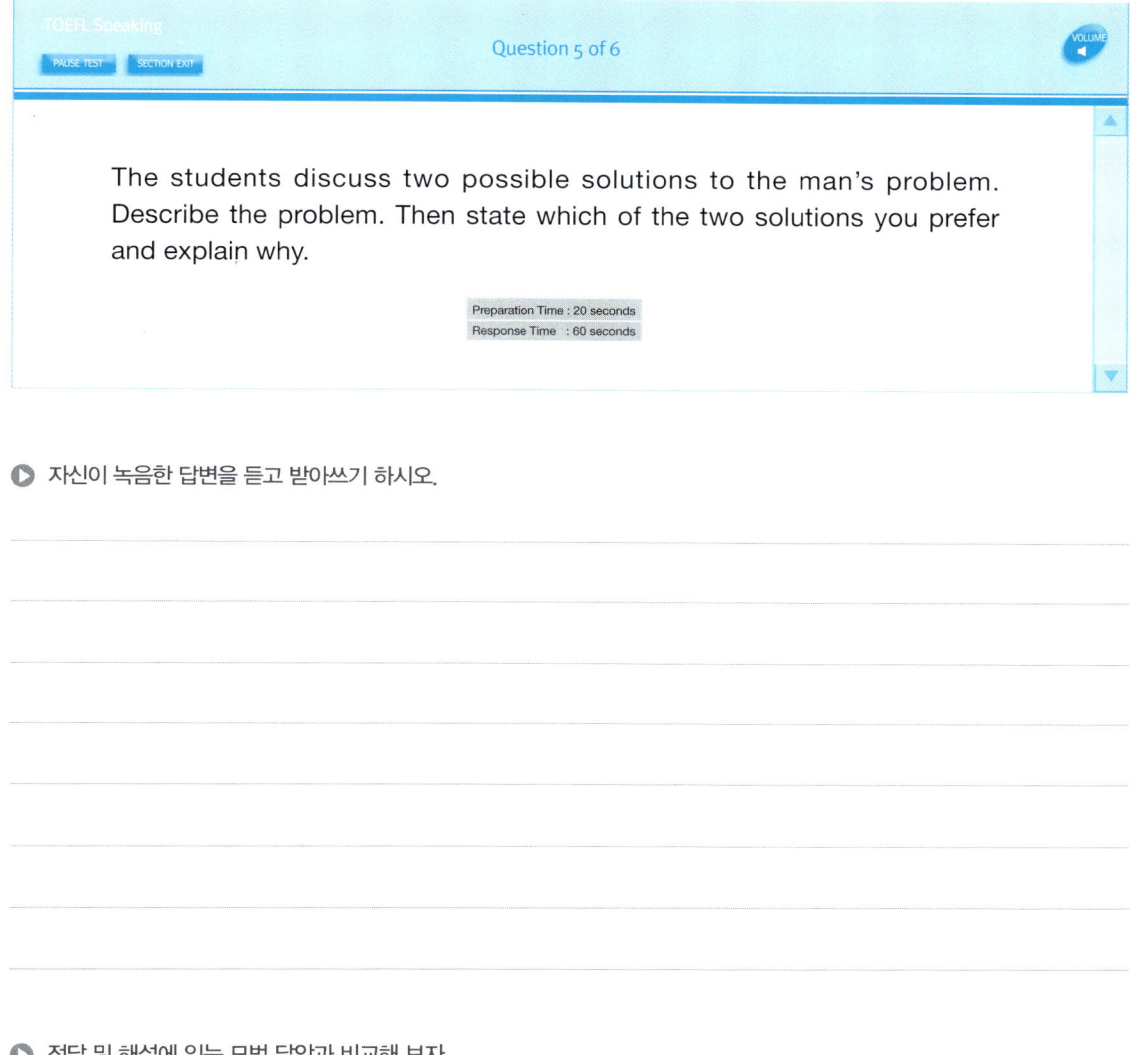

The students discuss two possible solutions to the man's problem. Describe the problem. Then state which of the two solutions you prefer and explain why.

Preparation Time : 20 seconds
Response Time   : 60 seconds

▶ 자신이 녹음한 답변을 듣고 받아쓰기 하시오.

▶ 정답 및 해설에 있는 모범 답안과 비교해 보자.

Exercise

7

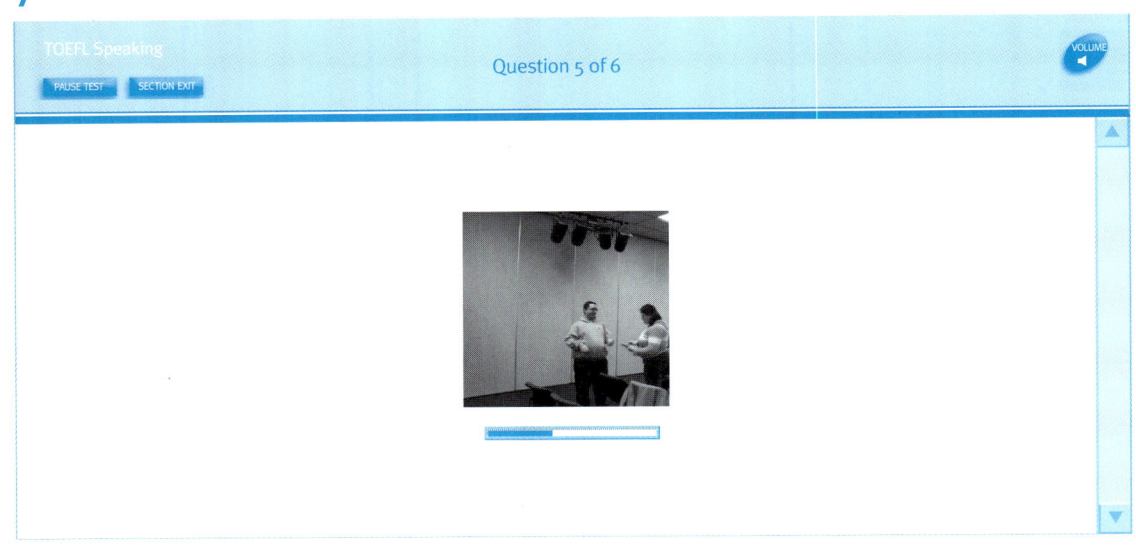

Problem: _____

Suggested solution 1: _____

Suggested solution 2: _____

My preference: _____

Why?: _____

_____

The students discuss two possible solutions to the woman's problem. Describe the problem. Then state which of the two solutions you prefer and explain why.

Preparation Time : 20 seconds
Response Time   : 60 seconds

▶ 자신이 녹음한 답변을 듣고 받아쓰기 하시오.

▶ 정답 및 해설에 있는 모범 답안과 비교해 보자.

Exercise

8

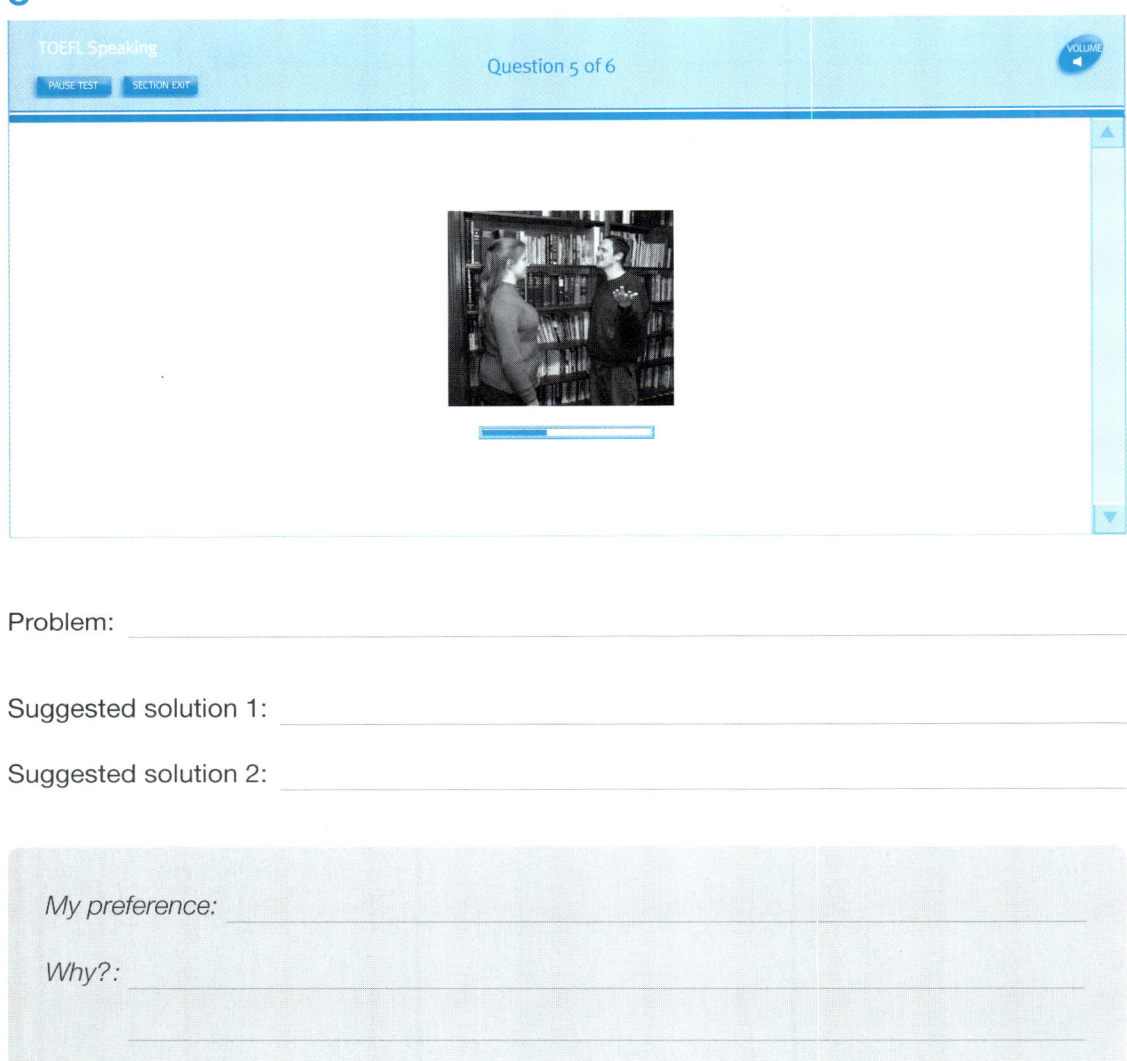

Problem: _____

Suggested solution 1: _____

Suggested solution 2: _____

My preference: _____

Why?: _____

_____

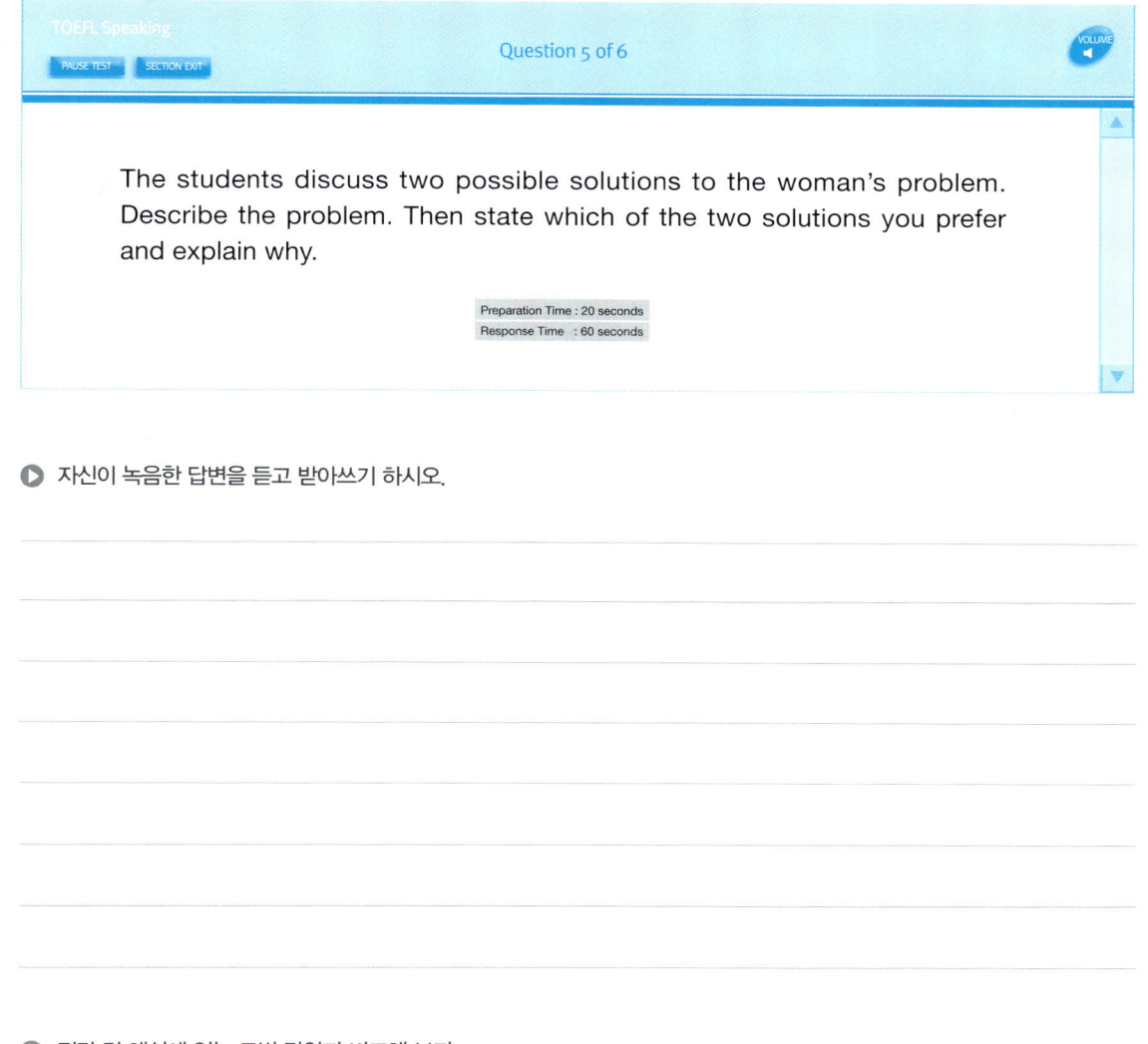

The students discuss two possible solutions to the woman's problem. Describe the problem. Then state which of the two solutions you prefer and explain why.

Preparation Time : 20 seconds
Response Time   : 60 seconds

▶ 자신이 녹음한 답변을 듣고 받아쓰기 하시오.

▶ 정답 및 해설에 있는 모범 답안과 비교해 보자.

Task 6

Summary

6 Summary

학술적인 주제에 대한 교수의 강의의 일부를 듣고 그 강의의 주제와 주어진 구체적 예를 요약하는 문제 유형이다. 답을 할 때 학술적인 강의의 주요 정보를 이해하는 능력과 그 정보를 분명하고 유창하게 논리적으로 전달하는 능력이 요구된다. 주어진 시간 내에 정확하고 완성도 있는 답을 전개하는 것이 중요하다.

■ 문제 유형

듣기	길이	90–120초 (230–280 단어)
	화자	교수, 강의자
	주제	일반적으로 서론 (도입 부분)과 본론으로 구성되며 서론에서는 배경 설명과 함께 강의의 주제가 주어진다. 본론에서는 주제와 관련된 소주제들과 구체적 예시가 주어진다. 용어나 개념을 설명하고 그것을 설명하는 실질적인 예를 든다. 강의 주제로는 생명과학, 사회과학, 자연과학, 인문과학 분야의 현상, 이론, 방법, 과정 등이 출제된다.
말하기	내용	강의 내용을 이해하고 강의자가 제시한 예를 사용하여 요약하시오.

■ 기출 주제

- American common culture
- Machine in the 19th century
- Use of color and emotion
- Time flow in movies
- Advertising strategy
- The benefits of positive externalities
- Substitutable goods and complementary goods

- Population of deer and pine trees
- Disruption in species' life cycle
- Babies' math ability
- Map making
- Data mining - two models
- Children's learning ability - mapping

■ 화면 구성

1 듣기: 학술적인 주제에 대한 강의를 90~120초간 청취한다.

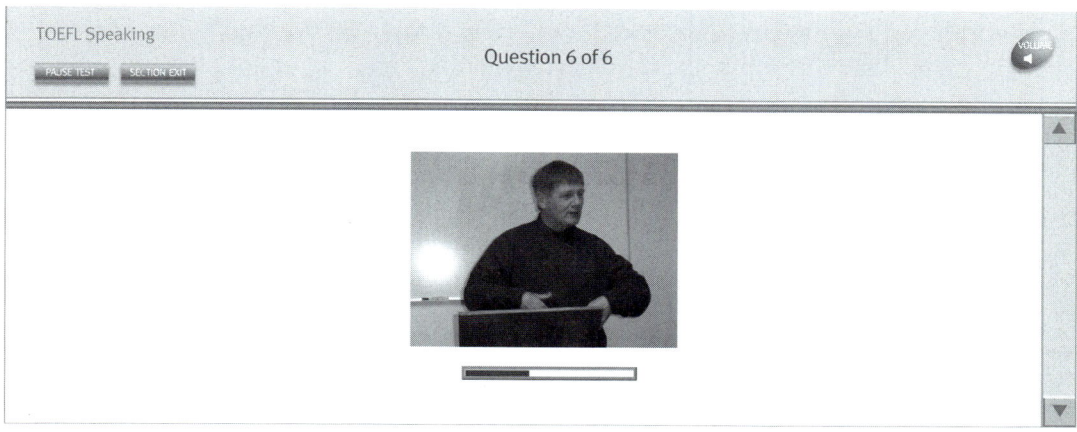

2 말하기: 강의의 주제와 세부적인 내용들을 요약하여 20초간 준비한 후 60초간 말한다.

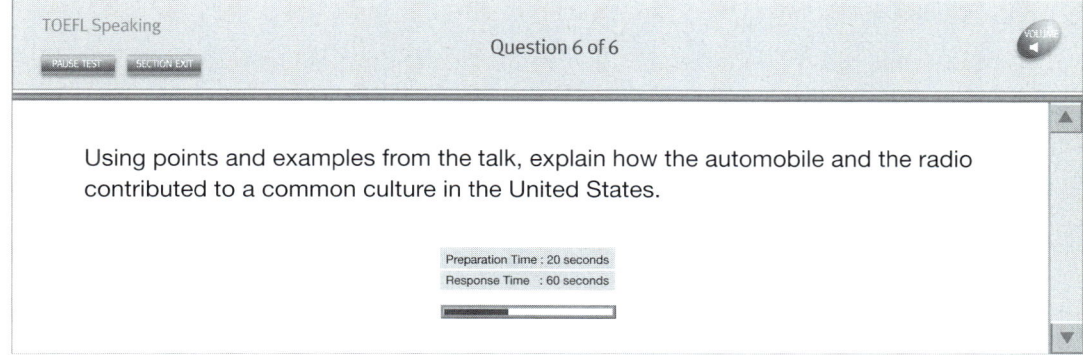

◻ Strategy

강의의 도입부를 듣고 이어질 내용 예측하기

도입부에서 배경 설명과 함께 강의의 주제가 주어진다. 때로 주제와 소주제가 같이 언급되는 경우도 있는데 이는 본론에서 주어질 내용을 예측하는데 중요한 정보가 된다. 주로 두 가지의 예, 방법, 요소들이 주어진다 는 것을 기억하면 예측하는데 도움이 된다.

강의의 주제를 언급하며 서두 시작하기

강의의 주제를 언급하면서 시작하거나, 주제의 정의를 말하는 것으로 시작해도 좋다. 너무 장황하거나 복잡 하게 시작하려 하지 말고 간단 명료하게 요점 중심으로 주제를 말하면 된다. 한 문장으로 말하는 것이 바람 직하다. 답은 강의에 초점을 맞추어 시작하면 된다.   예) The main topic of this lecture is ~

자신의 의견을 말하지 않기

수험자의 의견을 말하면 안 된다. 자신의 의견을 첨가하거나 강의에서 언급된 본래의 의미를 왜곡하지 말고 주어진 정보를 자기말로 바꾸어 요약한다. 또한 단순히 주어진 문장을 따라하지 말고 자신의 말로 바꾸거나 문장의 형태나 구조를 바꾸어 paraphrase해야 한다.

간결 명료하게 답하기

강의에서 주어진 서론 부분은 요약해서는 안 되며 언급된 주제의 개념 또한 요약할 필요가 없다. 주제와 그 에 대한 예를 위주로 요약하면 된다. 따라서 강의 내용을 전부 이해하려 하지 말고 필요한 정보를 얻는데 집 중해야 효과적으로 정확한 정보를 얻을 수 있다. 실질적으로 답에 필요한 정보는 주어진 강의의 20% 이하이 다. 미사여구를 피하고 요점 중심으로 답을 해야 한다.

> **Tip** Task 4와 Task 6의 차이점
> Task 4의 주제는 주로 심리학이 80%, 생물학이 20%가 출제되고 경영학과 관련된 주제는 주로 심리학과 연 결되어 출제되며 주제에 대한 예가 주어진다. 따라서 이 유형의 문제는 example question이라고 기억하면 된다.
> Task 6는 모든 영역에 걸쳐서 출제되며 그 형식도 다양하다. 주제에 대한 두 가지 방법, 요소, 예, 정의, 과정 등이 다양하게 주어진다. 하나의 ～이 주어지기도 하고 두 가지가 주어지고 그 중 하나만 요약하라고 주어지 기도 한다.

☐ Sample

▌ Listening

P: **1** Due to its vastness, a common national culture in the United States was slow to develop. About a century ago, there was little communication between the different areas of the United States. Due to this lack of communication, people in different regions were quite different from one another. For example, they all spoke, dressed, and behaved differently from one another. But because of the following two inventions, the communication between the regions started to greatly increase: **2** the automobile and the radio.

As you're aware, **3** automobiles began to be mass produced during the 1920's, decreasing the price and increasing their availability. Americans now had the ability to travel rather easily to nearby cities. The automobile also increased the ability to take trips to other parts of the country. This increased mobility helped to change attitudes in Americans and shorten the "bridge" between regions. For example, the people in small towns began to be more influenced by the styles and attitudes of the people from the big cities.

With the increased purchase of automobiles came the **4** increase in the ownership of the radio. Americans were able to listen to the same radio programs and musicians throughout the entire country. The terms and phrases that were on the popular shows and in music were catching on everywhere in the country. They also were able to hear the news and all about the important events happening all across the country, which brought the country closer together.

1 주제 제시   **2** 구체적 예시   **3** 첫 번째 근거 제시   **4** 두 번째 근거 제시

Q Using points and examples from the talk, explain how the automobile and the radio contributed to a common culture in the United States.

▌ Speaking

1 The main topic of the lecture is common culture in the United States. The professor tells the students that America did not have a common culture 100 years ago because people in different regions of the country did not communicate much with each other. The automobile and the radio changed this situation. **2** As an example, the professor explains that when automobiles became inexpensive, people from small towns could travel easily to cities or to other parts of the country. When they began to do this, they started acting like people from those other regions and started to dress and speak in the same way. **3** Another example is that when radio became popular, people from different parts of the country began listening to the same programs and the same news reports and began to speak alike and have similar experiences and ideas. **4** The professor explains that these similar ways of speaking, dressing, and thinking became the national culture of the United States.

1 주제 제시   **2** 첫 번째 예시   **3** 두 번째 예시   **4** 요약 정리

Mini Test

CD Possible Responses: Track 70

🔊 듣기 지문을 들으며 노트필기 공간에 주요 내용을 필기하시오.
필기 내용을 토대로 말하는 연습을 하시오.

1

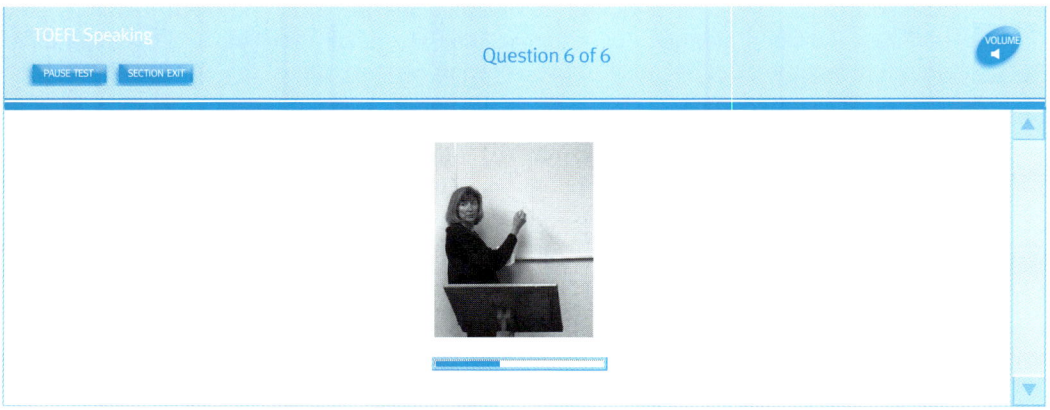

Topic: _____

Sub-topic: _____

   Detail: _____

_____

Q Using points and examples from the talk, explain how the population of deer influences the number of trees.

_____

_____

_____

_____

Useful Expressions

순서를 말할 때

- First of all ~
- Secondly ~
- Finally ~

2

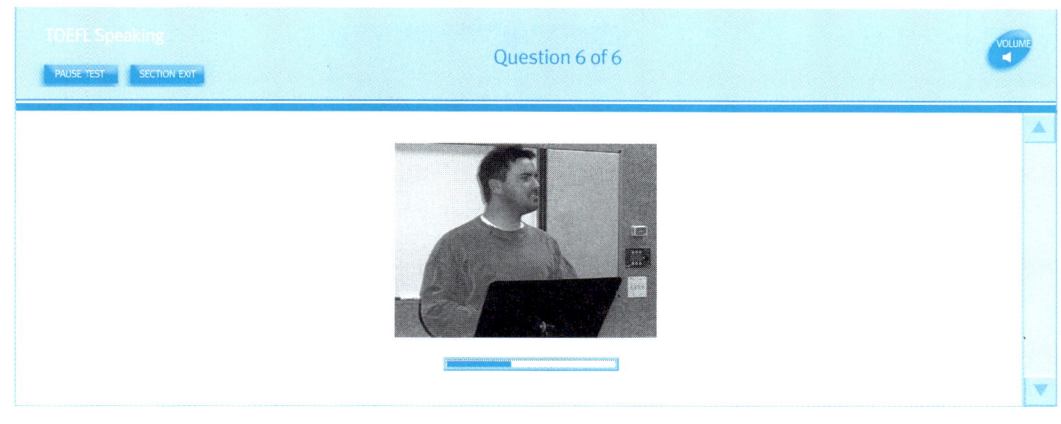

Topic:

Sub-topic:

   Detail:

Q Using points and examples from the talk, explain the photographers' impressions of machines in the 19th century.

Useful Expressions

결론을 말할 때

- What I gathered from this lecture is ~
- For these reasons I think ~
- This is the reason why ~

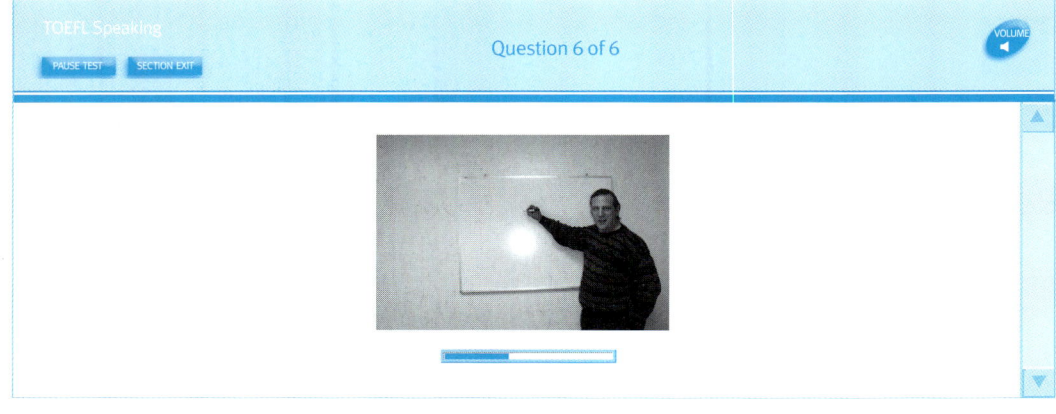

Topic:

Sub-topic:

Detail:

Q Using points and examples from the talk, explain the threat that an influx of new species have on a habitat.

Useful Expressions

전환할 때

- Similarly ~
- Likewise ~
- On top of that ~

4

Topic:

Sub-topic:

Detail:

Q Using points and examples from the talk, explain the use of color in art.

Useful Expressions

전환할 때

- However ~
- On the other hand ~
- In contrast ~

Exercise

🔈 듣기 지문을 들으며 노트필기 공간에 주요 내용을 필기하시오.
필기 내용을 토대로 말하는 연습을 하시오.

CD Possible Responses: Track 72~79

1

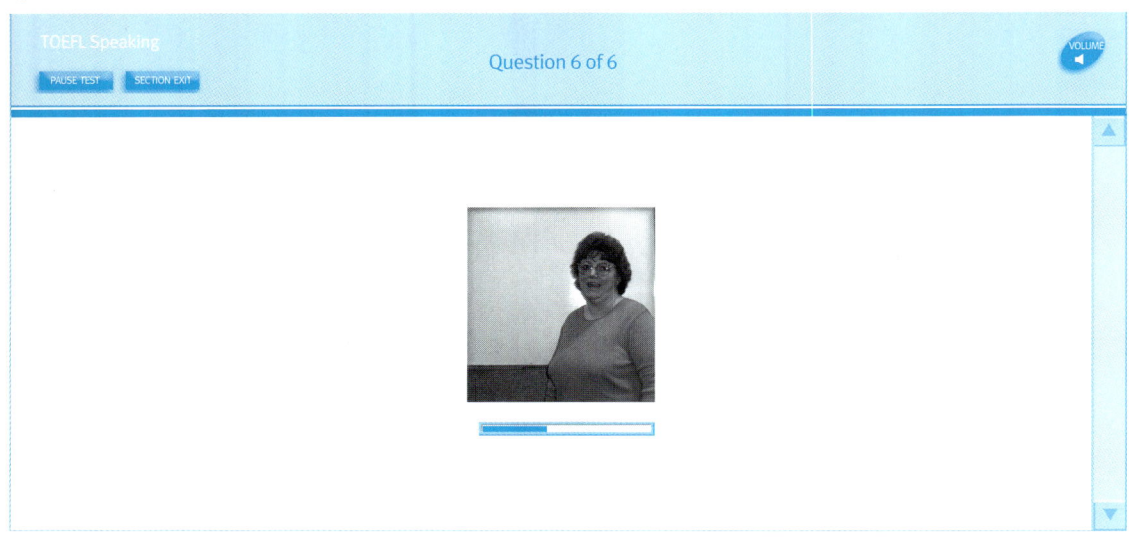

Topic: _____

Sub-topic 1: _____

    Detail: _____

Sub-topic 2: _____

    Detail: _____

Using points and examples from the talk, explain the different methods of portraying the change in time in movies.

Preparation Time : 20 seconds
Response Time   : 60 seconds

▶ 자신이 녹음한 답변을 듣고 받아쓰기 하시오.

▶ 정답 및 해설에 있는 모범 답안과 비교해 보자.

Exercise

2

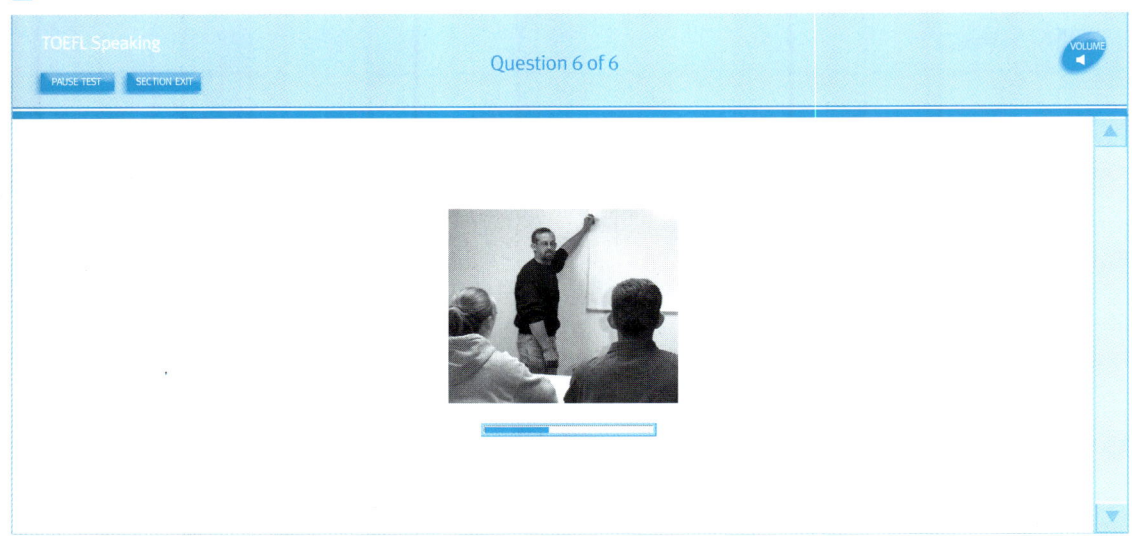

Topic: _____

Sub-topic 1: _____

  Detail: _____

Sub-topic 2: _____

  Detail: _____

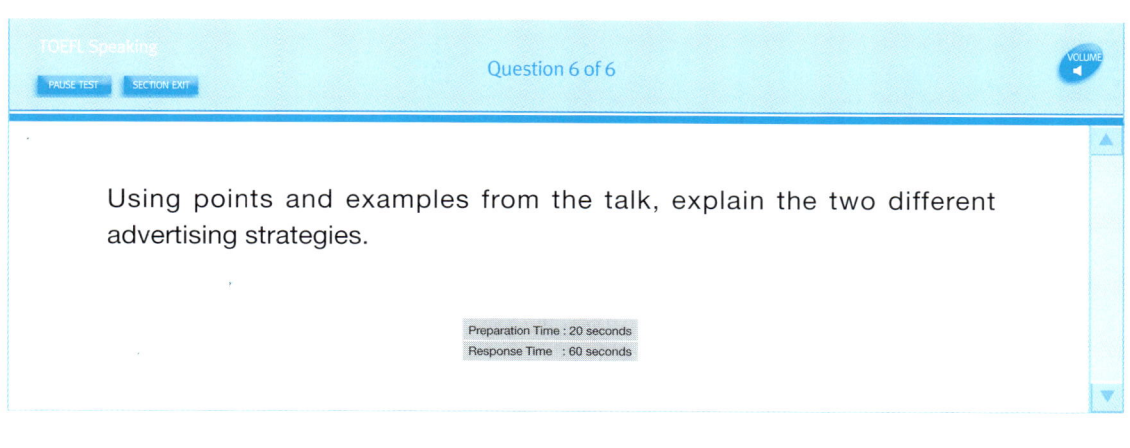

Using points and examples from the talk, explain the two different advertising strategies.

Preparation Time : 20 seconds
Response Time   : 60 seconds

▶ 자신이 녹음한 답변을 듣고 받아쓰기 하시오.

▶ 정답 및 해설에 있는 모범 답안과 비교해 보자.

Exercise

3

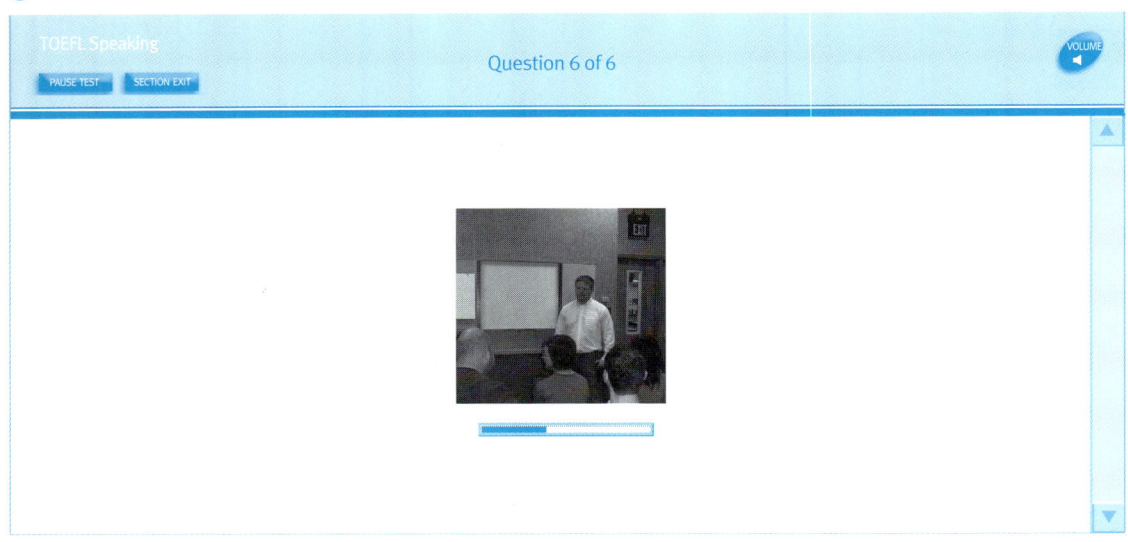

Topic:

Sub-topic 1:

     Detail:

Sub-topic 2:

     Detail:

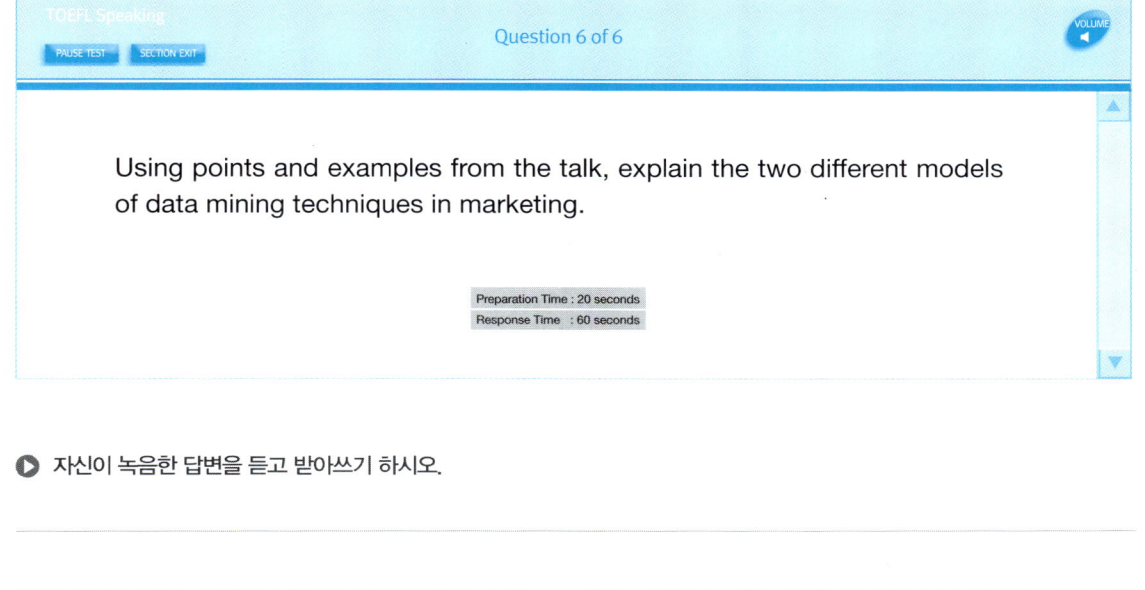

Using points and examples from the talk, explain the two different models of data mining techniques in marketing.

Preparation Time : 20 seconds
Response Time   : 60 seconds

▶ 자신이 녹음한 답변을 듣고 받아쓰기 하시오.

_____

_____

_____

_____

_____

_____

_____

▶ 정답 및 해설에 있는 모범 답안과 비교해 보자.

Exercise

4

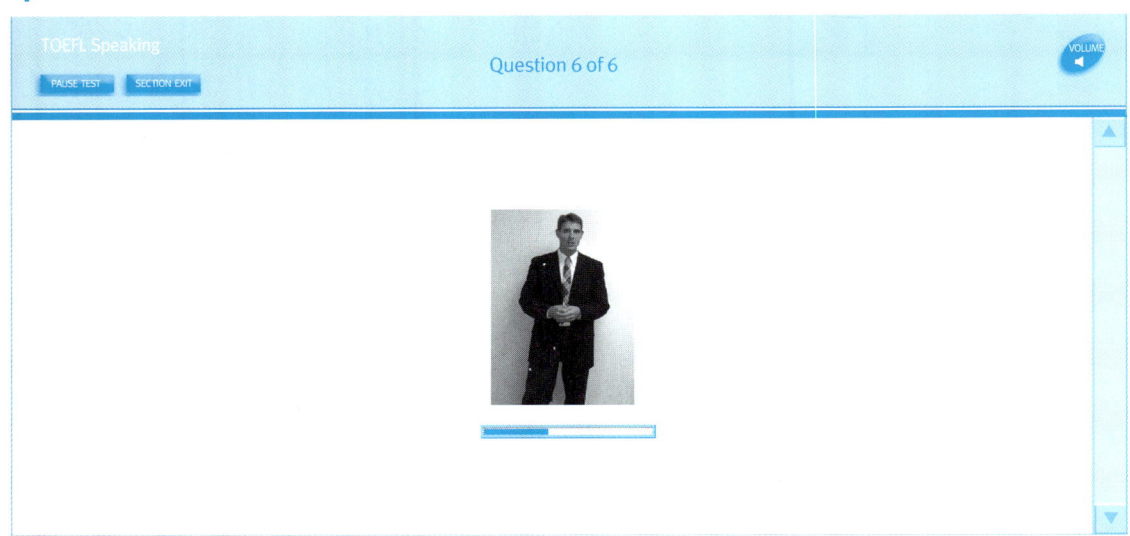

Topic: _____

Sub-topic 1: _____

    Detail: _____

Sub-topic 2: _____

    Detail: _____

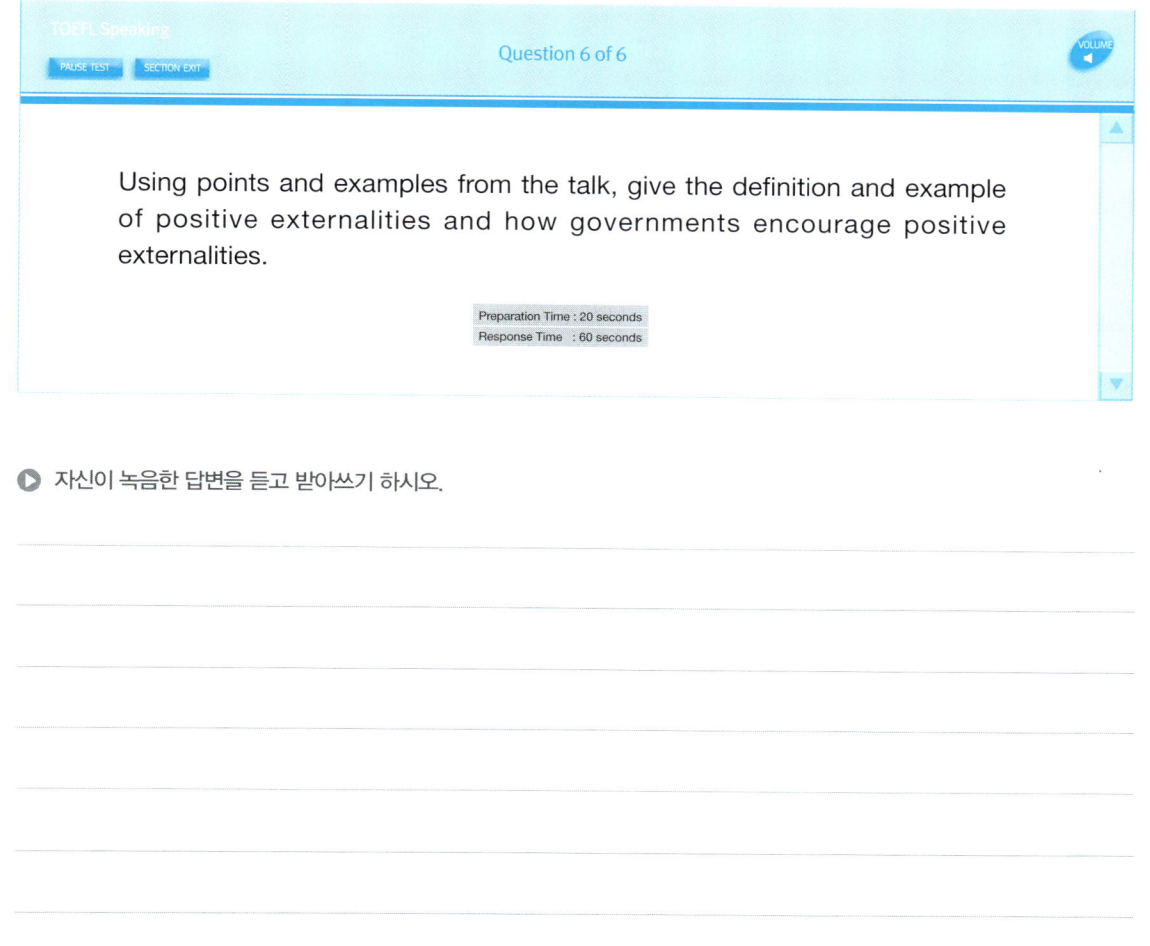

Using points and examples from the talk, give the definition and example of positive externalities and how governments encourage positive externalities.

Preparation Time : 20 seconds
Response Time   : 60 seconds

▶ 자신이 녹음한 답변을 듣고 받아쓰기 하시오.

▶ 정답 및 해설에 있는 모범 답안과 비교해 보자.

Exercise

5

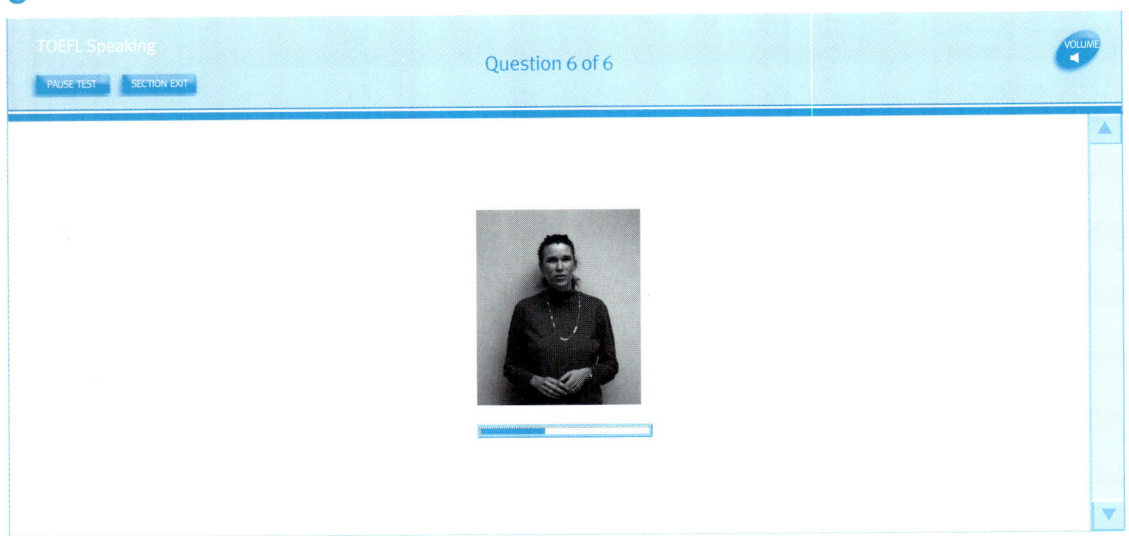

Topic: _____

Sub-topic 1: _____

    Detail: _____

Sub-topic 2: _____

    Detail: _____

Using points and examples from the talk, explain the two errors in the mapping process of children.

Preparation Time : 20 seconds
Response Time   : 60 seconds

▶ 자신이 녹음한 답변을 듣고 받아쓰기 하시오.

_____

_____

_____

_____

_____

_____

_____

_____

▶ 정답 및 해설에 있는 모범 답안과 비교해 보자.

Exercise

6

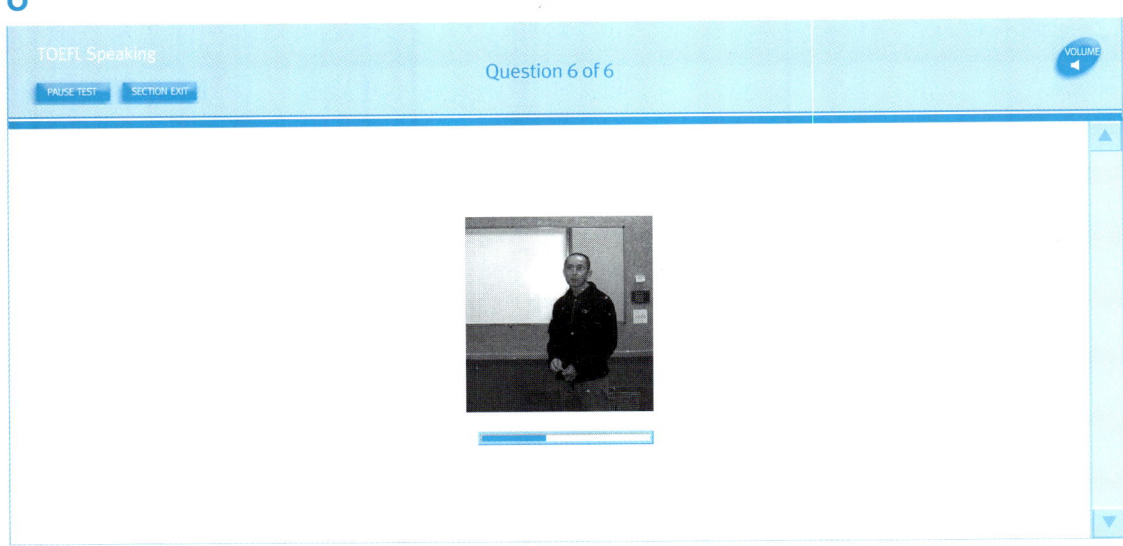

Topic:

Sub-topic 1:

    Detail:

Sub-topic 2:

    Detail:

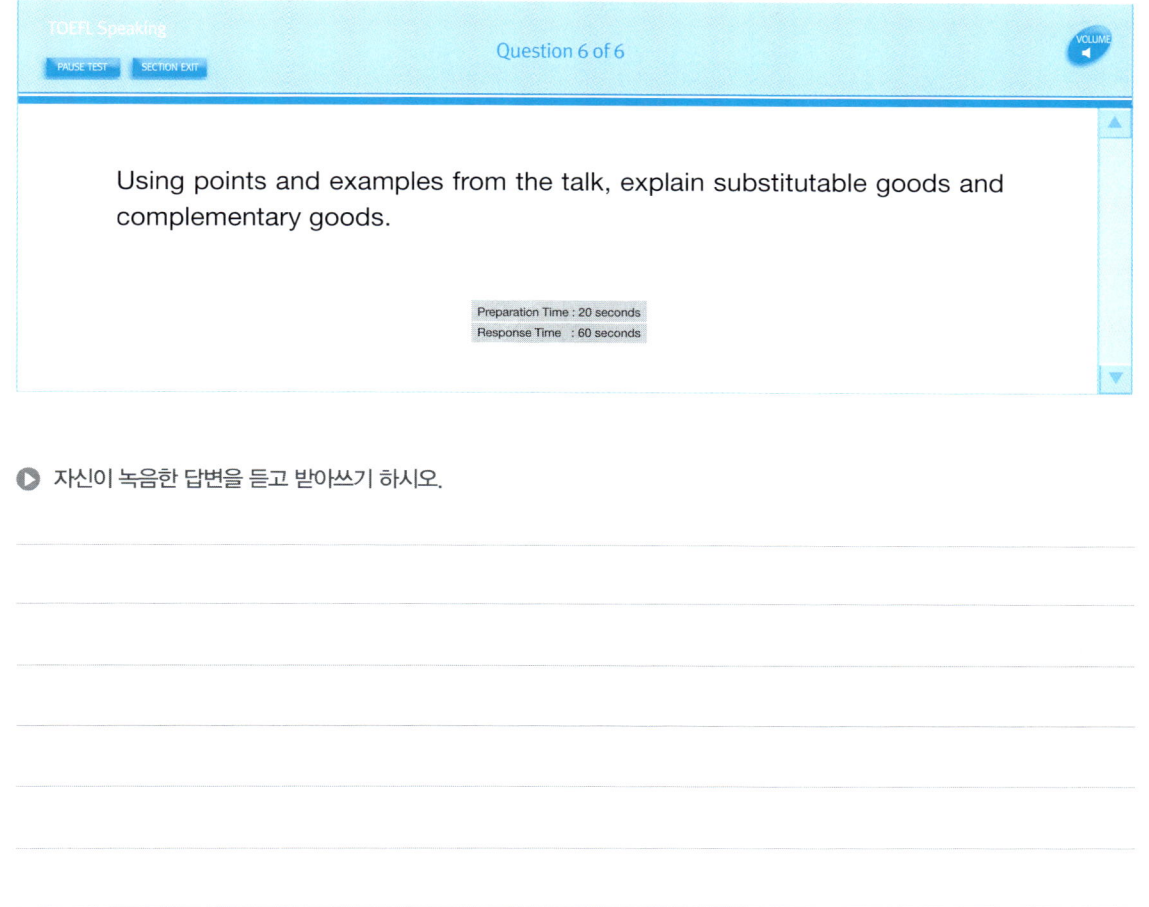

Using points and examples from the talk, explain substitutable goods and complementary goods.

Preparation Time : 20 seconds
Response Time   : 60 seconds

▶ 자신이 녹음한 답변을 듣고 받아쓰기 하시오.

▶ 정답 및 해설에 있는 모범 답안과 비교해 보자.

Exercise

7

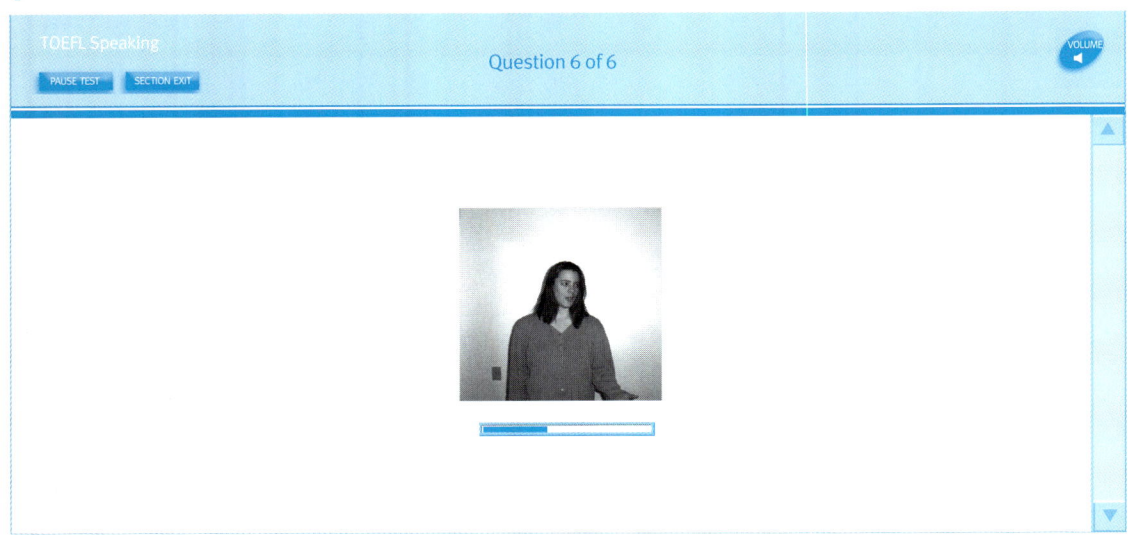

Topic:

Sub-topic 1:

   Detail:

Sub-topic 2:

   Detail:

Using points and examples from the talk, explain the experiment of 5-month-old babies and their ability to count.

Preparation Time : 20 seconds
Response Time   : 60 seconds

▶ 자신이 녹음한 답변을 듣고 받아쓰기 하시오.

▶ 정답 및 해설에 있는 모범 답안과 비교해 보자.

Exercise

8

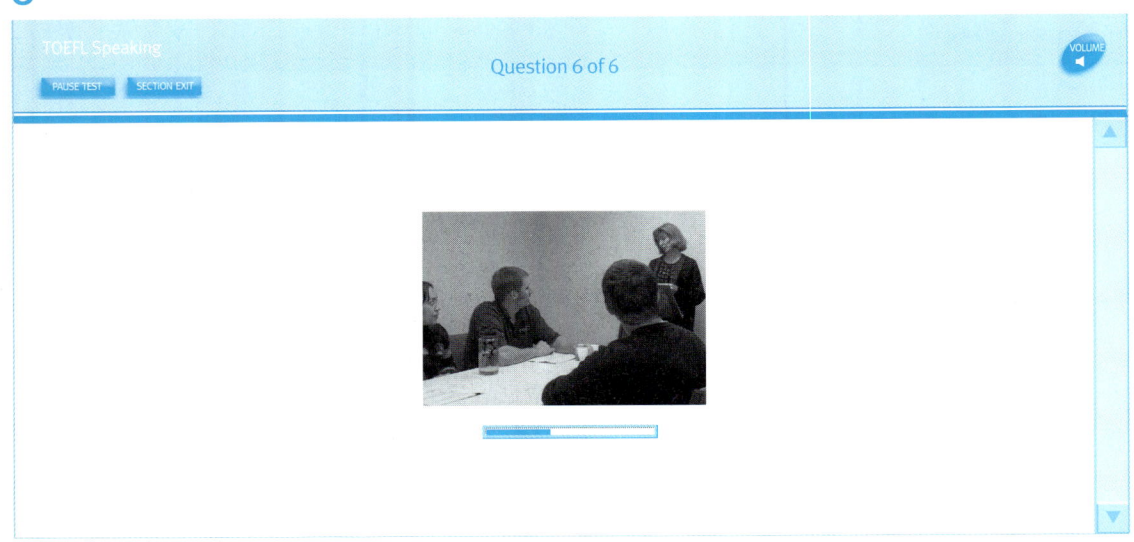

Topic: _____

Sub-topic 1: _____

    Detail: _____

Sub-topic 2: _____

    Detail: _____

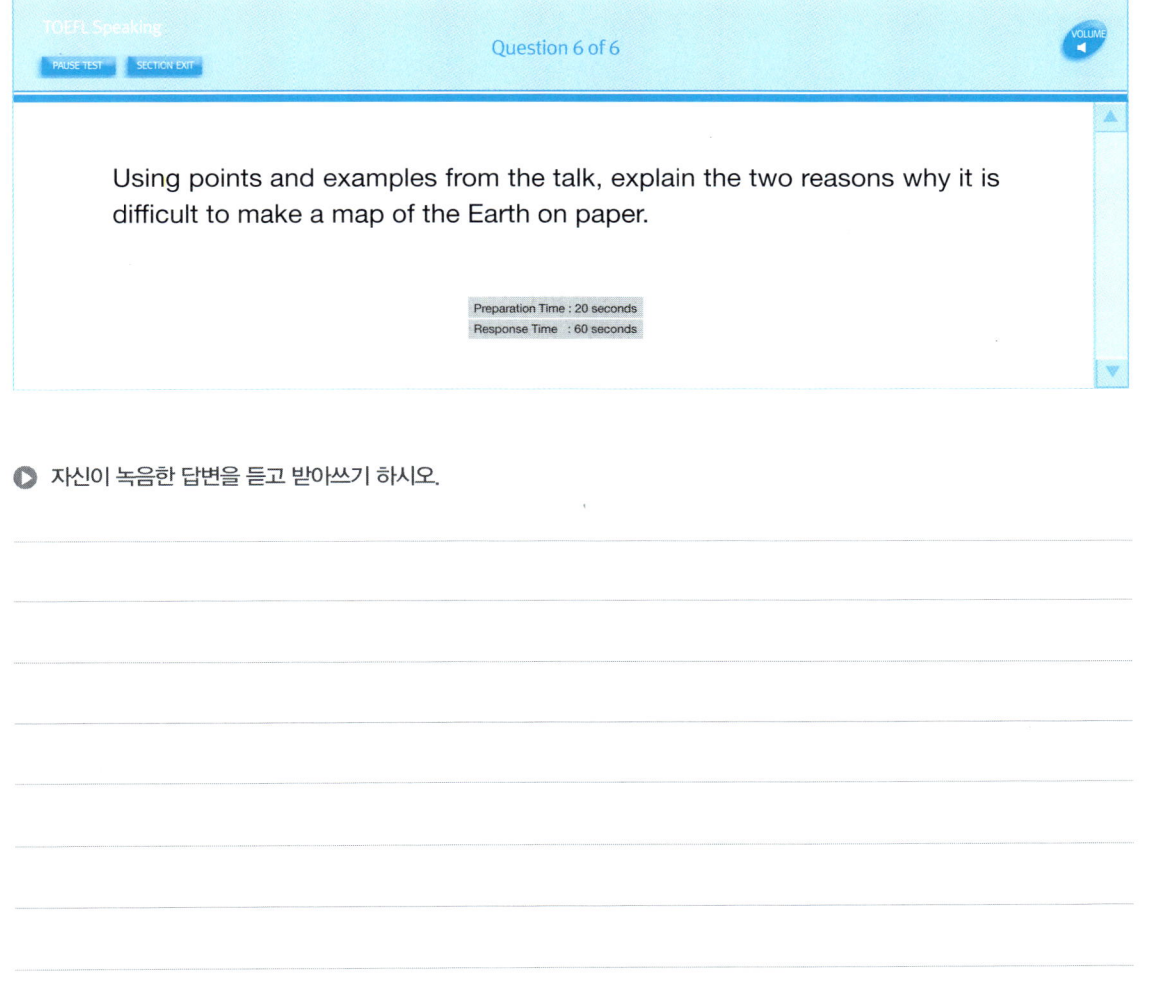

Using points and examples from the talk, explain the two reasons why it is difficult to make a map of the Earth on paper.

Preparation Time : 20 seconds
Response Time   : 60 seconds

⏵ 자신이 녹음한 답변을 듣고 받아쓰기 하시오.

⏵ 정답 및 해설에 있는 모범 답안과 비교해 보자.

Part 3

iBT Actual Test

Set 1

Set 1

🆎 Possible Responses: Track 81~86

1

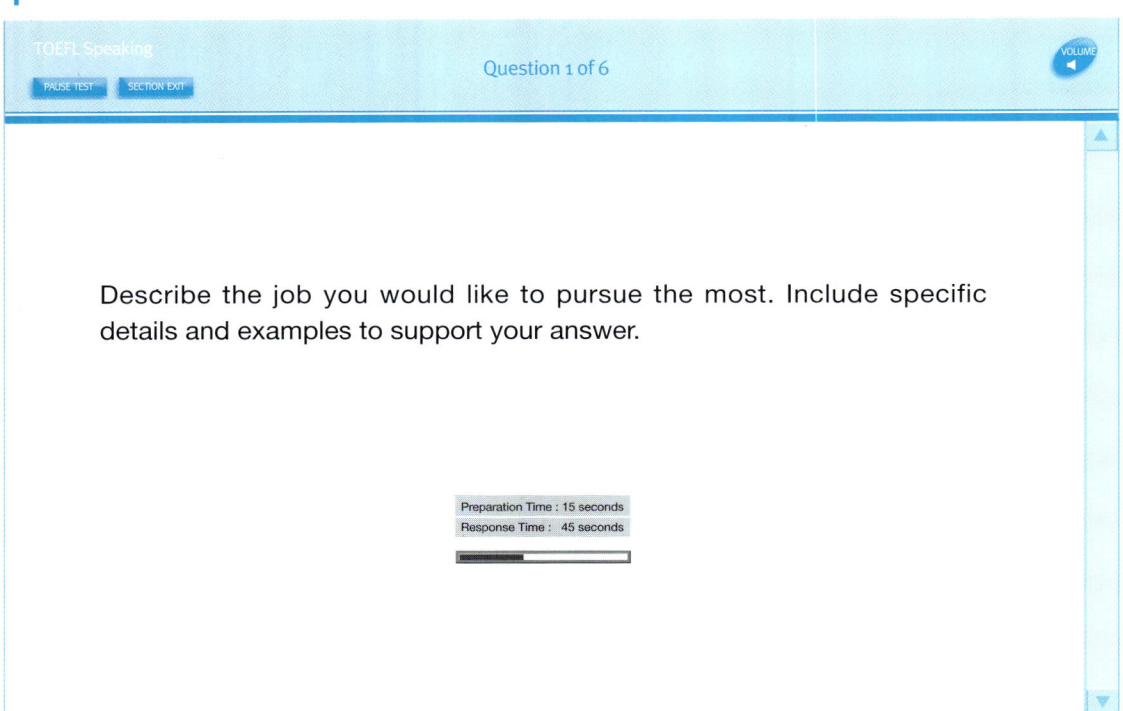

Describe the job you would like to pursue the most. Include specific details and examples to support your answer.

Preparation Time : 15 seconds
Response Time : 45 seconds

2

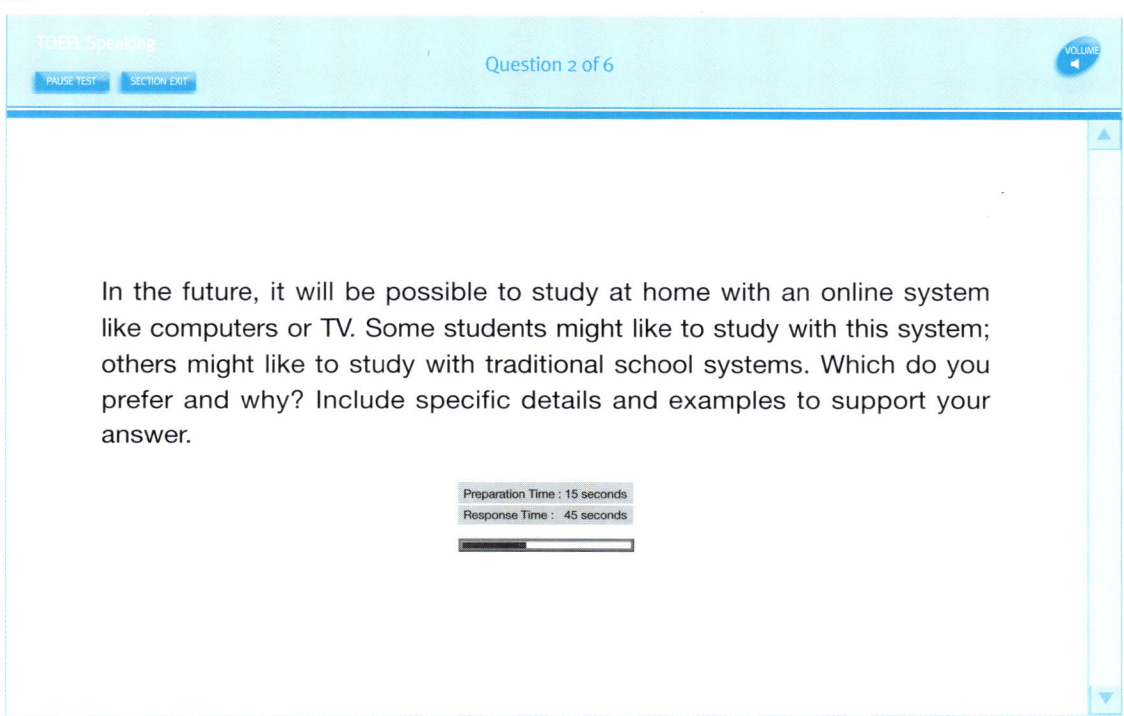

In the future, it will be possible to study at home with an online system like computers or TV. Some students might like to study with this system; others might like to study with traditional school systems. Which do you prefer and why? Include specific details and examples to support your answer.

Preparation Time : 15 seconds
Response Time :   45 seconds

Set 1

3

Reading time: 45 seconds

Policy Change

The university has made some changes to the class policy. Undergraduate students will now be able to join graduate classes, if needed. This will allow undergrad students to get a better understanding of the graduate school system and have a competitive start if they choose to go to graduate school. Also, it allows for a good introduction to the graduate program in our school.

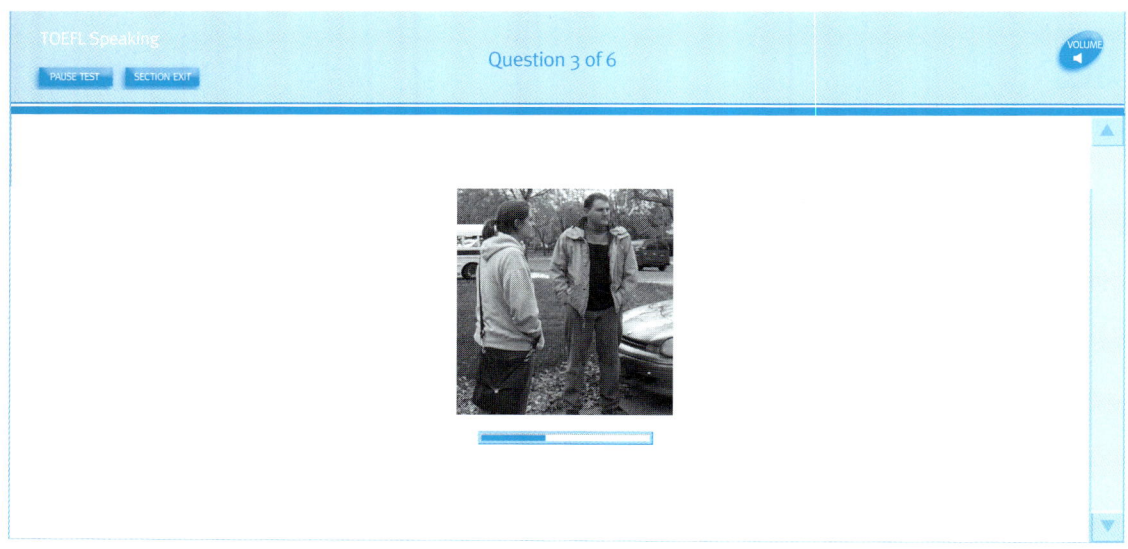

The man expresses his opinion of the university's plan to allow undergraduate students to take graduate courses. State his opinion and explain the reasons he gives for holding that opinion.

Preparation Time : 30 seconds
Response Time : 60 seconds

Set 1

4

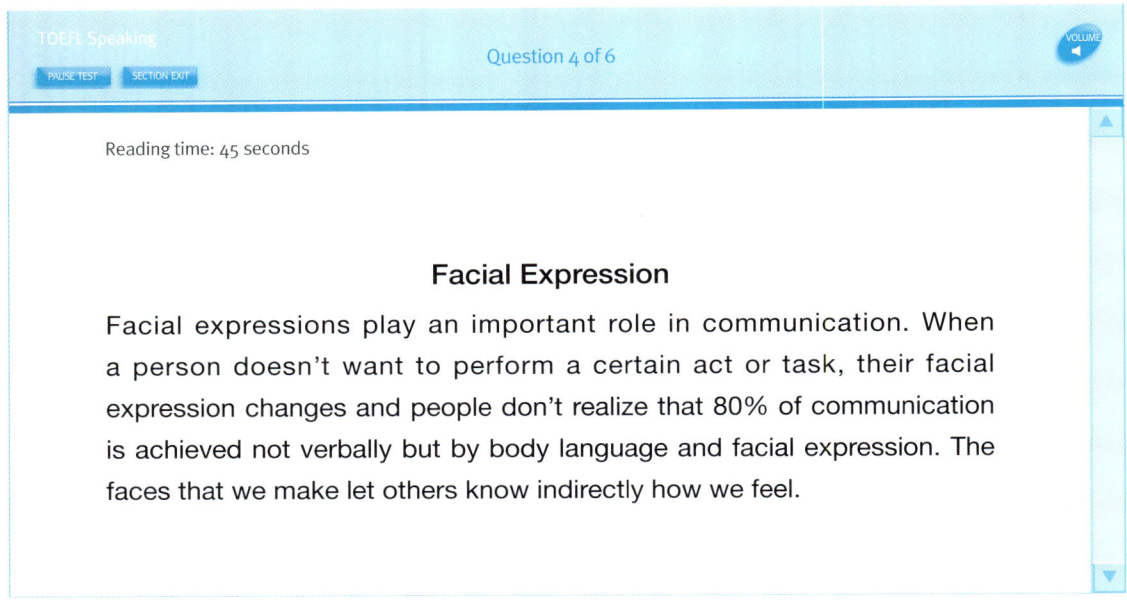

Reading time: 45 seconds

Facial Expression

Facial expressions play an important role in communication. When a person doesn't want to perform a certain act or task, their facial expression changes and people don't realize that 80% of communication is achieved not verbally but by body language and facial expression. The faces that we make let others know indirectly how we feel.

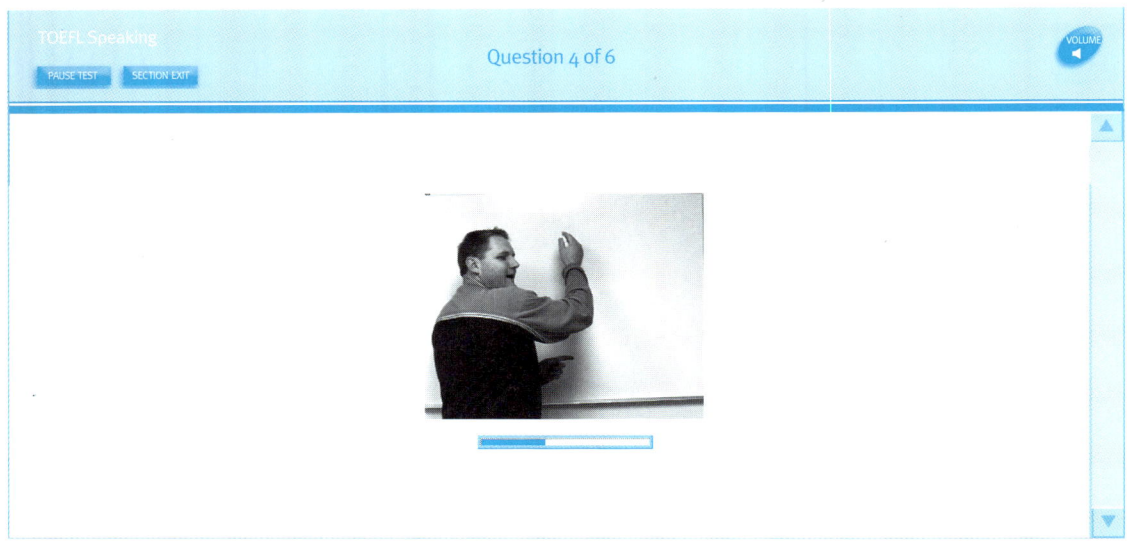

The professor talks about facial expression. Explain how the professor uses a 13-year-old boy to explain his views.

Preparation Time : 30 seconds
Response Time :   60 seconds

Set 1

5

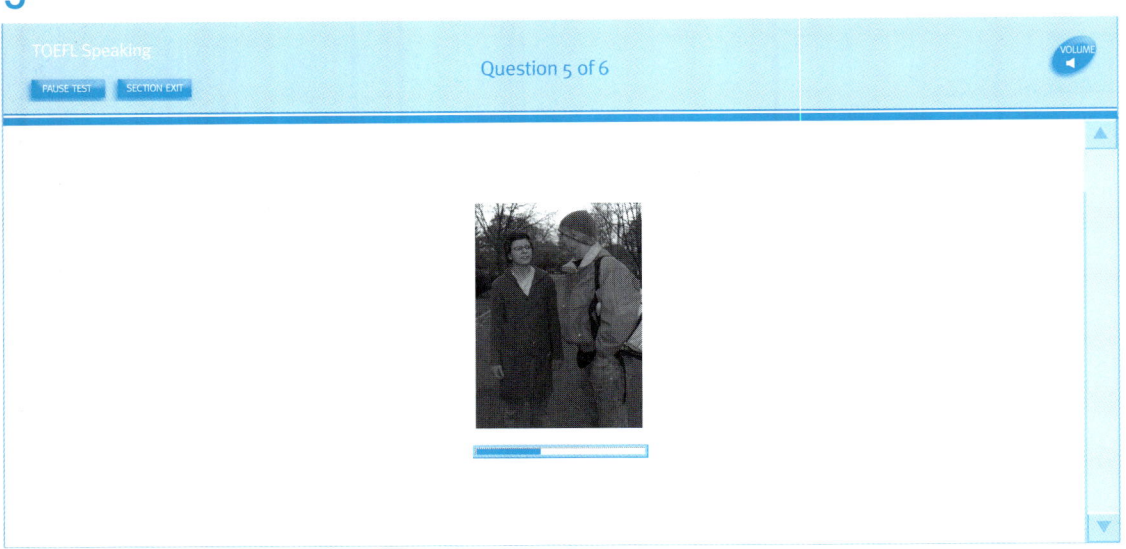

The students discuss two possible solutions to the man's problem. Describe the problem. Then state which of the two solutions you prefer and explain why.

Preparation Time : 20 seconds
Response Time : 60 seconds

6

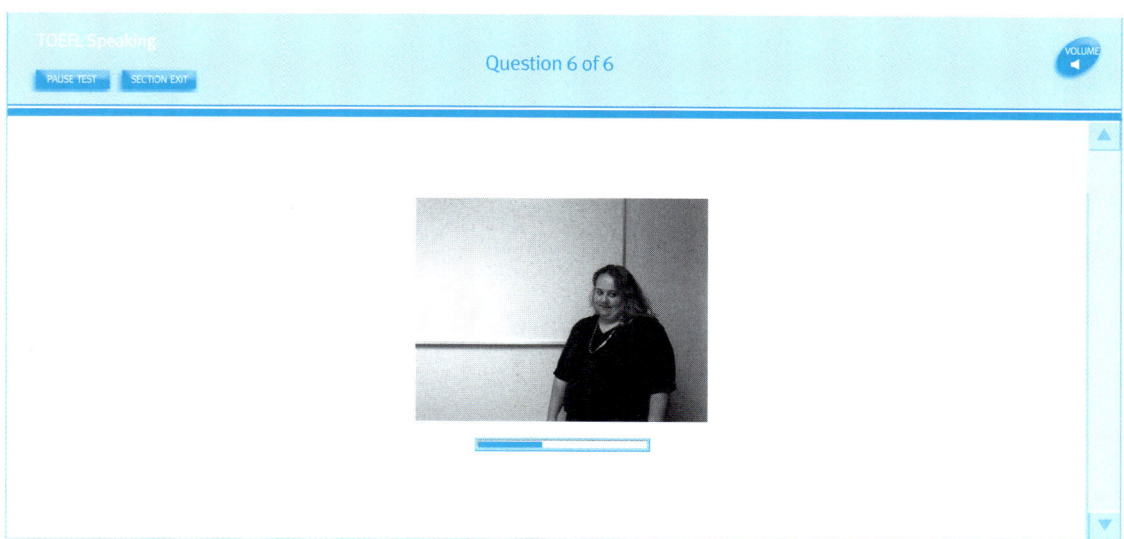

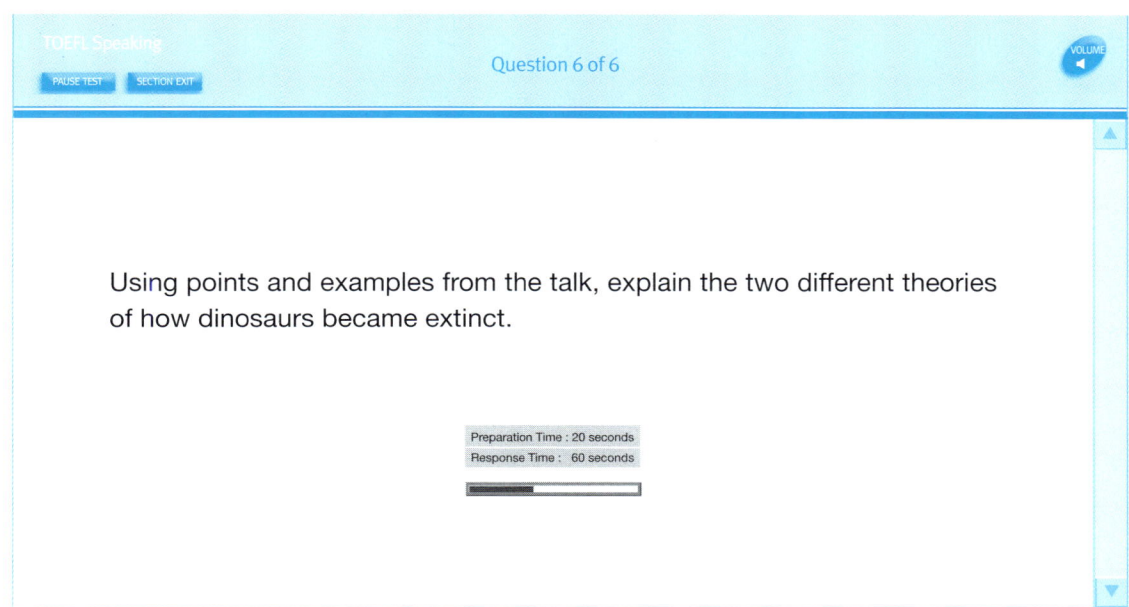

Using points and examples from the talk, explain the two different theories of how dinosaurs became extinct.

Preparation Time : 20 seconds
Response Time :   60 seconds

Set 2

Set 2

1

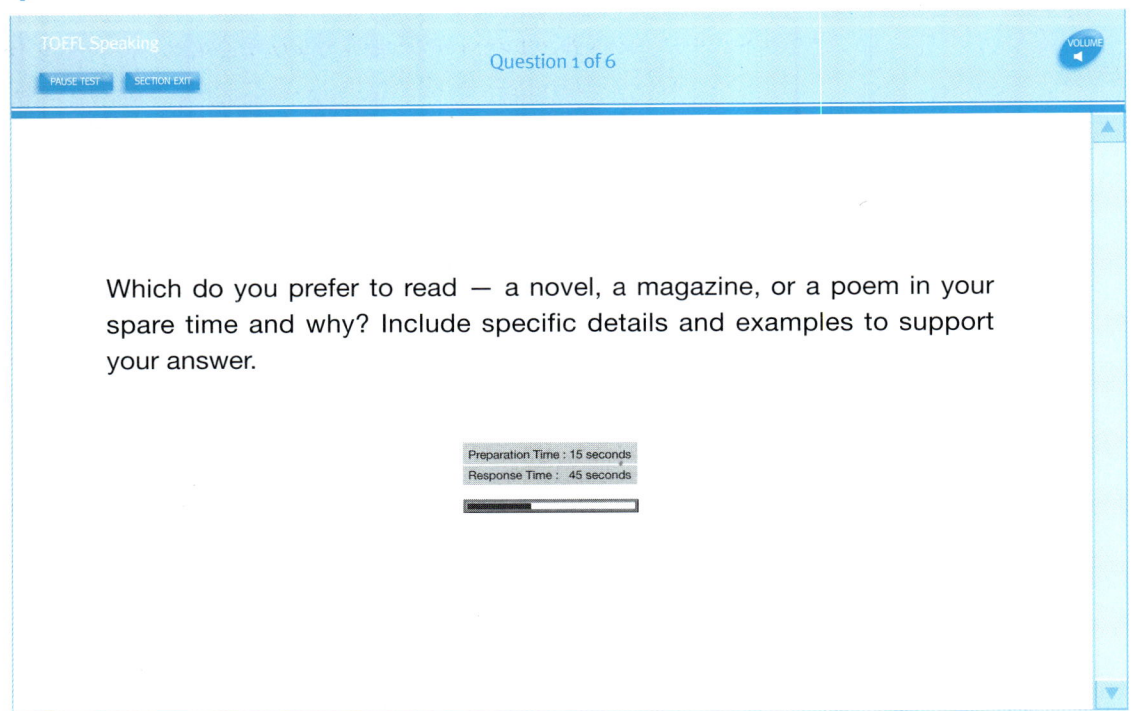

TOEFL Speaking

PAUSE TEST   SECTION EXIT

Question 1 of 6

VOLUME

Which do you prefer to read — a novel, a magazine, or a poem in your spare time and why? Include specific details and examples to support your answer.

Preparation Time : 15 seconds
Response Time :   45 seconds

2

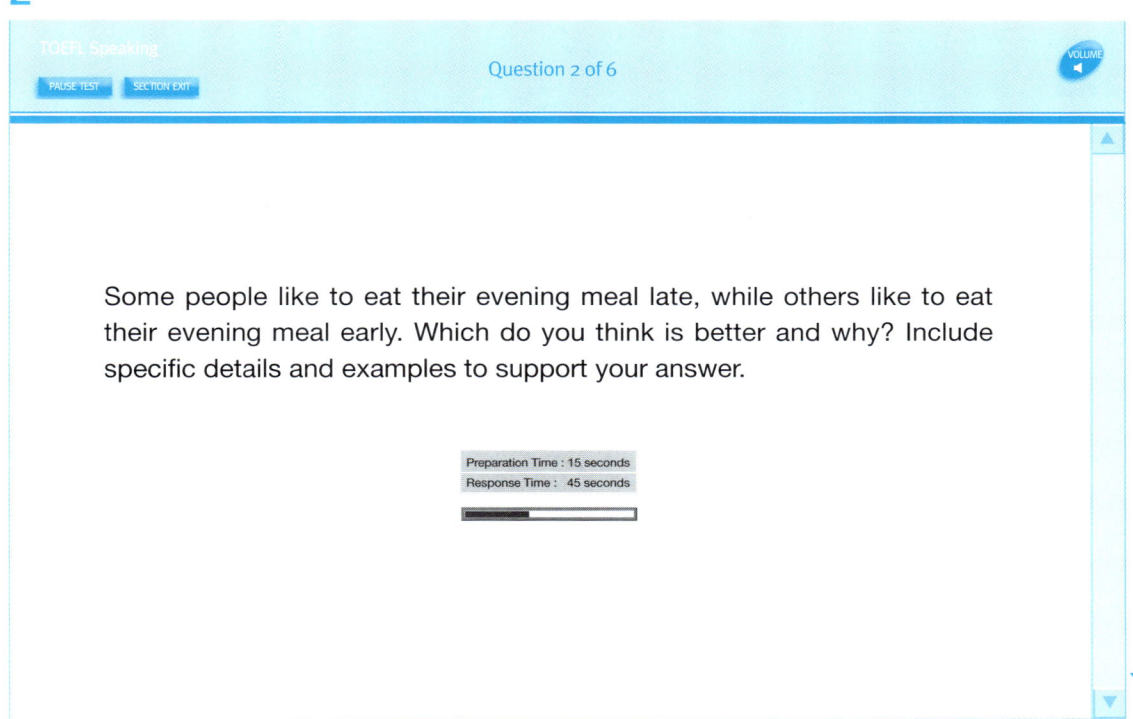

Some people like to eat their evening meal late, while others like to eat their evening meal early. Which do you think is better and why? Include specific details and examples to support your answer.

Preparation Time : 15 seconds
Response Time :   45 seconds

Set 2

3

Reading time: 45 seconds

Disturbance in the Rest Area

I would like to make a statement about the rest area in the student center. The rest area has turned into a loud and crowded place to visit in-between class. I'd like to request that the school administration remove the big screen located in the rest area. The big television screen is becoming a disturbance for the students who would like to study between classes and have a quiet study time to themselves. By removing the big screen television, we would be able to control the noise level and the overcrowding in the rest area.

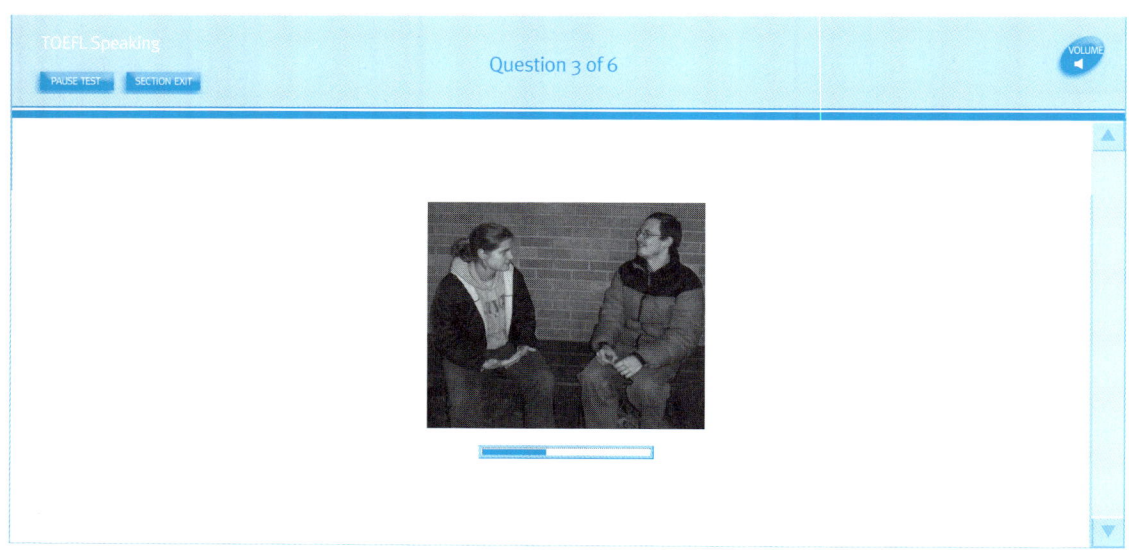

The man expresses his opinion of the university's plan to take away the big screen television in the rest area. State his opinion and explain the reasons he gives for holding that opinion.

Preparation Time : 30 seconds
Response Time : 60 seconds

Set 2

4

Reading time: 45 seconds

Credibility

When people make a speech, there are certain ways to build credibility. In a public speech, the speaker must be knowledgeable about the topic he or she is talking about. Also, the speaker must have confidence in the topic and exude this to the audience. If a speaker has vast knowledge about a subject, but does not come off as confident, the speaker appears like he or she does not know much about the topic at hand. And of course, it doesn't hurt for the speaker to be charismatic.

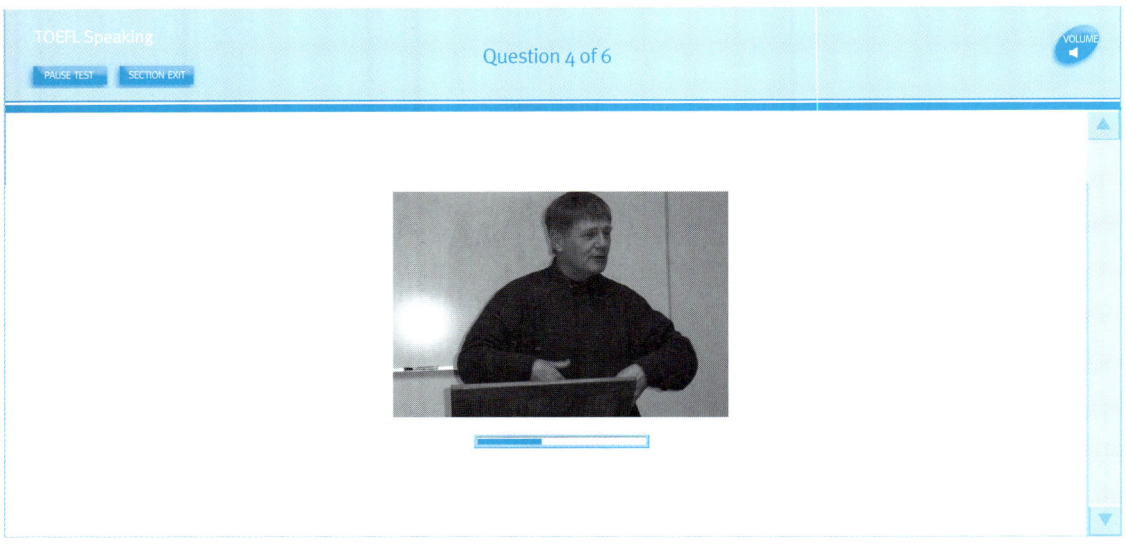

Using points and examples from the lecture, explain how politics is related to credibility.

Preparation Time : 30 seconds
Response Time : 60 seconds

Set 2

5

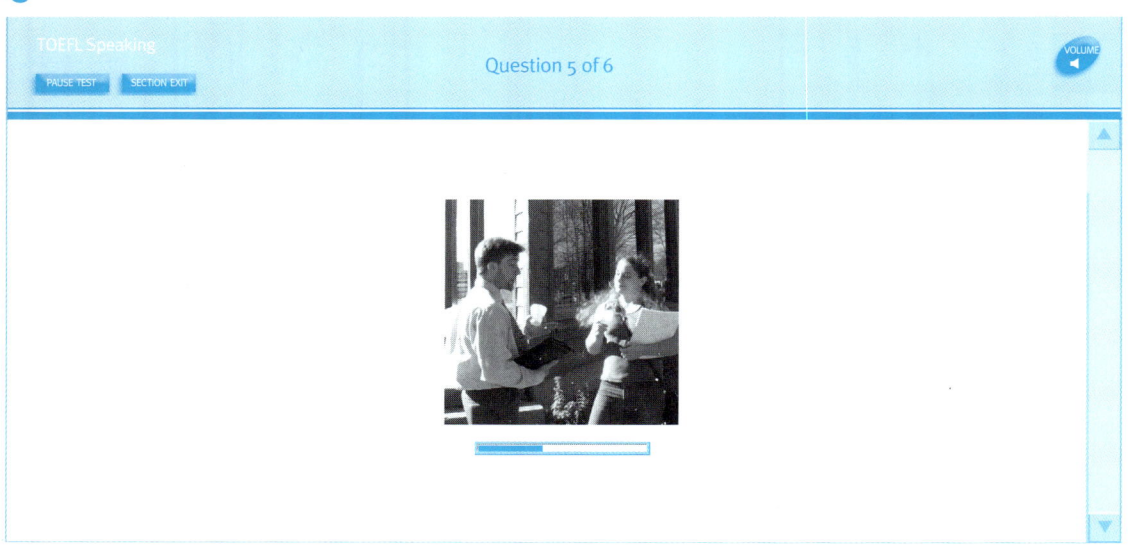

The students discuss two possible solutions to the woman's problem. Describe the problem. Then state which of the two solutions you prefer and explain why.

Preparation Time : 20 seconds
Response Time :   60 seconds

6

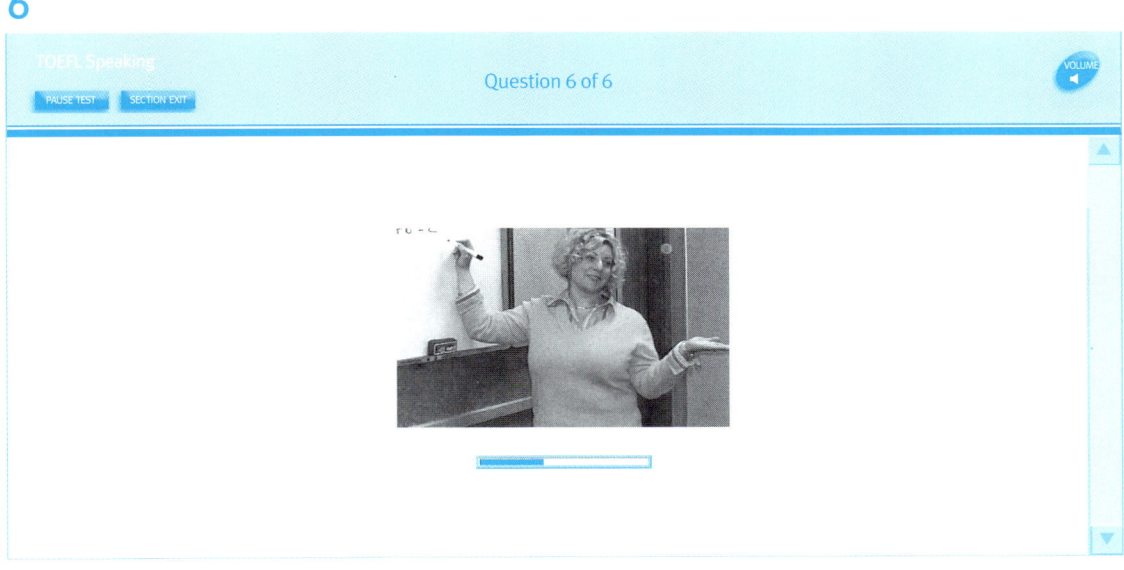

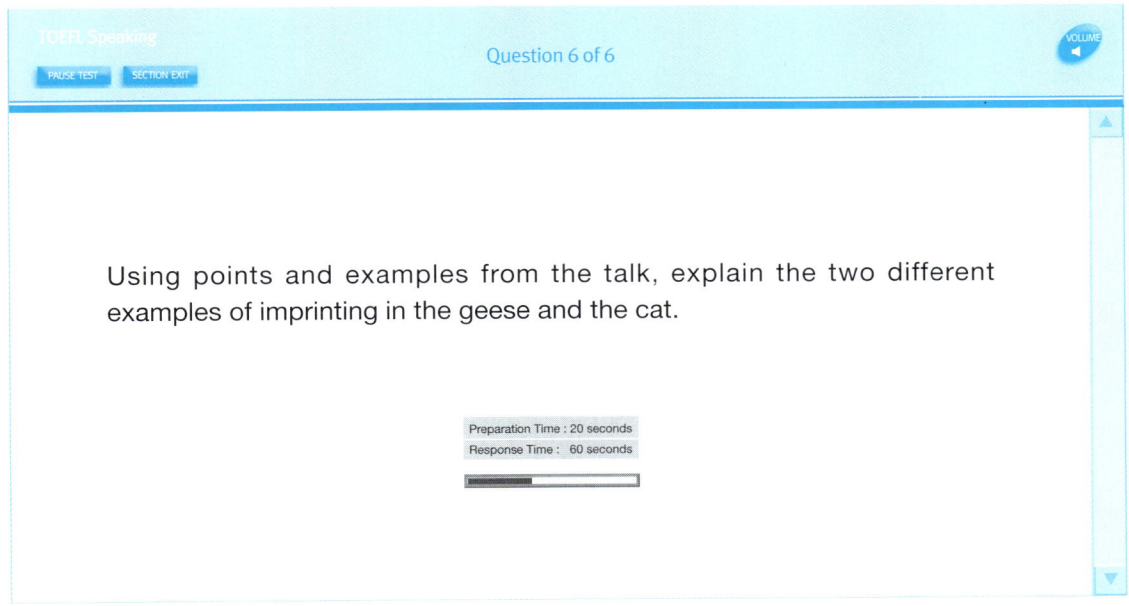

Using points and examples from the talk, explain the two different examples of imprinting in the geese and the cat.

Preparation Time : 20 seconds
Response Time :   60 seconds

The Best Solution for TOEFL iBT

HOW
TO
TOEFL ®

iBT

120

SPEAKING
정답 및 해설

넥서스

TASK 1 Personal Preference

◻ Sample

CD Possible Response: Track 1

Describe a friend who had the most influence on you during your university life. Include specific details and examples to support your answer.

I've had various kinds of friends during my university life, but Kevin had the most influence on me because he gave me a lot of advice. I met him when I was very confused about my future. He advised me to sit down and think about myself. Since then, I have tried to figure out my motivation in life. I realized that I was very interested in helping other people because I can be very patient with others. I was also interested in public speaking. So I decided to become a teacher. Now I'm very happy teaching at a school. He also encouraged me to develop presentation skills to transfer my knowledge to students more effectively. I will never forget his advice.

나는 대학 시절에 여러 친구들을 만났지만 Kevin이 나에게 충고를 많이 해주었기 때문에 가장 많은 영향을 주었다. 나는 미래에 대해 매우 혼란스러울 때 그를 만났다. 그는 나에게 차분하게 나 자신에 대해 생각해 보라고 했다. 그 이후로 나는 내 인생의 동기를 찾으려고 애썼다. 나는 내가 참을성이 많기 때문에 남을 돕는 것에 흥미가 많다는 것을 깨달았다. 또한 나는 사람들 앞에서 말하는 것에 관심이 많았다. 그래서 나는 선생님이 되기로 결심했다. 나는 지금 학교에서 가르치며 매우 행복하게 지내고 있다. 그는 또한 학생들에게 내 지식을 더 효과적으로 전달하기 위해 발표 능력을 키우라고 권했다. 나는 그의 충고를 결코 잊지 못할 것이다.

Mini Test

CD Possible Responses: Track 3~6

1 What is the most important characteristic of a good supervisor? Include specific details and examples to support your answer.

Which characteristic? _consideration_ 배려
Why? _makes people comfortable_ 사람들을 편안하게 하기 때문에
In detail? _people are not afraid of making mistakes_
사람들은 실수하는 것을 두려워하지 않는다

Possible response

I think the most important characteristic of a

good supervisor is consideration. It makes people comfortable. Considerate supervisor takes care of the employees' mistakes so that they are not afraid of making mistakes when they try doing something new.

나는 좋은 관리자의 가장 중요한 특성이 배려라고 생각한다. 그것은 사람들을 편안하게 한다. 사려 깊은 관리자는 직원들의 실수를 잘 처리해서 그들이 새로운 것을 시도할 때 실수하는 것에 대해 두려워하지 않도록 한다.

2 What do you consider to be the most important room in a house? Why is this room more important to you than any other room? Include specific details and examples to support your answer.

Which room? _living room_ 거실
Why? _building relationships_ 관계를 형성하기 때문에
In detail? _talk and have a chance to understand each other_ 이야기하고 서로를 이해할 수 있는 기회를 갖는다

Possible response

I think the living room is the most important room in a house because most people build relationships with family members and friends there. For example, when I have conflicts with my parents, I talk to my parents about them in that room and have a chance to understand each other.

나는 집에서 가장 중요한 방이 거실이라고 생각한다. 대부분의 사람들이 그곳에서 가족과 친구들과 관계를 형성하기 때문이다. 예를 들어, 부모님과 갈등이 있을 때 나는 그곳에서 그것에 대해 부모님과 이야기하고 서로를 이해할 수 있는 기회를 갖는다.

3 What do you want to accomplish in the future? Include specific details and examples to support your answer.

What? _my own business_ 개인 사업
Why? _make a lot of money to donate to a charitable organization_ 돈을 많이 벌어서 자선 기구에 기부하기 위해서
In detail? _orphanage_ 고아원

Possible response

I want to build up my own business in the future. Through my business, I want to make a lot of money to donate to charitable organizations such as orphanages.

나는 미래에 개인 사업을 하고 싶다. 내 사업을 통해 많은 돈을 벌어서 고아원 같은 자선 기구에 돈을 기부하고 싶다.

4 Describe the most enjoyable event in your childhood. Include specific details and examples to support your answer.

Which event? *my 11th birthday* 내 11번째 생일
Why? *a special memory at a family restaurant*
　　　패밀리 레스토랑에서의 특별한 기억 때문에
In detail? *a birthday song and pictures*
　　　생일 축하 노래와 사진들

Possible response

Among my childhood memories, my 11th birthday party was the most enjoyable event. The party took place at a family restaurant. A band in the restaurant sang a birthday song for me and I took pictures wearing a funny costume.

유년기의 많은 기억 중에 가장 즐거웠던 것은 나의 11번째 생일 파티였다. 파티는 패밀리 레스토랑에서 열렸다. 식당의 밴드가 나를 위해 생일 축하 노래를 불러주었고, 우스운 복장을 하고 사진을 찍었다.

5 What is the most important characteristic of a good co-worker? Include specific details and examples to support your answer.

Which characteristic? *cooperative mind* 협동심
Why? *work is efficient and enjoyable*
　　　업무가 효율적이고 즐겁기 때문에
In detail? *successful presentation (collect data, put on the computer)* 성공적인 발표 (자료수집, 자료 저장)

Possible response

I believe that the most important characteristic of a good co-worker is a cooperative mind. When we work together, cooperative colleagues help each other, so that work is efficient as well as enjoyable. Our last presentation was quite successful due to such cooperation: one of my colleagues collected data and the other one put the data on the computer and so on.

나는 좋은 동료가 되는 가장 중요한 특성이 협동심이라고 생각한다. 함께 일을 할 때 협동심 있는 동료들은 서로 돕기 때문에 일이 즐거울 뿐만 아니라 효율적이다. 우리의 지난번 발표는 이러한 협동심 때문에 꽤 성공적이었다. 내 동료 중 한 명은 자료를 모으고 다른 한 명은 그 자료를 컴퓨터에 입력했다.

6 Describe a book that affected you the most. Include specific details and examples to support your answer.

Which book? *The Korean War* 한국 전쟁
Why? *was able to understand the war more deeply*
　　　전쟁에 대해 더 깊이 이해할 수 있었기 때문에
In detail? *shows how the Korean people were damaged by the war*
　　　전쟁으로 한국 사람들이 얼마나 상처 받았는지 보여준다

Possible response

I think the book that affected me the most is a book called *The Korean War*. I was able to understand the circumstances and consequence of the war more deeply after reading the book. It shows how the Korean people were damaged by the war.

내가 가장 감명 받았던 책은 *한국 전쟁*이라는 책이다. 이 책을 읽음으로써 전쟁의 상황과 결과를 더 깊이 이해할 수 있었다. 이 책은 한국 사람들이 전쟁으로 인해 얼마나 상처 받았는지 보여준다.

7 Describe the most memorable event from the schools you attended. Include specific details and examples to support your answer.

Which event? *school festival at high school* 고등학교 축제
Why? *had a chance to participate in a school play*
　　　교내 연극에 참여할 수 있는 기회가 있었기 때문에
In detail? *gave motivation to be an actor*
　　　배우가 되는 동기를 주었다

Possible response

I have a lot of memories from my school days, but the school festival at my high school is the most memorable event for me because I had a chance to participate in a school play. I had a great time and the experience actually motivated me to pursue a career as an actor.

나는 학창 시절에 대한 많은 추억들이 있지만 교내 연극에 참여할 수 있는 기회가 있었기 때문에 고등학교 축제가 가장 기억에 남는다. 정말 즐거운 시간을 보냈으며, 그 경험은 실제로 나에게 연기자라는 직업을 추구하는 동기를 주었다.

8 Choose a city that you wish to visit that you've never been to. Include specific details and examples to support your answer.

Which city? *Paris* 파리
Why? *romantic city* 로맨틱한 도시이기 때문에
In detail? *talk over a cup of coffee at a cafe on Champs Élysées* 샹젤리제 거리에 있는 카페에서 커피 한잔을 마시기

Possible response

Among the cities that I've never been to, I really want

to visit Paris in France. I'd like to look around the romantic city and drink a cup of warm coffee at a cafe on Champs Élysées.

가보지 않은 도시 중에 나는 프랑스 파리에 정말 가보고 싶다. 그 낭만적인 도시를 둘러보고 샹젤리제 거리에 있는 카페에서 따뜻한 커피 한잔을 마시고 싶다.

9 What was the most important decision in your life? Include specific details and examples to support your answer.

Which decision? *choosing my major* 전공 선택
Why? *was able to prepare for my job efficiently*
효율적으로 직업을 준비할 수 있었기 때문에
In detail? *focused on the subjects related to my future job* 미래 직업과 연관이 있는 과목에 집중했다

Possible response

I believe that the most important decision in my life was choosing my major because I was able to prepare for my job more efficiently. For example, I focused on the subjects that were directly related to my future job and the knowledge I gained from these subjects is helpful in carrying out my job better now.

나는 전공을 선택한 것이 내 인생에 있어 가장 중요한 결정이었다고 생각한다. 보다 효율적으로 나의 직업을 준비할 수 있었기 때문이다. 예를 들어 나는 장래 직업과 직접적인 연관이 있는 과목들에 집중했고, 그 과목들로부터 쌓은 지식은 현재 나의 일을 보다 잘 하는데 도움이 되고 있다.

10 Describe the most disappointing moment in your life. Include specific details and examples to support your answer.

Which moment? *failed to enter the university that I wanted* 가고 싶었던 대학에 들어가지 못했을 때
Why? *had dreamed about studying with the professors there* 그곳에 계신 교수님들과 공부하는 것에 대해 꿈꿔왔기 때문에
In detail? *famous professors in the public administration department* 행정학과에 계신 저명한 교수들

Possible response

I think the most disappointing moment in my life was when I failed to enter the university that I wanted to attend. I was very upset because I had dreamed about studying with many of the professors there. The university had many famous professors in its public administration department.

내 인생에서 가장 실망했던 순간은 가고 싶었던 대학에 입학하지 못했던 것이다. 나는 그곳에 계신 교수님들과 공부하는 것을 꿈꿔왔기 때문에 매우 속이 상했다. 그 대학의 행정학과에는 저명한 교수님이 여러 분 계셨다.

11 Describe a challenge that you overcame. Include specific details and examples to support your answer.

What? *taking the college entrance exam*
대학 입학 시험을 치른 것
Why? *it was a big burden* 큰 부담이었기 때문에
In detail? *many subjects to study* 공부할 과목이 많았다

Possible response

I think taking the college entrance exam was a challenging experience that I overcame because it was a big burden for me. For example, there were many subjects that I had to study to enter the university such as English, math, science, sociology, etc. It was very stressful but I was able to enter the school I wanted.

나는 대학 입학 시험을 치른 것이 내가 극복했던 도전이었다고 생각한다. 그것은 나에게 큰 부담이었기 때문이다. 예를 들어 대학에 들어가기 위해 영어, 수학, 과학, 사회학 등 많은 과목을 공부해야 했다. 스트레스가 많이 쌓였지만 나는 원했던 학교에 들어갈 수 있었다.

12 Describe the best time of the year. Include specific details and examples to support your answer.

Which season? *winter* 겨울
Why? *enjoy winter sports* 겨울 스포츠를 즐기기 때문에
In detail? *skiing* 스키

Possible response

I think the best time of the year is winter because I enjoy winter sports. I go skiing every winter with my friends to escape from my routine life.

나는 겨울 스포츠를 즐기기 때문에 최고의 계절이 겨울이라고 생각한다. 나는 일상 생활로부터 벗어나기 위해 겨울마다 친구와 스키를 타러 간다.

13 What do you consider most when you choose a restaurant or a cafe? Include specific details and examples to support your answer.

Which feature? *the quality of the food* 음식의 질
Why? *like to have healthy dishes*
몸에 좋은 음식을 먹는 것을 좋아하기 때문에
In detail? *chemical ingredients* 화학 재료

Possible response

I consider the quality of the food first when I choose a restaurant. I really like to have healthy dishes not containing chemical ingredients, like M.S.G.

나는 레스토랑을 선택할 때 음식의 질을 가장 먼저 고려한다. 나는 조미료 같은 화학 재료가 들어있지 않은 몸에 좋은 음식을 먹는 것을 매우 좋아한다.

14 What sport do you think will become more popular in your country in ten years? Include specific details and examples to support your answer.

Which sports? _golf_ 골프

Why? _female golfers in LPGA_ LPGA에 있는 여성 프로 골프 선수들

In detail? _their successful games draw attention_
그들의 성공적인 경기가 관심을 끈다

Possible response

I think golf will become more popular in Korea in ten years. There are many professional female golfers in the LPGA league such as Seri Park and Michelle Wie. Their successful games continually draw more attention to golf in Korea and will make golf more popular.

나는 10년 내에 한국에서 골프가 더욱 인기가 많아질 것이라고 생각한다. LPGA 리그에는 박세리와 미셸 위 같은 여성 프로 골프 선수들이 많이 있다. 그들의 성공적인 경기는 한국에서 골프에 대한 더욱 많은 관심을 지속적으로 자아내고 있고, 골프의 인기를 더욱 높일 것이다.

15 Every country has its own traditional drinks. Which traditional drink is famous in your country? Include specific details and examples to support your answer.

Which drink? _rice wine_ 막걸리

Why? _celebrate family gathering_ 가족 모임을 축하하기 위해

In detail? _lunar New Year's Day and Korean
Thanksgiving Day_ 음력 설날과 추석

Possible response

Of all the popular traditional drinks in Korea, rice wine is the most famous. It is made of rice, which is the staple food of Koreans. Koreans drink rice wine to celebrate family gathering on lunar New Year's Day and Korean Thanksgiving Day.

한국에서 인기 있는 많은 전통 음료 중에 막걸리가 가장 유명하다. 막걸리는 한국인들의 주식인 쌀로 만들어진다. 한국인들은 음력 설날과 추석에 가족 모임을 축하하기 위해 막걸리를 마신다.

16 Describe a tourist attraction in your city. Include specific details and examples to support your answer.

Which place? _cultural center_ 문화센터

Why? _provides various cultural activities_
다양한 문화 활동을 제공하기 때문에

In detail? _yoga, cooking, foreign language courses_
요가, 요리, 외국어 강좌

Possible response

I think the cultural center in my town is very attractive to visitors. It provides visitors with various cultural activities. For example, they have yoga classes, cooking classes as well as foreign language courses for those who are interested.

나는 우리 동네 문화센터가 방문자들에게 매력적일 것이라고 생각한다. 이곳에서는 방문객들에게 다양한 문화 활동을 제공한다. 예를 들어 이곳에서는 관심이 있는 사람들을 위해 요가 수업, 요리 수업 및 외국어 강좌 등을 제공한다.

17 Choose a skill that is necessary to be successful in the world today. Include specific details and examples to support your answer.

Which skill? _being able to use the Internet_
인터넷을 사용할 수 있는 것

Why? _can help people succeed in their careers_
사람들로 하여금 직업에서 성공할 수 있도록 도와줄 수 있기 때문에

In detail? _share information, send and receive
documents_ 정보 공유, 서류 주고 받기

Possible response

I think being able to use the Internet is a very important skill. The Internet can help people succeed in their careers. These days, in many parts of business, the Internet is used. Through the Internet, people can share information about their business and also send and receive important documents.

나는 인터넷을 사용할 줄 아는 것이 매우 중요한 기술이라고 생각한다. 인터넷은 사람들로 하여금 직업에서 성공할 수 있도록 도와줄 수 있다. 오늘날 많은 사업장에서 인터넷이 사용된다. 인터넷을 통해서 사람들은 그들의 사업에 대한 정보를 공유하고 중요한 서류를 주고 받을 수 있다.

18 Describe a poem, a song, or a painting that is impressive to you. Include specific details and examples to support your answer.

What? _song_ 노래

Why? _reminds me of my first love_
첫사랑에 대한 기억이 떠오르기 때문에

In detail? _The power of love_ 사랑의 힘

Possible response

The song titled _The Power of Love_ is impressive to me because it reminds me of my first love. Whenever I listen to that song, I always remember the time I spent with my first love and how powerful the love was.

사랑의 힘이라는 곡은 내 첫사랑에 대한 기억이 떠오르기 때문에 인상 깊은 노래이다. 그 노래를 들을 때마다 항상 내 첫사랑과 보냈던 시간들이 생각나고 얼마나 많이 사랑했었는지 기억난다.

19 Describe one of your goals in life. Include specific details and examples to support your answer.

What? _becoming a teacher_ 선생님이 되는 것
Why? _want to help other people_ 다른 사람들을 도와주고 싶기 때문에
In detail? _give advice about how to study more efficiently_
더 효율적으로 공부하는 방법에 대해 충고해 준다

Possible response

One of my goals in life is becoming a teacher because I want to help other people. I especially want to help students who have trouble studying. For example, I can give them advice about how to study more efficiently because I have experience in that area, and I always enjoy helping others.

내 삶의 목표 중 하나는 다른 사람들을 도와주고 싶기 때문에 선생님이 되는 것이다. 나는 특히 공부할 때 어려움을 느끼는 학생들을 도와주고 싶다. 예를 들어 나는 내 경험을 비추어 더 효과적으로 공부하는 방법에 대해 충고해 줄 수 있다. 그리고 나는 늘 다른 사람을 도와주는 것을 즐긴다.

20 Describe a special opportunity that was given to you. Include specific details and examples to support your answer.

What? _studying abroad_ 외국에서 공부한 것
Why? _gave opportunity to speak to and to learn from people in different countries_ 다른 나라에서 온 사람들과 이야기하고 배울 수 있는 기회를 주었기 때문에
In detail? _Chinese words, Chinese food_
중국어 단어. 중국 음식

Possible response

Studying abroad was a special opportunity for me because it gave me an opportunity to speak to and to learn from people in different countries. For example, when I was in China, my new friends taught me how to say several Chinese words and how to cook some delicious Chinese food.

외국에서 공부한 것이 내게 주어진 특별한 기회였던 이유는 다른 나라에서 온 사람들과 이야기 하고 배울 수 있는 기회를 주었기 때문이다. 예를 들어 내가 중국에 있을 때 새로 만난 친구들은 나에게 여러 가지 중국어 단어와 맛있는 중국 음식을 만드는 방법을 가르쳐 주었다.

21 Describe a job you would like to have. Include specific details and examples to support your answer.

What? _judge_ 판사
Why? _help develop a fairer society_
보다 공정한 사회의 발전에 공헌하기 위해서
In detail? _protect people from corrupt judges_
타락한 판사들로부터 사람들을 보호한다

Possible response

If possible, I would really like to become a judge so I can help develop a fairer society. If I were a fair judge, I could help protect people from the few corrupt judges who only worry about making money and not being fair to the people they judge.

가능하다면 나는 보다 공정한 사회의 발전에 공헌하기 위해 판사가 되고 싶다. 만약 내가 공정한 판사라면, 돈을 버는 것에만 관심이 있고 판결을 내리는 사람들에게 공정하지 못한 몇몇 타락한 판사들로부터 사람들을 보호할 수 있을 것이다.

22 Describe a skill or something that you are good at. Include specific details and examples to support your answer.

What? _giving presentations_ 발표하기
Why? _gave a multi-media presentation and classmates were very impressed_
멀티미디어 발표를 했는데 학급 친구들이 매우 감동했다
In detail? _asked how l long had prepare for it_
얼마나 오랫동안 준비했는지 물었다

Possible response

I think I'm good at giving presentations. For example, last semester, I gave a multi-media presentation with handouts in my political science class, and most of my classmates were very impressed. They asked me how long I had prepared for my presentation. Of course, I received a good grade from my professor.

나는 발표에 재능이 있다고 생각한다. 예를 들어 지난 학기에 나는 정치학과 수업에서 유인물을 사용한 멀티미디어 발표를 했는데 대부분의 학급 친구들이 매우 감동했다. 그들은 나에게 얼마나 오랫동안 발표를 준비했는지 물었다. 물론 나는 교수님에게 좋은 점수를 받았다.

23 What is the most important characteristic of a good leader? Include specific details and examples to support your answer.

Which characteristic? _consideration_ 배려 (사려 깊음)
Why? _people usually respect other people who are considerate_ 사람들은 보통 사려 깊은 사람들을 존경한다
In detail? _a considerate leader focuses on why it happened and helps to correct it_ 사려 깊은 지도자는 왜 그러한 일이 발생했고 그것을 고치는데 초점을 둔다

Possible response

I think the most important characteristic of a good leader is consideration. Usually, people respect other people who are considerate, and a leader needs to be respected. When you make a mistake, a considerate leader focuses on why it happened and helps to correct it instead of just putting the blame on you.

나는 좋은 지도자의 가장 중요한 특성이 배려라고 생각한다. 사람들은 보통 사려 깊은 사람을 존경하며, 지도자는 존경을 받아야 한다. 실수를 했을 경우, 사려 깊은 지도자는 무조건 비난하는 것이 아니라 왜 그러한 일이 발생했고, 그것을 고치는데 초점을 둔다.

24 When do you miss your family or country the most? Include specific details and examples to support your answer.

When? *miss my parents when I go through a hard time*
힘든 일을 겪을 때 부모님이 그립다

Why? *they could give lots of advice*
그들은 많은 조언을 해줄 수 있기 때문에

In detail? *got help from my dad's advice when I failed a class* 낙제했을 때 아버지의 조언으로부터 도움을 받았다

Possible response

Whenever I go through a hard time, I miss my family, especially my parents, because they could give me lots of advice if they were with me. When I failed one of my classes last semester, I got a lot of help from my dad's advice because he is an experienced academic advisor.

나는 힘든 일을 겪을 때마다 가족, 특히 부모님이 그립다. 그들이 나와 함께 있다면 많은 조언을 해줄 수 있기 때문이다. 지난 학기에 한 과목을 낙제했을 때 나는 아버지의 조언으로부터 많은 도움을 받았다. 아버지께서는 경험이 풍부한 학업 상담자이시기 때문이다.

Exercise 🔊 Possible Responses: **Track 8~15**

1 Describe a person you admire most. Include specific details and examples to support your answer.

Thesis: *The person I admire most is my uncle, NamKyu.*
내가 가장 존경하는 사람은 남규 삼촌이다

Reason 1: *supported his mother and two siblings*
그의 어머니와 두 동생을 부양했다

Detail: *worked two jobs* 두 가지 일을 했다

Reason 2: *dropped out of college but continued to study at home* 대학을 중퇴했지만 집에서 공부를 계속했다

Detail: *acquired several certifications, was hired by LG* 자격증을 여러 개 취득했고 LG에 입사했다

Conclusion: *These are the reasons why admire him most.* 이와 같은 이유로 나는 그를 가장 존경한다

Possible response

The person I admire most is my uncle NamKyu for the following reasons. First, he was very dedicated. When he was a university student in Gumi, he lost his father due to cancer and had to move back to Seoul to help support his mother and two siblings. During that time, he had to work two jobs. Second, he was strong enough to overcome his difficulties. He had to drop out of college because of financial problems, but continued to study computers at home. He acquired several certifications and all of his hard work paid off when he was hired by LG, one of the biggest companies in Korea. After ten years, he helped send both of his siblings to college and bought two houses on his own. These are the reasons why I admire him most.

내가 가장 존경하는 사람은 다음과 같은 이유들 때문에 나의 남규 삼촌이다. 우선, 그는 매우 헌신적이었다. 그가 구미에서 대학생이었을 때 아버지께서 암으로 돌아가셔서 어머니와 두 명의 동생들을 부양하기 위해 서울로 돌아와야만 했다. 그 기간 동안, 그는 두 가지 일을 해야 했다. 두 번째로, 그는 어려움을 극복할 만큼 충분히 강했다. 그는 경제적인 문제로 대학을 중퇴해야 했지만 집에서 컴퓨터 공부를 계속했다. 그는 자격증을 여러 개 취득했고, 한국의 대기업 중 하나인 LG에 입사함으로써 열심히 일한 것에 대한 보상을 받았다. 10년 후, 그는 두 동생들이 대학에 갈 수 있도록 지원했고, 두 채의 집을 장만했다. 이와 같은 이유로 나는 그를 가장 존경한다.

2 Describe your favorite place in your city. Include specific details and examples to support your answer.

Thesis: *My favorite place in the city is the public library.*
내가 도시에서 가장 좋아하는 곳은 공립 도서관이다

Reason 1: *enjoy reading* 책 읽기를 즐긴다

Detail: *a huge selection of books* 많은 책이 있다

Reason 2: *a very quiet place* 매우 조용한 장소이다

Detail: *can relax, get away from the busy city*
휴식을 취한다, 바쁜 도시로부터 벗어난다

Conclusion: *The public library is my favorite place in the city.* 공립 도서관이 내가 도시에서 가장 좋아하는 곳이다

Possible response

There are many exciting places in my city, but my favorite is the public library for the following reasons. First, I enjoy reading and the public library has a huge selection of books available for check out from my major field to my hobby. I like reading different genres, and there are so many books to choose from. Second, the public library is a very quiet place where I can relax and get my work done. I go there to get away from the busy city and focus on what I need to get done. These are the reasons why the public library is my favorite place in the city.

내가 사는 도시에는 흥미로운 곳들이 많지만 내가 가장 좋아하는 곳은 다음과 같은 이유로 공립 도서관이다. 우선, 나는 책을 읽는 것을 좋아하며, 공립 도서관에는 전공서에서부터 나의 취미에 관한 책까지 대출할 수 있는 방대한 종류의 책들이 있다. 나는 다양한 장르의 책을 즐겨 보고, 도서관에는 선택의 폭이 넓다. 두 번째 이유는 공립 도서관이 편안히 쉴 수 있고 해야 할 일을 할 수 있는 매우 조용한 장소라는 것이다. 나는 바쁜 도시로부터 벗어나서 해야 할 일에 집중해야 할 때 도서관에 간다. 이러한 이유로 공립 도서관은 내가 도시에서 가장 좋아하는 장소이다.

3 Describe the most memorable gift you have ever received. Include specific details and examples to support your answer.

Thesis: *The most memorable gift I have received is a violin from my parents.* 내가 받은 선물 중에 가장 기억에 남는 선물은 부모님으로부터 받은 바이올린이다

Reason 1: *was able to make my parents happy*
부모님을 기쁘게 할 수 있었다

Detail: *my parents were pleased and proud*
부모님께서 기뻐하시고 자랑스러워 하셨다

Reason 2: *became a better violin player*
더 좋은 바이올린 연주자가 되었다

Detail: *played it during the school festival*
학교 축제에서 연주했다

Conclusion: *That's why I think the violin I received from my parents is the most memorable gift I've ever received.*
이러한 이유로 나는 부모님으로부터 받았던 바이올린이 지금까지 받았던 선물 중 가장 기억에 남는다고 생각한다

The most memorable gift I have received is a violin from my parents. First, I was able to make my parents happy with it. My parents seemed very pleased when I played the violin in front of them. Through that experience, I felt that my parents were proud of me and loved me very much. Second, I became a better violin player. I practiced it every chance I got. I played it during the school festival. It was a great experience for me. That's why I think the violin I received from my parents on my birthday is the most memorable gift I've ever received.

내가 받았던 가장 기억에 남는 선물은 부모님으로부터 받은 바이올린이다. 첫 번째로, 나는 그것으로 부모님을 기쁘게 해드릴 수 있었다. 부모님 앞에서

바이올린을 연주했을 때 그들은 매우 기뻐하셨다. 이 경험을 통해서 나는 부모님께서 나를 자랑스럽게 여기고 매우 사랑하신다는 것을 느꼈다. 두 번째로, 나는 더 좋은 바이올린 연주자가 되었다. 나는 기회가 생길 때마다 바이올린을 연습했고, 학교 축제에서 연주했다. 그것은 나에게 좋은 경험이었다. 이러한 이유로 나는 부모님으로부터 받았던 바이올린이 지금까지 받았던 선물 중 가장 기억에 남는다고 생각한다.

4 Describe what you do for relaxation. Include specific details and examples to support your answer.

Thesis: *I like to go to the gym to relax*
나는 헬스장에서 휴식하는 것을 좋아한다

Reason 1: *can lighten up my life* 삶을 가볍게 할 수 있다

Detail: *bicycling with music → escape from monotonous life* 음악을 들으며 자전거를 타면 단조로운 일상으로부터 벗어날 수 있다

Reason 2: *can refresh myself by doing work out*
운동을 하면 기력을 회복할 수 있다

Detail: *feel like a new man after a sauna and a shower* 사우나와 샤워를 하고 나면 새로운 사람이 된 것 같다

Conclusion: *That's why I like to go to the gym to relax in my spare time.* 이러한 이유로 나는 여가 시간에 헬스장에서 긴장을 푸는 것을 좋아한다

When I relax, I like to go to the gym for the following reasons. First, I can lighten up my life. By bicycling with music, I can completely escape from my monotonous life. Second, I can refresh myself by working out. After a good work out, I usually go to the sauna and unwind in there. I feel like a new man after sauna and a shower. When I go back to my normal life, I feel more energetic. This is why I like to go to the gym to relax in my spare time.

나는 휴식을 취할 때 다음과 같은 이유 때문에 헬스장에 가는 것을 좋아한다. 우선 나의 삶을 가볍게 할 수 있다. 음악을 들으며 자전거를 타면, 단조로운 일상으로부터 완전히 벗어날 수 있다. 두 번째로, 운동을 하면 기력을 회복할 수 있다. 충분히 운동을 하고 난 후 나는 보통 사우나에 가서 긴장을 푼다. 사우나와 샤워를 하고 나면 새로운 사람이 된 것 같은 기분이 든다. 일상으로 돌아가면 더 활력이 생긴다. 이러한 이유로 나는 여가 시간에 헬스장에서 긴장을 푸는 것을 좋아한다.

5 Describe the most important characteristic of a good parent. Include specific details and examples to support your answer.

Thesis: *The most important characteristic of a good parent is patience.* 좋은 부모의 가장 중요한 자질은 인내심이다

Reason 1: *parents have to understand their children* 부모는 그들의 아이들을 이해해야 한다

  Detail: *children are going to make mistakes* 아이들은 실수를 하게 되어있다

Reason 2: *having patience will help lower parents' stress levels* 인내심은 부모의 스트레스를 줄여 줄 것이다

  Detail: *children's misbehavior causes stress* 아이들의 잘못된 행동은 스트레스를 받게 된다

Conclusion: *Patience is the most important characteristic of a good parent.* 좋은 부모가 되는 가장 중요한 자질이 인내심이다.

Possible response

I believe that the most important characteristic of a good parent is patience. The first reason is that parents have to understand that their children are going to make mistakes. Therefore, they must be willing to be patient with their children through their growing pains. Second, having patience will help lower parents' stress levels. For example, parents are normally very busy at work, so when they come home and their children are misbehaving, this causes a lot of stress. Having patience will help them control themselves, thus lowering their stress levels. That's why I feel that patience is the most important characteristic of a good parent.

나는 좋은 부모의 가장 중요한 자질은 인내심이라고 생각한다. 첫 번째 이유는 부모는 자녀들이 언제든지 실수를 할 수 있다는 것을 이해해야 하기 때문이다. 따라서 그들은 자녀들이 실수를 통해서 배울 수 있을 때까지 기꺼이 참고 인내해야 한다. 두 번째로, 인내심이 있는 것은 부모의 스트레스를 낮추는데 도움이 될 것이다. 예를 들어 부모들은 보통 일을 하느라 매우 바쁘기 때문에, 집에 왔을 때 아이들이 잘못된 행동을 하게 되면 스트레스를 많이 받게 된다. 인내심이 있으면 그로 하여금 스스로를 제어할 수 있도록 도와 줄 것이며, 따라서 스트레스를 줄일 수 있을 것이다. 그래서 나는 좋은 부모가 되는 중요한 자질이 인내심이라고 생각한다.

6 Describe a place of historical significance that you would like to visit. Include specific details and examples to support your answer.

Thesis: *I would like to visit Kyungbok Palace in Seoul.* 나는 서울에 있는 경복궁을 방문하고 싶다

Reason 1: *learn about how the kings lived* 왕이 어떻게 살았는지 배운다

  Detail: *where they worked, how they spent their spare time* 왕들이 어디에서 일을 했고 어떻게 여가 시간을 보냈는지

Reason 2: *educational* 교육적이다

  Detail: *construction technology of the Joseon Dynasty* 조선 시대의 건축 기술

Conclusion: *These are the reasons why I would like to visit Kyungbok Palace in Seoul.* 이러한 이유로 나는 서울의 경복궁을 방문하고 싶다

Possible response

Of all the historical sites, I would like to visit Kyungbok Palace in Seoul. I'd like to learn about how the kings lived during ancient times. More specifically, I'm interested in where they worked and how they spent their spare time. Also, visiting Kyungbok Palace would be educational. Since I major in architecture, I'm very interested in the construction technology of the Joseon Dynasty. I'd like to see the special heating system they used at Kyungbok Palace that uses sunlight. These are the reasons why I would like to visit Kyungbok Palace in Seoul.

많은 역사 유적지 중 나는 서울에 있는 경복궁을 방문하고 싶다. 나는 고대에 왕이 어떻게 살았는지에 대해 배우고 싶다. 더 자세히 말해 나는 그들이 어디에서 일했고, 여가 시간을 어떻게 보냈는지에 대해 관심이 있다. 또한, 경복궁을 방문하는 것은 교육적일 것이다. 나는 건축학을 전공하고 있기 때문에 조선 시대의 건축 기술에 관심이 많다. 나는 경복궁에서 사용했던 햇빛을 이용하는 특수한 난방 시스템을 보고 싶다. 이러한 이유로 나는 서울의 경복궁을 방문하고 싶다

7 Which medium is more influential, television or radio and why? Include specific details and examples to support your answer.

Thesis: *I believe that television is more influential than radio for the following reasons.* 나는 다음과 같은 이유로 텔레비전이 라디오보다 더 영향력 있다고 생각한다

Reason 1: *television utilizes both hearing and visual senses* 텔레비전은 청각과 시각을 둘 다 활용한다

  Detail: *radio only utilizes one's hearing* 라디오는 단지 청각만 활용한다

Reason 2: *TV watching is a big part of people's lives* TV 시청은 사람들의 중요한 일상이다

  Detail: *news reports and infomercials* 뉴스 보도, 정보 광고

Conclusion: *That's why I believe that television is more influential than radio.* 이러한 이유로 나는 텔레비전이 라디오보다 더 영향력 있다고 생각한다

Possible response

I believe that television is more influential than radio for the following reasons. First, radio only utilizes one's hearing, but television utilizes both hearing and visual senses and is able to give more information. Second, in today's society, time consumed by TV watching is a big part of people's lives. Families spend a lot of time watching television and many news reports and infomercials influence people's lives everyday. That's why I believe that television is more influential than radio.

포함한다는 것이다. 그런 영화들은 손에 땀을 쥐게 한다. 이것이 내가 액션 영화를 가장 좋아하는 이유이다.

나는 다음과 같은 이유로 텔레비전이 라디오보다 더 영향력 있다고 생각한다. 첫 번째로, 라디오는 단지 청각만을 활용하지만 텔레비전은 청각과 시각을 둘 다 사용하고 더 많은 정보를 제공할 수 있다. 두 번째로, 현대 사회에서 TV 시청에 소요되는 시간은 사람들의 중요한 일상이다. 가족들은 텔레비전을 보면서 많은 시간을 보내고, 많은 뉴스 보도와 정보 광고는 사람들의 일상 생활에 큰 영향을 미친다. 이러한 이유로 나는 텔레비전이 라디오보다 더 영향력 있다고 생각한다.

8 Describe your favorite genre in movies. Include specific details and examples to support your answer.

Thesis: *I've watched various kinds of movie genre, but my favorite genre is action films for the following reasons.* 나는 여러 장르의 영화를 봤지만, 다음과 같은 이유 때문에 액션 영화를 가장 좋아한다

Reason 1: *the best special effects* 최고의 특수 효과

Detail: *very high budget, awesome cinematography* 매우 높은 예산, 멋진 촬영 기술

Reason 2: *usually involve a lot of suspense* 보통 많은 서스펜스를 포함한다

Detail: *keep me on the edge of my seat* 손에 땀을 쥐게 한다

Conclusion: *That's why action movies are my favorite genre.* 이것이 내가 액션 영화를 가장 좋아하는 이유이다

Possible response

I've watched various kinds of movie genres, but my favorite genre is action films for the following reasons. First, action films have the best special effects. They usually have a very high budget with awesome cinematography. I am fascinated by those awesome scenes in action movies. Another reason is that action movies usually involve a lot of suspense which builds up to a climax. Movies like that keep me on the edge of my seat. That's why action movies are my favorite genre.

나는 여러 장르의 영화를 봤지만, 다음과 같은 이유 때문에 액션 영화를 가장 좋아한다. 첫 번째로, 액션 영화는 최고의 특수 효과를 가지고 있다. 액션 영화는 일반적으로 매우 높은 예산을 확보하고 있고, 멋진 촬영 기술을 보여준다. 나는 액션 영화에서 이와 같은 굉장한 장면들에 큰 매력을 느낀다. 또 다른 이유는 보통 액션 영화는 클라이맥스에 이르기까지 많은 서스펜스를

TASK 2 Paired Choice

Sample
CD Possible Response: Track 16

Some people think that it is better to travel as part of a tour group when they are visiting a foreign country, while other people prefer to make their own travel plans so that they can travel independently. Which approach do you think is better and why? Include specific details and examples to support your answer.

> I have taken various tours, but I would rather make my own travel plans for a couple of reasons. First of all, people in a group tend to miss out on the exotic culture of the country they are visiting. For example, they usually stay in large hotels where they are served basic meals and do not get a chance to taste exotic food of that particular country. Secondly, another reason that I like to travel by myself is that I am an adventurous person, so I like to explore places that not many people have been to. These are the reasons why I like traveling alone.
>
> 나는 다양한 여행을 해왔지만 몇 가지 이유 때문에 나만의 여행 계획을 짜는 것을 선호한다. 우선, 그룹으로 여행하는 사람들은 그들이 방문하는 나라의 이국적인 문화를 체험하지 못하는 경향이 있다. 예를 들어 그들은 보통 큰 호텔에 투숙하고 기본적인 음식을 먹게 되기 때문에 그 나라 고유의 음식을 먹어볼 기회가 없다. 혼자 여행하길 좋아하는 또 다른 이유는 내가 모험심이 많아서 사람들이 많이 가보지 않은 곳을 탐험하는 것을 좋아하기 때문이다. 이것이 내가 혼자 여행하는 것을 좋아하는 이유이다.

Mini Test
CD Possible Responses: Track 18~22

1 Some students like to study at school, while others like to study at home. Which do you prefer and why? Include specific details and examples to support your answer.

Your preference? *study at school* 학교에서 공부하는 것
Why? *can use facilities for study* 학습 시설을 이용할 수 있기 때문에
In detail? *library* 도서관

Possible response

Although some people like to study at home, I like to study at school where I can use facilities for my study. For example, I can go to the library to get the information I need for my classes.

어떤 사람들은 집에서 공부하는 것을 좋아하지만, 나는 공부하는데 필요한 시설을 이용할 수 있는 학교에서 공부하는 것이 좋다. 예를 들어, 수업에 필요한 정보를 얻기 위해 도서관에 갈 수 있다.

2 When trying to find a job, some people think money is the most important factor, while others think their aptitude is more important. Which do you agree with and why? Include specific details and examples to support your answer.

Your opinion? *aptitude is a more important factor* 적성이 더 중요한 요소이다
Why? *motivated more* 더욱 동기 부여가 되기 때문에
In detail? *motivates us to do a better job or do our best* 일을 더 잘하거나 최선을 다하도록 동기를 부여한다

Possible response

I believe that aptitude is a more important factor than money because we are motivated more when we do something because we enjoy it rather than just make money out of it. Money makes us do our job, yet, aptitude motivates us to do a better job, or often, do our best. For example, if you enjoy teaching, you try to be not a teacher but a good teacher.

나는 적성이 돈보다 더 중요한 요소라고 믿는다. 그 이유는 어떤 일을 할 때 단지 돈을 버는 것보다 그것을 즐길 때 더욱 동기 부여가 되기 때문이다. 돈은 우리로 하여금 일을 하도록 만들지만, 적성은 우리로 하여금 일을 더 잘하거나, 종종 최선을 다하도록 동기를 부여한다. 예를 들어 가르치는 것을 즐기면, 단지 선생님이 아니라 좋은 선생님이 되기 위해 노력한다.

3 Some people like to participate in indoor activities while others like to participate in outdoor activities. Which do you prefer and why? Include specific details and examples to support your answer.

Your preference? *outdoor activities* 야외 활동
Why? *enjoy playing outdoor sports* 야외 스포츠를 좋아하기 때문에
In detail? *skiing in winter, swimming in summer* 겨울에는 스키를 타고 여름에는 수영을 한다

I prefer outdoor activities because I enjoy playing outdoor sports — skiing in winter and swimming in summer. When I ski in the mountains and swim in the ocean, I can enjoy not only playing these sports but also communing with nature, which I cannot do when participating in indoor activities.

나는 겨울에 스키를 타고 여름에 수영을 하는 등 야외 스포츠를 즐기기 때문에 야외 활동을 선호한다. 산에서 스키를 타고 바다에서 수영을 할 때, 나는 이러한 스포츠를 즐길 뿐만 아니라 자연과 교감할 수 있는데, 이것은 실내 활동으로부터는 얻을 수 없는 것이다.

4 Do you agree or disagree with the following statement? Telling the truth is always the best choice. Include specific details and examples to support your answer.

Your opinion? *honesty is not always the best*
정직이 언제나 최선인 것은 아니다

Why? *need to tell a white lie for better relationships*
더 나은 관계를 위해 선의의 거짓말을 해야 할 필요가 있기 때문에

In detail? *not to hurt one's feelings* 감정을 상하지 않게 하기 위해

I strongly disagree that telling the truth is always the best. Occasionally, we need to tell a white lie for better relationships. For example, if your friend asks you whether his new clothes look good on him, you might sometimes have to tell a lie, a white lie, not to hurt his feelings.

나는 진실을 말하는 것이 늘 최선이라는 것에 강력히 반대한다. 우리는 때로 더 나은 관계를 위해 선의의 거짓말을 해야 할 필요가 있다. 예를 들어 만약 친구가 새 옷이 잘 어울리냐고 묻는다면 그의 감정을 상하지 않게 하기 위해 때로는 선의의 거짓말을 해야 할 수도 있다.

5 Some people think most of what they learn happens outside of the classroom, while others think it happens in the classroom. Which do you agree with and why? Include specific details and examples to support your answer.

Your opinion? *learnng happens more outside of the classroom* 학습은 교실 밖에서 더 많이 이루어진다

Why? *learn the basics of right and wrong from people around them*
주변 사람들로부터 기본적인 옳고 그름에 대해 배우기 때문에

In detail? *parents teach children not to use bad words and how to speak more politely* 부모들은 자녀들에게 욕설을 하지 않고 더 공손하게 말하는 방법을 가르친다

I believe that most of what people learn happens outside of the classroom because we learn the basics of right and wrong more at home than inside of the classroom. Parents, in particular, teach their children not to use bad words and how to speak more politely to others.

나는 사람들이 학습하는 것의 대부분이 교실 밖에서 일어난다고 믿는데, 그 이유는 우리가 기본적인 옳고 그름에 대해 교실이 아닌 집에서 더 많이 배우기 때문이다. 특히 부모들은 그들의 자녀들에게 욕설을 하지 않고 다른 사람들에게 더 공손하게 말하는 방법을 가르친다.

6 Some people like to learn by listening to people around them such as friends and family, while others like to learn from their own experience. Which do you prefer and why? Include specific details and examples to support your answer.

Your preference? *learn from my own experiences*
스스로의 경험을 통해 배우기

Why? *some things can't be taught by someone*
다른 사람으로부터 배울 수 없는 것이 있기 때문에

In detail? *love* 사랑

I prefer to learn through my own experiences because there are some things that can't be taught by someone else. For example, I can learn what real love is when I actually love someone. What love is and how to love cannot be taught by someone else.

나는 다른 사람으로부터 배울 수 없는 것이 있기 때문에 스스로의 경험을 통해 배우는 것을 선호한다. 예를 들어, 내가 실제로 누군가를 사랑할 때 진정한 사랑이 무엇인지 배울 수 있다. 사랑이 무엇이고 어떻게 사랑하는지는 다른 사람이 가르쳐 줄 수 없는 것이다.

7 Some people like to watch movies during their free time, while others like to read books. Which do you prefer and why? Include specific details and examples to support your answer.

Your preference? *watching movies* 영화 보기
Why? *big fan of action movies* 액션 영화의 열렬한 팬이기 때문에
In detail? *computer graphics and sound effects*
컴퓨터 그래픽과 음향 효과

I prefer watching movies during my free time because I am a big fan of action movies. I love watching computer graphics and listening to great sound effects. To me, because of these reasons, movies are more exciting than books.

나는 액션 영화의 열렬한 팬이기 때문에 여가 시간에 영화를 보는 것을 선호한다. 나는 컴퓨터 그래픽을 보고 멋진 음향 효과를 듣는 것을 좋아한다. 나에게는 이러한 이유 때문에 책보다 영화가 더 흥미진진하다.

8 Some people prefer to study for their assignments in groups, while others like to study individually. Which do you prefer and why? Include specific details and examples to support your answer.

Your preference? *study in groups* 그룹에서 공부하기
Why? *easier to learn things* 더 쉽게 배울 수 있기 때문에
In detail? *explaining to each other helps to understand better* 서로에게 설명해주는 것이 더 잘 이해할 수 있도록 도와준다

Possible response

I prefer to study in groups because it is sometimes easier to learn things when I verbally discuss the material with other people. Explaining the material to others and also having other people explain the material to me help me understand the material better than studying alone.

나는 때로는 어떤 주제에 대해서 다른 사람들과 말로 토론할 때 더 쉽게 배울 수 있기 때문에 그룹에서 공부하는 것을 좋아한다. 자료에 대해 다른 사람에게 설명하거나 다른 사람이 나에게 설명해주는 것은 혼자 공부하는 것보다 더 잘 이해할 수 있도록 도와준다.

9 Some students like to live in a dormitory on campus, while other students like to live in their own apartment. Which do you prefer and why? Include specific details and examples to support your answer.

Your preference? *living in my own apartment* 내 아파트에서 사는 것
Why? *can have individual rooms* 개인 방을 쓸 수 있기 때문에
In detail? *living room, study room, bedroom* 거실, 공부방, 침실

Possible response

Although some people like to live in a dormitory, I prefer living in my own apartment because I have many individual rooms that I cannot have in the dormitory. For instance, I can have my own living room, bedroom, and study room.

어떤 사람들은 기숙사에서 사는 것을 좋아하지만, 나는 기숙사에서는 가질 수 없는 개인 방을 쓸 수 있기 때문에 내 아파트에서 사는 것을 좋아한다. 예를 들어, 나는 나만의 거실과 침실, 공부방을 가질 수 있다.

10 Some people are always in a hurry to go to places and get things done. Other people prefer to take their time and live life at a slower pace. Which do you prefer and why? Include specific details and examples to support your answer.

Your preference? *take my time* 시간 여유를 갖는 것
Why? *don't like to schedule out my life* 내 인생을 시간에 맞추어 계획하는 것을 좋아하지 않기 때문에
In detail? *have a flexible schedule so I can relax* 편안히 쉴 수 있도록 융통성 있는 스케줄을 갖는다

Possible response

I'm sometimes in a hurry, but I prefer to take my time and live life at a slower pace because I don't like to schedule out my life. I would rather have a flexible schedule so I can relax. Then, I can be more energetic when I go back to my normal life.

나는 때로는 서두르기도 하지만 내 인생을 시간에 맞추어 계획하는 것을 좋아하지 않기 때문에 시간 여유를 갖고 삶을 여유롭게 사는 것을 선호한다. 나는 편안히 쉴 수 있도록 융통성 있는 스케줄을 갖는 것을 선호한다. 그렇게 하면 일상 생활로 돌아갔을 때 더 힘이 나기 때문이다.

11 While traveling, some people like to get to their destinations quickly and others take their time to explore places here and there. Which do you prefer and why? Include specific details and examples to support your answer.

Your preference? *exploring here and there* 이곳 저곳 둘러보는 것
Why? *experience the area as much as possible* 그 지역을 가능한 많이 경험하기 위해서
In detail? *take pictures of beautiful places* 아름다운 곳의 사진을 찍는다

Possible response

While traveling, I like to explore here and there though it takes more time. I like to experience the area that I am exploring as much as possible. If I find a beautiful place that I feel like taking a picture of, I just stop there and go for it.

나는 여행할 때 시간이 조금 더 걸린다 할지라도 이곳 저곳 둘러보는 것을 좋아한다. 나는 내가 둘러보는 지역을 가능한 많이 경험하는 것을 좋아한다. 만일 사진을 찍고 싶은 아름다운 곳을 발견하면 나는 그냥 그곳에 머물고 사진을 찍는다.

12 Some people take a long time to make a decision and others make it immediately. Which do you prefer and why? Include specific details and examples to support your answer.

Your preference? *taking my time* 시간을 갖기

Why? *can consider all my possibilities and outcomes*
모든 가능성과 결과들을 고려할 수 있기 때문에

In detail? *might rush into problems* 문제가 생길 수도 있다

Possible response

I tend to take my time in making a decision. The reason is that I want to consider all my possibilities and outcomes beforehand. Otherwise, I might rush into problems and make careless choices.

나는 결정을 하는데 있어서 시간을 갖는 편이다. 그 이유는 결정하기 전에 모든 가능성과 결과들을 고려해 보고 싶기 때문이다. 그렇지 않으면, 문제가 생길 수도 있고 부주의한 결정을 하게 될지도 모른다.

13 Some people like to work for themselves or own a business. Others prefer to work for an employer. Would you rather be self-employed or work for someone else? Include specific details and examples to support your answer.

Your preference? *self-employed* 자영업

Why? *want to manage my company the way I would like* 나만의 방식대로 회사를 운영하고 싶기 때문에

In detail? *let employees work when they feel comfortable depend on their lifestyle* 직원들이 스스로의 생활 방식에 따라서 편하다고 느낄 때 일할 수 있도록 한다

Possible response

I'd rather be self-employed than be employed by someone else because I want to manage my company the way I would like. What I mean by 'my way' is that I would let employees work when they felt comfortable depending on their lifestyle.

나는 나만의 방식대로 회사를 운영하고 싶기 때문에 고용되는 것보다는 자영업을 하고 싶다. '나의 방식'이란 직원들이 스스로의 생활 방식에 따라서 편하다고 느낄 때 일할 수 있도록 하는 것을 의미한다.

14 Some people prefer to talk to their friends on the telephone. Other people write a letter or send an e-mail. Which means of communication do you like and why? Include specific details and examples to support your answer.

Your opinion? *talking on the phone* 전화로 연락하기

Why? *can feel the mood of my friends directly by voice*
친구들의 기분을 목소리로 직접 느낄 수 있기 때문에

In detail? *depressed → voice isn't energetic*
우울하면 목소리에 힘이 없다

Possible response

I prefer talking on the phone to keep in touch with my friends because I can sense the mood of my friends directly through their voices. If they are depressed, their voices aren't usually energetic, but if they are happy, their voices may be louder.

나는 친구들의 기분을 목소리로 직접 느낄 수 있기 때문에 전화로 친구들과 통화하며 연락하는 것을 선호한다. 친구들이 우울하면 그들의 목소리는 보통 힘이 없지만, 행복하다면 목소리가 더 클 수 있다.

15 Some students like to take large classes, while others like to attend small classes. Which do you prefer and why? Include specific details and examples to support your answer.

Your preference? *small classes* 학생수가 적은 수업

Why? *can study in a much better educational environment* 훨씬 나은 교육 환경에서 공부할 수 있기 때문에

In detail? *can get more attention from teachers*
선생님들로부터 더 많은 관심을 받을 수 있다

Possible response

I prefer attending small classes rather than taking large classes because I can study in a much better educational environment. For example, in a smaller class, I can get more attention from my teachers.

나는 훨씬 나은 교육 환경에서 공부할 수 있기 때문에 학생이 많은 수업을 듣는 것보다 학생수가 적은 수업을 듣는 것을 좋아한다. 예를 들어, 소규모 수업에서는 선생님들로부터 더 많은 관심을 받을 수 있다.

16 Some people believe that parents should limit their children's TV hours, while others believe that they should let them watch TV without limitations. Which view do you agree with and why? Include specific details and examples to support your answer.

Your opinion? *limit their children's TV hours*
자녀의 TV 시청 시간을 제한해야 한다

Why? *waste of time to watch useless programs*
쓸모없는 프로그램을 보는 것은 시간 낭비이기 때문에

In detail? *soap opera* 드라마

Possible response

I believe that parents should limit their children's TV hours because it is a waste of time to watch useless programs. Soap operas have a lot of themes that are harmful to children such as violence and other crimes.

나는 쓸모없는 프로그램을 보는 것은 시간 낭비이기 때문에 부모들이 자녀의 TV 시청 시간을 제한해야 한다고 생각한다. 낮 시간에 하는 드라마는 폭력이나 기타 범죄 등 어린이들에게 해로운 여러 가지 주제를 다루고 있다.

17 Do you agree or disagree with the following statement? Students should not be allowed to bring their cell phones to class. Include specific details and examples to support your answer.

> Your opinion? _should not bring their cell phones to class_ 수업 시간에 핸드폰을 가져와서는 안 된다
> Why? _disturb their studies_ 수업을 방해한다
> In detail? _text messages_ 문자

Possible response

I completely agree that students shouldn't bring their cell phones to class because they can disturb their studies. Even in class, when they get text messages, they feel like sending messages back. As they text message back and forth, they might miss important lecture points.

나는 핸드폰이 공부에 방해되기 때문에 수업 시간에 핸드폰을 가져와서는 안 된다는 의견에 전적으로 동의한다. 수업 중에도 문자를 받으면, 그들은 답 문자를 보내고 싶어한다. 그들이 문자를 주고 받을 때, 강의의 중요한 요점을 놓칠 수 있다.

18 Some people think business success is more important than friendship. What do you think is more important and why? Include specific details and examples to support your answer.

> Your opinion? _business success is more important_ 사업의 성공이 더 중요하다
> Why? _need to support my family financially_ 나의 가족을 경제적으로 부양해야 하기 때문에
> In detail? _buy food and pay for the education_ 식비와 교육비 제공

Possible response

I believe that business success is more important than friendship because I need to support my family financially. Although friendships are important and friends can help in times of need, my family and their needs are my responsibility. For example, I have to pay for my children's education, my family's housing, their clothing and their food.

나는 나의 가족을 경제적으로 부양해야 하기 때문에 우정보다는 사업의 성공이 더 중요하다고 믿는다. 비록 우정이 중요하고 필요한 경우 친구들이 도움을 줄 수 있지만, 가족과 그들의 필요는 내가 책임져야 한다. 예를 들어 나는 우리 아이들의 교육, 집, 의복, 음식에 대한 돈을 지불해야 한다.

19 Some people like to work on many things at the same time. Others like to do one thing at a time. Which do you prefer and why? Include specific details and examples to support your answer.

> Your preference? _do one thing at a time_ 일을 한번에 하나씩 하는 것
> Why? _multitasking can be hard to accomplish and dangerous_ 많은 일을 한번에 하는 것은 어렵고 위험할 수 있다
> In detail? _changing clothes while driving_ 운전하는 중에 옷을 갈아 입는 것

Possible response

I prefer to do one thing at a time. Multitasking can be hard to accomplish and sometimes dangerous. For example, a driver changing clothes while driving may involve not only himself but also others in an accident because such a task is not easy.

나는 일을 한번에 하나씩 하는 것을 좋아한다. 많은 일을 한번에 하는 것은 어렵고 때로는 위험할 수 있다. 예를 들어 운전자가 운전하는 중에 옷을 갈아 입는 것은 쉬운 일이 아니기 때문에 자신 뿐만 아니라 다른 사람도 사고에 처하게 할 수 있다.

20 Some students like to enroll as full-time students, while others prefer going to school part-time. Which do you prefer and why? Include specific details and examples to support your answer.

> Your preference? _full-time student_ 전임 학생
> Why? _can concentrate on my study better_ 공부에 더 집중할 수 있기 때문에
> In detail? _can spend more time studying_ 더 많은 시간을 공부에 투자할 수 있다

Possible response

I prefer to enroll as a full-time student because I can concentrate on my studies better. I can spend more time studying without being disturbed by other things. For example, I will not be distracted or prevented from studying by work or other outside responsibilities.

나는 공부에 더 집중할 수 있기 때문에 전임 학생이 되는 것을 선호한다. 나는 다른 것에 방해 받지 않고 공부하는 데 더 많은 시간을 투자할 수 있다. 예를 들어 일이나 다른 책임으로 인해 공부를 방해받거나 못하게 되지 않을 것이다.

21 Do you agree or disagree with the following statement? The best way to learn about a new city is visiting its landmarks or historical monuments. Include specific details and examples to support your answer.

Your opinion? *best way is visiting its landmarks or historical monuments* 역사적인 건물이나 기념물을 방문하는 것이 가장 좋은 방법이다

Why? *can gather interesting and in-depth information* 흥미롭고 자세한 정보를 얻을 수 있다

In detail? *Colosseum, Pantheon* 콜로세움, 판테온

Possible response

I agree that the best way to learn about a new city is visiting its landmarks or historical monuments because I can gather more interesting and in-depth information about the places I visit from these sites. For example, visiting Roman architectural sites, such as the Colosseum or the Pantheon, can provide us with a lot of information about the history of Rome.

나는 새로운 도시에 대해 배울 수 있는 가장 좋은 방법이 그곳의 역사적인 건물이나 기념물을 방문하는 것이라는 것에 동의한다. 그 이유는 이러한 곳에서부터 내가 방문하는 곳에 대한 흥미롭고 자세한 정보를 얻을 수 있기 때문이다. 예를 들어 콜로세움이나 판테온 같은 로마의 건축물을 방문하는 것은 로마 역사에 대한 정보를 많이 제공해 줄 수 있다.

22 Some people say that conserving old buildings is more important than constructing new buildings, while others believe constructing new buildings is more important. Which view do you agree with and why? Include specific details and examples to support your answer.

Your opinion? *preserving old building is more important* 옛 건물을 보존하는 것이 더 중요하다

Why? *will be able to gain valuable information from the old buildings* 오래된 건축물로부터 귀중한 정보를 얻을 수 있기 때문에

In detail? *Namdaemoon → history, importance in culture* 남대문의 역사와 문화에서의 중요성

Possible response

I believe that preserving old buildings is more important than constructing new buildings because the next generation will be able to gain valuable information from the old buildings that we leave behind. For example, if children visit Namdaemoon, they will discover a lot of information about its history and importance in our culture.

나는 다음 세대가 남기고 가는 오래된 건축물로부터 귀중한 정보를 얻을 수 있기 때문에 새로운 건물을 짓는 것보다 옛 건물을 보존하는 것이 더 중요하다고 믿는다. 예를 들어, 만약 어린이들이 남대문을 방문하면 그들은 그것의 역사와 문화의 중요성에 대한 많은 정보를 얻게 될 것이다.

23 Some people like to plan out their trips while others like to play it by ear. Which do you prefer and why? Include specific details and examples to support your answer.

Your preference? *make plans for my trips* 여행을 갈 때 계획 세우기

Why? *can budget more effectively* 예산을 더 효과적으로 짤 수 있기 때문에

In detail? *transportation, place to stay* 교통편, 묵을 곳

Possible response

I prefer to make plans for my trips because I can budget my money more wisely. Then I have more money to spend while on my trips if I want. For example, if I have a plan to go on a vacation to the West Sea, I try to figure out the form of transportation and the place to stay that will save me the most money.

나는 예산을 더 효과적으로 짤 수 있기 때문에 여행을 갈 때 계획을 세우는 것을 좋아한다. 그렇게 하면 원하는 경우 여행을 할 때 쓸 수 있는 돈이 더 많다. 예를 들어 만약 서해안으로 여행을 갈 계획이 있다면 나는 돈을 가장 절약하기 위해 이용할 수 있는 교통 수단과 묵을 곳을 알아보려고 노력한다.

24 Some people like to read a book until they finish it, while others like to start new books without finishing them. Which do you prefer and why? Include specific details and examples to support your answer.

Your preference? *read a book until I finish it* 책을 다 읽을 때까지 읽기

Why? *I can better understand the book I read* 내가 읽고 있는 책을 더 잘 이해할 수 있기 때문에

In detail? *information is overlapped* 정보가 겹친다

Possible response

I prefer reading a book until I finish it because I can better understand the book I am reading. For example, I once started reading a new book, *Yongaesomoon*, without finishing *General Lee*, which I'd already started to read. The information I had gained from *General Lee* overlapped with the information that I was learning from *Yongaesomoon* and I became confused.

나는 내가 읽고 있는 책을 더 잘 이해할 수 있기 때문에 다 읽을 때까지 그것을 읽는 것을 선호한다. 예를 들어 나는 이미 읽기 시작한 연개소문이라는 책을 끝내지 않고 *이순신* 장군이라는 책을 읽기 시작했다. *이순신* 장군에서 얻은 정보가 연개소문으로부터 알게 된 정보와 겹쳤고, 혼란스러워졌다.

25 Some individuals believe that people need to learn how to play a musical instrument from childhood. Do you agree or disagree with this idea? Include specific details and examples to support your answer.

Your opinion? *learn from childhood* 어릴 때부터 배워야 한다
Why? *children learn more easily* 어린이들이 더 쉽게 배우기 때문에
In detail? *my brother learned the piano when he was a child* 내 동생은 어렸을 때 피아노를 배웠다

Possible response

I believe that people need to learn how to play a musical instrument from childhood because children learn more easily than adults. For example, I didn't learn how to play the piano when I was young. I'm trying to learn to play the piano these days, but it is really hard. On the other hand, my brother learned it when he was a child. He learned it very quickly and easily.

나는 어린이들이 어른들보다 더 쉽게 배우기 때문에 어린 시절부터 악기를 연주하는 법을 배워야 한다고 생각한다. 예를 들어 나는 어렸을 때 피아노 치는 법을 배우지 않았다. 이제 피아노 치는 법을 배우려고 하고 있지만 정말 어렵다. 반면에 내 동생은 어렸을 때 피아노 치는 것을 배웠다. 그는 매우 빠르고 쉽게 그것을 배웠다.

26 Some people trust their first impressions about a person's character because they believe these judgments are generally correct, while others do not judge a person's character quickly because they believe first impressions are often wrong. Which do you agree with and why? Include specific details and examples to support your answer.

Your opinion? *shouldn't judge a person's character at first sight* 첫인상으로 사람의 성격을 판단해서는 안 된다
Why? *first impressions are often wrong* 첫인상은 종종 틀리기 때문에
In detail? *the first time I met my good friend, he did not seem kind* 내가 친한 친구를 처음 만났을 때 그는 친절해 보이지 않았다

Possible response

I don't think that we should judge a person's character at first sight because there is a lot of evidence that first impressions are often wrong. For example, the first time I met my good friend, he did not seem kind. However, the more I got to know him I realized that he was a very gentle and sincere person. My first impression was incorrect. So, we became very good friends.

나는 첫인상이 틀리다는 근거가 많기 때문에 첫인상으로 사람의 성격을 판단해서는 안 된다고 생각한다. 예를 들어 내가 친한 친구를 처음 만났을 때 그는 친절해 보이지 않았다. 하지만 점점 더 그를 알게 되면서 그가 매우 친절하고 진실된 사람이라는 것을 깨달았다. 내 첫인상이 틀렸던 것이다. 그래서 우리는 매우 좋은 친구가 되었다.

27 Some people say that childhood is the best time of one's life. Do you agree or disagree with this idea? Include specific details and examples to support your answer.

Your opinion? *childhood was the best time* 어린 시절이 가장 좋았다
Why? *learned about ethics* 윤리에 대해 배웠기 때문에
In detail? *it is nice to greet our neighbors* 이웃들에게 인사하는 것은 좋은 것이다

Possible response

I strongly believe that childhood was the best time in my life because I learned about ethics. It enabled me to understand what's right and wrong. For example, I learned important ethics such as it is nice to greet our neighbors whenever I meet them on the street, and it is wrong to steal other people's belongings.

나는 윤리에 대해 배웠기 때문에 어린 시절이 내 삶의 가장 좋은 시기였다고 생각한다. 윤리는 나로 하여금 무엇이 옳고 그른지 이해할 수 있도록 해주었다. 예를 들어 나는 이웃을 거리에서 만날 때 인사를 하는 것은 매우 좋은 일이고, 다른 사람의 물건을 훔치는 것을 잘못된 일이라는 등의 중요한 윤리를 배웠다.

28 Some people think trying new food is better than trying familiar foods all the time. Do you agree or disagree with this idea? Include specific details and examples to support your answer.

Your opinion? *trying new food* 새로운 음식을 시도하기
Why? *have the opportunity to try foods from different culture* 다른 문화의 음식을 맛볼 수 있는 기회를 주기 때문에
In detail? *curry* 카레

Possible response

I agree that it is better to try new dishes because it allows me to have the opportunity to try foods from a different culture. For example, I have tried eating an Indian ethnic dish, curry. I'd never had curry before, and it had a very different flavor from the foods that I was used to. It was very spicy, and trying a new food was an exciting experience for me.

나는 다른 문화의 음식을 맛볼 수 있는 기회를 주기 때문에 새로운 음식을 시도해 보는 것이 더 좋다는 것에 동의한다. 예를 들어 나는 인도의 전통 음식인 카레를 먹어 보았다. 전에 한번도 카레를 먹어본 적이 없었는데 익숙한 음식들과는 매우 다른 향이 났다. 그것은 많이 매웠고, 나에게는 새로운 음식을 먹어보는 것이 아주 신나는 경험이었다.

29 Do you agree or disagree with the following statement? Some people think high school students should wear school uniforms. Include specific details and examples to support your answer.

Your opinion? _should wear school uniforms_
교복을 입어야 한다

Why? _can build a sense of community_
공동체 의식을 기를 수 있기 때문에

In detail? _help someone wearing their school uniform_
자기 학교의 교복을 입는 사람을 돕는다

Possible response

I believe that high school students should wear school uniforms because they can build a sense of community. For example, if you see someone who is wearing your school uniform having some difficulties in public, you'll feel like helping them because you will probably think they are part of your community. Likewise, students wearing the same school uniform will feel a sense of community and pride.

나는 공동체 의식을 기를 수 있기 때문에 고등 학생들이 교복을 입어야 한다고 생각한다. 예를 들어 만약 같은 교복을 입고 있는 사람이 공개적으로 어려움을 겪고 있다면 그들이 아마도 자신의 공동체에 속해있다고 생각할 것이기 때문에 그들을 도우려고 할 것이다. 이와 마찬가지로 같은 교복을 입는 학생들은 공동체 의식과 자부심을 느낄 것이다.

30 Some people like to read newspapers or magazines to get information, while others watch TV or other media to get it. Which do you prefer and why? Include specific details and examples to support your answer.

Your preference? _reading newspaper_ 신문 읽기
Why? _can acquire various kinds of information from different points of view_
다른 관점의 다양한 정보를 얻을 수 있기 때문에

In detail? _presidential election_ 대통령 선거

Possible response

I prefer reading newspapers rather than watching TV or interacting with other media to get information because I can acquire various kinds of information from different points of view. Specifically, I can receive

information about the presidential election from a professional point of view because many experts express their opinions about it in different newspaper articles.

나는 정보를 얻기 위해 텔레비전이나 다른 매체를 보는 것보다 신문을 읽는 것을 선호한다. 다른 관점의 다양한 정보를 얻을 수 있기 때문이다. 구체적으로 말하자면 많은 전문가들이 대선에 대한 그들의 의견을 많은 신문 기사를 통해 밝히기 때문에 대선에 대한 전문적인 견해를 얻을 수 있다.

Exercise **CD** Possible Responses: Track 24~31

1 Some students like to study early in the morning, while others like to study late at night. Which method of studying do you think is better for students and why? Include specific details and examples to support your answer.

Thesis: _I think that students should study in the morning, rather than at night._
나는 학생들이 밤보다는 아침에 공부해야 한다고 생각한다

Reason 1: _students are well rested_ 학생들이 충분한 휴식을 취한다
Detail: _their minds get tired at night_
저녁에는 머리가 지치게 된다

Reason 2: _finish their work earlier → enjoy their nights_
일을 일찍 끝내고 저녁 시간을 즐길 수 있다
Detail: _hang out with their friends, stay home and read a book_
친구들과 밖에서 놀 수도 있고 집에서 책을 읽을 수도 있다

Conclusion: _For these reasons I think it's better for students to study in the morning._
이러한 이유로 나는 학생들이 아침에 공부하는 것이 더 좋다고 생각한다

Possible response

Some students like to study at night, but I think that students should study in the morning, rather than at night for a couple of reasons. First of all, students are well rested in the morning because it's the start of a new day. Their minds get tired at night because their brains have been active all day. Therefore, studying in the morning is more efficient. Secondly, if students study in the morning, they can finish their work earlier so they can enjoy their nights. For example, they can hang out with their friends or just stay home and read a book. For these reasons I think it's better for students to study in the morning.

어떤 학생들은 밤에 공부하는 것을 좋아하지만, 나는 몇 가지 이유 때문에 학생들이 밤보다는 아침에 공부해야 한다고 생각한다. 무엇보다도, 아침은

하루의 시작이기 때문에 학생들은 충분한 휴식을 취한 상태이다. 뇌가 하루 종일 활동했기 때문에 저녁에는 머리가 지치게 된다. 따라서 아침에 공부하는 것이 더 효율적이다. 두 번째로 학생들이 아침에 공부하면 일을 일찍 끝내고 저녁 시간을 즐길 수 있다. 예를 들어 친구들과 밖에서 놀 수도 있고 집에서 책을 읽을 수도 있다. 이러한 이유로 나는 학생들이 아침에 공부하는 것이 더 좋다고 생각한다.

2 Some students prefer gaining knowledge from their experiences, while others like to get knowledge from books. Which do you prefer and why? Include specific details and examples to support your answer.

Thesis: _I prefer to learn from books rather than through experience._
나는 경험보다는 책을 통해 배우는 것을 더 좋아한다
Reason 1: _unlimited amount of information_ 무한한 양의 정보
    Detail: _short amount of time_ 짧은 시간
Reason 2: _some information is not possible to get through experience_
    어떤 정보는 경험으로는 얻을 수 없다
    Detail: _other plants_ 다른 위성들
Conclusion: _These are the reasons why I prefer to learn through books._
    이것이 내가 책을 통해 배우는 것을 선호하는 이유이다

Possible response
Some people like to learn from their experiences, but I prefer to learn from books for a couple of reasons. First of all, I can easily get unlimited amount of information on any topic from books in a short amount of time. For example, you can read a book to understand how much energy you need to walk for 100km. Secondly, some information is not possible to get through experience. To be specific, we can get information about other planets by only books because it is impossible to go there individually. These are the reasons why I prefer to learn through books.

어떤 사람들은 경험을 통해 배우는 것을 좋아하지만, 나는 몇 가지 이유 때문에 경험보다는 책을 통해 배우는 것을 더 좋아한다. 무엇보다도, 짧은 시간에 책으로부터 어떤 주제에 대해서도 무한한 양의 정보를 손쉽게 얻을 수 있다. 예를 들어, 100킬로미터를 걷기 위해 필요한 에너지량을 책으로부터 쉽게 알 수 있다. 두 번째로, 어떤 정보는 경험으로는 얻을 수 없다. 구체적으로 말하면, 개인적으로 다른 위성에 가는 것은 불가능하기 때문에 단지 책을 통해서만 그것들에 관한 정보를 얻을 수 있다. 이것이 내가 책을 통해 배우는 것을 선호하는 이유이다.

3 When we decide an important policy, some people say the opinion of a group of people is better, while others insist that an expert's opinion is better.

Which do you agree with and why? Include specific details and examples to support your answer.

Thesis: _When deciding an important policy, an expert's opinion should be consulted._
    중요한 정책을 결정할 때는 전문가의 의견을 들어야 한다
Reason 1: _professional points of view_ 전문적 관점
    Detail: _professional approach would be beneficial_
    전문적으로 접근하는 것이 유익하다
Reason 2: _valuable time might be wasted in a majority vote_ 대다수 투표에 소중한 시간이 낭비될 수 있다
    Detail: _face the emergency with an uninformed group's opinion_
    잘 모르는 사람들의 의견을 듣고 긴급 상황 처리
Conclusion: _I strongly believe that an expert should be consulted before an important policy is discussed._ 중요한 정책을 토론하기 전에 전문가에게 자문을 구하는 것이 더 좋다고 생각한다

Possible response
A decision is often reached by majority rule, but when deciding an important policy, an expert's opinion should be consulted for a couple of reasons. First of all, we can get professional points of view from experts. For example, when a board of educators meets to decide a policy to change a curriculum, a professional approach would be beneficial rather than asking moms to vote on what would be best for their children. Secondly, valuable time might be wasted in a majority vote, or even to get a perfect majority gathered together. If the North Korean navy breaks into our territory, how can we face the emergency with an uninformed group's opinion? These are the reasons why I strongly believe that an expert should be consulted before an important policy is discussed.

다수결의 원칙이 보편적이기는 하지만, 중요한 정책을 결정할 때는 몇 가지 이유로 전문가의 의견을 들어야 한다. 무엇보다도, 우리는 전문가들로부터 전문적인 의견을 얻을 수 있다. 예를 들어, 커리큘럼을 바꾸기 위한 정책을 결정하기 위해 이사회가 모임을 가질 때 엄마들에게 어떤 것이 아이들을 위해 가장 좋은지 투표를 요청하는 것보다는 전문적으로 접근하는 것이 훨씬 유익할 것이다. 두 번째로, 대다수 또는 모든 사람의 투표를 요구함으로써 소중한 시간이 낭비될 수 있다. 만약 북한의 해군이 우리의 영역을 침범한다면, 정보에 대해 잘 모르는 사람들의 의견을 듣고 어떻게 이 긴급 상황을 처리할 수 있겠는가? 바로 이러한 이유로 나는 중요한 정책을 토론하기 전에 전문가에게 자문을 구하는 것이 더 좋다고 생각한다.

4 Some people say that students should study the subject they are interested in. Others say that they should concentrate on subjects they need for their jobs or careers. Which do you agree with and why?

Include specific details and examples to support your answer.

Possible response

Some students like to study the subject they are interested in, but I believe students should concentrate on subjects needed for their careers for a couple of reasons. First of all, we can prepare for our future jobs better. These days, employees are required to have a lot of abilities to take care of their duties. For example, if we want to work as an accountant, we need to study accounting rather than other subjects. Secondly, we can learn about the subject we are interested in by ourselves. For instance, if we are interested in history, we can learn about it by visiting historical sites or watching historical dramas. These are the reasons why I think that students should study the subjects that are needed for their jobs.

어떤 학생들은 그들이 관심 있는 과목을 공부하는 것을 좋아하지만, 나는 몇 가지 이유 때문에 학생들이 직업을 준비하는데 필요한 과목에 집중해야 한다고 생각한다. 우선, 미래의 직업을 더 잘 준비할 수 있다. 오늘날 직원들에게는 업무를 수행하기 위한 여러 능력들이 요구된다. 예를 들어, 회계사로 일하고 싶다면 다른 과목보다는 회계학을 공부해야 할 것이다. 두 번째로, 우리가 관심 있는 분야는 스스로 배울 수 있다. 예를 들어 역사에 관심이 있다면 역사 유적지를 방문하거나 역사극을 보면서 역사를 배울 수 있다. 이러한 이유로 나는 학생들이 직업을 준비하기 위한 과목을 공부해야 한다고 생각한다.

5 Some people like to surf the Internet to get information, while others like to get information from books in the library. Which do you prefer and why? Include specific details and examples to support your answer.

Possible response

I've gotten information from various sources, but I prefer surfing the Internet to get information for a couple of reasons. First of all, it is a lot more convenient. I can look up information immediately from anywhere that has an Internet connection. Secondly, I can get correct information very easily. For example, when I need information about American presidents, then I just type president, and the computer surfs the information by itself and lets me know about American presidents easily. Like this way, the Internet opens the door to all types of information. These are the reasons why I prefer surfing the Internet for information.

나는 다양한 경로로 정보를 수집하지만, 몇 가지 이유로 인터넷을 통해서 정보를 얻는 것을 선호한다. 무엇보다도, 인터넷을 통한 정보 수집은 훨씬 편리하다. 인터넷이 연결된 곳이면 어디에서든지 즉시 정보를 찾을 수 있다. 두 번째로, 올바른 정보를 쉽게 얻을 수 있다. 예를 들어, 미국 대통령들에 대한 정보가 필요한 경우에는 대통령의 이름을 간단히 입력하면 컴퓨터가 알아서 정보를 찾아 미국 대통령들에 대해 쉽게 알려준다. 이처럼 인터넷은 모든 종류의 정보에 접근할 수 있도록 해준다. 이것이 내가 인터넷으로 정보를 찾는 것을 좋아하는 이유이다.

6 Some people like to eat at home and others prefer eating out. Which do you prefer and why? Include specific details and examples to support your answer.

I usually eat at home, but I prefer to eat out at a restaurant rather than eating at home for a couple of reasons. First of all, it is convenient to dine at a restaurant. You don't have to clean up after you eat, and you can also get food delivered. Secondly, I can save time by eating out. I live alone so preparing food for me is a waste of time. With my busy schedule, I don't have time to prepare a meal and wash the dishes. These are the reasons why I prefer eating out rather than eating at home.

나는 보통 집에서 식사를 하지만 몇 가지 이유로 집에서 식사를 하는 것보다 외식하는 것을 더 좋아한다. 우선, 외식을 하는 것은 편리하다. 먹은 후에 치우지 않아도 되며 음식을 배달시킬 수도 있다. 두 번째로, 외식을 함으로써 시간을 절약할 수 있다. 나는 혼자 살기 때문에 음식을 준비하는 것은 시간 낭비이다. 바쁜 스케줄 때문에 나는 음식을 준비하고 설거지를 할 시간이 없다. 이것이 내가 집에서 먹는 것보다 외식을 선호하는 이유이다.

7 Some universities require students to attend classes decided upon by the school, while other students think that going to required classes should be optional for students. Which view do you agree with and why? Include specific details and examples to support your answer.

Thesis: *Students should be given the liberty to choose their own classes at universities.*
대학에서 학생들이 수업을 스스로 선택할 수 있도록 자유를 주어야 한다

Reason 1: *can concentrate more* 더 집중할 수 있다
Detail: *psychology* 심리학
Reason 2: *what classes are better for them and for their future* 어떤 수업이 그들의 미래를 위해 더 좋은지
Detail: *want to become a biologist-> biology subjects* 생물학자가 되고 싶다면 생물학 수업
Conclusion: *I think school should permit their students to choose their own classes.*
나는 학교가 학생들이 스스로 수업을 선택하도록 허락해야 한다

I agree that students should be given the liberty to choose their own classes at universities for a couple of reasons. First of all, students can concentrate more on the classes they choose. If they select a psychology class, it means they are interested in the course, and they will be more eager to study. Another reason is that the students might know what classes are better for them and for their future. For example, if they want to become a biologist, they will take classes related to biology subjects. It will not be necessary for them to study other subjects for their future plan. These are

the reasons why I think schools should permit their students to choose their own classes.

나는 몇 가지 이유 때문에 대학에서 학생들이 수업을 스스로 선택할 수 있도록 자유를 주어야 한다는 생각에 동의한다. 무엇보다도, 학생들은 그들이 선택한 수업에 더 집중할 수 있다. 만약 그들이 심리학 수업을 선택한다면, 이것은 그 과목에 관심이 있다는 것을 뜻하며, 따라서 더욱 열심히 공부할 것이다. 또 다른 이유는 학생들은 어떤 수업이 그들의 미래를 위해 더 좋은지 알 것이라는 것이다. 예를 들어, 생물학자가 되고 싶다면 생물학과 관련된 수업을 수강할 것이다. 그들은 미래의 계획을 위해 다른 과목을 공부할 필요가 없다. 이것이 내가 학교가 학생들이 스스로 수업을 선택하도록 허락해야 한다고 생각하는 이유이다.

8 Some students think grades encourage students to learn, while others think they place heavy burdens on them. Which view do you agree with and why? Include specific details and examples to support your answer.

Thesis: *Grades that students receive are the motivation for them to learn.*
학점은 학생들에게 학습에 대한 동기를 부여한다

Reason 1: *there will not be any form of evaluation to attach their accomplishments*
그들의 성과에 대한 평가가 없을 것이다
Detail: *encourage them to do better next time*
다음에 더 잘 하도록 격려할 것이다
Reason 2: *give the opportunity to figure out which subjects they are good at*
어떤 과목에 재능이 있는지 알 수 있는 기회를 준다
Detail: *develop talents in that particular subjects*
이러한 특정 과목에 대한 재능을 개발한다
Conclusion: *Grades motivate students to study harder.*
학점은 학생들에게 더 열심히 공부를 하려는 동기를 부여한다

I think grades sometimes place heavy burdens on students, but I feel that the grades that students receive are the motivation for them to learn for a couple of reasons. First of all, without grades, there will not be any form of evaluation to attach to their accomplishments. The marks students receive in classes will encourage them to do better next time. Another reason is that grades give the opportunity for students to figure out which subjects they are good at. Students can try to develop their talents in those particular subjects. These are the reasons why I think grades motivate students to study harder.

나는 때로 학점이 학생들에게 부담이 된다고 생각하지만, 몇 가지 이유로 학점이 학생들에게 학습에 대한 동기를 부여한다고 생각한다. 우선, 학점이 없다면 그들의 성과에 대한 평가가 없을 것이다. 수업에서 받는 학점은 다음

에 더 잘 하도록 격려할 것이다. 또 다른 이유는 학점이 학생들로 하여금 그들이 어떤 과목에 재능이 있는지 알 수 있는 기회를 준다는 것이다. 학생들은 이러한 특정 과목에 대한 재능을 개발하기 위해 노력할 수 있다. 이러한 이유로 나는 학점이 학생들에게 더 열심히 공부를 하려는 동기를 부여한다고 생각한다.

TASK 3 Fit and Explain

CD Possible Response: Track 32

☐ **Sample**

Reading

City University is planning to increase tuition and fees. Read the announcement about the increase from the president of City University. You will have 45 seconds to read the announcement. Begin reading now.

Announcement from the President

The university governing board has authorized an 8 percent increase in tuition and fees for all students next semester. For the past 5 years, the tuition and fees haven't changed. However, it is unavoidable that we increase the tuition and fees in order to better serve the student body. The university has a lot more students than it did five years ago, and we must hire more professors to meet the demands of the larger student body. We will also make a new commitment to research and technology, and will be modernizing our laboratory facilities to better meet our students' needs.

대학 이사회는 다음 학기 수업료를 8퍼센트 인상하는 것을 승인했습니다. 지난 5년간 수업료가 변경되지 않았으나, 학생들에게 보다 나은 서비스를 제공하기 위해 수업료 인상이 불가피합니다. 5년 전에 비해 학생수가 크게 증가했으므로, 많은 학생들의 요구를 충족하기 위해 더 많은 교수를 채용해야 합니다. 또한 새로운 연구와 기술에 보다 전념할 것이며 학생들의 필요를 충족시키기 위해 실험실을 현대화 할 예정입니다.

Listening

Now listen to two students as they discuss the announcement.

M Oh, great! Now we have to pay more for our tuition next semester.

W Yeah, I know, but I can understand why. When I was a freshman, classes were a lot smaller than they are now. There are so many new students now and it's hard to get any personal attention from the professors.

M Yeah, I guess you're right. You know, in some classes, it's even difficult to find a seat. And I couldn't take the biology course I wanted because it was already full when I tried to sign up.

W Another thing that I'm really worried about is whether I'll be able to find a job after I graduate.

M Why? You're one of the top students in your class, aren't you?

W I'm doing pretty well, but the facilities here are so old-fashioned. There are so many important experiments in biology that are being developed, but we don't have the facilities to try them here. Also, there isn't enough equipment in the laboratories. How can we compete for jobs with people who study in modern facilities? I think the extra tuition will be a great help.

남 이런, 이제 다음 학기에 학비를 더 많이 내야 해.

여 알아, 하지만 왜 그래야 하는지 이해해. 내가 신입생이었을 때는 수업별 학생수가 지금처럼 많지 않았어. 이제는 신입생들이 너무 많아서 교수님들에게 개인적으로 지도 받기가 어려워.

남 그래, 네 말이 맞기도 해. 어떤 수업은 자리를 찾기도 힘들어. 난 등록하려고 했던 생물학 수업이 이미 마감되어서 수강할 수가 없었어.

여 난 졸업 후에 직장을 구할 수 있을지도 정말 걱정돼.

남 왜? 너는 학급에서 우수생 중 한 명이지 않아?

여 꽤 잘하고 있기는 하지만 이곳 시설들은 너무 낡았어. 생물학 분야에 새롭게 개발되고 있는 중요한 실험들이 많은데, 여기에는 그 실험들을 해볼 시설이 없잖아. 그리고 실험실에 장비도 부족해. 현대적인 시설에서 공부하는 학생들과 경쟁해서 우리가 어떻게 직업을 얻을 수 있겠어? 난 추가 학비가 큰 도움이 될 거라고 생각해.

Speaking

The woman expresses her opinion about the announcement made by the university president. State her opinion and explain the reasons she gives for holding that opinion.

Possible response

The woman is concerned that the increase in tuition might be a burden on students, but she believes that the increase in tuition and fees will bring a lot of benefits to students. For example, students will be able to get more personal care from the professors. She also points out that the school needs to improve school facilities because most of the facilities in the school are out-of-date, especially the biology laboratory. More modern facilities will enable students to compete for better jobs. In the end, the woman feels that increasing tuition and fees is a good idea for the students on campus.

여자는 수업료 인상이 학생들에게 부담이 될지도 모른다는 것에 대해 걱정하지만, 학비 인상이 학생들에게 많은 이익을 제공할 것이라고 생각한다. 예를 들어, 학생들은 교수들로부터 개인적 지도를 더 많이 받을 수 있을 것이다. 그녀는 또한 교내에 있는 대부분의 시설들, 특히 생물 실험실의 시설들이 낡았기 때문에 개선해야 한다고 지적한다. 보다 현대적인 시설들은 학생들로

하여금 더 나은 직업을 위해 경쟁할 수 있도록 해 줄 것이다. 결국 여자는 학비를 인상하는 것이 교내 학생들을 위한 좋은 방안이라고 생각한다.

Mini Test

CD Possible Responses: Track 34

1

Reading

The university is planning to eliminate the evening classes. Read the announcement about the class elimination. You will have 45 seconds to read the announcement. Begin reading now.

Elimination of Evening Classes

The university has decided to eliminate evening classes. These days, the numbers of students who enroll in the classes are decreasing. Therefore, it would be a huge burden for the school to maintain evening classes. In order to better serve students, extra morning classes will be provided.

대학은 저녁 수업을 없애기로 결정했습니다. 요즘 등록생수가 점점 감소하고 있습니다. 따라서 저녁 수업을 유지하는 것은 학교에 매우 큰 부담이 될 것입니다. 학생들의 요구를 보다 잘 충족시켜 주기 위해 오전에 추가 수업이 개설될 것입니다.

Listening

Now listen to two students as they discuss the announcement.

M   I can't believe that our school has decided to cancel all the evening classes.

W   Same here.

M   The school insists that the number of students is getting smaller, but if there are fewer students in the classes, students can get more attention from professors and build up a closer relationship.

W   Yeah, I completely agree with you there.

남   학교가 저녁 수업을 전부 없애기로 했다는 게 믿기지가 않아.

여   나도 그래.

남   학교는 학생수가 점점 줄어든다고 하지만, 수업별 학생수가 적으면 학생들은 교수들로부터 더 많은 관심을 받고 더 친밀한 관계를 맺을 수 있을 거야.

여   맞아. 너랑 전적으로 동감이야.

Subject: *cancel all the evening classes* 저녁 수업을 전부 없애기

Opinion: *disagree* 반대

By whom: *man* 남자

Detail: *smaller classes → more attention*
          소규모 수업 → 더 많은 관심

Speaking

The man expresses his opinion of the university's plan to eliminate the evening classes. State his opinion and explain the reasons he gives for holding that opinion.

Possible response

The man disagrees with eliminating evening classes. The major reason is that if the school keeps evening classes, students can receive more attention from their teachers and can establish a better relationship with them.

남자는 저녁 수업을 없애는 것에 반대한다. 가장 큰 이유는 만약 학교가 저녁 수업을 계속한다면 학생들은 교수들로부터 더 많은 관심을 받을 수 있고 그들과 더 나은 관계를 형성할 수 있기 때문이다.

2

Reading

Read the announcement about the library expansion. You will have 45 seconds to read the announcement. Begin reading now.

Library Expansion

The university has decided to increase the size of the library. The school has been around for a long time, and therefore, has a lot of books to stack. Because there is not enough space in the library, school authorities have decided to build an additional wing to make more space for the books. With the construction of the additional wing, students will also benefit from more study space.

대학은 도서관의 규모를 확장하기로 결정했습니다. 학교가 오래되었기 때문에 보관할 책이 많습니다. 도서관에 공간이 부족하기 때문에 학교 당국은 책을 보관할 공간을 확보하기 위해 부속 건물을 추가하기로 했습니다. 부속 건물이 건축되면 학생들 또한 공부할 공간이 더 많아지는 혜택을 누리게 될 것입니다.

Listening

Now listen to two students as they discuss the announcement.

M   I don't think it's practical to enlarge the size of the library.

W   Why not? In addition to creating more space for the books, it would also create more study space.

M   I know, but it is much better to invest money on technological features such as microfilm or adding more computers.

W   Well, I guess you can look at it that way.

남   난 도서관의 규모를 늘리는 것은 실용적이지 않다고 생각해.

여   왜? 책을 놓을 공간이 더 많아지고 공부할 수 있는 공간도 늘어나잖아.

남 알아, 하지만 마이크로필름이나 컴퓨터를 더 설치하는 것 같은 기술적 부분에 돈을 투자하는 것이 훨씬 더 나아.

여 음, 그렇게 생각할 수도 있겠구나.

Subject: *enlarge the library* 도서관 확장

Opinion: *disagree* 반대

By whom: *man* 남자

Detail: *it is much better to invest on technological features* 기술적 부분에 투자하는 것이 훨씬 더 낫다

Speaking

The man expresses his opinion of the library expansion. State his opinion and explain the reasons he gives for holding that opinion.

Possible response

The man disagrees with the idea of expanding the library. The reason he is against it is that he believes it is better to invest money on modern facilities such as computers or microfilm. He feels that the school doesn't need to enlarge the size of the library due to these reasons.

남자는 도서관을 확장하는 방안에 동의하지 않는다. 그가 반대하는 이유는 컴퓨터 또는 마이크로필름 같은 현대식 시설에 돈을 투자하는 것이 더 좋다고 생각하기 때문이다. 그는 이러한 이유로 학교가 도서관의 크기를 확장할 필요가 없다고 느낀다.

3

Reading

A student has written an article in the school newspaper about changing the computer lab policy. Read the article about the change in the computer lab policy. You will have 45 seconds to read the article. Begin reading now.

Changing the Computer Lab Policy

I think it is a good idea to change the computer lab policy. These days, the school lab is so crowded that we have to wait for a long time to use it. It is quite time-consuming. The school should have students make reservations to use the lab. Also, students waiting outside the lab make a lot of noise and create disturbances in the halls. In my opinion, the school should consider all these situations.

저는 컴퓨터실 정책을 바꾸는 것이 좋은 생각이라고 생각합니다. 요즘에는 학교 컴퓨터실이 너무 붐벼서 사용하려면 오랫동안 기다려야 하고, 이것은 큰 시간 낭비입니다. 학교는 학생들이 컴퓨터실을 사용하려면 예약을 하도록 해야 합니다. 또한, 컴퓨터실 밖에서 기다리는 학생들이 매우 시끄럽고 복도에서 소란을 피웁니다. 저는 학교에서 이러한 모든 상황들을 고려해야 한다고 생각합니다.

Listening

Now listen to two students as they discuss the article.

W I don't think asking the students to make reservations at the lab is going to work.

M Yeah, I agree. I think there will be a lot of scheduling problems.

W If the students can't finish their work within the scheduled time, they will have to come back again to finish it. It'll be very inconvenient and students will complain about it all the time.

M Definitely.

여 나는 학생들에게 컴퓨터실을 예약하도록 한다는 게 효과적일 것 같지 않아.

남 그래. 나도 동의해. 내 생각엔 스케줄을 잡는데 문제가 많을 것 같아.

여 학생들이 정해진 시간 내에 일을 다 끝내지 못하면 다시 와서 끝내야 할 거야. 그건 정말 불편할 거고 학생들은 늘 이것에 대해 불평을 할 거야.

남 그렇고 말고.

Subject: *make reservations at the lab* 컴퓨터실에서 예약을 하도록 한다

Opinion: *disagree* 반대

By whom: *woman* 여자

Detail: *students will have to come back if they do not finish their work* 학생들은 일을 못 끝내면 다시 와야 할 것이다

Speaking

The woman expresses her opinion of the article. State her opinion and explain the reasons she gives for holding that opinion.

Possible response

The woman disagrees with the idea of making reservations to use the computer lab. The reason she is against it is that students who can't finish their work within the scheduled time will have to make another reservation. The woman feels that it is very inconvenient and will waste students' time.

여자는 컴퓨터실을 사용하기 위해 예약을 하도록 한다는 생각에 반대한다. 그녀가 반대하는 이유는 정해진 시간 내에 일을 다 끝내지 못한 학생들은 다시 예약을 해야 할 것이기 때문이다. 여자는 이것이 매우 불편하고 학생들의 시간을 낭비하게 할 것이라고 느낀다.

4

Reading

The university has announced a change in the university parking policy. Read the announcement about the change in the parking policy. You will have 45 seconds to read the announcement. Begin reading now.

University Parking Policy

The university has decided to limit the central parking lot for non-resident students only. Non-resident students have trouble finding parking spaces in the lot, and are often late for their classes. The main reason for this is that many resident students park their cars in the central parking lot. Considering regular complaints from non-resident students on this matter, the school authorities have decided to limit the central parking lot to non-resident students only. Resident students must park their cars off campus.

대학은 중앙 주차장을 비거주자 학생들만 사용하도록 제한하기로 결정했습니다. 비거주자 학생들은 주차장에서 주차 공간을 찾는데 어려움을 겪고 있으며 종종 수업에 지각을 하고 있습니다. 이것의 가장 큰 이유는 많은 거주 학생들이 중앙 주차장에 차를 주차하기 때문입니다. 이 문제에 대한 비거주자 학생들의 주기적인 불평을 고려하여 대학 당국은 중앙 주차장을 비거주자 학생들만 사용하도록 제한하기로 결정했습니다. 거주 학생들은 캠퍼스 밖에 주차해야 합니다.

Listening

Now listen to two students as they discuss the announcement.

M I don't think the new policy is necessary.

W No argument there.

M Non-resident students should arrive early enough to school to find a space. Actually, there is enough space in the central parking lot, but the problem is, most of the students want to park in the closest spaces to their classrooms. If students come to school earlier, there shouldn't be any problem.

W Absolutely. Most resident students don't use their cars on campus. They only use their cars to get off campus.

남 난 새로운 정책이 불필요하다고 생각해.

여 나도 동의해.

남 비거주자 학생들은 주차 공간을 찾기 위해 학교에 일찍 와야 해. 사실 중앙 주차장에는 주차 공간이 충분한데 대부분의 학생들이 교실에서 가장 가까운 곳에 주차하길 원하는 게 문제야. 학생들이 학교에 좀 더 일찍 온다면 아무 문제 없을 거야.

여 맞아. 대부분의 거주 학생들은 캠퍼스에서 차를 쓰지 않아. 학교에서 외출할 때만 자동차를 쓴다고.

Subject: *limiting central parking lot to non-resident students only* 비거주 학생들만 중앙 주차장을 사용하도록 제한

Opinion: *disagree* 반대

By whom: *man* 남자

Detail: *should come to school earlier* 더 일찍 학교에 와야 한다

Speaking

The man expresses his opinion of the announcement. State his opinion and explain the reasons he gives for holding that opinion.

Possible response

The man disagrees with the university's parking policy. He feels non-resident students are not diligent enough to come to school early enough to find a parking space. He thinks that there are plenty of parking places in the central parking lot, and problems will be solved if students come to school early. He does not think the university should limit the use of the central parking lot.

남자는 대학의 주차 정책에 동의하지 않는다. 그는 비거주자 학생들이 주차할 장소를 찾기 위해 충분히 일찍 학교에 올 만큼 근면하지 않다고 생각한다. 그는 중앙 주차장에는 주차 공간이 충분하다고 생각하며, 학생들이 학교에 일찍 온다면 문제가 해결될 것이라고 생각한다. 그는 대학이 중앙 주차장 사용을 제한해서는 안 된다고 생각한다.

Exercise

CD Possible Responses: Track 36~43

1

Reading

A student has written an article in the school newspaper about establishing a statue in the student center. Read the article about establishing a statue. You will have 45 seconds to read the article. Begin reading now.

Statue for the School

I feel that the school should reconsider establishing a statue of the founder of the school. I feel that putting up a school monument in the student center is a waste of effort; there are different ways to strengthen the school's image. Though the school authority said that the statue would make a good impression during open house week, I feel that the school should make realistic plans to improve major facilities such as the library and computer labs rather than establishing a statue for the campus.

저는 학교가 창립자의 동상을 세우는 것을 재고해야 한다고 생각합니다. 저는 학생 회관에 학교 기념비를 세우는 것은 노력의 낭비이며, 다른 방법으로 학교의 이미지를 강화할 수 있다고 생각합니다. 학교 당국은 동상이 오픈 하우스(학교 개방일) 주에 좋은 인상을 줄 것이라고 말했지만, 학교가 동상을 세우는 것보다 도서관과 컴퓨터실 같은 주요 기관을 개선하는 현실적인 계획을 세워야 한다고 생각합니다.

Listening

Now listen to two students as they discuss the

article.

W I support the school's plan to build a statue of the founder for open house week. How about you?

M Really? I have been to the student center. It didn't look empty at all. Putting a statue might clutter up the place.

W Yeah, I read about it in the school paper. But I feel that adding something like a statue can totally change the student centers' mood for the open house. Just doing that will create a positive outlook for the school.

M Well, I still think it's wiser to spend money on new equipment in the library or the health center instead.

W Just putting new machines and modern technology in the library won't help. The statue will draw more attention from prospective applicants who will improve the reputation of our university. It will be very beneficial for both our university and the visitors.

M Yeah, you have a point there.

여 나는 대학이 오픈 하우스가 열리는 주를 위해서 학교 창설자의 동상을 세우겠다는 계획에 동의해. 넌 어때?

남 정말? 난 학생 회관에 가봤는데 전혀 여유가 없었어. 동상을 놓으면 그곳을 복잡하게만 할 거야.

여 그래, 학교 신문에서 읽었어. 하지만 난 동상 같은 걸 놓으면 오픈 하우스 때 학생 회관의 분위기를 완전히 바꿀 수 있다고 생각해. 그렇게만 해도 학교의 전망을 긍정적으로 만들 거야.

남 글쎄, 난 여전히 그 돈을 도서관이나 의료 센터에 필요한 새 기구를 사는데 쓰는 것이 더 현명하다고 생각해.

여 도서관에 새로운 기계와 현대적 시설을 설치하는 것만으로는 도움이 되지 않아. 동상은 우리 대학의 명성을 드높일 비전 있는 지원자들로부터 많은 관심을 유도할 수 있을 거야. 이건 우리 학교나 방문자들 모두에게 매우 유익할 거야.

남 그래, 네 말도 일리가 있구나.

Subject: *building a statue for open house week*
오픈 하우스 주를 위해 동상을 세우는 것

Woman's opinion: *create a positive outlook for the school* 학교의 전망을 긍정적으로 만들 것이다

Detail: *draw more attention from prospective applicants* 비전 있는 지원자들로부터 많은 관심을 유도할 것이다

Man's opinion: *might clutter up space* 공간을 복잡하게 할 수 있다

Detail: *wiser to spend money on library or health center* 도서관이나 의료 센터에 돈을 쓰는 것이 더 현명하다

Speaking

The woman expresses her opinion of the university's plan to build a new statue. State her opinion and explain the reasons she gives for holding that opinion.

The woman disagrees with the student's letter in the school paper for several reasons. First of all, she feels that a statue in the student center will help the school atmosphere. Putting a statue in the student center will give a sense of school spirit and might boost the morale of the school. Secondly, the statue will grab potential applicants' attention and help to improve the university's reputation, especially during open house week. Therefore, the woman feels that it is a very good idea to build a statue on campus.

여자는 몇 가지 이유 때문에 교내 신문에 실린 학생의 편지에 동의하지 않는다. 우선 그녀는 학생 회관에 동상을 세우는 것이 학교 분위기를 도울 것이라고 생각한다. 학생 회관에 동상을 세우는 것은 학교 정신을 부여할 것이고, 학교의 사기를 올릴 수도 있다. 두 번째로 동상은 특히 오픈 하우스 주에 잠재적인 지원자들의 관심을 유도하고, 대학의 평판을 개선하는 데 도움을 줄 것이다. 그러므로 여자는 캠퍼스에 동상을 세우는 것이 매우 좋은 생각이라고 느낀다.

2

Reading

Read the announcement about the new dean of the humanities department. You will have 45 seconds to read the announcement. Begin reading now.

New Dean of the Humanities Department

Attention Students: As you all know, we have been interviewing candidates to become the new dean of the Humanities department for the past month. It is my pleasure to announce the hiring of Dr. Jonathan Lee as the new dean of Humanities. Dr. Lee received a Ph.D. from Stanford University and has been a valued member of our faculty for the past 15 years. He is replacing Dr. Larry Smith, who has been a dedicated member of our faculty for 25 years. We wish Dr. Smith the best of luck after his retirement and are very pleased that Dr. Lee has accepted the position. Thank you students and faculty for your attention during this announcement.

학생들에게 알립니다: 여러분께서 모두 알고 있듯이, 우리는 지난 달부터 인문과학대의 새로운 학장을 뽑기 위해 후보자들의 면접을 보았습니다. 인문과학대의 새로운 학장으로 Jonathan Lee 박사를 고용하게 되었음을 발표하게 되어 기쁘게 생각합니다. Lee 박사는 스탠포드 대학에서 박사 학위를 받고, 지난 15년간 우리 학교의 중요한 교수진 일원이었습니다. 그는 25년동안 헌신적인 교수진 일원이었던 Larry Smith 박사를 대신하게 되었습니다. Smith 박사에게 퇴임 후 진심으로 행운을 빌며, Lee 박사가 직위를 수락한 것을 매우 기쁘게 생각합니다. 이 공고에 관심을 가져주신 학생 여러분과 교수진들에게 감사를 표합니다.

Now listen to two students as they discuss the announcement.

M I wish they had hired the other candidate instead of Dr. Lee.

W Why's that? Have you had a bad experience with him?

M To tell the truth, he was my counselor last semester and he didn't really help me much. He wouldn't listen to any of my comments and gave me poor advice. It was a terrible experience for me. I've never seen such a counselor before.

W Oh, really? I have never met the man myself, but I have only heard good things about him.

M Yeah, so did I, but as my counselor he was horrible. Some of the classes he told me to take did not even count towards my major. For example, I had to take some classes related to my major, biology to graduate, but he recommended that I take some subjects related to chemistry. Thanks to his advice, I had to enroll for an extra semester.

W No way... that's terrible. I can see why you're upset.

남 Lee 박사 대신에 다른 후보자를 고용했더라면 좋았을 텐데.

여 이유가 뭔데? 그분이랑 안 좋은 경험이라도 있어?

남 실은 지난 학기에 그분이 내 카운슬러였는데, 별로 도움이 되지 않았어. 내가 하는 말을 전혀 듣지 않았고, 해주신 충고도 별로였어. 정말 나쁜 경험이었지. 그런 카운슬러는 한번도 만나본 적이 없었거든 .

여 정말? 난 그분을 직접 만난 적은 없지만, 좋은 말만 들었는데.

남 나도 그랬어. 하지만 카운슬러로서 그는 최악이었어. 그가 들으라고 했던 몇몇 과목들은 심지어 내 전공과 전혀 관계가 없었어. 예를 들어서, 졸업을 하려면 전공인 생물학과 관련된 수업을 들어야만 했는데. 그는 화학과 관계된 과목을 들으라고 조언했거든. 그의 충고 때문에 난 한 학기를 더 등록해야만 했어.

여 저런... 정말 안됐구나. 네가 왜 기분이 안 좋은지 알 것 같아.

Subject: *hiring of a new dean of the Humanities Department* 인문과학대의 새 학장 취임

Man's opinion: *was his counselor but did not help much* 그의 카운슬러였지만 별로 도움이 되지 않았다

Detail: *didn't listen to his comments, gave wrong advice* 그가 하는 말을 듣지 않았고 잘못된 조언을 해주었다

Woman's opinion: *have only heard good things about him* 그에 대해서는 좋은 말만 들었다

Detail: *can see why the man is upset* 남자가 기분이 안 좋은 이유를 알 것 같다

The man expresses his opinion of the university's hiring of a new dean of the Humanities department. State his opinion and explain the reasons he gives for holding that opinion.

Possible response

The man disagrees with the hiring of Dr. Lee as the new dean for several reasons. The first reason is that he feels he was not a good counselor before. For example, he didn't listen to his comments carefully and didn't give him useful advice. The second reason is that the classes he told him to take didn't relate to his major, and he had to register for another semester because of his incorrect advice. It was a very bad experience for him. Therefore, the man feels it is not a good idea to hire Dr. Lee.

남자는 몇 가지 이유 때문에 새로운 학장으로 Lee 박사를 고용하는 것에 동의하지 않는다. 첫 번째 이유는 그가 좋은 카운슬러가 아니었다고 느끼기 때문이다. 예를 들어, 그는 그의 말을 잘 듣지 않았고, 유용한 조언을 해주지도 않았다. 두 번째 이유는 그가 그에게 들으라고 했던 수업은 남자의 전공과 관계가 없었고, 그의 틀린 충고 때문에 한 학기를 더 등록해야만 했기 때문이다. 그러므로 남자는 Lee 박사를 학장으로 고용하는 것이 좋은 생각이 아니라고 느낀다.

3

The university is planning to hire a part-time computer lab assistant. Read the announcement about the part-time position. You will have 45 seconds to read the announcement. Begin reading now.

Now Hiring: Computer Lab Assistant

Attention Students: The computer lab is hiring a part-time associate to assist with daily lab functions. The hours are from 5:00 pm to 9:00 pm, Monday through Friday, and the pay is $7.00 an hour. So, all computer majors who are interested in a part-time position and would like to gain some valuable experience, please turn in your applications and resumes at the computer lab. This position is for computer majors only. Thank you for your attention.

학생들에게 알립니다: 컴퓨터실에서 일상적인 기본적 기능을 도와줄 파트타임 아르바이트생을 모집합니다. 근무 시간은 월요일부터 금요일까지 5시부터 9시까지이며, 급여는 한 시간에 7달러입니다. 이 파트타임 직에 관심이 있고 소중한 경험을 얻고자 하는 모든 컴퓨터 전공자들은 컴퓨터실에 지원서와 이력서를 제출해 주시기 바랍니다. 컴퓨터 전공자만 응시 가능합니다. 관심 가져주셔서 감사합니다.

Now listen to two students as they discuss the announcement.

W That's great that they are only hiring computer majors for that position.

M I guess, but I don't see why they can't hire any student for the job. I would even think about working there if I needed the extra money.

W Well, I had a bad experience the last time I was using the lab. I was having problems with the printer and when I asked for help, the guy working there couldn't help me. He said that he was a sociology major and that he didn't know too much about computers or printers. I was thinking to myself, "Why are you working here then?"

M Yeah, I understand that, but you don't have to be a computer major to know about computers. I'm not a computer major but I'm computer literate.

W Well, the experience working in the computer lab would benefit computer majors in their field. That position would be more beneficial to them than it would be for other students.

M Yeah, it probably would.

여 그 자리에 컴퓨터 전공자들만 고용하겠다는 건 좋은 결정인 것 같아.

남 그럴지도 모르지만 왜 아무 학생이나 고용하려 하지 않는지는 잘 모르겠어. 나도 만약 돈이 필요하면 거기서 일하는 것을 고려해 볼텐데 말이야.

여 음. 난 지난번에 컴퓨터실에서 안 좋은 경험을 했어. 프린터에 문제가 있어서 도와 달라고 했는데. 거기서 일하는 사람이 도와주지 못했어. 그는 자신이 사회학 전공이라서 컴퓨터와 프린터에 대해서 잘 모른다고 했어. 난 속으로 생각했지. "그럼 넌 왜 여기서 일하는 거야?"라고.

남 그래. 그건 이해하지만 컴퓨터에 대해 잘 알기 위해서 꼭 컴퓨터를 전공할 필요는 없어. 난 컴퓨터 전공자는 아니지만 컴퓨터에 대해서 잘 알거든.

여 글쎄. 컴퓨터실에서 일한 경험은 컴퓨터 전공자들의 분야에서 도움이 될 거야. 그 자리는 다른 학생들보다 컴퓨터 전공자들한테 더 유용할 거야.

남 그래, 아마 그렇겠지.

Subject: *hiring for a part-time job at the computer lab*
컴퓨터실의 파트타임직 채용

Woman's opinion: *agree with hiring only computer majors* 컴퓨터 전공생만 채용하는 것에 동의한다

Detail: *sociology major couldn't help her last time, benefit computer majors in their field*
지난번에 사회학 전공생이 도와주지 못했다. 컴퓨터 전공생들의 분야에서 도움이 될 것이다

Man's opinion: *don't see why they can't hire any student for the job*
왜 아무 학생이나 고용하려 하지 않는지 잘 모르겠다

Detail: *you don't have to be a computer major to know about computers*
컴퓨터에 대해 잘 알기 위해서 꼭 컴퓨터를 전공할 필요는 없다

Speaking

The woman expresses her opinion of the announcement. State her opinion and explain the reasons she gives for holding that opinion.

Possible response

The woman agrees with the computer lab hiring only computer majors for several reasons. The first reason she agrees with the idea is that she had a bad experience in the computer lab before. She had trouble with a printer, but she couldn't get help from someone who was working there at that time because, being a sociology major, he didn't know about the machine. The second reason is that working as an assistant at a computer lab would be a good experience for someone in the computer field. Therefore, she agrees with the computer lab hiring only computer majors.

여자는 몇 가지 이유 때문에 컴퓨터실에서 컴퓨터 전공자들만 고용하는 것에 동의한다. 그녀가 동의하는 첫 번째 이유는 전에 그녀가 컴퓨터실에서 나쁜 경험을 겪었기 때문이다. 프린터를 쓰는데 문제가 있었는데, 그 당시 그곳에서 일하던 사람은 사회학 전공이었으며 프린터에 대해서 몰랐기 때문에 아무런 도움을 받을 수 없었다. 두 번째 이유는 컴퓨터실에서 조수로 일하는 것은 컴퓨터를 전공하는 사람에게 좋은 경험이 될 것이기 때문이다. 그러므로 그녀는 컴퓨터실에서 컴퓨터 전공자들만 고용하는 것에 동의한다.

4

Reading

Read the announcement about the change in the final exam. You will have 45 seconds to read the announcement. Begin reading now.

Change in the Final Exam

A history professor has announced that his final exam will be an oral presentation. However, it is mandatory that all students prepare for their presentations with an assigned partner. The reason for this is that students can learn a lot by working together. Students can learn how to cooperate and can share their ideas and knowledge. It will be very beneficial for the class.

한 역사 과목 교수는 기말고사가 구두 발표가 될 것이라고 발표했다. 그러나 모든 학생들은 지명된 파트너와 함께 발표를 준비해야 한다. 그 이유는 함께 일하면서 많은 것을 배울 수 있기 때문이다. 학생들은 같이 일하면서 협력하는 방법에 대해 배우고 생각과 지식을 공유할 수 있다. 이것은 수업에 매우 유용할 것이다.

Listening

Now listen to two students as they discuss the announcement.

W I don't want to do this presentation. Why can't we just have a multiple-choice test like all the other classes?

M What makes you say that?

W My roommate had to do this kind of project before. She was assigned a terrible partner who did not want to get together at all to work on the presentation or show up for the presentation itself. Thus, it dramatically hurt her final grade.

M That sounds like a very unique case. Maybe it was just bad luck.

W Maybe you're right, but who can guarantee that I don't get assigned a bad partner like my roommate did? Furthermore, at the end of the semester, students are very busy preparing for their final exams and papers. It's not going to be easy to focus on preparing for a presentation. I think that the professor should put himself in his students' shoes.

M You're probably right. He should have been more careful.

여 난 이 발표를 하고 싶지 않아. 왜 다른 수업에서처럼 그냥 선다형 시험을 볼 수 없는 걸까?

남 왜 그렇게 생각하는데?

여 내 룸메이트가 전에 이런 프로젝트를 해야 했는데, 안 좋은 파트너를 만나서 발표 준비를 전혀 하고 싶어하지 않았고, 심지어 발표에 나타나지도 않았대. 그래서 학점을 완전히 망쳤대.

남 그건 매우 드문 경우인 것 같아. 운이 나빴던 걸 거야.

여 네 말이 맞을지도 모르지만 내 룸메이트처럼 나쁜 파트너를 만나지 않는다는 것을 누가 보장할 수 있겠어? 더구나 학기말에는 학생들이 기말고사와 보고서 준비에 정신이 없잖아. 발표 준비에 전념하기가 쉽지 않을 거야. 교수님께서 학생들의 입장에서 생각하셔야 할 것 같아.

남 네 말이 맞을지도 모르겠다. 교수님께서 좀더 신중하셨어야 했어.

Subject: *doing a presentation with a partner for the final exam* 기말고사로 파트너와 함께 발표를 하는 것

Woman's opinion: *don't want to do the presentation* 발표를 하고 싶지 않다

Detail: *don't want to get a bad partner, will be busy preparing for final exams and papers* 안 좋은 파트너를 만나고 싶지 않다, 기말고사와 보고서 준비로 바쁠 것이다

Man's opinion: *woman's friend had bad luck* 여자의 친구는 운이 나빴다

Detail: *professor should have been more careful* 교수님께서 좀더 신중하셨어야 했다

Speaking

The woman expresses her opinion of the change in the final exam. State her opinion and explain the reasons she gives for holding that opinion.

Possible response

The woman is against having to do an oral presentation for her final exam. She has two reasons for holding her opinion. The first reason is that her roommate had a bad experience in the past. She had a terrible partner who would not cooperate so she received a very low grade. The second reason is that most students are usually very busy at the end of the semester preparing for their final exams and term papers so that they can't concentrate on their projects. These are the reasons why she disagrees with the professor's plan.

여자는 기말고사로 구두 발표를 해야 하는 것에 반대한다. 그녀는 이 의견에 대해 두 가지 이유가 있다. 첫 번째 이유는 그녀의 룸메이트가 과거에 나쁜 경험을 했기 때문이다. 그녀는 협력하려고 하지 않는 파트너 때문에 매우 낮은 점수를 받았다. 두 번째 이유는 대부분의 학생들이 학기말에는 보통 기말고사와 보고서 준비로 매우 바쁘기 때문에 프로젝트에 집중할 수 없기 때문이다. 이러한 이유로 그녀는 교수의 계획에 반대한다.

5

Reading

The university has announced the plan to change the school's health center into an alumni center. Read the annoucement about the school's plan to change the health center. You will have 45 seconds to read the announcement. Begin reading now.

Health Center

The university has decided to turn the school's health center into an alumni center. With the new university hospital nearby, students will be able to get better service at the hospital with insurance benefits. An increase in graduating students requires the school to have a department to organize and keep a log of past graduates.

대학은 교내 보건소를 졸업생 회관으로 바꾸기로 결정했다. 근처에 대학 병원이 새로 생겼기 때문에 학생들은 보험 혜택을 받아 더 좋은 서비스를 받을 수 있을 것이다. 졸업생이 증가했으므로 학교는 졸업생 명단을 조직하고 관리할 부서가 필요하다.

Listening

Now listen to two students as they discuss the announcement.

M I don't think the school should turn the health center into an alumni center. What about you?

W I'm not sure because I don't really use that facility. I do see that there might be some problems with the change.

M Actually, the university hospital is fifteen minutes from the school. This can cause problems when people are in serious need of a health center close by.

W Even if I just want to go and get some medicine for a cold or something small, I probably wouldn't go because it's too far.

M　Colds and minor injuries have to be checked quickly or they could get worse. A minor problem can become a major problem. Also, if a student doesn't have a car, it might be difficult to get to after the bus stops running at night. The health center should be on campus.

W　You're probably right.

남　나는 학교가 보건소를 졸업생 회관으로 변경해서는 안 된다고 생각해. 넌 어떻게 생각해?

여　난 그 시설을 별로 이용하지 않기 때문에 잘 모르겠어. 변경하면 문제가 생길 것 같긴 해.

남　사실 대학 병원은 학교에서 15분 거리야. 보건소가 바로 옆에 있어야 될 심각한 상황에서는 문제가 될 수 있어.

여　만약 감기나 사소한 질병 때문에 병원에 가서 약을 얻어야 한다고 해도 너무 멀어서 가지 않을 것 같아.

남　감기나 작은 부상도 심각해지기 전에 빨리 검사 받지 않으면 악화될 수 있어. 작은 문제가 큰 문제가 될 수 있잖아. 그리고 만약 학생이 차가 없다면 밤에 버스가 끊긴 후에는 그곳에 가기가 힘들 거야. 보건소는 교내에 있어야 해.

여　그래, 네 말이 맞는 것 같아.

Subject: *turning the health center into an alumni center*
보건소를 졸업생 회관으로 변경하는 것

Man's opinion: *don't think the school should turn the health center into an alumni center* 학교가 보건소를 졸업생 회관으로 변경해서는 안 된다고 생각한다

Detail: *university hospital is far away, might be difficult to get to the hospital at night* 대학 병원이 멀다, 밤에 병원에 가기가 힘들 수도 있다

Woman's opinion: *not sure because she doesn't really use that facility* 그 시설을 별로 이용하지 않기 때문에 잘 모르겠다

Detail: *thinks the man is probably right* 아마도 남자의 말이 맞는 것 같다

Speaking

The man expresses his opinion of the university's plan to close the health center. State his opinion and explain the reasons he gives for holding that opinion.

Possible response

The man disagrees with the school's plan to change the health center to an alumni center. The first reason he is against the idea is because of the distance from the university hospital. Small injuries from sports and minor symptoms can cause serious problems if they are not treated promptly. Furthermore, the off-campus location of the new hospital will be a problem for students because transportation may not be available at night. For these reasons, the man strongly disagrees with the school's plan to change the health center to an alumni center.

남자는 보건소를 졸업생 회관으로 바꾼다는 학교의 계획에 동의하지 않는다. 그가 그 생각에 반대하는 첫 번째 이유는 대학 병원으로부터의 거리 때문이다. 학생들이 운동하면서 당한 작은 부상이나 가벼운 증상들은 신속하게 치료하지 않으면 심각한 문제를 일으킬 수 있다. 게다가, 캠퍼스 밖에 위치한 새로운 병원에는 밤에 가는 교통편이 없을 수도 있기 때문에 학생들에게 문제가 될 수 있다. 이러한 이유로 남자는 보건소를 졸업생 회관으로 바꾼다는 학교의 계획에 강하게 반대한다.

6

Reading

Read the announcement about the change of menu in the university dining services. You will have 45 seconds to read the announcement. Begin reading now.

Dining Service

The university dining services are planning to change the menu for the upcoming semester. The plan consists of changing all hot foods in the cafeterias and dorm meal serving areas to cold foods in the mornings. The cold foods will be healthier and cheaper than the hot foods. This plan is due to the increase in health concerns for our fellow students at the university.

대학 식당 서비스는 다음 학기에 메뉴를 바꿀 계획이다. 이 계획에는 아침 시간에 카페테리아와 기숙사의 식사 제공 구역에서 제공되는 모든 더운 음식을 찬 음식으로 바꾸는 것이 포함된다. 찬 음식은 건강에 더 좋고 더운 음식보다 가격이 저렴할 것이다. 이 계획은 대학내 학생들의 건강에 대한 관심이 증가한 데 따른 것이다.

Listening

Now listen to two students as they discuss the announcement.

M　They are finally serving healthier cold foods rather than the fatty and high in cholesterol hot foods.

W　Well, I'm not thrilled about it. I was always used to the hot foods and they really gave me a lot of energy.

M　Well, I prefer cold foods rather than hot foods. Cold foods are supposed to be healthier than the hot foods that were served at school.

W　Hot foods have more usable energy for your body. They are not processed foods like the cold foods served in the dining areas.

M　But cold food is cheaper for students since they don't need to be cooked.

W　Those who prefer hot foods will walk all the way off campus to buy hot foods and that will cost more money. I think the university has to consider this decision again.

남   드디어 기름지고 콜레스테롤이 많은 더운 음식 대신 건강에 좋은 찬 음식을 제공하기로 했구나.
여   글쎄. 난 별로라고 생각해. 난 늘 더운 음식을 먹었고 그 음식은 나에게 에너지를 많이 주었거든.
남   난 더운 음식보다 찬 음식이 좋아. 찬 음식은 학교에서 주는 더운 음식보다 건강에 더 좋다고 하잖아.
여   더운 음식은 몸에서 사용할 수 있는 에너지가 더 많아. 그 음식들은 식당에서 제공하는 찬 음식처럼 가공된 음식이 아니라고.
남   하지만 찬 음식은 요리를 할 필요가 없어서 학생들이 사먹기가 더 저렴해.
여   더운 음식을 좋아하는 학생들은 더운 음식을 사러 학교 밖으로 나갈 거고, 결국 더 비싸게 될 거야. 난 대학이 이 결정을 재고해야 한다고 생각해.

Subject: *serving cold foods in the cafeteria*
카페테리아에서 찬 음식을 제공하는 것
Woman's opinion: *not thrilled about it* 별로라고 생각한다
Detail: *hot foods gave her a lot of energy, will cost more money to buy hot foods off campus*
더운 음식은 에너지를 많이 준다, 학교 밖에서 더운 음식을 사는 것은 돈이 더 많이 들 것이다
Man's opinion: *prefer cold foods* 찬 음식을 선호한다
Detail: *healthier, cheaper* 건강에 더 좋다, 더 저렴하다

Speaking

The woman expresses her opinion of the university's plan to change the dining service. State her opinion and explain the reasons she gives for holding that opinion.

Possible response

The woman strongly disagrees with the school announcement for several reasons. First, she thinks that hot foods give more energy compared to cold foods. Second, it can be more expensive for the students because those who want hot foods will travel off campus to get their breakfasts. Therefore, the woman is strongly against the school's plan to change all hot foods into cold foods during breakfast.

여자는 몇 가지 이유 때문에 학교 공고에 대하여 강하게 반대한다. 첫 번째로 그녀는 더운 음식이 찬 음식보다 더 많은 에너지를 준다고 생각한다. 두 번째로 더운 음식을 원하는 사람들이 아침을 먹기 위해 캠퍼스 밖으로 갈 것이기 때문에 돈을 더 많이 쓰게 될 수 있다. 그러므로 여자는 아침에 모든 더운 음식을 찬 음식으로 바꾸고자 하는 학교의 계획에 강하게 반대한다.

7

Reading

The university has announced new writing requirements for science majors. Read the announcement about new writing requirements. You will have 45 seconds to read the announcement. Begin reading now.

Writing Requirements for Science Majors

For science majors, there were no writing requirements after the first semester of the freshman year. However, the school board has decided to add 12 more intensive writing requirements for graduation. The reason is that students who are enrolled in science have poor essay writing skills, and the department of science has decided to increase the credit hours to help students graduate easier.

과학 전공자들에게는 일학년 첫 학기 이후에는 작문 필수 과목이 없었다. 그러나 학교 이사회는 졸업 필수 과목으로 집중 작문 과정 열 두 과목을 추가하기로 결정했다. 그 이유는 과학 학부에 등록하는 학생들의 작문 능력이 부족하기 때문이며, 과학 학과는 학생들이 졸업을 더 쉽게 할 수 있도록 돕기 위해 이수 단위를 늘리기로 결정했다.

Listening

Now listen to two students as they discuss the announcement.

W   Did you hear about the new writing requirements for graduation? I personally don't need more writing.
M   That's great! I was thinking it would be great to have a few more writing classes for English. My writing was always weak, and I would like to take more classes.
W   Really? I don't like writing; I always felt that I could concentrate on mathematics more.
M   I think it'll be great to get better at writing. Most of the time, people try to just get by, but writing skills are very important for students who want to go to graduate school, since there are a lot of paper assignments.
W   I guess you're right. I could always get better in writing, although I still don't know if it's necessary.
M   Well, writing is important because it is used in all fields of study; as you know, it is basic for all communications. Getting better at it won't hurt you at all.

여   졸업을 위해 새로 작문을 요구하겠다는 소식 들었니? 개인적으로 난 더 이상 글을 쓰고 싶지 않아.
남   잘됐다! 영어 작문 과목을 몇 개 더 들으면 좋겠다고 생각하고 있었거든. 난 늘 작문 실력이 부족했기 때문에 수업을 더 들으면 좋을 것 같아.
여   정말? 난 글을 쓰는 게 싫어. 난 항상 수학에 더 집중할 수 있다고 느꼈어.
남   난 작문을 더 잘 할 수 있다면 아주 좋을 거라고 생각해. 대부분의 경우에 사람들은 단지 과목을 패스하는 데 만족하지만 작문 기술은 대학원에

가고 싶은 학생들에게는 매우 중요해. 대학원에서는 작문 과제가 많잖아.
여 네 말이 맞는 것 같기도 해. 작문을 더 잘 한다면 좋을 것 같아. 여전히 그게 필요한 것인지는 모르겠지만 말야.
남 작문은 모든 학문분야에서 사용되기 때문에 중요해. 너도 알다시피 작문은 모든 의사 소통의 기본이잖아. 작문을 더 잘하게 되는 건 전혀 해로울 일이 없어.

Subject: *new writing requirements for graduation*
졸업을 위해 새로 작문을 요구하는 것

Man's opinion: *would like to take more classes*
수업을 더 듣고 싶다

Detail: *it'll be great to get better at writing*
작문을 더 잘하게 되면 좋을 것이다

Woman's opinion: *don't like writing* 글을 쓰는 것이 싫다

Detail: *don't know if it's necessary* 필요한 것인지는 모르겠다

Speaking

The man expresses his opinion of the university's plan to increase the writing requirements. State his opinion and explain the reasons he gives for holding that opinion.

Possible response

The man strongly agrees with the university's decision which requires 12 more intensive writing courses for graduation. First of all, he feels that he will have more chances to get better at writing. He thinks that he is not good at writing and it will be helpful to take a few more writing classes to improve his writing skills. Secondly, having good writing skills will benefit students who want to go to graduate school because graduate students usually have many papers to write. Actually, writing skill is required in all areas of study. The man strongly agrees with the university's decision to change the graduation requirements for the field of science.

남자는 졸업을 하기 위해 작문 집중 과정을 12개 더 수강해야 한다는 대학의 결정에 전적으로 동의한다. 우선 그는 작문 실력을 개선할 기회가 될 것이라고 느낀다. 그는 자신이 글쓰기를 잘 하지 못하며, 작문 실력을 강화하기 위하여 수업을 몇 개 더 들으면 좋을 것이라고 생각한다. 두 번째로 대학원에서는 일반적으로 보고서를 많이 써야 하기 때문에 작문 실력이 좋은 것은 대학원에 진학하고자 하는 학생들에게 유용하다. 사실 작문 능력은 모든 분야의 학문에서 요구된다. 남자는 과학 분야에서 작문을 졸업 필수로 변경하는 결정에 대해 전폭적인 지지를 보낸다.

8

Reading

Read the announcement about building a new dorm off campus. You will have 45 seconds to read the announcement. Begin reading now.

Building a New Dorm Off Campus

The university has decided to build the school dormitory outside of campus due to limited space on campus. The dormitory will be located away from campus 10 minutes by bus in the local community. A network of campus police and community police will monitor students' security. There will be shuttle bus bus services for students without cars during the weekday.

대학은 캠퍼스의 제한된 공간 때문에 캠퍼스 밖에 학교 기숙사를 짓기로 결정했다. 기숙사는 버스로 10분 거리인 인근 지역에 위치할 것이다. 캠퍼스 경찰과 지역사회 경찰이 학생들의 안전을 관리할 것이다. 주중에는 자동차가 없는 학생들을 위해 셔틀 버스 서비스가 제공될 것이다.

Listening

Now listen to two students as they discuss the announcement.

W I don't think I want to live in the dormitories next semester.

M Yeah, I heard what the school is trying to do. I don't think it's a bad idea to build the new dormitory off campus.

W Well, the traffic will be outrageous and commuters will be late for school. Students will be unhappy and stressed out. Imagine them struggling every morning in order to get to their classes on time.

M I understand, but there will be shuttle buses available.

W The distance will also cause students to miss most of the student activities held at school. It will be difficult to go to pep rallies and social club gatherings.

M I guess you're right. So, what have you decided to do?

W Well, I might as well just rent an apartment with a couple of roommates.

여 난 다음 학기에 기숙사에 살고 싶지 않아.
남 응, 나도 학교가 계획한 것을 들었어. 난 그 생각이 나쁘다고 생각하지 않아.
여 글쎄, 교통 체증이 심각할 거고, 통학하는 학생들은 학교에 지각할 거야. 학생들은 불쾌하고 스트레스를 많이 받게 될 거야. 매일 아침마다 수업에 제 시간에 가려고 애를 쓰는 모습을 상상해봐.
남 이해는 하지만 학생들은 셔틀 버스를 이용할 수 있을 거야.
여 거리 때문에 여러 교내 학생 활동에 참가할 수 없게 될 거야. 학급 모임이나 서클활동에 참가하는 게 어려울 거야.
남 그래, 네 말이 맞는 것 같구나. 그래서 넌 어떻게 하기로 했어?
여 글쎄, 룸메이트 몇 명과 함께 아파트를 빌리는 게 나을 것 같아.

Subject: *building the new dormitory off campus*
새 기숙사를 캠퍼스 밖에 건축하는 것

Woman's opinion: *don't want to live in the dormitories*
기숙사에서 살고 싶지 않다

Detail: *traffic will be outrageous, will be difficult to go to student activities*
교통 체증이 심각할 것이다. 교내 활동에 가는 것이 힘들 것이다

Man's opinion: *don't think it's a bad idea*
나쁜 생각인 것 같지 않다

Detail: *shuttle buses will be available, additional security* 셔틀 버스를 이용할 수 있을 것이다. 안전도 보강된다

Speaking

The woman expresses her opinion of the university's plan to build the dormitory off campus. State her opinion and explain the reasons she gives for holding that opinion.

Possible response

The woman disagrees with the idea of building the new dormitory off campus. The first reason she is against the idea is that she is worried about traffic to and from school. Students won't be happy if they are late for school because of the traffic. The second reason is that students' activities and club gatherings will not be easy to attend considering the long distance from the dorms. The woman disagrees with the dormitory being built off campus and gives her point of view on where she stands on the decision.

여자는 캠퍼스 밖에 새 기숙사를 짓는 계획에 동의하지 않는다. 계획에 반대하는 첫 번째 이유는 학교를 오고 갈 때 교통 체증을 걱정하기 때문이다. 만약 교통 체증 때문에 학교에 지각하게 된다면 학생들은 기분이 좋지 않을 것이다. 두 번째 이유는 기숙사로부터 학교까지의 먼 거리 때문에 학생 활동이나 서클모임에 참가하는 것이 쉽지 않을 것이기 때문이다. 여자는 캠퍼스 밖에 기술사를 짓는 것에 대해 반대하며 이 결정에 대한 자신의 견해를 밝히고 있다.

□ Sample

CD Possible Response: Track 44

Reading

Now read the passage about moral persuasion. You will have 45 seconds to read the passage. Begin reading now.

Moral Persuasion

Environmental ethics is the study of the moral relationship of human beings to the environment. The focus is environmental literature on wilderness, and possible future developments of the discipline. Putting out natural fires, culling feral animals or destroying some individual members of overpopulated indigenous species is necessary for the protection of the integrity of a certain ecosystem. Also, encouraging people to recycle garbage is a way to protect the environment.

환경 윤리란 인간과 환경의 윤리 관계를 연구하는 학문이다. 야생과 관련된 환경 문학 및 학문의 추후 발달 가능성에 초점을 두고 있다. 자연적으로 발생된 불을 끄고 야생 동물을 짝짓게 하거나 종의 개체수가 너무 많은 경우, 개체수를 조절하는 것은 특정 생태계를 보전하기 위해 필요하다. 또한 사람들로 하여금 쓰레기를 재활용할 것을 권장하는 것은 환경을 보호하기 위한 하나의 방법이다.

Listening

Now listen to part of a lecture in an advertisement class. The professor talks about moral persuasion.

P   Today, we'll talk about measures the Environmental Protection Agency is taking to educate the public about environmental ethics. Conserving the environment is a very important issue that the EPA is focusing on in a number of ways.

Alright, so to start the campaign, the Environmental Protection Agency has begun two approaches to enforce environmental ethics. First they introduced a friendly bear and named it "Smokey the Bear" to remind all citizens about forest fires and safety in the woods. Smokey the Bear received its name from the great American Brown Bear cub which acts as the mascot to represent the forests of the USA. The campaign chose this character to teach about saving animals by watching out for forest fires and the safety of the animals.

Another approach the EPA used was encouraging recycling by putting up signs and placing trash bins in convenient locations. This sparked the beginning of teaching the public about the ethics and discipline of our environment. This started with putting recycling bins in front of each house. With these two campaigns, the EPA will enforce moral persuasion on all citizens by enforcing ethics and discipline towards the environment.

오늘은 환경 보호 기관에서 일반인들에게 환경 윤리를 교육하기 위해 취하고 있는 조치에 대해 이야기 해 보고자 합니다. 환경 보존은 환경 보호 기관에서 여러 가지 면에서 중점을 두고 있는 중요한 이슈입니다. 자, 이 캠페인을 시작하기 위해 환경 보호 기관에서는 환경 윤리를 강화하기 위한 두 가지 접근을 개시했습니다. 우선, 그들은 산불과 숲의 안전에 대해 모든 시민들이 명심할 수 있도록 친근한 곰을 소개했고, 이 곰을 "Smokey the Bear"라고 이름 붙였습니다. Smokey the Bear는 미국의 숲을 상징하는 마스코트인 아메리칸 갈색 새끼 곰에서 이름을 얻게 되었습니다. 이 캠페인은 산불을 조심하고 동물들의 안전을 유의하는 것을 통해 동물들을 구할 수 있다는 것을 가르쳐주기 위해 이 캐릭터를 선택했습니다.

환경 보호 기관이 사용한 또 다른 방법은 표지판을 세우고 편리한 위치에 쓰레기통을 설치하여 쓰레기 재활용을 권장한 것입니다. 이것은 시민들에게 환경의 윤리와 규칙에 대해 가르치는 시발점이 되었습니다. 이것은 각 개인의 집 앞에 재활용 쓰레기통을 놓는 것부터 시작했습니다. 이와 같은 두 가지의 캠페인을 통해 환경 보호 기관은 환경에 대한 윤리와 교육을 실시함으로써 모든 시민들에게 윤리적 설득을 강화할 것입니다.

Speaking

The professor talks about how a campaign is organized to encourage moral discipline. Explain how environmental ethics are enforced by using two examples.

Possible response

The professor talks about two campaigns to enforce environmental ethics on the public. According to this lecture, Smokey the Bear is used to encourage people to be careful about forest fires which can endanger wildlife. For example, the American Brown Bear cub is used as the mascot of the forests in the USA because this campaign teaches how we can save the animals by watching out for forest fires. He also points out that recycling should be enforced by placing recycling containers near homes. The professor thinks by taking these two actions, the ecosystem will become more balanced.

교수는 대중에게 환경 윤리를 시행하기 위해 시작된 두 가지의 캠페인에 대하여 말하고 있다. 이 강의에 따르면, "Smokey the Bear"는 야생 동물들을 위험에 처하게 할 수 있는 산불을 조심하라고 사람들에게 고무시키기 위해 사용되었다. 예를 들어 이 캠페인은 산불을 조심하는 것을 통해 어떻게 동물을 구제할 수 있는지 가르치고 있기 때문에 새끼 아메리칸 갈색 곰을 미국에 있는 숲의 마스코트로 사용한다. 그는 또한 집 근처에 재활용 쓰레기통을 설치하여 재활용을 강화해야 한다고 지적하고 있다. 교수는 이 두 가지 방법을 통해 생태계가 보다 더 균형을 이룰 수 있다고 생각한다.

Mini Test   **CD** Possible Responses: **Track 46**

1

Reading

Now read the passage about supranational organizations. You will have 45 seconds to read the passage. Begin reading now.

Supranational Organizations

Many studies have shown that it is more effective and practical to work together in groups than by oneself. It is much easier to solve problems and achieve goals when you work with others. The reason for supranational organizations is based on this principle. Supranational organizations work together globally to efficiently achieve.

많은 연구들이 개인적으로 일을 하는 것보다 그룹 내에서 함께 일하는 것이 더 효과적이고 실질적이라는 것을 증명해 왔다. 타인과 함께 일을 하면 문제를 해결하고 목표를 이루기가 훨씬 수월하다. 초국가적인 조직들은 이와 같은 원칙에 근거하여 조직되었다. 초국가적인 조직들은 그들의 목표를 이루기 위해 전세계적으로 함께 일을 한다.

Listening

Now listen to part of a lecture in an international relations class. The professor talks about supranational organizations.

P Alright, so today we'll discuss supranational organizations. These organizations benefit people internationally through a number of ways. There are many different supranational organizations today, but we'll focus on one type of group and talk about the benefits.

First, let's talk about the WHO or World Health Organization. This organization exists in over 130 different countries. The WHO has provided vital benefits to people around the globe by providing immediate access to healthcare. In a health emergency, people do not have to wait for a long time. Also, if people are traveling and face health problems, instead of searching for a reputable hospital or doctor, people can look for the WHO

to seek treatment. Because of this supranational organization, people can put their minds at ease when looking for reliable and safe healthcare very quickly.

자, 오늘은 초국가적인 조직들에 관하여 이야기 해 보겠습니다. 이러한 조직들은 여러 가지 방법을 통해 국제적으로 사람들에게 많은 이익을 제공합니다. 오늘날에는 다양한 초국가적인 조직들이 많이 있지만 그 중 하나의 그룹과 그 이익들에 초점을 맞춰 보겠습니다.

우선 세계보건기구(WHO)에 관하여 이야기 해 봅시다. 이 기관은 130개 이상의 나라에서 존재하고 있습니다. WHO는 즉각적으로 건강 관리를 받을 수 있도록 하여 세계 인류에게 꼭 필요한 이익을 제공해오고 있습니다. 건강상 긴박한 상황에 처한 경우에 오래 기다리지 않아도 됩니다. 또한 여행을 하다가 건강에 문제가 발생했을 때 명성이 있는 병원이나 의사를 찾는 대신에 치료를 받기 위해 WHO를 찾으면 됩니다. 이 초국가적인 조직의 존재로 인해 사람들은 신뢰할 수 있고 안전한 건강 조치를 급히 찾아야 할 때 마음을 편하게 가질 수 있습니다.

Subject: _supranational organizations_ 초국가적인 조직들

Detail: _1. in 130 countries_ 130개 나라에 있다

2. provide health care 건강 관리를 제공한다

Speaking

The professor talks about a supranational organization and their main goals. Explain the idea of a supranational organization.

Possible response

The professor talks about supranational organizations. According to this lecture, an organization, like the WHO, provides benefits to people internationally. For example, the WHO provides immediate access to healthcare to people all over the world. People do not have to wait for a long time in a health emergency. Also, the WHO makes it easier for travelers to get medical attention. Tourists don't have to search for reputable hospitals; they can just find safe and reliable healthcare at the WHO. This is how the professor explains the idea of supranational organizations.

교수는 초국가적인 조직에 관하여 말하고 있다. 이 강의에 따르면, WHO와 같은 조직은 국제적으로 사람들에게 이익을 제공한다. 예를 들어 WHO는 전 세계적으로 사람들에게 건강 조치를 즉각적으로 제공할 수 있다. 사람들은 건강상 위급한 상황에서 오래 기다릴 필요가 없다. 또한 WHO는 여행자들이 쉽게 치료를 받을 수 있도록 한다. 그들은 명성 있는 병원을 찾을 필요 없이 WHO가 제공하는 안전하고 믿을 만한 건강 조치를 찾을 수 있다. 교수는 위처럼 초국가적인 조직에 대한 개념을 설명하고 있다.

2

Reading

Now read the passage about diffusion of responsibility. You will have 45 seconds to read the passage. Begin reading now.

Diffusion of Responsibility

The diffusion of responsibility says that the more people that are around, the less chance someone will help another person. A common explanation of this phenomenon is that, with others present, observers all assume that someone else is going to intervene; thus, they each refrain from doing so. People may also assume that other bystanders may be more qualified to help, such as a doctor or police officer, and their intervention would thus be unneeded.

책임의 전가란 주위에 사람이 많으면 많을수록 다른 사람을 도울 기회가 더 줄어들 것이라는 뜻을 갖는다. 이러한 현상에 대한 일반적인 설명은 다른 사람들이 있는 경우 상황을 지켜보던 사람들은 누군가가 도와줄 것이라고 생각하기 때문에 각자 직접 돕는 것을 피한다는 것이다. 사람들은 또한 의사나 경찰과 같은 다른 사람들이 도움을 주는데 더 자격이 있기 때문에 그들이 개입할 필요가 없다고 생각할 수도 있다.

Listening

Now listen to part of a lecture in a psychology class. The professor talks about diffusion of responsibility.

P   OK, so as an example of this diffusion of responsibility, let's take a look at this situation. If a car broke down during the morning rush hour, people think that others will help the motorist. As a result, people do not stop to help the person with the broken car, and do not feel responsible. As another example, let's say you witnessed a car accident. There are many cars passing by, and a police car is coming soon. Most likely, you will not stop your car to help the drivers. On the other hand, if it was early in the morning or very late at night you might feel more inclined to help because there are no other people around. If this was on the freeway with no cars passing by and no police or help arriving soon, you might feel more responsible and get out of your car to check on the car accident.

좋습니다. 그러면 책임의 전가에 대한 예로 다음 상황을 살펴봅시다. 만약 어떤 차가 아침 출퇴근 시간에 고장이 났다면, 사람들은 다른 사람들이 그 운전자를 도울 것이라고 생각할 것입니다. 결과적으로 사람들은 고장이 난 자동차의 운전자를 돕기 위해 멈추지 않고 이에 대해 책임을 느끼지 않습니다. 또 다른 예로 여러분이 자동차 사고를 목격했다고 합시다. 많은 차들이 지나가고 있고, 경찰차가 곧 도착할 것입니다. 아마도 여러분은 운전자를 돕기 위해 차를 멈추지 않을 것입니다. 한편, 만약 이 사고가 이른 아침에 발생했거나 늦은 밤에 일어났다면, 주위에 다른 사람들이 없기 때문에 도와주어야 한다고 느낄 가능성이 클 것입니다. 만약 이 사고가 지나가는 차가 전혀 없는 고속도로에서 발생했고 경찰차나 도움이 전혀 올 가능성이 없다면 여러분은 더욱 책임을 느낄 수도 있고 차에서 나와 사고를 확인할 것입니다.

Subject: *diffusion of responsibility* 책임의 전가
Detail: *car breaks down → help vs. not help*
자동차가 고장난다 → 돕는다 vs. 돕지 않는다

Speaking

The professor discusses the diffusion of responsibility. Explain the idea of diffusion of responsibility.

Possible response

The professor talks about the diffusion of responsibility. According to this lecture, the more people that are around, the less chance there is that someone will help another person. For example, the professor talks about a car breaking down during the morning rush hour. She says that because there are so many other motorists, people do not stop and help the people in the car, and they do not feel any responsibility for them. They think someone else will help. Another example she uses is if you see a car accident late at night. Since there are no other cars around, you feel more of a responsibility to help because you can't defer the responsibility to someone else. You feel obligated. This is how the professor explains the idea of diffusion of responsibility.

교수는 책임 전가에 대해 말하고 있다. 이 강의에 따르면 주변에 사람이 많을수록 다른 사람을 도와줄 기회가 적다고 한다. 예를 들어 교수는 아침 출퇴근 시간에 자동차가 고장 나는 것에 대해 이야기한다. 그는 다른 운전자들이 많기 때문에 사람들은 고장난 차의 운전자를 도와주기 위해 멈추지 않고, 이에 대한 책임도 느끼지 않는다고 말한다. 그들은 다른 사람이 도울 것이라고 생각하는 것이다. 교수가 제시한 또 다른 예는 늦은 밤에 자동차 사고를 보게 되는 경우이다. 주변에 다른 차들이 없기 때문에 다른 사람에게 책임을 전가할 수 없으므로 도와주어야 한다는 책임을 더 느끼게 된다. 즉 의무감을 느끼는 것이다. 교수는 이러한 방식으로 책임의 전가에 대한 개념을 설명하고 있다.

3

Reading

Now read the passage about the positive effect. You will have 45 seconds to read the passage. Begin reading now.

The Positive Effect

In psychology and cognitive science, the positive effect is the tendency of people, when they evaluate the causes of the behaviors of a person they like. The term positive effect also refers to how people's emotional attention is different. Studies have found that people are more likely to pay attention to positive rather than negative connotations.

심리학과 인지과학에서 긍정적 효과란 사람들이 그들이 좋아하는 사람의 행동의 원인들을 평가할 때 나타나는 경향을 의미한다. 긍정적 효과라는 말은 또한 사람의 감정적 주목이 어떻게 다른지를 나타내기도 한다. 연구에 따르면 사람들은 부정적인 암시보다는 긍정적인 암시에 더 많은 관심을 갖는다.

교수는 긍정적 효과에 관하여 말하고 있다. 강의에 따르면, 사람들은 긍정적인 말에 더 적극적인 반응을 보인다. 예를 들면, 사람들은 "오늘은 대체적으로 맑고 비가 올 확률이 50%이다"라고 말하는 일기 예보보다 "오늘은 부분적으로 흐리고 비가 올 확률이 50%이다"라고 하는 일기 예보를 들을 때 우산을 더 많이 들고 나간다.

Listening

Now listen to part of a lecture in a psychology class. The professor talks about the positive effect.

P　Today we will discuss the positive effect. Let's start with the terminology. People have a tendency to have a positive response to positive connotations. I will discuss an example of a weather forecast.

The weather forecaster broadcasts in two different ways. In the first case, he says, "Today is going to be partly cloudy with a 50% chance of rain." The other way of broadcasting is saying that the weather is going to be fairly sunny with a 50% chance of rain. Both of these forecasts are exactly the same, yet more people take their umbrellas in the first case than in the second because of the positive wording of the forecast.

오늘은 긍정적인 효과에 대하여 토론해 보겠어요. 우선 용어부터 살펴보도록 하죠. 사람들은 긍정적인 암시에 대해 긍정적인 반응을 보이는 경향이 있어요. 일기 예보에 대한 예를 들어봅시다.

기상캐스터는 두 가지 방법으로 일기를 예보해요. 첫 번째 방법은 "오늘은 부분적으로 흐리고 비가 올 확률이 50%입니다"라고 말하는 것이에요. 또 다른 일기 예보 방법은 날씨가 맑고 비가 올 확률이 50%라고 말하는 것이에요. 이 두 가지 일기 예보는 동일하지만 두 번째 경우보다 첫 번째 경우에 더 많은 사람들이 우산을 가져가요. 그 이유는 이 예보에 긍정적인 표현이 사용되었기 때문이에요.

Subject: *positive effect* 긍정적 효과

Detail: *weather forecast* 일기 예보

┌ *50% rain+partly rainy → umbrella*
│　비가 올 확률 50% + 맑음 → 우산
└ *50% rain+fairly sunny* 비가 올 확률 50% + 맑음

Speaking

The professor discusses positive effect. Explain how people show their interest in positive effect.

Possible response

The professor talks about the positive effect. According to the lecture, people respond to positive wording more eagerly. For example, people take their umbrellas when they hear the weather forecast saying, "Today is going to be partly cloudy with a 50% chance of rain" rather than saying, "fairly sunny with a 50% chance of rain."

4

Reading

Now read the passage about short-term memory. You will have 45 seconds to read the passage. Begin reading now.

Short-term Memory

Short-term memory is that part of memory which stores a limited amount of information for a few seconds. This can be contrasted to long-term memory, in which a seemingly unlimited amount of information is stored indefinitely. Short-term memory can be described as the capacity for holding in mind, in an active, highly available state, a small amount of information. The information held in short-term memory may be recently processed sensory input, items recently retrieved from long-term memory or the results of recent mental processing, although that is more generally related to the concept of working memory. In general, when new information comes in, old information goes out.

단기 기억은 몇 초간 제한된 양의 정보를 저장하는 기억의 일부이다. 이것은 무한한 양의 정보를 무기한으로 저장하는 장기 기억과 대조될 수 있다. 단기 기억은 활동적이고 언제든지 사용 가능한 상태의 정보를 머리 속에 소량으로 저장하는 능력으로 묘사될 수 있다. 단기 기억에 저장되는 정보는 최근에 감지된 감각적 정보, 장기 기억으로부터 최근에 기억된 것들 혹은 비록 작동 기억이라는 개념과 일반적으로 연관되지만 최근 정신적 과정의 결과일 수도 있다. 일반적으로 새로운 정보가 들어오면 옛 정보는 지워진다.

Listening

Now listen to part of a lecture in a psychology class. The professor talks about short-term memory.

P　We will discuss short-term memory in today's lecture. I remember one time when I went into a bookstore with a list of books that I was interested in. When I entered the bookstore, I remembered that I had left the list in my car, but was able to remember the name of the books on the list. When I was about to look for the books, I randomly saw my friend and talked about a few books with him. After a while, I couldn't remember any books on the list except the books my friend was talking about. This is because when we receive new information, old information fades away. This is called interference, which means the superposition of two or more waves resulting in a new wave pattern.

오늘 강의에서는 단기 기억에 대해 이야기 해 보겠어요. 제가 관심이 있던 책 목록을 가지고 서점에 갔던 것이 기억이 나네요. 서점에 들어 갔을 때, 그 목록을 차에 두고 왔다는 것이 기억 났지만 목록에 적혀 있던 책 제목을 기억할 수 있었어요. 그 책들을 찾아보려고 했을 때 우연 히 친구를 보았고 그와 함께 책 몇 권에 대해 이야기를 했어요. 잠시 후, 그 친구가 이야기한 책들을 제외하고는 목록에 있던 책을 한 권도 기억 할 수가 없었죠. 이것은 우리가 새로운 정보를 받게 되면 옛 정보가 지 워지기 때문이에요. 이것은 간섭이라고 불리는데, 두 개 혹은 그 이상의 파장이 서로 겹치게 되어 새로운 파장 양식을 생성하는 것을 의미해요.

Subject: *short-term memory* 단기 기억

Detail: *bookstore → met a friend → talked about books → couldn't remember the books on his list* 서점 → 친구를 만남 → 책에 대해 이야기를 했음 → 목록에 있던 책을 기억할 수 없었음

Speaking

The professor discusses short-term memory. Explain the example of short-term memory.

Possible response

The professor talks about short-term memory. According to this lecture, when new information comes in, old information easily fades away. The professor gives an example of his experience in a bookstore. To be specific, when he talked about a new list of books with his friend, who he met in the bookstore by accident, he forgot the old list of the books he had prepared before he entered the bookstore.

교수는 단기 기억에 대해 이야기 하고 있다. 이 강의에 따르면 새로운 정보 가 들어오면, 옛 정보는 쉽게 지워진다고 한다. 교수는 서점에서 자신이 겪었 던 경험을 예로 들고 있다. 구체적으로 말하면, 그가 서점에서 우연히 만난 친구와 새로운 책들에 관하여 이야기한 후, 그는 서점에 오기 전에 준비했던 책 목록에 대해 기억할 수 없었다.

Exercise

CD Possible Responses: Track 48~55

1

Reading

Now read the passage about mental script. You will have 45 seconds to read the passage. Begin reading now.

Mental Script

Humans are inclined to remember events that didn't happen if their happening is part of their mental script. Also, they find it hard to remember stories that they don't understand because they don't fit into their scripts. People develop their mental scripts through their experiences and own knowledge acquired in different situations. In any given situation, each person acts and responds differently. This is because each person has different expectations because of their mental scripts even though the environment is the same. In many ways, this situation will cause misunderstandings in communicating with each other.

인간은 만약 한 사건이 그들의 정신적 원본의 일부이면 발생하지 않은 사건이라도 그것을 기억하는 경향이 있다. 또한 이해하지 못한 이야기 는 그들의 원본에 포함되지 않았기 때문에 기억하는데 어려움을 겪는 다. 사람들은 경험과 다양한 상황에서 얻은 지식을 통해 자신만의 정신 적 원본을 개발한다. 어떠한 상황에서든 개개인은 각기 다른 행동과 반 응을 보인다. 이것은 각 개인은 같은 환경에서도 정신적 원본에 의해 다 른 기대를 하기 때문이다. 많은 경우 이러한 상황은 서로 의사소통을 할 때 오해를 낳게 된다.

Listening

Now listen to part of a lecture in a psychology class. The professor talks about mental script.

P   Until now, we have been studying mental script. Now, I'd like to talk about an incident that happened to me at a restaurant related to mental scripts. I was at a restaurant and a waiter asked me a question, "Do you know the name of this song?" I couldn't answer because I didn't expect to hear that question at a restaurant. I expected to be asked "What would you like to order?" instead. But to the waiter, this question was very normal because they usually ask those questions of their regular customers.

Another interesting phenomenon is that the old information which is not recently used is unconsciously remembered. For example, when you are singing a new song, and you unexpectedly remember an old song, they overlap. Another example is when you memorize a new address and can't remember the old address. It's as if the old address has been deleted and the new address has been inserted. It's weird how these things happen. This is the way the mental script works; the new address was inserted into the script of our brains. Everyone has a method of remembering and recalling which contributes to how fast we can recall certain memories of our lives.

지금까지 우리는 정신적 원본에 대해 공부해 왔습니다. 제가 식당에서

겪은 정신적 원본과 관련된 일에 대해 이야기 해 보겠습니다. 식당에 있을 때 웨이터가 저에게 "이 노래의 제목을 아시나요?"라고 질문했습니다. 저는 식당에서 이러한 질문을 받을 것이라고 예상하지 못했기 때문에 대답할 수가 없었습니다. 이 질문 대신 "무엇을 주문하시겠습니까?"라는 질문을 기대하고 있었던 것입니다. 그러나 그 웨이터에게는 이것이 일반적인 질문이었습니다. 왜냐하면 그들은 단골 손님들에게 종종 이러한 질문을 하곤 하니까요.

또 다른 흥미로운 현상은 최근에 사용하지 않았던 오래된 정보가 무의식 중에 기억된다는 것입니다. 예를 들면, 새로운 노래를 부를 때 무의식 중에 옛날 노래를 기억하게 되고 새로운 노래와 겹치게 되는 경우가 있죠. 또 다른 예로 새 주소를 외우면 옛날 주소가 기억 나지 않는 경우가 있습니다. 이것은 마치 옛 주소가 삭제되고 새 주소가 입력된 것이나 마찬가지입니다. 이런 일이 어떻게 일어나는지 정말 이상하죠. 정신적 원본은 바로 이러한 방식으로 작용합니다. 즉, 새로운 주소가 우리의 뇌의 원본에 입력되는 것이죠. 모든 사람은 기억하고 회상하는 방법을 가지고 있는데 이것은 우리의 삶에서 얼마나 빨리 특정 기억들을 회상할 수 있는지를 결정합니다.

Subject: *incident related to mental scripts*
정신적 원본과 관련된 사례

Detail: 1. *couldn't answer an unexpected question at a restaurant* 식당에서 예상하지 못한 질문에 대답할 수 없었다
2. *old information which is not recently used is unconsciously remembered*
최근에 사용하지 않았던 오래된 정보가 무의식 중에 기억된다

The professor talks about mental script. Explain how the professor explains mental script through her own personal experiences.

Possible response

The professor talks about the mental script and relates it to her personal story of what happened in a restaurant. According to the lecture, the professor has experienced her own mental script in some situations. For example, she explains her experience in the restaurant when a waiter asked her the name of a song. Her mental scrip didn't allow the professor to recall her memory because she didn't expect that kind of question at the restaurant. She also points out how the mental script works unconsciously when singing a song or memorizing a new address. The professor thinks that everyone has a script in their neural network and there is a special way of recalling a certain piece of information.

교수는 정신적 원본과 자신이 식당에서 개인적으로 경험한 일을 연관지어 설명하고 있다. 강의에 따르면, 교수는 특정 상황에서 정신적 원본을 경험했다. 예를 들어, 그는 웨이터가 노래의 제목을 물었던 식당에서의 경험에 대해 설명한다. 식당에서 들을 것이라고 예상하지 못했던 질문이기 때문에 그의 정신적 원본은 교수로 하여금 기억을 회상하지 못하도록 했다. 교수는 또한 노래를 부를 때나 새로운 주소를 외울 때 정신적 원본이 무의식적으로 작용하는 것에 대해 지적하고 있다. 교수는 모든 사람은 신경 조직망에 원본을 가지고 있으며 특정 정보를 회상하는 데에는 특별한 방법이 있다고 생각한다.

2

Now read the passage about animal coloration. You will have 45 seconds to read the passage. Begin reading now.

Animal Coloration

Animal coloration has evolved in many species that have been subjected to the pressures of predation as well as in predatory species. Such colors help predators and prey. Animals and insects use their coloration as a tool for their survival. In many cases, animals and insects use their coloration as a defense against predators or as a way to hunt for prey. They stealthily approach their prey by being camouflaged by their coloration. An animal's coloration can be a very useful tool.

동물의 채색은 피식자와 포식자와의 관계에서 많은 종(種)에 걸쳐 진화되어왔다. 이러한 채색은 포식자와 피식자를 돕는다. 동물과 곤충들은 생존을 위한 도구로서 그들의 채색을 이용한다. 많은 경우에 동물과 곤충들은 포식자로부터 자신을 보호하기 위해 또는 피식자를 포획하기 위해 채색을 사용한다. 그들은 채색으로 위장된 상태로 먹이감에게 몰래 접근한다. 동물의 채색은 매우 유용한 도구가 될 수 있다.

Now listen to part of a lecture in a biology class. The professor talks about animal coloration.

P So as we've discussed, animals can use their coloration for defense or as a tool to hunt. Now we're not talking about the changing of colors, but a creature utilizing its natural color schemes.

The zebra uses its stripes as a form of camouflage. It doesn't matter that the zebra's stripes are black and white and the lines of the grass are yellow, brown or green because the zebra's main predator, the lion, is colorblind. The pattern of the camouflage is much more important than its color when hiding from these predators. If a zebra is standing still in matching surroundings, a lion may overlook it completely. The dappling effect of the grass and the shadows also helps the "pajama-ed horse" to blend in.

The black panther uses its thick, dark coat of fur for stealth purposes. It is a largely nocturnal animal so it tends to do most of its hunting at night. Due to the fact that its coat is very dark or black, the black panther can easily sneak up on its prey and attack. The prey usually does not notice the black panther until it is too late.

그래서 우리가 토론했듯이 동물들은 방어를 하기 위해 혹은 사냥의 도구로서 그들의 채색을 사용할 수 있습니다. 이것은 색이 변화한다는 것이 아니라 생물이 자연적인 채색을 활용한다는 것을 뜻합니다.

얼룩말은 위장의 형태로 얼룩무늬를 사용합니다. 얼룩말의 무늬가 검은 색과 흰색으로 이루어졌고 풀은 노랗거나, 갈색이거나 녹색이라는 것은 크게 상관이 없습니다. 왜냐하면 얼룩말의 주요 포식자인 사자는 색맹이기 때문입니다. 포식자로부터 숨을 때는 채색보다 위장의 형태가 훨씬 더 중요합니다. 만약 얼룩말이 주위의 색과 어울리는 곳에서 움직이지 않고 서 있다면, 사자는 아마 그 얼룩말을 완전히 간과하게 될 것입니다. 풀과 그림자의 얼룩진 효과 또한 이 "파자마 무늬의 말"을 주변과 잘 조화되도록 도와줍니다.

흑표범은 눈에 잘 띄지 않게 하는 목적으로 그들의 두껍고 검은 털을 사용합니다. 이들은 주로 야행성 동물이기 때문에 대부분 밤에 사냥을 하는 경향이 있습니다. 털이 매우 짙은색이거나 검은색이기 때문에 그들은 쉽고 은밀하게 먹이에 접근해서 공격할 수 있습니다. 일반적으로 먹이들이 흑표범을 발견할 때는 이미 늦은 경우가 많습니다.

Subject: *camouflage in zebra, black panther*
얼룩막, 흑표범의 위장

Detail: *1. zebra → stripes as a form of camouflage, pattern of the camouflage is much more important than its color* 얼룩말은 위장의 형태로 얼룩무늬를 이용한다. 채색보다 위장의 형태가 더 중요하다

2. black panther → thick, dark coat of fur for camouflage 위장으로 두껍고 검은 털을 사용한다

Speaking

Explain how the two examples of the zebra and the black panther relate to animals using their coloration for survival.

Possible response

The professor talks about animal coloration. According to this lecture, the two examples of the zebra and the black panther relate to animals using their coloration for survival in the following ways. For example, the zebra uses its stripes as a defense against predators such as the lion. The pattern of the stripes confuses the lion and camouflages the zebra with the blades of grass. He also points out that the black panther uses its dark fur to sneak up on its prey. It hunts at night so the black panther approaches its prey almost unnoticeably. The professor thinks these are the ways that the zebra and the black panther use their coloration for survival.

교수는 동물의 채색에 대해 말하고 있다. 이 강의에 따르면 얼룩말과 흑표범의 두 가지 예는 다음과 같은 방법으로 생존하기 위해 채색을 이용하는 동물들과 관계가 있다. 예를 들어 얼룩말은 사자와 같은 포식자들로부터 스스로를 방어하기 위해 그들의 얼룩무늬를 사용한다. 얼룩무늬는 사자를 혼란스럽게 하고 풀과 조화되어 얼룩말을 위장해준다. 그는 또한 흑표범이 먹이에게 살금살금 접근하기 위해 짙은 털을 이용한다고 설명한다. 흑표범은 밤에 사냥을 하기 때문에 먹이가 눈치채지 못하게 접근하여 사냥한다. 교수는 이러

한 방법을 통해 얼룩말과 흑표범이 생존을 위해 채색을 이용한다고 생각한다.

3

Reading

Now read the passage about buyer's remorse. You will have 45 seconds to read the passage. Begin reading now.

Buyer's Remorse

Buyer's remorse is an emotional condition whereby a person feels remorse or regret after the purchase of an item. It is frequently associated with the purchase of high value items such as property and cars. In consumer psychology, buyer's remorse is taken into high consideration by companies. Thus, every company makes an effort to prevent buyer's remorse in various ways. To combat buyer's remorse, the salesman takes care to give full and complete information before buyers purchase their products.

구매자의 후회란 물건을 구입한 후 후회하는 느낌을 갖는 감정적 조건이다. 이것은 부동산이나 자동차와 같은 고가품을 구매하는 경우에 종종 발생한다. 소비자 심리학에서 구매자의 후회는 회사의 입장에서 중요한 것으로 여겨진다. 따라서 모든 회사는 다양한 방법을 사용하여 구매자의 후회를 방지하기 위해서 노력한다. 구매자의 후회를 방지하기 위해 영업 사원은 소비자들이 물건을 구매하기 전에 상세하고 완전한 정보를 주기 위해 노력한다.

Listening

Now listen to part of a lecture in a business class. The professor talks about buyer's remorse.

P The best example of buyer's remorse is when I bought my car recently. At the dealership I was talking to the salesman, and he said that at the time the car was the best choice that I could have made. So, I went ahead and purchased the car. Of course, I did some research before choosing the type of car I wanted. But when I actually drove the car out of the dealership, I had doubts as to whether or not I had made the best choice. I was confused because I was not sure if my purchase of that car was a good one.

Now, let me talk about how a salesman makes an effort to prevent buyer's remorse. The salesman reassured me that the car that I had purchased was the consumer's top pick and reminded me why I had chosen this car. That gave me reassurance about the car that I had purchased. The salesman also calls periodically to ask me how I am doing, and most importantly, if I have had any problems with my car. The way the salesman dealt with my buyer's remorse was with outstanding customer service; giving calls and sending thank you notes to the customer. This is exactly how I came to reassure myself that the car that I had purchased was the best choice for me.

구매자의 후회에 대한 가장 좋은 예는 제가 최근에 자동차를 샀을 때입니다. 자동차 대리점에서 판매 사원과 이야기를 할 당시 그는 저에게 그 자동차가 최선의 선택이라고 말했습니다. 그래서 저는 그 자동차를 구입했습니다. 물론 원하는 차종을 고르기 전에 많이 조사해 보았지만, 실제로 대리점에서 차를 몰고 나왔을 때는 최선의 선택을 한 것인지에 대해 확신할 수가 없었습니다. 자동차를 잘 구입한 것인지에 대한 확신이 없었기 때문에 저는 혼란스러웠습니다.

자, 그러면 판매원이 구매자의 후회를 방지하기 위해 어떻게 노력하는지에 대해 이야기 해 보겠습니다. 그 판매원은 제가 구입한 자동차가 소비자들이 가장 많이 선택한 차라고 안심시켜 주었고 왜 제가 이 차를 선택했었는지 다시 한번 상기시켜 주었습니다. 그것은 저에게 구입한 차에 대한 확신을 갖도록 해주었습니다. 그는 또한 정기적으로 전화해서 안부를 물으며, 차에 이상은 없는지 물어봅니다. 이 판매원은 전화를 하고 감사 카드를 보내는 등의 훌륭한 고객 서비스를 통해 저의 구매자의 후회를 처리했습니다. 바로 이것이 제가 구입한 자동차가 최선의 선택이었다는 확신을 갖게 해준 방법이었습니다.

Subject: *example of buyer's remorse* 구매자의 후회에 대한 예
Detail: *1. purchased a car but felt buyer's remorse*
자동차를 샀지만 구매자의 후회를 느꼈다
2. salesman dealt with buyer's remorse with outstanding customer service
판매원은 훌륭한 고객 서비스를 통해 구매자의 후회를 처리했다

Speaking

The professor discusses buyer's remorse. Explain how the professor explains it through her experience.

Possible response

The professor talks about her experience with buyer's remorse, which she felt at the car dealership. According to the lecture, the professor had recently purchased a car, and she felt buyer's remorse because she doubted whether the actual purchase was a good buy or not. However, the salesman gave her reassurance about her purchase by providing excellent customer service. The salesman called her regularly to ask her whether there were any problems with the car.

교수는 그가 차를 샀을 때 구매자의 후회를 느꼈던 경험에 대하여 말하고 있다. 강의에 따르면 교수는 최근에 차를 샀는데 정말 좋은 차를 산 것인지 아닌지에 대한 확신이 없었기 때문에 구매자의 후회를 느꼈다고 한다. 그러나 판매원은 훌륭한 고객 서비스를 통해 구입한 것에 대한 확신을 주었다. 판매원은 그녀에게 주기적으로 전화하여 자동차에 문제는 없는지 물어보았다.

4

Reading

Now read the passage about secondary ecological succession. You will have 45 seconds to read the passage. Begin reading now.

Secondary Ecological Succession

Nature has a way of fixing its own problems in a natural setting. Without human intervention, nature has the ability to solve problems. The important thing here is that trees coexist to give each plant a chance to grow and to allow enough time for a budding seed to grow into another tree. Nature fixes the problem where different types of trees both need sunlight and water. Nature only allows for one type of tree to grow or reproduce per season. The change in seasons kills one type of tree and then the other type of tree starts to grow.

자연은 그 환경 내에서 스스로 문제를 해결할 수 있는 방법을 가지고 있다. 사람들의 간섭이 없으면 자연은 문제를 해결할 수 있는 능력을 갖고 있다. 여기서 중요한 것은 나무들이 각 식물들이 자랄 수 있는 기회를 주고 씨앗이 나무로 자랄 수 있도록 충분한 시간을 주기 위해 공존한다는 것이다. 자연은 다른 종류의 나무들이 각기 햇빛과 물을 필요로 하는 경우의 문제를 스스로 해결한다. 자연은 한 계절에 한 종류의 나무만 자라도록 허락한다. 계절 변화로 인해 한 종류의 나무가 죽게 되며 또 다른 종류의 나무가 자라기 시작한다.

Listening

Now listen to part of a lecture in an ecology class. The professor talks about secondary ecological succession.

P Nature has an interesting way of helping plants grow. Today, I'd like to talk about the natural cycle that Mother Nature creates for different types of trees. For example, the raspberry tree is a typical plant that needs a lot of sunlight and water. If tall trees around the raspberry die, the raspberry tree grows up and this tree naturally coexists with other baby trees in the vicinity by sharing. After the other baby trees that are around the raspberry grow up and absorb most of the sunlight, which prevents enough sunlight from reaching the raspberry, the raspberry tree dies. But the seeds which are in the ground begin to sprout and to grow. In the meantime, the other trees around it begin to wither and allows the raspberry tree to absorb all the sunlight and grow up. Soon, the other trees begin to wither and die because of the raspberry tree. There is always a balance throughout nature and the living things in it. This balance is adjusted and fixed naturally by nature.

자연은 식물들이 자라도록 돕는 흥미로운 방법을 가지고 있어요. 오늘은 다양한 종류의 나무를 위해 자연이 만들어낸 순환 과정에 대해 이야기 해 보겠어요. 예를 들어 산딸기 나무는 많은 양의 햇빛과 물을 필요로 하는 전형적인 식물이에요. 만약 산딸기 주변의 큰 나무들이 죽으면 산딸기 나무가 자라게 되는데. 이 나무는 자연스럽게 주위의 작은 나무들과 공존하게 되어요. 산딸기 나무 주변에 있던 다른 작은 나무들이

자라서 대부분의 햇빛을 흡수하게 되면 산딸기를 위한 햇빛이 부족하게 되고, 산딸기 나무가 죽게 되죠. 하지만 땅 속에 있는 씨앗들이 싹트고 자라기 시작해요. 곧 주위의 다른 나무들이 시들게 되고 산딸기 나무가 모든 햇빛을 흡수하고 자랄 수 있게 되어요. 이처럼 자연과 생물들 사이에는 늘 균형이 존재해요. 그리고 이 균형은 자연에 의해서 조절되어요.

Subject: *natural cycle that helps plants to grow*
식물을 자라도록 돕는 자연적 순환 과정

Detail: *1. tall trees die → raspberry trees grow → baby trees grow → raspberry trees die → raspberry seed grows → kills the other trees*
큰 나무가 죽는다 → 산딸기 나무가 자란다 → 작은 나무들이 자란다 → 산딸기 나무가 죽는다 → 산딸기 씨앗이 자란다 → 다른 나무들이 죽는다
2. balance is adjusted and fixed naturally
균형은 자연적으로 조절된다

Speaking

The professor discusses secondary ecological succession. Explain how the raspberry tree coexists in nature with other trees.

Possible response

The professor talks about the natural cycle that Mother Nature maintains for the different types of trees. The professor states that the balance is always fixed naturally by nature. For example, when the tall trees which block sunlight around the raspberry tree which block sunlight die, the raspberry tree grows up and also the baby trees around it coexist. Then, other trees become big and tall, and they tend to overshadow the raspberry tree and end up killing the raspberry because it needs a lot of sunlight. Then the raspberry seeds in the ground start to grow and this cycle repeats. In this way, nature always recovers by itself.

교수는 자연이 다른 종류의 나무들을 위해 유지하는 자연적인 순환 과정에 대해 이야기하고 있다. 교수는 자연으로 인해 균형이 언제나 유지된다고 언급한다. 예를 들어 산딸기 나무 주위에서 햇빛을 차단하던 큰 나무가 죽으면 산딸기 나무가 자라게 되고 그 주변에 있던 작은 나무들과 공존하게 된다. 그 후, 다른 나무들이 키가 자라면 산딸기 나무에 그림자를 드리우게 되는데, 햇빛을 많이 필요로 하는 산딸기는 결국 죽게 된다. 그러면 땅 속에 있던 산딸기 씨앗이 자라기 시작하고 이와 같은 과정이 반복된다. 이처럼 자연은 항상 스스로 재생한다.

5
Reading

Now read the passage about instinctive behavior of animals. You will have 45 seconds to read the passage. Begin reading now.

Instinctive Behavior

Animals have specific instinctive behavior when around their habitation. Animals act instinctively to warn or send different messages to their fellow animals that an intruder is near. But in some animals, instinctive behavior is often modified by the outside world. When they feel they are in danger they behave wildly, but when they feel they are not threatened, they behave gently. These instinctive behaviors are indigenous in the area that the animals live. These animals are very territorial and guard their territory from any friend or foe.

동물들은 그들이 사는 곳 주변에서 특정한 본능적 행동을 한다. 동물들은 그들의 동족들에게 주위에 침입자가 있다고 경고하거나 다른 메시지를 전하기 위하여 본능적으로 행동한다. 그러나 일부 동물의 경우, 본능적 행동은 종종 외부 세계로 인해 수정된다. 그들이 위험을 느낄 때는 거칠게 행동하지만 안전하다고 느끼면 얌전하게 행동한다. 이와 같은 본능적인 행동들은 동물들이 사는 지역에 기인한다. 이 동물들은 매우 영역적이고 친구나 적으로부터 그들의 영역을 지킨다.

Listening

Now listen to part of a lecture in a biology class. The professor talks about instinctive behavior of animals.

P   Now let me talk about instinctive behavior in specific animals. I'd like to take an example of the prairie dog. This animal is very territorial by nature and has an innate behavior that warns other prairie dogs of any intruder. Prairie dogs bark loudly when an intruder is near and jumps up and down to warn others. If they feel threatened, they will jump and bark. Their behavior is instinctive because out of reflex they get excited, but actually, it gets the other animals' attention.

But the prairie dogs do not always behave instinctively. Innate behavior is often modified by learning from the outside world. For example, when prairie dogs first see a person approaching them, they bark and jump to let others know there is a person. But they calm down when the person does not become a threat to them and they feel safe. Then the person can walk around the prairie dog's territory. There is no learned conditioning for prairie dogs; every time the same person comes they will act and alert others. They will not remember the face of the person, but by repeating the same activities, innate behavior is changed and they behave very gently once they know the person doesn't threaten them. That means the prairie dogs know who friends and enemies are.

자, 그러면 특정 동물의 본능적 행동에 대해 이야기 해 보겠습니다. 프레리도그의 예를 들어 보겠습니다. 이 동물은 본능적으로 매우 영역적이고 침입자가 있는 경우 다른 개들을 경고하는 본능적 행동을 합니다. 프레리도그는 침입자가 가까이 있으면 크게 짖고 위 아래로 뛰면서 동족들에게 경고를 보냅니다. 만약 그들이 위협당하고 있다고 느끼면 그들은 뛰고 짖을 것입니다. 이들의 행동은 본능적입니다. 왜냐하면 이들은 반사적으로 흥분을 한 것이지만 이것이 실제로 다른 프레리도그들의 주목을 끌기 때문입니다.

그러나 프레리도그들이 항상 이처럼 본능적으로 행동하는 것은 아닙니다. 본능적인 행동은 종종 외부 세계의 학습으로 인해 수정됩니다. 예를 들어 프레리도그는 사람이 다가오는 것을 처음 보면 다른 개들에게 알리기 위해 짖고 뜁니다. 그러나 사람이 그들을 위협하지 않는다는 것을 알게 되고 안전하다고 느끼는 순간 순해집니다. 그러면 사람은 그 개의 영역 주위를 걸어 다닐 수 있습니다. 프레리도그에게 학습된 조건화는 없습니다. 같은 사람이 올 때마다 그들은 다른 동물을 경고하는 행동을 할 것입니다. 그들은 그 사람의 얼굴을 기억하지 못하지만, 같은 행동을 반복함으로써 본능적 행동은 변화되고 사람들이 그들을 위협하지 않는다는 것을 알게 되면 그들은 매우 얌전하게 행동합니다. 그것은 프레리도그들이 누가 친구이고 누가 적인지 안다는 것을 의미합니다.

Subject: *instinctive behavior in prairie dogs*
프레리도그들의 본능적 행동

Detail: *1. bark loudly when there is an intruder, warns others* 침입자가 있으면 크게 짖는다, 다른 개들을 경고한다
2. innate behavior is often modified by learning 본능적 행동은 종종 학습으로 인해 수정된다

Speaking

The professor talks about the instinctive behavior of animals. Explain how prairie dogs behave.

Possible response

The professor talks about instinctive behavior in prairie dogs. According to this lecture, animals behave instinctively to protect themselves. For example, prairie dogs have an instinctive behavior when an intruder is near their territory. Because prairie dogs are very territorial, they will jump up and down to warn other prairie dogs of the intruder. She also points out that instinctive behavior is modified by learning from the outside world. Prairie dogs do not remember the faces of people. So, whenever the same person shows up, they get excited as if it was the first time. After prairie dogs get used to the intruder and they know the person doesn't threaten them, they calm down.

교수는 프레리도그의 본능적 행동에 대해 이야기하고 있다. 이 강의에 따르면, 동물들은 스스로를 보호하기 위해 본능적으로 행동한다. 예를 들어 프레리도그는 침입자가 그들의 영역 근처에 있을 때 취하는 본능적 행동이 있다. 그들은 매우 영역적인 동물이기 때문에 침입자가 왔다는 것을 다른 프레리도그들에게 경고하기 위해 위 아래로 뛸 것이다. 그는 또한 본능적인 행동이 외부 세계의 학습으로 인해 수정된다는 것에 대해 설명한다. 프레리도그는 사람들의 얼굴을 기억하지 못한다. 따라서 같은 사람이 나타날 때마다 마치 처음 본 것처럼 흥분한다. 침입자에 익숙해지고 그가 위협하지 않는다는 것

을 알게 되면 그들은 얌전해진다.

6

Reading

Now read the passage about assumption. You will have 45 seconds to read the passage. Begin reading now.

Assumption

An assumption is something taken for granted or accepted as the truth without proof. Assumptions are made constantly when most individuals believe that other people act upon their assumptions. Ordinary people generally believe that most others act upon their own assumptions.

가설이란 증거 없이 당연한 사실처럼 받아들여지는 것을 의미한다. 가설은 타인이 자신의 가정에 근거하여 행동할 것이라고 사람들이 믿을 때 끊임없이 형성된다. 보통 사람들은 대부분의 사람들이 자신이 가정하는 대로 행동할 것이라고 믿는다.

Listening

Now listen to part of a lecture in a psychology class. The professor talks about assumption.

P Today, I'd like to introduce one exciting experiment to prove the theory that an assumption is not always right. This theory is held by a psychologist. The psychologist has done an experiment on a group. This experiment asked the group a question. The experiment asked the group, "Would you shout in a library if you had to?" The results were astounding — half of the group said "yes" and the other half said "no."

In the second trial, the group which said "yes" were asked a different question. They were asked, "If you asked other people the same question about shouting in a library, what would they say?" The assumption was that other people would do as they would do, in other words, they would say yes, but the result was totally different from what they had assumed. The results were that only half of the new group said yes and the other half did not. This result was completely different from the original group that had expected all of them to say yes. It is a common belief that people generalize and assume that their actions or decisions are right and that others will probably act the same way as themselves. But as you see from this experiment, it was proven that assumptions are not always correct.

오늘은 가설이 늘 옳은 것은 아니라는 가설을 증명하기 위한 흥미로운 실험을 소개하고자 해요. 이 가설은 한 심리학자가 세운 것인데, 그

는 한 그룹을 대상으로 실험을 했어요. 이 실험은 그룹에게 한 가지 질문을 했죠. "만약 해야 한다면 도서관에서 소리를 지를 것입니까?"라는 질문이었어요. 결과는 놀라웠어요. 절반은 "예", 나머지 절반은 "아니오"라고 했죠.

두 번째 시도로 "예"라고 대답한 사람들에게 다른 질문을 했어요. "다른 사람들에게 도서관에서 소리를 치는 것에 대한 같은 질문을 하면, 어떻게 대답할 것 같습니까?"라는 질문이었어요. 여기서 가정했던 것은 다른 사람들도 그들과 똑같이 소리를 지른다는 것이었어요. 즉 "예"라고 대답할 것을 가정했던 것이죠. 하지만 결과는 그들이 가정했던 것과는 완전히 달랐어요. 결과에 따르면 새로운 그룹의 절반만이 "예"라고 대답했고, 나머지 절반은 그렇게 대답하지 않았어요. 이 결과는 모든 사람들이 "예"라고 대답할 것이라고 예측했던 기존 그룹과는 완전히 달랐어요. 사람들이 일반화하고 그들의 행동이나 결정이 옳고 다른 사람들도 그들처럼 행동할 것이라는 것은 일반적인 사실이에요. 하지만 이 실험에서 볼 수 있듯이 가정이 늘 맞는 것은 아니라는 것이 증명되었어요.

Subject: *experiment to prove the theory that an assumption is not always right*
가설이 늘 옳은 것은 아니라는 가설을 증명하기 위한 실험

Detail: *1. Would you shout in a library if you had to? → 50% yes, 50% no* 만약 해야 한다면 도서관에서 소리를 지를 것입니까? → 50% 예, 50% 아니오

2. 'yes' group: If you asked other people the same question about shouting in a library, what would they say? → expected 100% yes, but result was 50% yes, 50% no "예"라고 대답한 그룹: 다른 사람들에게 도서관에서 소리를 치는 것에 대한 같은 질문을 하면, 어떻게 대답할 것 같습니까? → 100% 예를 예상했지만, 결과는 50% 예, 50% 아니오

Speaking

The professor talks about assumption. Explain how the experiment explains people's assumption.

Possible response

The professor talks about an experiment to analyze assumptions. According to this lecture, a psychologist did an experiment on a group. The study asked two questions of the group. The first question was if they would shout in a library if they had to. The results showed that half of the group said "yes" and the other half said "no." The second question was asked to the people who had answered "yes" to the first question. They were asked if they thought other people would shout in a library if they had to. They assumed that the new group would answer the same way they did, but in actuality, only half of the new group answered that way. The other half did not follow their assumptions. So, the professor thinks that this experiment proved that assumptions are not always correct.

교수는 가정에 대해 분석하기 위한 실험에 대해 이야기한다. 이 강의에 따르

면, 한 심리학자가 한 그룹을 대상으로 실험을 했다. 그 연구에서는 그룹에게 두 가지의 질문을 했다. 첫 번째 질문은 만약 해야 한다면 도서관에서 소리를 지를 것인가였다. 그 결과 절반은 "그렇다", 나머지 절반은 "아니다"라고 대답했다. 두 번째 질문은 첫 번째 질문에 "그렇다"라고 대답한 사람들을 대상으로 했다. 그들은 다른 사람들 역시 필요한 경우, 도서관에서 소리를 칠 것이라고 생각하는가였다. 그들은 새 그룹 역시 그들과 똑같이 대답할 것이라고 가정했지만 실제로는 절반만이 그렇게 대답을 했고, 나머지는 그들의 가정을 따르지 않았다. 따라서 교수는 이 실험이 가정이 늘 옳은 것은 아니라는 것을 증명했다고 생각한다.

7

Reading

Now read the passage about cognitive dissonance. You will have 45 seconds to read the passage. Begin reading now.

Cognitive Dissonance

In psychology, cognitive dissonance is the perception of incompatibility between two cognitions. A cognition is any element of knowledge, including attitude, emotion, belief, or behavior. People don't want to change their behavior when they are acting according to their beliefs. To reduce the amount of dissonance between thoughts, people have the consciousness to acquire or invent new thoughts or beliefs, or to modify their existing beliefs.

심리학에서 인지 부조화란 두 가지의 인지가 서로 양립할 수 없다는 것을 뜻한다. 인지는 행동, 감정, 믿음, 행위를 포함하는 지식의 요소이다. 사람들은 자신의 믿음에 따라 행동할 때 스스로의 태도를 바꾸는 것을 원하지 않는다. 두 생각 사이의 부조화를 줄이기 위해, 사람들은 새로운 생각과 믿음을 획득하거나 현재 그들의 믿음을 수정하려는 자각을 가지고 있다.

Listening

Now listen to part of a lecture in a psychology class. The professor talks about cognitive dissonance.

P   We have been discussing cognitive dissonance. Now, through this lecture, I'd like introduce an example of cognitive dissonance from my experience in high school and think about how to reduce cognitive dissonance.

I remember having a lot of conflict in thoughts, especially during high school. We all go through a lot of change at this point in our lifetime. I had been addicted to video games, which didn't help me with my studies at all during high school. Although I had always thought I had to study chemistry, I couldn't put that into practice. By my senior year, many people became worried about graduation, and I personally got worried because I felt that I had to do well in all subjects in high school. With chemistry being my worst subject, I became even more worried. Then one day, I changed my mind. I had thrown out my worries about chemistry and decided to study only the subjects that were related to sociology because I wanted to be a sociologist in the future.

The change helped me to concentrate only on what was helpful to my career and that helped me change my way of thinking. Conflict due to cognitive dissonance creates a driving force which allows the person to be better and more well off than before. It allows the mind to reach new levels of understanding of oneself and the problem at hand.

우리는 인지 부조화에 대해 이야기하고 있습니다. 이 강의를 통해서 저는 고등학교 때 겪었던 인지 부조화의 예를 소개하고 어떻게 인지 부조화를 줄일 수 있는지에 대해 생각해 보았으면 합니다.

저는 특히 고등학교에 다닐 때 많은 생각으로 혼란스러웠던 것이 기억이 납니다. 우리는 모두 이 시기에 인생에 있어서 많은 변화를 겪지요. 저는 당시 비디오 게임에 중독이 되어 있었고, 이것은 전혀 학업에 도움이 되지 않았습니다. 늘 화학을 공부해야겠다고 생각했지만 그것을 실천하지는 못했습니다. 고등하고 3학년 때는 많은 학생들이 졸업에 대해 걱정을 하는데, 저는 개인적으로 고등학교 때 모든 과목을 잘 해야 한다고 느꼈기 때문에 걱정을 했습니다. 가장 못하는 과목이 화학이었기 때문에 더욱 걱정이 많아졌죠. 그러던 어느 날, 저는 생각을 바꾸었습니다. 화학에 대한 걱정을 던져 버리고 사회학과 관련된 과목만 열심히 공부하기로 했습니다. 왜냐하면 저는 미래에 사회학자가 되고 싶었으니까요.

그 변화는 내 직업에 도움이 될 수 있는 것에만 집중하도록 도와주었고, 사고방식을 바꾸도록 도와주었습니다. 인지 부조화로 인한 갈등은 상황을 보다 개선시켜주는 원동력을 창조합니다. 이것은 자기 자신과 현재 직면한 문제들에 대한 이해의 폭을 넓혀줍니다.

Subject: *example of cognitive dissonance, how to reduce cognitive dissonance*
인지 부조화에 대한 예, 인지 부조화를 줄이는 방법

Detail: *1. worried about chemistry* 화학에 대해 걱정했다
2. decided to study only the subjects related to sociology → wanted to be a sociologist in the future 사회학 관련 과목만 공부하기로 결심했다 → 미래에 사회학자가 되고 싶었다

The professor talks about cognitive dissonance. Explain how the professor explains it through her personal experience.

Possible response

The professor talks about cognitive dissonance, which is the incompatibility of two thoughts. The professor explains her experience with cognitive dissonance

during high school. She states that she had a very simple life during high school and that she was completely absorbed in video games. Her main worry was chemistry class, but she decided to throw away her worries about chemistry and to embark on what she wanted to do, which was sociology. Sociology was related to her future career because she wanted to be a sociologist. The change helped her to focus on her studies as well as change her way of thinking. So, the professor thinks that her cognitive dissonance changed her way of thinking and helped her to better understand herself.

교수는 두 가지의 생각이 양립할 수 없다는 것을 뜻하는 인지 부조화에 대해서 말하고 있다. 교수는 고등학교 시절에 인지 부조화를 겪었던 경험에 대해 설명한다. 그녀는 고등학교 때 매우 단순한 생활을 했고 비디오 게임에 완전히 빠져서 지냈다고 말한다. 그녀가 주로 걱정했던 것은 화학이었지만 화학에 대한 걱정을 버리고 하고 싶었던 것, 즉 사회학을 공부하기 시작했다. 그녀는 사회학자가 되고 싶었기 때문에 사회학은 그녀의 미래의 직업과 연관이 있었다. 그 변화는 그녀를 공부에 집중할 수 있도록 도와주었을 뿐만 아니라 그녀의 사고 방식을 변화시켰다. 따라서 교수는 인지 부조화가 자신의 사고 방식을 변화시키고 스스로를 보다 잘 이해하도록 도와주었다고 생각한다.

8

Now read the passage about role conflict. You will have 45 seconds to read the passage. Begin reading now.

Role Conflict

Role conflict is a conflict among the roles corresponding to two or more statuses. Today, people juggle many responsibilities created by their various statuses and roles in an attempt to create a more peaceful environment. But people often fail to carry out their various roles, so they cannot satisfy everyone who is involved in the situation. The main reason for this is that while they are choosing their roles, they cannot carry out their other roles. This happens because as time goes by, modern society gets more complicated. This problem is getting more serious in society among people both inside and outside of the home.

역할 갈등이란 두 개 혹은 그 이상의 신분을 대응하는 역할 사이의 갈등이다. 오늘날 사람들은 보다 평화로운 환경을 조성하기 위해서 그들의 다양한 신분과 역할로 인해 생긴 책임을 부담하고 있다. 그러나 사람들은 종종 그들의 다양한 역할을 수행하는 것을 실패하기 때문에 그 상황에 연관된 모든 사람들을 만족시킬 수는 없다. 이것의 주요한 이유는 그들이 그들의 역할을 선택하는 동안 다른 역할을 수행할 수 없기 때문이다. 시간이 지날수록 현대 사회가 점점 복잡해지기 때문에 이러한 일이 발생한다. 이 문제는 오늘날 사회에서 가정 안팎으로 점점 더 심각해지고 있다.

Now listen to part of a lecture in a psychology class. The professor talks about role conflict.

P   One's role in society is quite an underestimated factor as to how a person is perceived and received. People have a way of stereotyping people according to how they are viewed. This creates a conflict between how people are perceived and the roles that they fill. I will describe this through examples.

A full-time student attends a university. He also works full-time to pay for his classes. Now in the following scenario, his role is in conflict. One of his professors asked him to come to his class at 3 p.m. But the problem is, his boss at his job has asked him to come to work by 3 p.m. as well. Now if he chooses to go to class rather than his job, then he will be perceived as a bad employee, but a good student. If he chooses to go to his job and skip his class, he will be perceived as a good employee, but a bad student. As I mentioned above, the student's role in either scenario will be positive and negative.

Another example is that of a professor whose role is in conflict in the following scenario. He teaches at a nearby university, and he is able to spend a lot of time with his family. One day, a university which is 30 miles away from his house offers him a teaching position with excellent benefits. If he stays at his current university, he will be able to spend more time with his family, but will not receive the same type of benefits the new university provides.

사회에서의 한 사람의 역할은 그가 어떻게 인지되고 받아들여지느냐는 부분에 있어 간과되고 있는 요인입니다. 사람들은 타인을 어떻게 인지하느냐에 따라 편견을 갖는 경향이 있습니다. 이것은 사람들이 어떻게 인지되고, 어떠한 역할을 수행하는지 사이에 갈등을 야기합니다. 이것에 대해 예를 들어보겠습니다.

대학에 다니는 한 학생이 있습니다. 그는 학비를 벌기 위해 정규직으로 일을 하고 있습니다. 자, 이제 다음과 같은 상황에서 그는 역할 갈등을 겪게 됩니다. 그의 교수 한 명이 3시까지 오라고 했습니다. 그러나 문제는 그의 상사 또한 3시까지 오라고 했다는 것입니다. 만약 그가 학교에 가면 그는 나쁜 사원으로 인지될 것이지만 좋은 학생이 될 것입니다. 만약 그가 수업에 가지 않고 일을 하러 간다면 그는 좋은 사원으로 인지되겠지만 나쁜 학생으로 간주될 것입니다. 위에서 언급했듯이 양쪽 상황에서 모두 이 학생은 긍정적, 부정적으로 인지됩니다.

또 다른 예는 다음과 같은 상황에서 역할 갈등을 겪고 있는 교수입니다. 그는 집 근처에 있는 대학에서 강의를 하고 있어서 가족과 함께 많은 시간을 보낼 수 있습니다. 어느날, 그의 집으로부터 30 마일 떨어진 어느 대학에서 더 나은 조건을 제시했습니다. 만약 그가 현재 가르치고 있는 대학에 머물러 있으면 그의 가족과 함께 더 많은 시간을 보낼 수 있지만, 새로운 대학에서 제공하는 혜택을 받지 못할 것입니다.

Subject: *role conflict* 역할 갈등

Detail: *1. full-time student: school vs. work*
대학생: 학교 vs. 직장

2. professor: current university vs. new university 교수: 현재 대학 vs. 새로운 대학

The professor talks about role conflict. Explain how role conflict is illustrated by using the given examples.

Possible response

The professor talks about role conflict. The professor explains about role conflict by using two examples. In the first example, a student who also has a full-time job experiences role conflict when he is required to come by 3 o'clock by both his professor and his boss. The conflict of roles is between his role as a student and his role as an employee. In the second example, a professor is in conflict between taking a job further from his house for more money or staying close to home to spend time with his family. The conflict of roles is between being a family man and concentrating on his career. The professor explains the concept of role conflict by using these examples.

교수는 역할 갈등에 대해 이야기하고 있다. 교수는 두 가지의 예를 들어 역할 갈등에 대해 설명한다. 첫 번째 예시에서 정규직으로 일을 하고 있는 한 학생은 교수와 상사 양쪽에서 3시까지 오라는 요구를 받고 역할 갈등을 겪는다. 이 역할 갈등은 학생과 고용인으로서의 그의 역할 간에 발생한다. 두 번째 예시에서 한 교수는 더 많은 돈을 위해 집에서 멀리 떨어진 곳에서 일할 것인가 아니면 그의 가족과 함께 시간을 보내기 위해 집 가까이에 머물 것인가를 갈등하고 있다. 이 역할 갈등은 가족의 일원으로 충실할 것인지 직업에 열중할 것인지 간에 발생한다. 교수는 이러한 예시를 사용하여 역할 갈등에 대해 설명하고 있다.

TASK 5 Problem and Solution

□ Sample

CD Possible Response: Track 56

Listening

Now listen to a conversation between two students.

M Hey, Linda! How's it going?

W Hi, Mike. I'm fine, I guess, but my schoolwork is really stressing me out.

M Yeah? What's the matter?

W Well, I have to write a paper, prepare for two exams, and finish my math homework. It's just too much to handle. One minute I'm trying to concentrate on studying for one of my exams, and the next minute I'm wondering when I can finish that math homework.

M Wow, sounds like you have much more work than you can handle. Look, have you met some of your professors... I mean, have you tried to explain your situation? You might be able to get an extension on your paper or your math homework...

W But I'm worried whether I'll be able to get the same grade as other students if I get an extension.

M Well, another thing that you might do is to make a schedule for yourself. That's what I do when I feel overwhelmed.

W What do you mean?

M Well, I mean, try to make your own schedule for the next few days on how much time to spend on each assignment...

W Oh! That's a good idea. I'll try it.

남 안녕, Linda. 어떻게 지내?

여 안녕, Mike. 난 잘 지내. 그런데 학교 공부 때문에 정말 스트레스 받아.

남 그래? 무슨 일인데?

여 음, 보고서도 써야 하고 시험도 두 개나 있고 수학 숙제도 끝내야 해. 다 하기에 너무 많아. 시험 공부에 집중하려고 하다가도 언제 수학 숙제를 끝낼 수 있을지 고민하게 돼.

남 와, 감당할 수 있는 것보다 해야 할 일이 많은 것 같구나. 교수님들은 만나봤어? 그러니까, 네 상황을 설명하려고 시도해 봤어? 보고서나 수학 숙제를 연기할 수 있을지도 몰라.

여 그렇지만 연기되면 다른 학생들과 같은 점수를 받을 수 있을지 걱정이야.

남 음, 다른 방법은 너만의 계획표를 만들어 보는 거야. 할 일이 너무 많을 때 내가 하는 방법이지.

여 무슨 말이야?

남 음, 그러니까 다음 며칠 동안에 각 과제들을 하는데 얼마나 시간을 할당할지 스스로의 계획을 세워보라는 말이야.

여 와! 그거 좋은 생각이다. 그렇게 해볼게.

Speaking

The students discuss two possible solutions to the woman's problem. Describe the problem. Then state which of the two solutions you prefer and explain why.

Possible response

The woman's problem is that she can't handle her school workload. She has to write her term paper, prepare for two exams, and finish her math homework. The man suggests meeting her professors to get an extension on her term paper. But the problem is that even though her professors might be willing to give her an extension, they might somehow penalize her for it by grading her assignments more severely. The other idea like preparing a schedule seems better because she can carry out her tasks one at a time and if she learns how to organize a schedule now, it will help her throughout her academic career. So, I support her making a schedule that she can handle.

여자의 문제는 학교 공부가 너무 많아서 감당할 수가 없다는 것이다. 그녀는 보고서를 써야 하고, 두 개의 시험을 준비해야 하며 수학 숙제를 끝내야 한다. 남자는 그녀에게 보고서 기한을 연장하기 위해 교수님들을 만나보라고 권유한다. 그러나 문제는 만약 교수들이 기한을 연장해 준다고 하더라도 과제 점수를 더 엄격하게 줌으로써 약간의 불이익을 당할 수 있다는 것이다. 계획표를 준비한다는 다른 의견이 더 나은 것 같다. 한번에 하나씩 일을 처리할 수 있고 지금 일정을 조절하는 것을 배우면 학업 과정에 도움이 될 것이기 때문이다. 그래서 나는 그녀가 잘 지킬 수 있는 계획을 세우는 것을 더 지지한다.

Mini Test

CD Possible Responses: Track 58

1

Listening

Now listen to a conversation between two students.

W Hey! How's it going, John?

M Everything's going well, except one thing.

W Yeah? You want to tell me what's bothering you?

M Well, I have a group project to finish tonight, but it's my father's birthday today and we are having a party at my cousin's house. I don't know what to do.

W Why don't you talk to the members in the project? Maybe they will understand your situation.

M But I don't think it is fair for them to have to finish the project by themselves.

W Well, then, you could go to the party a little bit earlier and spend time with your family and tell your parents you have a project to finish and leave earlier. I'm sure your family would understand your situation.

M That could be a solution. Thank you for your advice.

W You're welcome.

여 안녕, 어떻게 지내, John?

남 한 가지만 빼고는 잘 지내고 있어.

여 그래? 무엇 때문에 그러는지 말해줄래?

남 그룹 프로젝트를 오늘밤에 끝내야 하는데, 오늘이 아버지 생신이라서 사촌 집에서 파티를 하기로 했어. 어떻게 해야 할지 모르겠어.

여 프로젝트를 함께 하는 사람들에게 이야기 해 보지 그래? 네 상황을 이해해 줄지도 몰라.

남 하지만 그들끼리 프로젝트를 끝내야 하는 건 공평한 것 같지 않아.

여 음, 그러면 파티에 조금 일찍 가서 가족들과 시간을 보내고 프로젝트를 끝내야 한다고 부모님께 말씀 드리고 일찍 나오는 건 어때? 가족들이라면 네 상황을 분명 이해해 줄 거야.

남 그렇게 하면 되겠다. 조언해줘서 고마워.

여 천만에.

Problem: *has a group project to finish, has to go to a birthday party*
끝내야 할 그룹 프로젝트가 있다, 생일파티에 가야 한다

Solution 1: *talk to the members in the project*
프로젝트 그룹 멤버들에게 말해라

Response → *not fair* 공평하지 않다

Solution 2: *leave father's birthday party earlier*
아버지의 생신 파티에서 일찍 출발해라

Response → *could be a solution* 해결책이 될 수 있다

Speaking

The students discuss two possible solutions to the man's problem. Describe the problem. Then state which of the two solutions you prefer and explain why.

Possible response

The man's problem is that he has a group project to finish, but he can't join the group because he has to attend his father's birthday party. The woman first suggests that he explain his situation to the members in the group, but he thinks it's not fair to make them work on the project by themselves. I think the other idea, going to his father's birthday party early and leaving early is better because he can then attend the party as well as join the group to prepare for the project. If he can work on the project with them, he will not feel guilty. Also, he will feel more satisfied if he contributes to the group project. So, I support going to the party early and leaving early to do his work with the other members in the group.

남자의 문제는 끝내야 할 프로젝트가 있는데 아버지의 생신 파티에 가야 하기 때문에 참여할 수 없다는 것이다. 여자는 먼저 조원들에게 상황을 설명하라고 제안하지만 남자는 그들에게 프로젝트를 하라고 하는 것은 공평하지 않다고 생각한다. 나는 생일 파티에 일찍 가서 조금 일찍 출발하라는 다른 제안이 더 좋다고 생각한다. 왜냐하면 그렇게 하면 파티에도 갈 수 있고 그룹에 참여해서 프로젝트를 준비할 수 있기 때문이다. 함께 일을 할 수 있으면 그는 죄책감을 느끼지 않을 것이다. 또한 그룹 프로젝트에 참여하면 더욱 만족감을 느낄 것이다. 따라서 나는 조원들과 함께 프로젝트를 하기 위해 파티에 일찍 가서 빨리 되돌아오는 것을 지지한다.

2

Listening

Now listen to a conversation between two students.

W Excuse me. Could you help me?

M Sure. How can I help you?

W To tell the truth, I'm a freshman and I left my class schedule in the dormitory, so I don't know where my classroom is.

M In that case, why don't you go to the student center and make a copy of your schedule? It won't take too long.

W I know, but my first class is psychology and I don't want to be late because it's one of my favorite classes.

M Then, actually, there are only three lecture rooms in the building, so one of the rooms would be your classroom. Try those three rooms one by one. It would be easy to get to because there is an elevator.

W Well, the problem is I have never met the professor before.

M Oh, then you might have some trouble finding the right classroom.

여 실례합니다. 좀 도와 주시겠어요?

남 물론입니다. 무엇을 도와드릴까요?

여 실은 저는 신입생인데 수업 스케줄을 기숙사에 놓고 와서 제 강의실이 어딘지 잘 모르겠어요.

남 그렇다면 학생 회관에 가서 스케줄을 복사하는 게 어떠세요? 오래 걸리지는 않을 거예요.

여 네, 그건 알지만 첫 수업이 심리학인데 제가 제일 좋아하는 수업 중 하나라서 지각하고 싶지 않아요.

남 그렇다면 사실 이 건물에는 강의실이 3개 밖에 없으니까 그 중 하나가 당신의 강의실일 거예요. 강의실 3개를 하나씩 확인해 보세요. 엘리베이터가 있으니까 쉽게 가실 수 있을 거예요.

여 하지만 문제는 아직 교수님을 만나본 적이 없거든요.

남 아, 그렇다면 맞는 교실을 찾기가 좀 힘들겠네요.

Problem: *left class schedule in the dormitory → don't
know where the classroom is* 강의 계획서를 기숙사
에 놓고 와서 강의실이 어디인지 잘 모른다

Solution 1: *go to the student center and copy your
schedule* 학생 회관에 가서 수업 스케줄을 복사해라

Response → *don't want to be late for the class*
수업에 지각하길 원하지 않는다

Solution 2: *try the three classrooms one by one*
강의실 3개를 하나씩 확인해라

Response → *have never met the professor before*
교수님을 만나본 적이 없다

Speaking

The students discuss two possible solutions to the
woman's problem. Describe the problem. Then state
which of the two solutions you prefer and explain
why.

Possible response

The woman's problem is that she can't find her
classroom because she left her class schedule in her
dorm room. The man first suggests that she make a
copy of her schedule in the student center. But she
thinks that she might be late for her class because
it will take some time. I think that the other idea,
checking all three classrooms one by one, is a better
choice. Even if she tries going into every room, it
shouldn't take much time to find the room because
there are only three rooms in the building. Plus, she
doesn't need to worry about being late for the class
because it will be much quicker than making a copy of
her schedule in the student center. So, I support the
second suggestion.

여자의 문제는 자신의 수업 스케줄을 기숙사에 놓고 와서 강의실을 찾을 수
없다는 것이다. 남자는 먼저 학생 회관에 가서 스케줄을 복사하라고 제안한다.
그러나 여자는 시간이 좀 걸리기 때문에 수업에 늦을지도 모른다고 생각한
다. 나는 강의실 3개를 하나씩 살펴보라는 두 번째 제안이 더 나은 선택이라
고 생각한다. 모든 강의실을 하나씩 확인한다고 해도 그 건물에는 강의실이
3개 밖에 없기 때문에 시간이 그렇게 많이 걸리지 않을 것이다. 또한 학생 회
관에서 수업 스케줄을 복사하는 것보다 훨씬 빠를 것이기 때문에 수업에 늦
을 염려가 없다. 그래서 나는 두 번째 제안을 지지한다.

3

Listening

Now listen to a conversation between two students.

W Hey, Steve! How are you doing?

M I'm okay, but there is something that's really
bothering me. I don't know how to take care of it.

W What is it? Is there anything I can do to help you

out?

M Thanks. Well, I invited a philosophy professor to
give a lecture next week, but the students don't
seem to be interested because his lecture is kind
of boring. I would feel bad if only half of the room
is filled.

W Stop worrying about it and just send an email to
everyone to encourage him or her to participate in
the lecture.

M I'm not sure if it will work.

W Otherwise, you can ask the professor to change
his teaching method. Like allowing students
to discuss a certain topic, and then doing a
presentation. Most students prefer this kind of
lecture these days, you know.

M If I do that, then I have to propose the professor
change his teaching style and the content of the
lecture just to entertain the students. I don't think
it's the right way to go.

여 안녕, Steve. 잘 지내니?
남 잘 지내. 그런데 날 괴롭게 하는 게 한 가지 있어. 어떻게 처리해야 할지
모르겠어.
여 무슨 일인데? 내가 도와줄 거라도 있니?
남 고마워. 다음 주에 철학 교수님 한 분을 초빙해서 강의를 하시기로 했
는데 그분의 강의가 약간 지루한 편이라서 학생들이 관심이 없어 보여.
강의실이 절반 밖에 차지 않으면 너무 죄송할 것 같아.
여 걱정하지 말고 모두에게 이메일을 보내서 강의에 참석하도록 권해봐.
남 그게 효과가 있을지 잘 모르겠어.
여 아니면 교수님께 강의 방식을 바꿔달라고 제안을 할 수도 있겠지. 예를
들어서 학생들에게 특정 주제에 대해 토론을 하게 하고 발표를 하도록
하는 거야. 너도 알다시피 요즘에는 대부분의 학생들이 이런 강의를 선
호하잖아.
남 그렇게 하면 단지 학생들의 즐거움을 위해 교수님께 교수 방식과 강의
내용을 변경해 달라고 제안해야 하잖아. 그건 올바른 방법이 아닌 것
같아.

Problem: *invited a philosophy professor → the students
don't seem to be interested in the lecture*
철학 교수를 초빙했다 → 학생들이 강의에 관심이 없는 것 같다

Solution 1: *send an email to everyone to encourage
participation*
참여를 권하기 위해 학생들에게 이메일을 보내라

Response → *not sure if it will work* 효과가 있을지 확실하지 않다

Solution 2: *suggest the professor to change his teaching
method* 교수에게 강의 방식을 바꿔달라고 제안해라

Response → *don't think it's a right way to go*
옳은 방법인 것 같지 않다

Speaking

The students discuss two possible solutions to the

man's problem. Describe the problem. Then state which of the two solutions you prefer and explain why.

Possible response

The man's problem is that he invited a philosophy professor for a lecture, but the students are not interested because his lecture is boring. The woman suggests that he ask the professor to change his teaching style and contents of the lecture. But the man thinks that is very rude to do so. I think the other idea, like sending emails to all the students to encourage them to attend the lecture is a better choice because even though it's not guaranteed that the students will attend, it will have an advertising effect and can increase the students' participation. Plus, it will not offend the professor. If the man asks the professor to change his teaching style, he might be upset.

남자의 문제는 강연을 위해 철학 교수님 한 분을 초빙했는데 학생들이 강의가 지루해서 관심을 보이지 않는다는 것이다. 여자는 교수에게 강의 방식과 내용을 변경해 달라고 요청하라고 제안한다. 그러나 남자는 그렇게 하는 것이 매우 무례하다고 생각한다. 나는 강의에 참여하도록 유도하기 위하여 모든 학생들에게 이메일을 보내는 것이 더 나은 선택이라고 생각한다. 왜냐하면 비록 모든 학생들이 참가할지 확실하지는 않지만 광고 효과가 있을 것이고 학생들의 참여를 높일 수 있기 때문이다. 또한 이 방법은 교수를 기분 나쁘게 하지 않을 것이다. 만약 남자가 교수에게 교수 방법을 변경해 달라고 말하면 교수는 마음이 상할 수도 있다.

4

Listening

Now listen to a conversation between two students.

W Hi, Danny. You seem upset. What's the matter?

M Hey, Sarah. Well, I am directing a play for the school festival, but the main actor is very hot-tempered. He gets angry with the other actors very easily.

W Really? That's quite a big problem.

M So I'm thinking that I should do the acting instead of him. I know the lines. You think I can do it?

W I understand what you mean. But don't you have a lot of work to do as a director, such as directing and taking care of other actors and actresses?

M Yeah, you're right. I should try to persuade him to get along with the others. You know, it's very important to be able to work with others, right?

W Yeah! That could be the best solution.

여 안녕, Danny. 기분이 언짢아 보이네. 무슨 일이야?

남 안녕, Sarah. 학교 축제에서 공연할 연극을 감독하고 있는데 주연 배우가 성격이 너무 급해. 다른 배우들에게 너무 쉽게 화를 내.

여 그래? 꽤 큰 문제구나.

남 그래서 내가 대신 연기를 해야겠다고 생각 중이야. 대사는 알거든. 내가 할 수 있을 것 같니?

여 무슨 말인지는 알겠는데, 감독으로서 해야 하는 일이 많지 않니? 감독을 하고 남녀 배우들을 돌보는 것 같은 일 말이야.

남 그래, 네 말이 맞아. 다른 사람들과 잘 지내라고 그를 설득해 봐야겠어. 너도 알다시피 다른 사람들과 잘 지낼 줄 아는 건 매우 중요하잖아, 그렇지?

여 그럼! 그게 가장 좋은 방법일 것 같아.

Problem: *the main actor is very hot-tempered*
주연 배우의 성격이 너무 급하다

Solution 1: *do the acting instead of him* 그 대신 연기한다

Response → *have a lot of work to do as a director*
감독으로서 해야 할 일이 많다

Solution 2: *persuade him to get along with others*
다른 사람들과 잘 지내라고 설득한다

Response → *could be the best solution* 최선의 방법일 것이다

Speaking

The students discuss two possible solutions to the man's problem. Describe the problem. Then state which of the two solutions you prefer and explain why.

Possible response

The man's problem is that he is the director of a play in the school festival, but the main actor is very hot-tempered and causes problems with the other cast members. The man considers playing the lead role instead of the main actor. But the problem is that he is very busy as the director. I think that the other idea of persuading the main actor to get along with the other cast members is a better choice because then, the man can just focus on directing. If he does both directing and acting, he might not do a good job with either because he can't concentrate on one job. Also, he can build a good relationship with the main actor by giving him suggestions on working with others. If he fires the actor, it could damage their relationship in the long run. So, I support persuading the main actor to get along with others.

남자의 문제는 자신이 학교 축제 연극의 감독인데, 주연 배우의 성격이 너무 급하고 다른 배우들과 문제를 일으키고 있다는 것이다. 남자는 주연 배우 대신 직접 연기를 하는 것을 고려한다. 그러나 문제는 그는 감독으로서 해야 할 일이 많기 때문에 매우 바쁘다는 것이다. 나는 주연 배우를 설득하여 다른 사람들과 잘 지내도록 하는 것이 더 나은 방법이라고 생각한다. 그 이유는 그렇게 하면 남자는 감독하는 일에 좀 더 집중할 수 있기 때문이다. 만약 그가 감독과 연기를 같이 한다면 집중을 할 수 없기 때문에 어느 것도 제대로 할 수 없을 것이다. 또한 타인과 함께 일하는 것에 대해 조언을 해주는 것을 통해 주연을 맡은 배우와 좋은 관계를 유지할 수 있다. 만약 그가 그 연기자를 해고하면 장기적으로는 둘의 관계에 피해를 미칠 수 있다. 그래서 나는 다른 사람들과 잘 지내도록 주연 배우를 설득하는 의견을 지지한다.

1

Listening

Now listen to a conversation between a student and a professor.

M Professor Smith, do you have a second?

W Yeah, sure, Brian. What's up?

M Well, I have this issue and was wondering if I could speak with you about it.

W All right, go ahead.

M See, I have to enroll in a Conservation Biology course, and many people recommended your class. I really want to take your course, but when I tried to register, it was already full.

W Oh, Brian. I appreciate you saying that, but you're right... that class is already full. I really can't take any more students. The university won't allow me to do so.

M I understand, but is there any possibility that I could enroll?

W I guess you could try to register on the first day of class. There might be some students who have dropped the course. Then you can add on.

M Yeah, I'll probably do that, but that still doesn't guarantee anything. I need the class in order to graduate.

W I see. Well, in that case, you should enroll in a different section. There are some really good professors teaching the same course in another section such as on the weekends or in the evenings.

M Yeah, I guess, but I was really hoping to take your class. I thought I might understand the subject better because you introduce everything very easily. Well, we'll see if anyone drops on the first day.

W I hope a spot opens up for you.

남 Smith 교수님, 잠깐 시간 되시나요?

여 물론이에요, Brian. 무슨 일인가요?

남 저, 문제가 좀 있는데 교수님과 상의를 해도 될까요?

여 그래요, 말해보세요.

남 보존 생물학 수업을 들어야 하는데, 많은 사람들이 교수님의 수업을 추천해 주었어요. 교수님의 수업을 꼭 듣고 싶은데 등록하려고 하니까 이미 자리가 다 찼더라고요.

여 그렇게 말해줘서 고맙군요, Brian. 말한대로 그 수업은 이미 다 찼어요. 더 이상 학생을 받기는 힘들어요. 학교측에서도 그렇게 하는 것을 허락하지 않을 거예요.

남 네, 알겠습니다. 그런데 등록할 수 있는 다른 방법이 전혀 없나요?

여 수업 첫날 다시 등록을 해보는 게 어때요? 강의를 취소한 학생들이 있을 수 있거든요. 그러면 등록할 수 있을 거예요.

남 네, 그렇게 해보겠지만 여전히 보장되진 않잖아요. 졸업을 하려면 이 수업을 꼭 들어야 하거든요.

여 그렇군요. 그런 경우라면 다른 수업을 등록하는 게 나을 거예요. 같은 과목을 주말이나 저녁에 가르치는 아주 훌륭한 교수님들 수업도 있거든요.

남 네, 그렇지만 저는 교수님 수업을 듣고 싶었어요. 교수님께서는 모든 걸 쉽게 설명하셔서 이해가 더 잘 될 것 같았거든요. 첫날 수강을 취소하는 학생들이 있는지 기다려 봐야겠네요.

여 들어올 자리가 나면 좋겠군요.

Problem: *want to enroll in Professor Smith's Conservation Biology class, but the class is full* Smith교수의 보존 생물학 수업을 등록하고 싶지만 이미 수업이 마감되었다

Suggested solution 1:
try to register on the first day of class
수업 첫날 다시 등록을 해본다

Suggested solution 2:
enroll in a different section 다른 수업을 등록한다

Speaking

The student and the professor discuss two possible solutions to the man's problem. Describe the problem. Then state which of the two solutions you prefer and explain why.

Possible response

The man's problem is that he wants to enroll in Professor Smith's Conservation Biology class, but it is already full. He needs to take the course this semester in order to graduate. The woman suggests that he try to register again on the first day, but it cannot be guaranteed whether there will be an available spot in the class. I think enrolling in a different section with a different professor is a better choice than waiting for someone to drop on the first day. If he waits too long, the other sections might become full as well, and there is a possibility that no one will drop Professor Smith's class. So, I support taking a different section.

남자의 문제는 Smith 교수의 보존 생물학 수업을 듣고 싶은데 이미 자리가 다 찼다는 것이다. 그는 이번 학기에 졸업하기 위해서 이 수업을 수강해야 한다. 여자는 수업 첫날 다시 등록을 해보라고 제안하지만 등록할 자리가 있을지 보장할 수 없다. 나는 첫날 누군가 수업을 취소하기를 기다리는 것보다 다른 교수가 하는 다른 수업을 등록하는 것이 더 나은 선택이라고 생각한다. 만약 그가 너무 오래 기다리면 다른 수업도 자리가 다 차게 될 수 있고 아무도 Smith 교수의 수업을 취소하지 않을 가능성도 있기 때문이다. 그래서 나는 다른 수업을 들을 것을 지지한다.

2

Listening

Now listen to a conversation between two students.

M Hi, Anne! I'm so glad to see you.

W Hey, Jerry! Is everything all right? What happened?

M I've been stressing out about this field trip to the museum that we're taking the kids to.

W Really, don't stress out about that.

M It's not the actual trip that I'm worried about... the school van broke down.

W If I were in your shoes, I would take it to a mechanic and get it fixed.

M Well, I tried calling around and talking to mechanics, but they all told me that it sounds like a pretty big problem. They estimate that it might be fairly expensive. Also, it might take awhile, so we would have to reschedule the trip.

W Oh, that's terrible. The kids would be so disappointed. They must have looked forward to the trip all week. Don't you have a friend who has a van? Can't you borrow his car for a day?

M Yeah, I do. I thought about that as well, but my friend uses his van for work. I'm not sure if he can afford to let me borrow it for an entire day.

W I see... What are you going to do then?

M I'm not sure, but I'll have to figure something out.

남 안녕, Anne, 만나서 정말 반가워.

여 안녕, Jerry. 잘 지내니? 별일 없어?

남 아이들 데리고 박물관 현장 학습을 가는 것 때문에 스트레스를 받고 있어.

여 그런 것 때문에 스트레스 받지 마.

남 현장 학습 때문에 걱정되는 게 아니라... 학교버스가 고장이 났어.

여 내가 너라면 정비사에게 가서 고치겠어.

남 음. 정비사들에게 전화해봤는데 다들 큰 고장인 것 같다고 했어. 돈이 꽤 많이 들 거라고 예상하더라고. 게다가 시간이 좀 걸릴 수도 있어서 계획을 변경해야 할 지도 몰라.

여 저런, 안됐구나. 아이들이 실망하겠네. 일주일 내내 기대했을 텐데. 봉고차를 갖고 있는 친구가 있지 않아? 그에게 하루만 차를 빌릴 수 없어?

남 응. 맞아. 나도 그 생각을 했는데 그는 일을 할 때 차를 써야 하거든. 하루 종일 나에게 차를 빌려줄 수 있을지 잘 모르겠어.

여 그렇구나... 그럼 어떻게 할 생각이야?

남 모르겠어. 하지만 방법을 생각해 봐야지.

Problem: *has to take the kids on a field trip, but the school van broke down* 아이들을 데리고 현장 학습을 가야 하는데, 학교버스가 고장났다

Suggested solution 1:
take it to a mechanic and get it fixed 정비사에게 가서 고친다

Suggested solution 2:
borrow a van from a friend 친구에게 차를 빌린다

The students discuss two possible solutions to the man's problem. Describe the problem. Then state which of the two solutions you prefer and explain why.

Possible response

The man's problem is that he was supposed to take the students on a field trip to a museum, but their school van broke down. The woman suggests asking to borrow a van from a friend. The problem is that his friend uses his van for work and might not be able to lend it to the man. I think the other idea, getting the van fixed and rescheduling the field trip is better than borrowing a van from a friend. The van has to be repaired eventually and taking a group of children in a friend's van is a pretty big liability. So I support getting the van fixed rather than borrowing a van from a friend.

남자의 문제는 학생들을 데리고 박물관으로 현장 학습을 가기로 했는데 학교버스가 고장이 났다는 것이다. 여자는 친구로부터 봉고차를 빌릴 것을 제안한다. 문제는 그의 친구가 일 때문에 차를 써야 하기 때문에 남자에게 차를 빌려줄 수 없을지도 모른다는 것이다. 나는 차를 고치고 현장 학습 계획을 변경하는 다른 의견이 친구에게 차를 빌리는 것보다 낫다고 생각한다. 결국 차는 고쳐야 할 것이며 친구의 차에 아이들을 태우는 것은 부담이 크기 때문이다. 그래서 나는 친구로부터 차를 빌리는 것보다 고치는 것을 지지한다.

3

Listening

Now listen to a conversation between two students.

M Hi, Jane. I heard you hurt your leg. Are you okay?

W Hi, Stan. It's just a sprain, but it's kind of uncomfortable.

M What a shame. How are you going to get to school everyday?

W I don't know what I'm going to do. I have to teach downtown, but I can't drive with this leg.

M Well, maybe you could find a friend that lives near your area and carpool. That would be a great way to get downtown.

W Actually, I do have a friend that can take me downtown, but I have to wait an hour for him on the way back. I think that's a waste of time, and he also might feel burdened.

M You can wait at a coffee shop until he finishes. I am sure he won't feel burdened. He might actually enjoy the company. But if you're uncomfortable with that, how about taking a cab? The fare isn't that costly.

W That's another solution but I don't have money to spend on a cab. I'll think about it a bit more. Thanks for the advice, Stan.

남 안녕, Jane. 다리를 다쳤다고 들었어. 괜찮아?

여 안녕, Stan. 삔 것 뿐인데, 약간 불편해.

남 안됐구나. 학교에는 매일 어떻게 가려고 해?

여 어떻게 해야 할지 모르겠어. 시내에서 수업을 해야 하는데 이 다리로는 운전을 할 수가 없어.

남 음, 근처에 사는 친구와 카풀을 하는 건 어때? 시내까지 가는데 아주 좋은 방법일 것 같은데.

여 사실 시내에 태워다 줄 수 있는 친구가 있긴 한데, 돌아오는 길에 한 시간이나 그를 기다려야 해. 그건 시간 낭비이고 그도 부담스러울 것 같아.

남 그가 끝날 때까지 커피숍에서 기다리면 되잖아. 부담을 느끼진 않을 거야. 동행이 있어서 즐거울 수도 있어. 하지만 정 네가 불편하면 택시를 타는 건 어때? 요금이 그렇게 비싸지는 않아.

여 좋은 생각인데 난 택시에 쓸만한 돈은 없어. 조금 더 생각해볼게. 조언 고마워, Stan.

Problem: *hurt her leg but has to go downtown to teach* 다리를 다쳤는데 시내에서 수업을 해야 한다

Suggested solution 1:
carpool with a friend 친구와 카풀을 한다

Suggested solution 2:
take a cab 택시를 탄다

Speaking

The students discuss two possible solutions to the woman's problem. Describe the problem. Then state which of the two solutions you prefer and explain why.

Possible response

The woman's problem is that she sprained her leg, so it is difficult for her to get downtown where she has to teach students. The man suggests finding a person that lives near her so that they can carpool. She has a friend who can carpool, but she has to wait an hour for him on the way back. She feels it's a waste of time to wait. She is also worried that her friend might feel burdened about it. I think the other idea, taking a cab, is better because even though taking a cab is expensive, it is a safe and quick way to get to her destination on time. Also, she doesn't need to feel burdened about asking her friend to give her a ride. So, I support taking a cab rather than carpooling.

여자의 문제는 다리를 삐어서 학생들을 가르치러 시내까지 가는데 어려움을 겪고 있다는 것이다. 남자는 그녀와 가까운 곳에 사는 사람을 찾아서 카풀을 할 것을 제안한다. 그녀는 카풀을 할 친구가 있지만 집에 돌아오기 위해 그를 한 시간이나 기다려야 한다. 그녀는 그것이 시간 낭비라고 느낀다. 또한 그녀는 친구가 부담을 느낄 수 있다는 것에 대해 걱정한다. 나는 택시를 타면 된다는 다른 의견이 더 낫다고 생각한다. 택시를 타는 것은 비싸기는 하지만 제시간에 목적지에 갈 수 있는 안전하고 빠른 방법이기 때문이다. 또한 친구에게 차를 태워달라고 부탁하지 않아도 되므로 부담도 없을 것이다. 그래서 나는 카풀을 하는 것보다 택시를 타는 것을 지지한다.

4

Listening

Now listen to a conversation between two students.

M Hey, Jenny. What's the matter? You don't look too happy.

W Well, I have a problem with my sociology professor.

M What is it?

W I'm not too happy about my grade from last week's exam. He gave me a lower grade on the essay section. But compared to my friend's answer, I should have gotten full points for that section.

M Did you try to go directly to the professor to ask him about it? The direct approach is always efficient and saves a lot of time.

W Well, not yet. I don't feel comfortable confronting a professor about grades. I get nervous and can't seem to find the right words.

M Then, how about this. Try discussing your grade with the teacher's assistant. I heard they are close to the professors. Maybe he or she can ask the professor for you.

W They both sound like a solution. I'll have to think about which approach I'll take.

남 안녕, Jenny. 무슨 일이야? 기분이 안 좋아 보이네.

여 응. 사회학 수업 교수 때문에 문제가 좀 있어.

남 뭔데?

여 지난 주에 본 시험 점수가 만족스럽지 않아. 에세이 부분에서 낮은 점수를 주셨거든. 하지만 내 친구가 쓴 답과 비교해 보면, 그 부분에서 만점을 받았어야 해.

남 교수님을 직접 찾아가서 시험에 대해 이야기 해 보았니? 직접적인 방법은 늘 효과적이고 시간을 많이 절약해 주잖아.

여 아니, 아직. 난 교수님들과 성적에 대해 논의할 때 맘이 편하지 않거든. 긴장을 해서 말을 제대로 못해.

남 그럼 이건 어때. 조교를 찾아가서 의논해봐. 그들은 교수님들과 친하다고 들었어. 너 대신 교수님께 여쭈어볼 수 있을지도 몰라.

여 두 가지 다 해결 방법 같은데. 어떤 방법으로 접근할지 생각을 해 봐야 겠어.

Problem: *not happy about her grade from last week's exam* 지난 주에 본 시험 점수에 대해 불만이 있다

Suggested solution 1:
go directly to the professor to ask him about it 교수님을 직접 찾아가서 이야기 해본다

Suggested solution 2:
try discussing with the teacher's assistant 조교를 찾아가서 의논한다

Speaking

The students discuss two possible solutions to the woman's problem. Describe the problem. Then state which of the two solutions you prefer and explain why.

Possible response

The woman thinks that her professor gave a wrong evaluation on her previous exam. The man suggests that talking to the professor might be the fastest and most effective way to solve the problem, but the woman does not feel comfortable and gets nervous when she talks to professors about grades. I think the other idea, addressing the problem directly with the teacher's assistant, is better because the TA is closer to the professor and can talk to the professor very easily. Also, she may feel much more comfortable because she doesn't need to talk to the professor herself. So, I support talking to the TA about her grade.

여자는 교수가 이전에 본 시험에 대해 잘못된 결과를 주었다고 생각한다. 남자는 교수를 찾아가서 이야기하는 것이 문제를 해결할 수 있는 가장 빠르고 효과적인 방법일 것이라고 제안하지만 여자는 성적에 대해 교수와 이야기할 때 불편하고 긴장을 한다. 나는 조교를 찾아가 문제를 해결하는 다른 제안이 낫다고 생각한다. 조교는 교수와 가깝기 때문에 교수에게 더 수월하게 이야기 할 수 있기 때문이다. 또한 그녀가 직접 교수에게 이야기하지 않아도 되기 때문에 훨씬 더 편안할 것이다. 그래서 나는 조교에게 학점에 대하여 이야기하는 것을 지지한다.

5

Listening

Now listen to a conversation between two students.

M Hi, Stephanie. Did you apply for the summer internship?

W Hi, Greg. Well, I applied for one, but I haven't gotten any response from the company yet.

M Did you apply for housing as well?

W Nope, I couldn't apply for on campus housing, either. I don't know where I am going to stay for the next semester because it totally depends on my internship.

M Here's what you can do. You can stay at home with your parents and go to school from your house. Actually, I went to school from my house, and even though it was two hours away, I got to save a lot of money.

W I'm not so sure if I could I travel for two hours to school everyday.

M You can also rent housing near the school. That way you can be closer to school and don't have to fight traffic.

W I think that might be a little pricey, although it is a good idea to save time spent on the road to study more or to utilize the school's facilities.

M You have solutions laid out for you. I hope you

make the right decision so that you won't have any regrets.

W Yeah, I will keep your advice in mind. Thanks.

남 안녕, Stephanie. 여름 인턴쉽은 지원했니?

여 안녕, Greg. 한 군데 지원했는데 아직 회사로부터 연락을 못 받았어.

남 주택 신청도 했니?

여 아니, 기숙사도 신청할 수가 없었어. 전적으로 인턴쉽에 달려있기 때문에 다음 학기에 어디에서 살아야 할지 모르거든.

남 이렇게 하는 건 어때. 집에서 부모님과 살고 학교까지 통학해. 실은 난 집에서 다녔는데, 비록 2시간이나 떨어져 있었지만 돈을 많이 모을 수 있었어.

여 매일 2시간씩 통학할 수 있을지 잘 모르겠어.

남 아니면 학교 근처에 집을 임대할 수도 있어. 그렇게 하면 학교 근처에 있을 수 있고 교통 문제에 대해 걱정할 필요가 없을 거야.

여 그건 돈이 많이 들 것 같아. 비록 길에서 보내는 시간을 절약하고 공부나 학교 시설 활용에 시간을 쓸 수 있어서 좋긴 하지만 말야.

남 몇 가지 해결책이 있네. 후회하지 않도록 좋은 선택을 하길 바래.

여 응, 네 조언 명심할게. 고마워.

> Problem: *don't know where to stay for the next semester* 다음 학기에 어디에서 살아야 할지 모른다
>
> Suggested solution 1:
> *stay at home with parents and go to school from her house* 집에서 부모님과 살고 학교에 통학한다
>
> Suggested solution 2:
> *rent housing near the school* 학교 근처에 집을 임대한다

Speaking

The students discuss two possible solutions to the woman's problem. Describe the problem. Then state which of the two solutions you prefer and explain why.

Possible response

The woman's problem is that she didn't get any response from the company for her summer internship. So, she didn't apply for on campus housing, and she needs to find a place that is feasible for her to live in. The man suggests that she stay at home and commute to school from home. The problem with this is that it takes too much time. I think the other idea, getting on campus housing, is better because even though it is a little pricey, it would definitely be convenient for her. Also, she doesn't need to worry about traffic and would feel free from the burden of wasting time on the road. So, I support the idea of getting housing near campus.

여자의 문제는 여름 인턴쉽에 대해 회사로부터 답을 못 받았다는 것이다. 그래서 그녀는 기숙사를 신청하지 않았기 때문에 머물만한 적당한 장소를 찾아야 한다. 남자는 그녀에게 집에서 지내고 학교에 통학할 것을 제안한다. 이

것의 문제는 시간이 너무 오래 걸린다는 것이다. 나는 학교 근처에서 거주지를 찾는다는 다른 제안이 더 낫다고 생각한다. 비록 돈이 많이 들겠지만 그녀에게 분명히 편리할 것이기 때문이다. 또한 교통 문제에 대해 걱정할 필요가 없으며 길에서 시간을 낭비한다는 부담으로부터 해방될 것이다. 그래서 나는 학교 근처에 집을 얻는 것을 지지한다.

6

Listening

Now listen to a conversation between two students.

W   Hello, James. How's the publishing of the photo magazine going?

M   It was going well until I ran into a slight problem. There aren't enough photos to publish in the magazine. I don't know what to do.

W   I see. I heard that you tried to get more photos from other sources, but couldn't.

M   That's right. Do you have any ideas?

W   How about lowering the selection standards? Then you would have enough photos to publish. I don't think the magazine calls for only high quality photos.

M   But the problem is that choosing photos that are not good will damage the magazine's reputation. A lot of students are really looking forward to having a great photo magazine.

W   Yeah, that's true. Then what about this? Try to release the magazine once every two months, rather than every month.

M   That's a good idea, but students will expect to have it every month. After all, the name of the magazine is *Campus Photo Monthly*.

W   Hmm, I don't know. I hope you work it out soon.

M   I hope so, too.

여   안녕, James. 사진 잡지 출간은 어떻게 되고 있어?

남   약간 문제가 생기기 전까진 아주 잘 되고 있었어. 잡지에 실을 만한 사진이 부족해서 어떻게 해야 할지 모르겠어.

여   그렇구나. 다른 곳에서 사진을 구하려고 했는데 못 구했다고 들었어.

남   맞아. 혹시 생각나는 방법이라도 있어?

여   사진 선택 기준을 낮추는 건 어때? 그러면 발행할 만한 사진이 충분할 거야. 잡지에 질이 높은 사진만 필요한 건 아니라고 생각해.

남   그렇지만 질이 낮은 사진을 선택하면 잡지의 평판이 나빠질 거야. 많은 학생들이 훌륭한 사진 잡지를 기대하고 있어.

여   그건 그래. 그럼 이건 어때? 잡지를 매달 내는 게 아니라 두 달에 한번씩 발행하는 거야.

남   좋은 생각이지만 학생들은 매달 발행되는 걸 기대할 거야. 무엇보다 잡지 이름이 *Campus Photo Monthly*(월간 캠퍼스 사진)잖아.

여   흠, 난 잘 모르겠다. 곧 해결되길 바랄게.

남   나도 그랬으면 좋겠어.

Problem: *not enough photos to publish in the photo magazine* 사진 잡지에 실을 만한 사진이 부족하다

Suggested solution 1:
   lower the selection standards
   사진 선택 기준을 낮춘다

Suggested solution 2:
   release the magazine once every two months 잡지를 두 달에 한번씩 발행한다

Speaking

The students discuss two possible solutions to the man's problem. Describe the problem. Then state which of the two solutions you prefer and explain why.

Possible response

The man's problem is that he doesn't have enough photos to publish in the school magazine. He tried to get more photos from other sources, but he failed. The woman suggests that he lower his selection standards. The problem is that choosing photos that are not qualified will harm the magazine's reputation. I think publishing the magazine every two months is much better than publishing it every month because although students expect the magazine every month, it would help him prevent damaging the magazine's reputation with low quality pictures. Also, when he gets more good pictures later, he can publish the magazine once a month. So, I support publishing the magazine every other month.

남자의 문제는 학교 잡지에 실을 만한 사진이 충분하지 않다는 것이다. 그는 다른 곳에서 사진을 더 구해보려고 했지만 실패했다. 여자는 남자에게 사진 선택 기준을 낮추라고 조언한다. 질이 낮은 사진을 선택하는 것의 문제는 잡지의 평판에 누를 끼칠 것이라는 점이다. 나는 매달 잡지를 발행하는 것이 아니라 두 달에 한번씩 잡지를 출간하는 것이 훨씬 낫다고 생각한다. 비록 학생들은 매달 잡지가 출간되기를 기대하겠지만, 낮은 질의 사진으로 인해 잡지의 평판이 나빠지는 것을 막을 수 있기 때문이다. 또한 좋은 사진을 더 많이 확보하면 매달 잡지를 출간할 수 있을 것이다. 그러므로 나는 두 달에 한번 잡지를 출간하는 것을 지지한다.

7

Listening

Now listen to a conversation between two students.

M   Hi, Kathy, how are you doing?

W   Not so well.

M   What's wrong?

W   Our school is offering a French history class that I really want to take this semester. The professor is very famous in the field. But the problem is that my sister just had her baby in another country, and my brother-in-law is going away on a business trip. So I have to go and take care of her.

M I see your problem. Why don't you go ahead and take the class and visit her after the semester? I'm sure your sister has a good neighbor or friend who'll look after her.

W Well, I'm afraid my sister will be disappointed. She is really looking forward to seeing me, you know?

M Well... Then how about taking the course next time? Try taking the class during the summer. You can get a lot of information about the class from your friends who take the class this semester, and then you will get a better grade as well.

W That would be great, but I'm not sure they're offering the course this summer.

M Well, I'll keep my fingers crossed for you.

W Thanks.

남 안녕, Kathy, 어떻게 지내?

여 별로 잘 못 지내.

남 무슨 일이야?

여 학교에서 이번 학기에 정말 듣고 싶은 프랑스 역사 수업을 개설했어. 그 분야에서 아주 유명한 교수님이시거든. 그런데 문제는 언니가 다른 나라에서 막 출산을 했는데 형부가 출장을 가신다는 거야. 그래서 내가 가서 언니를 돌봐야 해.

남 문제가 뭔지 알겠어. 그냥 수업을 듣고 학기가 끝난 후에 언니를 방문하는 게 어때? 언니를 돌봐줄 좋은 이웃이나 친구가 분명 있을 거야.

여 그렇게 하면 언니가 실망할 것 같아. 날 보는 걸 기대하고 있거든.

남 음... 그럼 수업을 다음에 듣는 건 어때? 여름 학기 때 들어봐. 이번 학기에 이 수업을 들은 친구들에게서 정보를 많이 받을 수 있을 거야. 그러면 더 좋은 점수를 받을 수 있을지도 몰라.

여 그러면 좋겠지만, 이번 여름에 수업이 열릴지 모르겠어.

남 음, 행운을 빌어줄게.

여 고마워.

Problem: *want to take a French history class but has to go help her sister with her new baby*
프랑스 역사 수업을 듣고 싶지만 언니의 새로 태어난 아기를 돌보는 것을 도와주어야 한다

Suggested solution 1:
take the class and visit her after the semester
수업을 듣고 학기가 끝난 후 방문한다

Suggested solution 2:
take the class during the summer
여름에 수업을 듣는다

Speaking

The students discuss two possible solutions to the woman's problem. Describe the problem. Then state which of the two solutions you prefer and explain why.

Possible response

The woman is in conflict between two situations. She wants to take a French history course, but her sister needs her help with her new baby. She is given the following two suggestions. First, the man suggests taking the class and visiting her sister after the semester, but the problem is that her sister will not be happy. The other idea, going to her sister's and taking the class during the summer, is much better because helping family is very important. One day, when she needs her sister's help, she will probably do the same for her. Also, she can take the French history class next time. So I support visiting her sister to take care of her and taking the class next semester.

여자는 두 상황 사이에 갈등을 겪고 있다. 그녀는 프랑스 역사 수업을 듣고 싶지만 그녀의 언니가 새로 태어난 아기를 돌보는 데 도움을 필요로 한다. 그녀는 다음 두 가지 제안을 받는다. 남자는 먼저 수업을 듣고 학기가 끝난 후에 언니를 방문하라는 제안을 한다. 그러나 이것의 문제는 언니가 마음이 상할 것이라는 것이다. 언니를 찾아가고 수업은 여름에 들으라는 다른 제안이 더 나은 방법이다. 그 이유는 가족을 돕는 일은 매우 중요하기 때문이다. 언젠가 그녀 역시 언니의 도움이 필요할 것이고, 그녀도 아마 똑같이 해줄 것이다. 또한 프랑스 역사 수업은 다음에도 들을 수 있다. 그러므로 나는 언니를 돌보기 위해 가고 수업은 다음 학기에 듣는 것을 지지한다.

8

Listening

Now listen to a conversation between two students.

W Hey, Eddie. Long time, no see!

M Hi, Jodie. How have you been?

W I've been pretty good, but I have been under a lot of stress lately.

M Oh yeah? What are you so stressed about?

W I have a group project for my economics class. We were supposed to meet tonight, but I can't go because I have another important meeting for my science class. The professor said that it is mandatory to attend.

M Well, if I were you, I would call the group members and ask them to put off the meeting for sometime later this week.

W Then our project will not meet the deadline. We have to hand in all the materials that we had prepared this week and then discuss them. I don't want to let them down. You know what I mean, right?

M In that case, I guess you could just send all your materials to your members through email and explain your situation. I'm sure they will understand your situation.

W Yeah, that could be an alternative. I'll think about it. Thanks.

여 안녕, Eddie. 정말 오랜만이야!

남 안녕, Jodie. 어떻게 지냈어?

여 잘 지냈어. 그런데 최근에 스트레스를 많이 받고 있어.

남 그래? 무엇 때문에 그렇게 스트레스를 받는데?

여 경제학 수업에서 그룹 프로젝트가 있어. 오늘밤에 만나기로 했거든. 그런데 과학 수업에서도 중요한 모임이 있어서 갈 수가 없어. 교수님께서 참석이 필수라고 하셨어.

남 음. 내가 너라면 조원들에게 전화해서 이번 주 후반에 다른 날로 미루자고 부탁하겠어.

여 그러면 우리 과제는 기한을 못 맞춰. 준비한 자료를 이번 주에 전부 제출하고 토론해야 하거든. 조원들을 실망시키고 싶지 않아. 무슨 뜻인지 알지?

남 그렇다면 네 자료를 전부 이메일로 보내고 상황을 설명하면 될 거야. 분명히 네 상황을 이해해 줄 거야.

여 응. 그런 방법이 있겠구나. 생각해 볼게. 고마워.

Problem: *has a group project in economics class but needs to attend a meeting in science class*
경제학 수업에서 그룹 프로젝트가 있지만 과학 수업 모임에 참석해야 한다

Suggested solution 1:
call the group members and put off the meeting 조원들에게 전화해서 모임을 미룬다

Suggested solution 2:
send materials to the members through email 조원들에게 이메일로 자료를 보낸다

Speaking

The students discuss two possible solutions to the woman's problem. Describe the problem. Then state which of the two solutions you prefer and explain why.

Possible response

The woman's problem is that she has to be at two meetings at the same time but she can only go to her science class meeting. She is given two suggestions. The man first suggests rescheduling the other meeting, but the problem is that the project won't meet the deadline. I think emailing all her materials to her group members and explaining why she can't attend is a better idea. She has to attend the more important meeting of the two, which is the science class meeting. The other members of the group will understand because they have probably been in similar situations. As long as she has her work finished, she should be OK. So I support the second suggestion.

여자의 문제는 두 개의 모임이 겹쳤는데 과학 수업 모임에만 갈 수 있다는 것이다. 그녀는 두 가지 제안을 받는다. 남자는 먼저 다른 모임을 재조정하라고 제안하지만 문제는 프로젝트가 기한을 못 맞춘다는 것이다. 나는 그녀의 자료를 전부 조원들에게 이메일로 보내고 왜 참석할 수 없는지를 설명하는 것이 더 좋은 제안이라고 생각한다. 그녀는 둘 중 더 중요한 모임인 과학 수업 모임에 참석해야 하기 때문이다. 다른 멤버들도 아마도 비슷한 경험이 있을 것이므로 그녀를 이해할 것이다. 그녀가 맡은 일을 다 했다면 괜찮을 것이다. 그러므로 나는 두 번째 제안을 지지한다.

TASK 6 Summary

Sample

CD Possible Response: Track 68

Listening

Now listen to part of a talk in a United States history class.

P Due to its vastness, a common national culture in the United States was slow to develop. About a century ago, there was little communication between the different areas of the United States. Due to this lack of communication, people in different regions were quite different from one another. For example, they all spoke, dressed, and behaved differently from one another. But because of the following two inventions, the communication between the regions started to greatly increase: the automobile and the radio.

As you're aware, automobiles began to be mass produced during the 1920's, decreasing the price and increasing their availability. Americans now had the ability to travel rather easily to nearby cities. The automobile also increased the ability to take trips to other parts of the country. This increased mobility helped to change attitudes in Americans and shorten the "bridge" between regions. For example, the people in small towns began to be more influenced by the styles and attitudes of the people from the big cities.

With the increased purchase of automobiles came the increase in the ownership of the radio. Americans were able to listen to the same radio programs and musicians throughout the entire country. The terms and phrases that were on the popular shows and in music were catching on everywhere in the country. They also were able to hear the news and all about the important events happening all across the country, which brought the country closer together.

거대한 크기 때문에 미국의 공통적인 문화는 천천히 발전했습니다. 1세기 전에 미국의 다른 지역간에는 의사 소통이 거의 없었습니다. 이러한 의사소통의 부족으로 인해 다른 지역에 사는 사람들은 서로 매우 달랐습니다. 예를 들어 그들은 각각 말하거나 옷을 입거나 행동하는 양식이 달랐습니다. 그러나 다음 두 가지 발명품으로 인해 지역간의 의사 소통이 크게 증가했습니다. 이것은 바로 자동차와 라디오입니다.

여러분들도 알다시피 1920년에 자동차가 다량 생산되기 시작했고, 이로 인해 가격이 낮아졌고, 활용도는 증가했습니다. 미국인들은 이제 인근 도시로 쉽게 갈 수 있게 되었습니다. 자동차는 또한 다른 지방으로 여행을 갈 수 있게 해 주었습니다. 이러한 이동성의 증가는 미국인들의 태도에 변화를 가져왔고 지역간의 "격차"를 줄여주었습니다. 예를 들어, 소도시에 사는 사람들은 대도시 사람들의 스타일과 태도로부터 영향을 받기 시작했습니다.

자동차의 구입이 증가하면서 라디오의 소유도 들어났습니다. 미국인들은 전 지역에서 같은 라디오 프로그램과 음악가들을 들을 수 있었습니다. 인기 있는 쇼와 음악에서 사용되는 용어와 구절은 나라의 어디서나 보고 들을 수 있었습니다. 그들은 또한 나라 전체에서 발생한 뉴스와 중요한 사건들에 대해서 들을 수 있었고, 이것은 미국을 단합할 수 있도록 해주었습니다.

Speaking

Using points and examples from the talk, explain how the automobile and the radio contributed to a common culture in the United States.

Possible response

The main topic of the lecture is common culture in the United States. The professor tells the students that America did not have a common culture 100 years ago because people in different regions of the country did not communicate much with each other. The automobile and the radio changed this situation. As an example, the professor explains that when automobiles became inexpensive, people from small towns could travel easily to cities or to other parts of the country. When they began to do this, they started acting like people from those other regions and started to dress and speak in the same way. Another example is that when radio became popular, people from different parts of the country began listening to the same programs and the same news reports and began to speak alike and have similar experiences and ideas. The professor explains that these similar ways of speaking, dressing, and thinking became the national culture of the United States.

이 강의의 주제는 미국의 공통 문화이다. 교수는 학생들에게 미국의 다른 지역에 거주하는 사람들이 서로 의사 소통을 하지 않아서 100년 전에는 공통된 문화가 없었다고 설명한다. 자동차와 라디오가 이 상황을 변화시켰다. 그 예로 교수는 자동차가 저렴해져서 소도시에 사는 사람들이 다른 도시나 지역으로 쉽게 여행을 갈 수 있었다고 설명한다. 이렇게 하기 시작하자 그들은 다른 지역에 사는 사람들처럼 행동하고 옷을 입고 말하기 시작했다. 또 다른 예는 라디오가 인기가 많아지자 다른 지역에 사는 사람들이 같은 프로그램과 뉴스를 보고 같은 투로 말하고 비슷한 경험과 생각을 갖기 시작했다는 것이다. 교수는 이처럼 비슷하게 말하고 옷을 입고 생각하는 것이 미국의 문화가 되었다고 설명한다.

1

Listening

Now listen to part of a talk in an ecology class.

P　Now, let's talk about how the population of the deer influences the number of pine trees. We will take a look at the outcome of the research done by a group of environmental scientists. Their study was carried out to understand the increase in the population of pine trees relative to the population of the deer.

Scientists have noticed that in order for new pine trees to grow, it is a difficult and long process. The pinecones that bear the seeds must be broken apart and buried into the ground. The deer community in the mountainous area of Santa Cruz use pinecones as a source of food. The deer breaks open the hard pinecone, and then drops the seeds into the ground where the deer's hoof grinds it into the ground. This contributes to the increase in population of pine trees in the mountains.

자, 그럼 이제 사슴 개체수가 소나무 개체수를 증가시키는데 어떻게 영향을 미치는지 이야기 해 보겠어요. 환경 과학자들이 조사한 연구의 결과를 살펴보겠습니다. 그들의 조사는 사슴 개체수의 증가에 따라 소나무 개체수가 어떻게 증가되는지 이해하는 것이었어요.

과학자들은 새로운 소나무가 자라는 것은 어렵고 긴 과정이라는 것을 알게 되었어요. 씨앗을 담고 있는 솔방울이 부서지고 땅에 묻혀야 된다는 것을 알았죠. 산타크루즈의 산악 지대에 사는 사슴들에게는 솔방울이 주 식량이에요. 사슴은 딱딱한 솔방울을 부수고 씨앗을 땅에 떨어뜨리는데 사슴의 발이 그것들이 땅속으로 파묻히게 하죠. 이것이 산에 있는 소나무 개체수를 늘리는데 공헌하는 것이에요.

Topic: *influence of the population of the deer on number of pine trees* 사슴 개체수가 소나무 개체수에 미치는 영향
Sub-topic: *research* 연구
Detail: *deer break open the pinecone → seed drops into the ground → deer's hoof grinds it in the ground → increase of pine trees* 사슴이 솔방울을 깨뜨려 연다 → 땅에 씨앗이 떨어진다 → 사슴의 발로 인해 땅에 파묻힌다 → 소나무 개체수가 증가한다

Speaking

Using points and examples from the talk, explain how the population of deer influences the number of trees.

Possible response

The main topic of the lecture is how the population

of deer influences the increase in the population of pine trees. What I gathered from this lecture is that the increase in pine trees is caused by the deer. For example, the deer helps by eating through the tough shell of the pinecone, dropping the seeds, and stepping on the seeds on the ground. As a result, the number of pine trees is increased.

이 강의의 주제는 사슴 개체수가 소나무의 개체수 증가에 어떻게 영향을 미치는가 하는 것이다. 이 강의를 통해 이해한 것은 소나무 개체수의 증가는 사슴에 의해 야기된다는 것이다. 예를 들어 사슴은 딱딱한 솔방울 속의 씨앗을 먹으면서 땅에 씨앗을 떨어뜨리고, 그것을 밟아 땅속에 심는다. 그 결과로 소나무 개체수가 늘어난다.

2

Listening

Now listen to part of a talk in a photography class.

P　People's lifestyles have been affected by machines all throughout the world where technology is changing the face of the Earth every second. Today I would like to discuss how machines influenced photographers in the 19th century.

In the 19th century, machines were big and bulky, and people who worked with machines were blue-collar workers. These devices were a means to cut jobs for human workers, and people, especially, photographers had a negative point of view regarding the invention of machines. Photographers took pictures of a farmer lying on a stack of hay to emphasize the simplification of life or nature and kept the machine out of their pictures.

빠르게 발전하는 기술이 지구의 모습을 끊임없이 변화시키고 있는 세계 곳곳에서 사람들의 삶은 기계들에 의해 영향을 받아 왔습니다. 오늘은 기계가 19세기의 사진작가에게 어떠한 영향을 미쳤는지에 대해 이야기 해 보고자 합니다.

19세기에 기계들은 부피가 컸고, 기계를 다루던 사람들은 육체 노동자였습니다. 이 기계들은 인력을 필요로 하는 일을 감소시켰고, 이로 인해 사람들, 그 중 특히 사진작가들은 기계의 발명을 부정적으로 보았습니다. 작가들은 삶의 단순화 혹은 자연을 강조하기 위해 농부가 건초 위에 누워 있는 사진을 찍었고 사진에 기계를 등장시키지 않았습니다.

Topic: *influence of machines on photographers in the 19th century* 19세기에 기계가 사진작가에게 미친 영향
Sub-topic: *machines and blue-collar workers* 기계와 육체 노동자
Detail: *1. photographers had a negative point of view* 사진작가들은 부정적인 견해를 갖고 있었다

2. took pictures of a farmer lying on a stack of hay 건초 위에 누워 있는 농부의 사진을 찍었다

Using points and examples from the talk, explain the photographers' impressions of machines in the 19th century.

The main topic of the lecture is about the photographers' impressions of machines in the 19th century. What I gathered from this lecture is that photographers disliked machines because they replaced human workers at that time. As a result, photographers took photos of humans, such as farmers, and nature. They revealed their negative view about machines through such photographs.

이 강의의 주제는 19세기 사진작가들이 기계에 대해 가진 인상이다. 내가 이 강의를 통해 알게된 것은 사진작가들은 기계들이 사람들의 일을 대신하게 되었기 때문에 기계를 싫어했다는 것이다. 그 결과 사진작가들은 농부와 같은 사람들과 자연의 사진들을 찍었다. 그들은 이러한 사진을 통해 기계에 대한 그들의 부정적인 시선을 드러냈다.

3

Listening

Now listen to part of a talk in an ecology class.

P There are serious natural causes that can throw off the balance of certain environments. When an influx of new species is introduced to a certain area, the stable balanced life cycle can be disturbed. For example, a simple acacia tree can ruin an environment. The acacia tree can affect the area because of its characteristics; it tends to destroy other plants that are smaller than it because it blocks sunlight. Because it overshadows the smaller trees with its wide leaves and tall trunk, it absorbs all the sunlight. Introducing this species could destroy a whole area or even a country. To prevent these dangers, customs agents are strict on imports regarding the seeds of certain plants.

특정한 자연 환경의 균형을 깨뜨릴 수 있는 심각한 자연 현상들이 있습니다. 새로운 종자가 특정한 지역에 들어오면, 안정된 삶의 균형이 깨질 수 있습니다. 그 예로 한 그루의 아카시아 나무가 환경을 파괴할 수 있습니다. 아카시아 나무는 그것의 특징 때문에 한 지역에 영향을 미칠 수 있습니다. 이들은 햇빛을 가리기 때문에 자신보다 작은 나무들을 파괴시키는 경향이 있습니다. 아카시아 나무는 넓은 잎과 큰 키로 작은 나무를 그늘지게 하기 때문에 햇빛을 전부 흡수해 버립니다. 이런 종을 들여오게 되면 한 지역, 심지어는 한 나라를 망칠 수도 있습니다. 이러한 위기를 막기 위해, 관세 당국은 특정한 나무의 씨앗에 대한 수입을 엄격하게 관리합니다.

Topic: _natural causes that can throw off the balance in environments_ 자연 환경을 균형을 깰 수 있는 자연 현상들

Sub-topic: _acacia tree_ 아카시아 나무

Detail: _1. acacia tree blocks sunlight with wide leaves and tall trunk_ 아카시아 나무는 넓은 잎과 큰 키로 햇빛을 가린다

2. can destroy a whole area or even a country 한 지역이나 심지어 한 나라를 망칠 수도 있다

Using points and examples from the talk, explain the threat that an influx of new species have on a habitat.

The main topic of the lecture is how the introduction of a new species of tree can disturb the balance of a certain area. The professor gives the example of an acacia tree where the quality of this tree destroys all other plants living around the tree. The acacia tree is tall and blocks sunlight and slowly destroys all other smaller trees around itself.

강의의 주제는 한 지역에 유입된 새로운 종의 나무가 그 지역의 균형을 어떻게 깨뜨릴 수 있는지이다. 교수는 아카시아 나무가 갖고 있는 특성이 어떻게 주위의 모든 식물들을 파괴시키는지에 대한 예를 들고 있다. 아카시아 나무는 키가 크고 햇빛을 막기 때문에 주위의 모든 작은 나무들을 서서히 파괴시킨다.

4

Listening

Now listen to part of a talk in an art class.

P The uses of colors in art can elicit different emotions. Different colors represent messages and have a different significance. Okay, first let's take the example of the color red. Red can bring out very strong emotions, as it is a very powerful color. Red can excite a person, or draw out feelings of anger. If a room or painting has lots of red tones, the viewer can, in turn, feel powerful, or have intense feelings of fury. On the other hand, a color such as blue can have a totally opposite effect than a color like red. Blue is a cool color, and it feels smooth and suave, like the ocean breeze or the blue sky. When someone sees blue, they may feel refreshed and lighthearted because it may remind them of cool things such as the ocean or a gentle zephyr.

예술에 있어서 색상의 사용은 다른 감정들을 이끌어 낼 수 있어요. 각기 다른 색상들은 메시지를 나타내고 다른 의미를 갖고 있죠. 자, 그러면 첫 번째로 빨간 색상을 예로 들어봅시다. 빨간색은 매우 강렬한 색상이기 때문에 강한 감정을 불러 일으킬 수 있어요. 빨간색은 사람을 흥분하게 하거나 분노를 불러 일으킬 수 있어요. 만약 방이나 그림에 빨간 톤이 많이 사용되었다면 보는 사람은 힘을 느낄 수 있거나 강렬한 분노

를 느낄 수 있죠. 한편, 파란색과 같은 색상은 빨간색과는 완전히 반대되는 영향을 미칠 수 있어요. 파란색은 시원한 색상이고 마치 대양에서 부는 산들바람이나 파란 하늘처럼 부드럽고 원만한 느낌을 갖게 해요. 파란색을 보면 사람들은 대양이나 부드러운 산들바람처럼 시원한 것이 떠오르게 할 수 있기 때문에 신선함과 상쾌함을 느낄 수 있어요.

Topic: *use of colors in art* 예술에 있어서 색상의 사용

Sub-topic: *different colors have different significance*
각기 다른 색상들은 다른 의미를 갖는다

Detail: 1. *red: excite a person, bring out anger*
사람을 흥분하게 한다. 분노를 불러 일으킨다

2. *blue: refreshed* 상쾌함

Speaking

Using points and examples from the talk, explain the use of color in art.

Possible response

The main topic of the lecture is different emotions conveyed through colors. The professor explains how people use colors to communicate emotions in art. For example, people can use red to express strong emotions, to excite a person, or to express feelings of anger. In contrast, blue can be used in a totally different way compared to red. It represents being smooth and suave and may make people feel refreshed and relaxed.

강의의 주제는 색상을 통해 전달되는 다양한 감정들이다. 교수는 사람들이 예술에서 감정을 전달하기 위한 수단으로 색상을 사용하는 방법에 대해 설명한다. 예를 들어 사람들은 강한 감정을 나타내거나 흥분하게 하거나 화가 난 감정을 표현하기 위해 빨간색을 사용할 수 있다. 이와 대조적으로 파란색은 빨간색과 완전히 다르게 사용된다. 이것은 부드럽고 유순한 것을 나타내고 사람들로 하여금 신선하고 편안하게 느끼도록 할 수 있다.

Exercise
CD Possible Responses: Track 72~79

1

Listening

Now listen to part of a talk in a film class.

P It is interesting to understand how the flow of time is displayed to the viewers in a theater. It is very difficult to make a visually smooth connection of time through film. People usually don't realize how difficult it is to display the natural advancement of time by visual means. Movies employ various visual effects to show how time advances. Usually, many visual gimmicks are used, like a wheel of a train turning, to portray the advancement of time. Among these tricks, one prominent way is to actually show a clock or a calendar advancing quickly. This method is to use a clock and to make it go fast to give a sense of time changing quickly. Another prominent way of showing time advancing in a movie is by showing how a person's appearance — frequently the main character's — changes as the years go by. There is some resemblance to the young and old character even though they are different people; this gives the viewer a relationship between the two. For example, the film might show a boy in one of the scenes and then fade into a grown-up who is middle-aged.

영화에서 관객들에게 시간의 흐름을 표현하는 방식은 매우 흥미롭습니다. 영화를 통해 시각적으로 시간의 흐름을 매끈하게 연결하기란 어렵습니다. 사람들은 대부분 시각적인 방법으로 자연스러운 시간의 흐름을 보여주는 것에 따르는 어려움을 깨닫지 못합니다. 영화는 시간이 어떻게 흘러가는지 보여주기 위해 다양한 시각 효과를 활용합니다. 일반적으로 기차 바퀴가 돌아가는 등의 다양한 시각적 방법을 사용하여 시간이 흘러가는 것을 묘사합니다.
이러한 방법들 중에 한 가지 중요한 방법은 실제로 시계나 달력이 빨리 지나가는 것을 보여주는 것입니다. 이 방법은 시계를 사용하여 빨리 가도록 하고 이를 통해 시간이 빨리 흘러가는 것을 느끼게 하는 것입니다.
영화에서 시간의 흐름을 보여주는 또 다른 좋은 방법은 사람의 모습. 특히 주인공의 모습이 시간이 지나면서 어떻게 변하는지를 보여 주는 것입니다. 비록 사람이 다르다 해도 젊은 나이의 인물과 나이가 든 인물 간에는 유사한 부분이 있습니다. 바로 이것이 관객들에게 두 사람의 관계를 보여줍니다. 예를 들어 영화의 한 장면에서는 한 소년을 보여준 후, 그 소년이 중년으로 성장한 모습을 보여줄 수 있습니다.

Topic: *how the flow of time is portrayed in films*
영화에서 시간의 흐름을 묘사하는 방법

Sub-topic 1: *show a clock or a calendar advancing quickly* 시계나 달력이 빨리 지나가는 것을 보여주는 것

Detail: *gives a sense of time changing quickly*
시간이 빨리 흘러가는 것을 느끼게 한다

Sub-topic 2: *showing how a person's appearance changes* 사람의 모습이 어떻게 변하는지 보여주는 것

Detail: *a boy in one scene → a grown-up in next scene* 한 장면에서는 소년이 등장 → 다음 장면에서는 성인이 등장

Speaking

Using points and examples from the talk, explain the different methods of portraying the change in time in movies.

The main topic of the lecture is the ways to show how the flow of time is portrayed in films. The professor tells the students two most prominent ways used to portray the flow of time. The first way is by simply showing a clock or a calendar on the wall advancing quickly. Another way stated by the professor is to show different scenes with a person. For instance, a film can show a boy in one of the scenes, and then fade into a grown-up who is a middle-aged person to show that the person is older now and that many years have gone by. The professor thinks that these are the most prominent methods to portray the flow of time.

이 강의의 주제는 영화에서 시간의 흐름이 어떻게 묘사되는지 보여주는 것이다. 교수는 학생들에게 시간의 흐름을 묘사하기 위해 가장 흔히 사용되는 두 가지 방법에 대해 이야기한다. 첫 번째 방법은 단순히 벽에 있는 시계나 달력이 빠르게 움직이는 것을 보여주는 것이다. 교수가 언급하는 또 다른 방법은 사람이 등장하는 다른 장면을 보여주는 것이다. 예를 들어 영화는 한 장면에서 소년을 보여주고, 그가 나이가 들었으며 시간이 많이 지났다는 것을 보여주기 위해 다음 장면에서 중년의 성인을 보여줄 수 있다. 교수는 이 두 가지가 시간의 흐름을 묘사하는 가장 좋은 방법이라고 생각한다.

2

Listening

Now listen to part of a talk in a business class.

P   Now, we'll talk about advertising strategies that are the most important business activities to introduce their products to the public to maximize their benefits.

There are many advertising strategies that companies use to sell a product or a line of products. The most popular way as you may already know is to hire a celebrity to advertise the product. Many celebrities pose for certain products to give an impression to the consumer. Using a celebrity can be a clever way not only to impress people but also to disguise a product. For example, a car company advertising a new car, which isn't so fast, might hire a racecar driver. In the commercial, the racecar driver will give the impression that the car is fast. The consumer might feel that the car is fast because what they see is a celebrity as well as an expert in the field of auto racing. Through this advertising strategy, the company will create more revenue.

Another strategy would be to constantly repeat a comment or a catchy phrase. This prominent method is repeating a word or phrase. I know we've all experienced this advertising strategy used by the media. To set an example, people watch television advertisements about cars, and they are repeatedly told the word 'roomy', 'spacious', and 'cheap.' These words tend to target certain people who are looking for a multi-purpose vehicle that is within their budget. By repeating those words, it gets potential consumers interested in the product. If so, it has done its job.

자, 이제 이윤을 극대화하기 위하여 그들의 생산품을 대중에게 소개하는 가장 중요한 경제 활동인 광고 전략에 대해 이야기 해 보겠어요.

그들의 상품을 팔기 위해 회사들이 이용하는 많은 광고 전략들이 있어요. 여러분이 이미 아는 것처럼 가장 인기 있는 방법은 상품을 광고하기 위해 유명인을 쓰는 거에요. 많은 유명인들이 고객들에게 제품에 대한 좋은 인상을 주기 위해 광고를 찍죠. 유명인을 사용하는 것은 사람들에게 좋은 인상을 줄 뿐만 아니라 제품을 위장하기에 좋은 방법이에요. 예를 들어 그다지 빠르지 않은 자동차를 광고하기 위해 자동차 회사는 경주용 자동차 선수를 광고에 사용할 수 있어요. 광고에서는 경주용 자동차 선수가 차가 빠르다는 인상을 줄 거에요. 소비자들은 유명인인 동시에 경주용 자동차 선수인 사람을 보게 되기 때문에 자동차가 빠르다고 느끼게 될 수 있어요. 이 광고 전략을 통해 회사는 더 큰 수익을 창출할 수 있게 되죠.

또 다른 전략은 기발한 문구를 일정하게 반복하는 거에요. 자주 사용되는 이 방법은 단어나 구절을 반복하는 방법이에요. 우리들 모두 방송에서 사용되는 이 광고 전략을 경험해 본 적이 있을 거에요. 예를 들어 자동차 광고를 볼 때면 '공간이 넓은', '공간이 충분한', '저렴한'과 같은 단어를 반복해서 듣게 되어요. 이 단어들은 예산 범위 내에서 다용도로 쓸 수 있는 자동차를 찾는 사람을 목표로 하고 있어요. 이와 같은 단어들을 반복함으로써, 미래의 고객으로부터 제품에 대한 관심을 얻게 되어요. 그렇게 되면, 이들의 목표는 달성된 것이에요.

Topic: *advertising strategies* 광고 전략
Sub-topic 1:   *hire a celebrity to advertise the product*
   상품을 광고하기 위해 유명인을 고용한다
   Detail: *a race car driver → disguise the product → create more revenue* 경주용 자동차 선수 → 상품을 위장한다 → 더 큰 수익을 창출한다
Sub-topic 2:   *repeat a catchy phrase* 기발한 문구를 반복한다
   Detail: *roomy, spacious, and cheap → get the customers' interest in their product → sell more product* 공간이 넓은, 공간이 충분한, 저렴한 → 상품에 대한 소비자의 관심을 끈다 → 더 많은 상품을 판매한다

Speaking

Using points and examples from the talk, explain the two different advertising strategies.

Possible response

The main topic of the lecture is advertising strategies. The professor teaches the students two major advertising strategies. The first method is having a celebrity advertise the product, and the second is to repeat a keyword. To give an example of the first method, the professor explains how a car advertisement using a racecar driver can be effective in sales of a car. Consumers might be impressed by the celebrity and think that the car is really fast, even if it's not true. Another advertising method is to repeat words like 'roomy' or 'spacious' to describe a car so it will give the viewer an impression that the car has a lot of room. The professor asserts that these two advertising strategies are very helpful in getting customers' attention.

이 강의의 주제는 광고 전략이다. 교수는 학생들에게 두 가지 주요 광고 전략에 대해 가르쳐준다. 첫 번째 방법은 유명인을 이용하여 제품을 광고하는 것이고 두 번째 방법은 키워드를 반복하는 것이다. 첫 번째 방법의 예를 들기 위해 교수는 경주용 자동차 선수를 사용하는 자동차 광고가 판매에 있어 효과적일 수 있다고 설명한다. 고객들은 유명인 때문에 감탄하게 되고 비록 사실이 아니더라도 그 자동차가 빠를 것이라고 생각하게 될 것이다. 또 다른 광고 방법은 자동차를 묘사하기 위해 '공간이 넓은' 또는 '공간이 충분한' 등의 단어를 반복해서 고객들에게 이 차에 공간이 많다는 인상을 심어주는 것이다. 교수는 이 두 가지 방법이 고객의 관심을 끄는데 매우 유용하다고 주장하고 있다.

3

Now listen to part of a talk in a business class.

P   Data mining is, in some ways, an extension of statistics, with a few artificial intelligence and machine learning twists thrown in. Like statistics, data mining is not a business solution; it is just the underlying technology. There are two models associated with data mining.

Descriptive models are used to profile an individual customer's characteristics in a customer population. They are designed not to forecast any behavior, but only to compare one type of customer with another. For example, a company gave free flashlights to customers who filled out a survey to get individual information. According to the survey, many customers of the store were in their 30's. By utilizing this promotion, the company was able to categorize its customers into different groups, such as the average age group of its customers. The model doesn't predict anything about these individuals' future behavior — it simply produces a list of customers in a similar age group with similar interests.

A predictive model is simply an equation used to predict something. A predictive model can be formed by using data gathered from a descriptive model. In a simple but effective example, a predictive model is formed by collecting shoe sizes and heights from a group of people. I make a quick x/y plot that shows how generally taller people have larger shoes sizes than shorter people. Then I can use a computer statistics program to determine an equation that allows me to predict someone's shoe size if I know his height. Based on the predictive model, shoe stores can predict what size run of shoes they should hold on inventory by surveying the average height of its customers.

자료 수집이란 어떤 의미에서 통계의 연장선에 있어요. 여기에는 몇 가지 인공적인 지식과 기계에 대한 지식이 추가되어 있죠. 통계와 마찬가지로 자료 수집은 사업적 해결책이 아니에요. 이것은 단지 그것의 기술적인 기반일 뿐이죠. 자료 수집과 관련된 두 가지 모델이 있어요.

기술 모델은 고객 집단에서 개개인의 특성에 대한 프로필을 만들기 위해 사용되어요. 이것은 어떤 행동을 예상하기 위해서가 아니라, 특정 타입의 고객을 다른 타입의 고객과 비교하기 위해 고안되는 것이에요. 예를 들어, 한 회사가 개인 정보를 얻기 위해 실시한 조사에 참여한 사람들에게 공짜로 손전등을 주었다고 하죠. 조사에 따르면 상점에 오는 많은 고객들이 30대였어요. 이 판촉을 활용해서 회사는 고객들을 다양한 그룹, 예를 들어 연령대별로 분류할 수 있었어요. 이 모델은 개개인의 미래 행동에 관해서는 그 어떤 것도 예측하지 않았어요. 이것은 단지 비슷한 관심사를 가진 비슷한 연령대의 고객 명단을 작성한 것뿐이었어요.

예측 모델은 간단히 말해 무엇인가를 예측하기 위해 사용되는 방정식이에요. 예측 모델은 기술 모델로부터 모아진 자료를 토대로 고안될 수 있어요. 단순하지만 효과적인 예를 들어보면, 그룹의 사람들에게서 신발 사이즈와 신장을 모아서 예측 모델을 만들 수 있어요. 키가 큰 사람들이 일반적으로 키가 작은 사람들보다 신발 사이즈가 더 크다는 것을 나타내는 간단한 x/y 공식을 만든 후, 컴퓨터 통계 프로그램을 사용해서 누군가의 키를 아는 경우 신발 사이즈를 예측할 수 있도록 해주는 방정식을 만들 수 있죠. 이와 같은 예측 모델을 기반으로 하면 신발 가게는 고객들의 평균 신장을 조사해서 그들이 어떤 사이즈의 신발을 구비하고 있어야 하는지 예측할 수 있어요.

Topic: *models of data mining in the field of marketing*
마케팅 분야의 자료 수집 모델

Sub-topic 1: *descriptive model = a comparative model*
기술 모델 = 비교적인 모델

Detail: *profile a customer population* 고객 인구 비교

Sub-topic 2: *predictive model → computer aided software → predict certain information*
예측 모델 → 컴퓨터 보조 소프트웨어 → 특정 자료 예측

Detail: *height, shoe size → predict other customers' sizes* 신장, 신발 사이즈 → 다른 고객의 신발 사이즈 예측

Using points and examples from the talk, explain the two different models of data mining techniques in marketing.

Possible response

The main topic of the lecture is models of data mining in the field of marketing. The professor explains two models of data mining — the descriptive model and the predictive model. The descriptive model is a comparative model used to basically profile a customer population and compare it to other groups of customers. The descriptive model uses tools such as demographic data to profile each customer in certain areas. Another model, the predictive model, uses computer aided software to predict certain information. For instance, inputting the data of a person, like height and shoe size, will help to predict other customers' shoe sizes and thus, future shoe size preferences. The professor thinks that these two models are not a business solution, but the underlying technology.

이 강의의 주제는 마케팅 분야의 자료 수집 모델이다. 교수는 기술 모델과 예측 모델이라는 자료 수집의 두 가지 모델에 대해 설명한다. 기술 모델은 기본적으로 고객 인구에 대한 자료를 수집하여 다른 고객 그룹과 비교하는 비교적 모델이다. 기술 모델은 인구 조사 등의 도구를 사용하여 특정 지역의 고객 개개인의 자료를 수집한다. 또 다른 모델인 예측 모델은 특정 자료를 예측하기 위해 컴퓨터 보조 소프트웨어를 사용한다. 그 예로 개인의 신장과 신발 사이즈 등의 자료를 입력하면 다른 고객들의 신발 사이즈를 예측하는 데 도움이 되고, 따라서 선호하는 신발 사이즈를 예측할 수 있다. 교수는 이 두 가지 모델이 사업적 해결책이 아니라 기반이 되는 기술이라고 생각한다.

4

Listening

Now listen to part of a talk in an economics class.

P In economics, an externality is a cost or benefit from an economic transaction that parties "external" to the transaction receive. Externalities can be either positive, when an external benefit is generated, or negative, when an external cost is imposed upon others. In this lecture, I would like to discuss the benefits of positive externalities which are usually caused by government.

Let's say one local company decided to change their old bus, which uses gasoline, to a new bus that uses electricity to help save the environment. The problem was that the company was very small and didn't have enough money to accomplish their plan. So, the company decided to ask the government to help to pay for the new bus. Luckily, the government understood their situation and helped the company. Since then, people have used electronic buses, which do not pollute the air. The townspeople are able to enjoy cleaner air thanks to the new buses. In this case, the local

people had nothing to do with this scenario, but got to enjoy cleaner air because of the help of the government. This is a good example of a positive externality.

경제학에서, 외부 효과란 경제 활동의 제3자들이 비용을 물거나 이익을 얻게 되는 것을 뜻합니다. 외부 효과는 외형적인 이익이 생기는 경우 긍정적일 수 있으며, 그 비용이 다른 사람에게 부과될 때 부정적일 수 있습니다. 이 강의에서는 보통 정부에 의해 야기되는 긍정적 외부 효과에 대해 이야기 해 보겠습니다.

지방의 한 회사가 환경 보호를 위해 휘발유를 사용하는 기존의 버스를 전기를 사용하는 버스로 바꾸기로 결정했다고 합시다. 문제는 그 회사가 매우 작고 그들의 계획을 달성할 만한 자금이 부족하다는 것이었습니다. 그래서 그 회사는 정부에게 버스를 구입할 비용을 부탁하기로 결정했습니다. 운 좋게도 정부는 그들의 상황을 이해했고, 회사를 도와주었습니다. 그 이후 사람들은 공기를 오염시키지 않는 전기 버스를 이용했습니다. 새로운 버스 덕분에 시민들은 더 깨끗한 공기를 즐길 수 있게 되었습니다. 이 경우, 시민들은 이 상황과 아무런 연관이 없지만 정부의 도움 때문에 더 깨끗한 공기를 즐길 수 있게 되었습니다. 이것이 긍정적 외부 효과가 무엇인지 보여주는 좋은 예입니다.

Topic: *positive externalities* 긍정적 외부 효과
Sub-topic 1: *externality* 외부 효과
  Detail: *can be positive or negative*
        긍정적이거나 부정적일 수 있다
Sub-topic 2: *changing the bus with the help of the government* 정부의 도움을 받아 버스를 변경
  Detail: *gasoline bus → electronic buses → people enjoy cleaner air* 휘발유 버스 → 전기 버스 → 사람들이 더 깨끗한 공기를 즐김

Speaking

Using points and examples from the talk, give the definition and example of positive externalities and how governments encourage positive externalities.

Possible response

The main topic of this lecture is positive externalities. What I gathered from this lecture is that positive externalities are usually caused by government activities. The professor gives an example of a local company that made a plan to change their buses because the buses used gasoline, which polluted the air. The company didn't have the funds to buy electronic buses and asked the government for help. The government helped the company to convert the buses. As a result, the townspeople were able to enjoy fresh air. Actually, the townspeople didn't do anything at all to help the company to buy the electronic buses, but the people enjoyed the cleaner air because the government helped the company to buy them. This is an example of how positive externalities create benefits for external parties.

이 강의의 주제는 긍정적 외부 효과이다. 이 강의를 통해 알게 된 것은 긍정적 외부 효과가 보통 정부의 활동에 의해 야기된다는 것이다. 교수는 지방의 회사가 버스가 휘발유를 사용하여 공기를 오염시키기 때문에 버스를 바꿀 계획을 세운 것에 대해 예를 든다. 회사는 전기 버스를 구입할 자금이 없었기 때문에 정부에게 도움을 요청했다. 정부는 회사가 버스를 바꿀 수 있도록 도와주었다. 그 결과, 도시에 사는 시민들은 신선한 공기를 즐길 수 있게 되었다. 실질적으로 시민들은 그 회사가 전기 버스를 구입하는데 아무런 도움을 주지 않았지만, 정부가 그 회사를 도왔기 때문에 깨끗한 공기를 누릴 수 있게 되었다. 이것이 바로 긍정적 외부 효과가 제3자에게 유익함을 창출하는 것에 대한 예시이다.

5

Now listen to part of a talk in a child education class.

P Children have amazing learning abilities. A one-year-old child has the ability of the mapping process, which is the ability to put together images with words and to categorize them. For example, if you indicate "horse" in front of a child, he can recognize it as a type of animal if he or she has been taught the category of "animal." There are two downfalls to this mapping process in children: too broad or too specific.

A common error that children make is that they understand in a broad mapping process. When they learn that a horse has four legs, they often generalize that all four-legged animals are horses. In other words, even if they see a cow, they might think it is a horse.

The opposite of the broad mapping process would be a specific mapping process. This happens when children think that only one item is named a specific thing. For example, if a kid's doll is called "Doll" then the kid might think that only one doll is called "Doll." Most children tend to be specific when they have a toy that they have grown attached to, and the name "Doll" is known to them as "My Doll."

Children have these astounding ways of mapping their knowledge. Though they tend to be too broad or too specific at times, this ability to map certain images in their initial developmental stage is intriguing.

아이들은 놀랄만한 학습 능력을 가지고 있어요. 한 살짜리 어린이는 과정을 형상화하는 능력이 있는데, 이것은 이미지와 단어를 연관 지어 분류하는 능력이에요. 예를 들어 어린이 앞에서 "말"을 가리키면 그 어린이는 "동물"이라는 카테고리를 배웠을 경우 그것을 동물의 일종이라고 인식할 수 있어요. 아이들의 형상화 과정에는 너무 일반화 하거나 너무 특정화 한다는 두 가지 함정이 있어요.

아이들이 흔히 저지르는 실수는 형상화 하는 과정에서 일반화 한다는 것이에요. 그들은 말이 다리가 4개라는 것을 배우게 되면 다리가 4개인 동물은 모두 말이라고 일반화해요. 다시 말해 그들은 소를 본다고 해도, 이것을 말이라고 생각할 수 있어요.

일반화 형상 과정과 반대되는 것은 특정화 하는 것이에요. 이것은 아이들이 각각의 물건에 특정한 이름 하나만이 주어진다고 생각할 때 발생해요. 예를 들어 한 아이의 인형이 "Doll"이라고 불리면, 그 아이는 단지 그 인형만이 "Doll"이라는 이름을 갖는 것이라고 생각할 수 있어요. 대부분의 어린이들은 그들이 애착을 갖고 있는 장난감에 대해 특정화 하는 경향이 있어요. 그래서 "Doll"이라는 이름은 그들에게는 "내 Doll"을 나타내게 되죠.

아이들은 이처럼 그들의 지식을 형상화하는 놀라운 방법을 가지고 있어요. 비록 때때로 너무 일반화하거나 너무 특정화 하는 경향이 있지만, 초기 발달 단계에서 특정 이미지를 형상화하는 능력은 매우 흥미로워요.

Topic: *children's learning ability → two downfalls*
어린이의 학습 능력 → 두 가지 함정

Sub-topic 1: *broad mapping process* 일반화
Detail: *horse has four legs → all animals with four legs are horses* 말은 다리가 4개이다 → 4개의 다리를 가진 동물은 모두 말이다

Sub-topic 2: *specific mapping process* 특정화
Detail: *doll → toy's name becomes "Doll"*
인형의 이름이 "Doll"이 된다

Using points and examples from the talk, explain the two errors in the mapping process of children.

Possible response

The main topic of the lecture is about the mapping ability of children. According to the professor, children possess interesting mapping abilities which have downfalls in them as well: too broad or too specific. As an example of the broad mapping process, the professor explains that when people teach children that a horse has four legs, they might believe that all animals with four legs, such as cows or tigers, are horses. The specific mapping process is when you teach a child that the toy they play with is called "doll"; then the toy's name becomes "doll." The professor thinks that though there are some errors when kids learn, their ability to map images is amazing.

강의의 주제는 어린이들의 형상화 능력이다. 교수에 따르면 어린이들은 흥미로운 형상화 능력을 갖고 있지만 일반화 하거나 특정화 하는 단점도 있다. 일반화에 대한 예로 교수는 사람들이 어린이에게 말은 다리가 4개라고 가르쳐 주면, 어린이들은 소나 호랑이처럼 다리가 4개인 모든 동물을 말이라고 생각할 수도 있다고 설명한다. 특정화는 어린이에게 그들이 갖고 노는 장난감이 "인형"이라고 가르쳐 주면, 그 장난감의 이름이 "인형"이 되는 것을 뜻한다. 교수는 어린이가 학습할 때 비록 약간의 오류가 발생하지만, 이미지를 형상화하는 그들의 능력이 놀랍다고 생각한다.

6

Now listen to part of a talk in an economics class.

P　Today, I'd like to discuss the relationship between substitutable and complementary products. The prices of closely related goods influence the demand for a product. An increase in the price of one will cause an increase in demand for the other. These types of related goods are either called substitutes or complements. When two products perform similar functions or fulfill similar needs, they are substitutes. There is a direct relationship between the price of a product and the demand for substitutes. For example, butter and margarine are substitutes. Higher butter prices will increase the demand for margarine as consumers substitute it for the more expensive butter. Similarly, higher coffee prices will increase the demand for such substitutes as coca and tea.

Other closely related products are consumed jointly. An increase in the price of one will cause the demand for the other to fall. Goods that go together are called complements. For complements, there is an inverse relationship between the price of one and the demand for the other. For example, as the experience of the 1980s illustrates, higher CD prices caused the demand for CD players to decline. On the other hand, lower CD prices caused the demand for CD players to increase during the 1990s. Up to now, we have discussed how substitutable and complementary products are related to each other. Tomorrow, I'll talk about consumer's behaviors more.

오늘은 대체 가능하고 상호 보완적인 제품의 관계에 대해 논의하고자 합니다. 밀접한 연관이 있는 제품들의 가격은 제품의 수요에 영향을 미칩니다. 한 제품의 가격이 올라가면, 다른 제품에 대한 수요가 증가하게 됩니다. 이처럼 서로 연관이 있는 상품들은 대체품 또는 보완재라고 불립니다. 두 제품이 유사한 기능을 수행하거나, 유사한 필요를 충족시켜줄 때 그들은 대체품이라고 합니다. 상품의 가격과 대체품의 수요 사이에는 직접적인 관계가 있습니다. 예를 들어 버터와 마가린은 대체품입니다. 버터 가격이 높아지면 가격이 더 높은 버터 대신 마가린에 대한 수요가 증가할 것입니다. 이와 유사하게 커피 가격이 높아지면 코코아나 차와 같은 대체품에 대한 수요가 증가하게 됩니다.

밀접하게 관계가 있는 다른 제품들은 공동으로 소비됩니다. 하나의 가격이 올라가면 다른 하나에 대한 수요가 감소하게 됩니다. 이처럼 함께 소비되는 상품을 보완재라고 합니다. 보완품의 경우, 한 제품의 가격과 다른 제품의 수요는 역관계에 있습니다. 예를 들어 1980년대의 경험에서 알 수 있듯이 CD 가격의 상승은 CD 플레이어의 수요를 감소시켰습니다. 반면에, 1990년대에 CD 가격이 내리자 CD 플레이어의 수요가 증가하였습니다. 자, 지금까지는 대체품과 보완재가 서로 어떤 관계가 있는지에 대해 이야기 해 보았습니다. 내일은 소비자의 행동에 대해 좀 더 이야기 해 보겠습니다.

Topic: *two types of related goods → substitutable & complementary goods* 2개의 연관된 상품 → 대체품, 보완재
Sub-topic 1: *substitutable goods* 대체품
　Detail: *price of butter increase → demand for margarine increase* 버터 가격 상승 → 마가린 수요 상승
Sub-topic 2: *complementary goods* 보완재
　Detail: *prices of CD increase → demand for CD player decrease* CD 가격 상승 → CD 플레이어 수요 하락

Using points and examples from the talk, explain substitutable goods and complementary goods.

Possible response

The main topic of this lecture is about the relationship between substitutable and complementary goods. What I gathered from this lecture is that substitutable goods substitute for each other and these types of goods have a direct relationship to each other. For example, the lecturer states that if the price of butter increases, the demand for its substitutes, such as margarine, will increase. The professor also states that complementary goods are consumed jointly, but have an inverse relationship to each other. For instance, during the 1980's, the prices of CDs increased, which caused the demand for its complementary item, the CD player, to decline. This lecture describes how substitutable and complementary products influence each other.

이 강의의 주제는 대체품과 보완재간의 관계이다. 이 강의를 통해 이해한 것은 대체품은 서로를 대체하며, 이러한 상품들은 서로 직접적인 관계를 가지고 있다라는 것이다. 예를 들어 교수는 버터의 가격이 오르면, 마가린 같은 대체품의 수요가 증가할 것이라고 말한다. 교수는 또한 보완재는 함께 소비되지만, 역관계를 갖는다고 말한다. 예를 들어 1980대에 CD 가격이 올랐는데, 이것은 서로 보완 관계에 있는 CD 플레이어의 수요를 하락하게 했다. 이 강의는 대체품과 보완재가 서로에게 어떻게 영향을 미치는지에 대해 묘사하고 있다.

7

Now listen to part of a talk in a child development class.

P　Some researchers had been studying babies' intelligence levels and recognized that they had an ability to count as early as five months old. So, they set out a hypothesis to test it. Today, we'll be talking about the hypothesis that babies can count as early as five months of age. Six babies, all about five months old, were in an experiment to test this hypothesis. They were testing how babies would react if they didn't see what they expected. First, they showed a doll on a table to the babies. Then the doll disappeared behind a screen. When the screen was removed, the babies showed no response because the doll was still there. In the next stage, they showed two dolls to the babies and then hid them behind a screen. When the screen was removed, the babies only saw one doll on the table. Their reaction showed that they were surprised because they expected to see two dolls, but saw only one.

According to this experiment, it seems possible that babies, in fact, possess the ability to count when they are very young. If this hypothesis is true, perhaps we should raise another question — should we take advantage of this ability by teaching children mathematics at a younger age? They seem to have a great, untapped potential, but is it necessary for parents to pressure young children?

일부 연구원들이 아기의 지능에 대해 연구해 왔는데, 아기들이 5개월쯤 되었을 때부터 수를 세는 능력을 가지고 있다는 것을 알게 되었습니다. 그래서 그들은 그것을 실험하기 위해 가설을 설정했습니다. 오늘은 5개월 된 아기가 수를 셀 수 있다는 가설에 대해 이야기 해 보겠습니다. 약 5개월 정도 된 6명의 아기들이 이 가설을 확인하기 위한 실험에 참여했습니다. 이 실험은 아기들이 볼 것이라고 예상했던 것을 보지 못했을 때 어떤 반응을 보이는지를 실험하는 것이었습니다.

우선 아기들에게 테이블에 있는 인형 한 개를 보여주었습니다. 그런 후 인형은 스크린 뒤로 사라졌습니다. 스크린을 치웠을 때 인형이 여전히 그곳에 있었기 때문에 아기들은 아무런 반응을 보이지 않았습니다. 다음 단계에서는 아기들에게 두 개의 인형을 보여주고, 스크린 뒤에 인형들을 숨겼습니다. 스크린을 치우자 아기들은 테이블에 인형이 한 개밖에 없다는 것을 보게 되었습니다. 그들의 반응은 두 개의 인형을 볼 것을 예상했는데 단지 한 개를 보았기 때문에 놀랐다는 것을 나타냈습니다. 이 실험에 따르면 아기들이 실제로 매우 어렸을 때부터 수를 셀 수 있는 능력을 갖고 있다는 것이 가능한 것처럼 보입니다. 만약 이 가설이 사실이라면, 우리는 또 다른 질문을 할 수 있을 것입니다 – 어린이들에게 어렸을 때부터 수학을 가르쳐서 이 능력을 활용해야 될까요? 그들은 미개발된 훌륭한 잠재력을 가지고 있는 것처럼 보이지만, 부모들이 아이들을 압박하는 것이 필요한 것일까요?

Topic: *babies' ability to count → experiment*
수를 셀 수 있는 아기들의 능력 → 실험

Sub-topic 1: *one doll on the table → screen removed → one doll on the table* 테이블에 인형 1개 → 스크린 치움 → 테이블에 인형 1개

Detail: *shows no reaction → expected* 무반응 → 예측했음

Sub-topic 2: *two dolls on the table → screen removed → one doll on the table* 테이블에 인형 2개 → 스크린 치움 → 테이블에 인형 1개

Detail: *shows reaction (surprised) → unexpected* 반응 (놀람) → 예측하지 못했음

Speaking

Using points and examples from the talk, explain the experiment of 5-month-old babies and their ability to count.

Possible response

The main topic of this lecture is to see if babies can count as early as five months of age. Two experiments were carried out in order to test this hypothesis. In the first experiment, a doll was placed on a table and then hidden behind a screen. When the screen was removed, the doll was still on the table and the babies did not react. A doll on the table was what the babies had expected to see. However, in the next experiment, two dolls were placed on the table and then covered with a screen. When the screen was removed, there was only one doll remaining. The babies were surprised because they had expected to see two dolls on the table. The babies responded differently to each experiment because of what they had expected to see, and this shows how they might be able to count at a very young age.

이 강의의 주제는 5개월쯤 된 아기들이 숫자를 셀 수 있는 지적 능력이 있는지 확인하는 것이다. 이 가설을 시험하기 위해 두 개의 실험을 실시하였다. 첫 번째 실험에서는 인형 한 개를 테이블에 놓은 후 스크린 뒤에 감추었다. 스크린을 치우자 인형이 여전히 테이블에 있었고 아기들은 반응을 보이지 않았다. 아기들은 테이블에 인형 한 개가 있을 것이라고 예측했던 것이었다. 그러나 다음 실험에서는 테이블에 인형 두 개를 놓았다. 스크린을 치우자 테이블에는 인형이 한 개만 남아있었다. 아기들은 테이블에 인형 두 개를 볼 것이라고 예측했기 때문에 놀랐다. 아기들은 그들이 볼 것이라고 예측했던 것 때문에 각 실험에 다르게 반응했다. 그리고 이것은 아기들이 아주 어렸을 때부터 수를 셀 수 있을지도 모른다는 것을 보여준다.

8

Listening

Now listen to part of a talk in a geology class.

P Today, let's talk about creating a map. There is some difficulty in map-making because of the curvature of the Earth. When we map out the entire planet Earth, people make a lot of mistakes by trying to put something that is three-dimensional onto a flat piece of paper, thus distorting the actual size and distance of each continent. This would be the first problem. The most accurate representation of the Earth is not on paper, but on a globe because it is a 3D shape.

Another problem of creating a map is that the distance between points can be very deceiving. On a 2D map, it seems as if two places are close, but in actuality, it is farther than expected. The reason is that there could be mountains or canyons between the two points that the map doesn't show. It only shows a flat piece of land. So, if someone were traveling using a 2D map, they could be in for a surprise as to the amount of time it takes to get to their destination because it may appear close on the map, but they wouldn't have taken into consideration, climbing up a mountain.

오늘은 지도를 만드는 것에 대해 이야기 해 봅시다. 지구의 만곡 때문에 지도를 만드는데 약간의 어려움이 따릅니다. 우리가 지구 전체를 그릴 때 3차원의 것을 평평한 종이에 그리려고 하기 때문에 각 대륙의 크기와 거리를 왜곡하는 실수를 자주 하게 됩니다. 이것이 첫 번째 문제가 됩니다. 지구가 3차원이기 때문에 가장 정확하게 지구를 표현하는 것은 종이 위가 아니라 둥근 구 위에 그리는 것입니다.

지도를 만드는 또 다른 어려움은 지점과 지점 사이의 거리를 착각할 수 있다는 것입니다. 2차원 지도상에서는 두 장소가 마치 가까운 것처럼 보일 수 있지만 실제로는 예상했던 것보다 먼 경우가 있습니다. 그 이유는 실제로는 두 장소 사이에 산이나 협곡이 있는데 지도는 그것을 보여주지 않기 때문입니다. 지도는 단지 평평한 땅만을 나타냅니다. 그래서 만약 어떤 사람이 2차원의 지도를 가지고 여행을 한다면 목적지에 도달하는 시간 때문에 놀랄 수도 있습니다. 지도에서는 가깝게 보일 수 있지만 산을 올라야 한다는 것은 고려하지 않았을 것이기 때문입니다.

Topic: _creating a map_ 지도 만들기
Sub-topic 1: _the size and distance is inaccurate_
　　　　크기와 거리가 정확하지 않다
Detail: _most companies draw maps on a sheet of paper_ 대부분의 회사들은 종이에 지도를 보여준다
Sub-topic 2: _on a 2D map, the distance can be deceiving_ 2차원에서의 지도에서는 거리를 착각할 수 있다
Detail: _mountains or canyons between the two points does not appear on the map_ 두 지점 사이에 위치한 산이나 협곡은 지도에 나타나지 않기 때문에

Speaking

Using points and examples from the talk, explain the two reasons why it is difficult to make a map of the Earth on paper.

Possible response

The lecture is mainly about the difficulties in making a map. Creating a map of the world isn't easy because of the distortion caused by getting a 3-dimensional object onto a flat 2-dimensional piece of paper. The professor states that the size and distance will be inaccurate because most companies show an atlas on a sheet of paper. Another difficulty is that on a 2-dimensional map, two points seem closer than they actually are, but in actuality, they are a lot farther apart because of features such as mountains and canyons. Thus, the professor thinks that making a map is very difficult.

강의는 주로 지도를 만드는 데 따르는 어려움에 관한 것이다. 3차원의 것을 평평한 2차원의 종이 위에 나타내는 것을 통해 야기되는 왜곡 때문에 세계지도를 만드는 것은 쉽지 않다. 교수는 대부분의 회사들이 지형을 종이 위에 나타내기 때문에 크기와 거리가 정확하지 않을 것이라고 말한다. 또 다른 어려운 점은 2차원의 지도에서는 두 지점이 실제보다 더 가깝게 보이지만 실제로는 산이나 협곡 같은 것 때문에 그것이 훨씬 더 멀다. 그래서 교수는 지도를 만드는 것은 어려운 일이라고 생각한다.

iBT Actual Test

Possible Responses: Track 81~86

Set 1

1 Describe the job you would like to pursue the most. Include specific details and examples to support your answer.

Possible response

A job that I would like to pursue is that of an actor for the following reasons. First, I have always enjoyed performing arts since I was a child, and it is a passion of mine to perform in front of an audience. Performing in front of the public gives me confidence in myself. Second, I would like to be an actor in order to become rich and famous. Actors seem to have an enjoyable life because they have a lot of money. For example, actors usually drive very expensive cars, live in extravagant houses, and wear expensive designer label clothes. I would like to pursue acting because I want to enjoy my life in these ways.

내가 갖고 싶은 직업은 다음과 같은 이유로 배우이다. 우선, 나는 항상 어릴 때부터 연기하는 것을 즐겼고, 관객들 앞에서 연기하는 것이 나의 열정이다. 다른 사람들 앞에서 연기하는 것은 자신감을 갖게 한다. 두 번째로, 나는 부자가 되고 유명해지기 위해 배우가 되고 싶다. 배우들은 돈이 많기 때문에 인생을 즐겁게 사는 것 같다. 예를 들어 배우들은 보통 매우 비싼 차를 운전하고, 고급 주택에서 살고, 비싼 브랜드의 옷을 입는다. 나는 이렇게 인생을 즐기고 싶기 때문에 연기를 하고 싶다.

2 In the future, it will be possible to study at home with an online system like computers or TV. Some students might like to study with this system; others might like to study with traditional school systems. Which do you prefer and why? Include specific details and examples to support your answer.

Possible response

I prefer to study with an online system rather than with the traditional method of taking a bus to school and sitting in a classroom because there are many benefits to online schooling. First, an online system can easily be adjusted according to the students' schedule. Also, students can use the online study system anytime, anywhere. An online system also would benefit those who are far away from local traditional schooling. They could still get a quality education through an online system. Transportation costs could be saved by enrolling in an online study program. In my opinion, the next step in traditional study would be to have it available online.

나는 버스를 타고 학교에 가서 교실에서 수업을 받는 전통적인 방법보다 온라인으로 공부하는 것을 더 좋아한다. 그 이유는 온라인 학습에 따르는 많은 장점들 때문이다. 우선, 온라인 시스템은 학생들의 스케줄에 맞춰 쉽게 조정될 수 있다. 또한 학생들은 온라인 시스템을 언제, 어디서나 사용할 수 있다. 또한 온라인 학습은 지역 학교로부터 멀리 떨어져 사는 학생들에게도 도움이 될 것이다. 그들은 온라인 시스템을 통해서 양질의 교육을 받을 수 있다. 온라인 학습 프로그램에 등록함으로써 교통비를 아낄 수도 있을 것이다. 내 생각에는 전통적 학습 방법이 추구해야 하는 다음 단계는 온라인으로 학습이 가능하도록 하는 것이다.

3

Reading

The University has decided to change the class policy. Read the announcement about the university's plan to allow undergraduate students to take graduate courses. You will have 45 seconds to read the announcement. Begin reading now.

Policy Change

The university has made some changes to the class policy. Undergraduate students will now be able to join graduate classes, if needed. This will allow undergrad students to get a better understanding of the graduate school system and have a competitive start if they choose to go to graduate school. Also, it allows for a good introduction to the graduate program in our school.

대학은 수업 정책을 일부 변경했다. 이제 학부생들도 필요하다면 대학원 수업을 수강할 수 있다. 이는 학부생들로 하여금 대학원 시스템에 대해 보다 잘 이해하고 대학원에 진학하는 경우 보다 유리한 시작을 할 수 있도록 할 것이다. 이것은 또한 우리 학교 대학원 프로그램에 대한 유익한 소개가 될 것이다.

Listening

Now listen to two students as they discuss the announcement.

W There is a new policy change. I'm sure you've heard about it.

M I sure did. I don't think it's a good idea. There are no benefits for a graduate student if an undergrad attends a required graduate course.

W Why is that a big problem? It would be great to take some graduate courses in advance. Undergrad students could get much help from graduate students.

M Well, graduate classes are small in number so they spend a lot of time discussing specific topics and exchanging opinions. If there are more students in the class, they won't be able to carry out discussions effectively.

W I guess that could be a problem, but if the school limits the class size, it won't be too much of a problem.

M On top of that, the pace of the graduate program is much faster than undergrad school. But if undergraduate students take the class, they might slow down the class schedule. Also, undergrad students might lose a chance to meet new people in different graduate schools if they attend graduate classes at the same university.

여 정책이 새롭게 변경되었대. 너도 물론 들었겠지.
남 물론이지. 난 그게 좋은 생각인 것 같지 않아. 학부생이 대학원 필수 과목을 듣게 되면 대학원생에게는 전혀 도움이 되지 않아.
여 그게 왜 큰 문제야? 대학원 수업을 미리 들을 수 있으면 정말 좋을 거야. 학부생들은 대학원생들에게 많은 도움을 받을 수 있잖아.
남 글쎄, 대학원 수업은 학생수가 많지 않아서 특정 주제에 대해 토론하고 의견을 교환하면서 많은 시간을 보내는데, 수업에 학생들이 더 많아지면 토론을 효과적으로 할 수 없을 거야.
여 문제가 될 수는 있겠지만, 학교에서 수강 인원을 제한한다면 그렇게 큰 문제가 되지는 않을 거야.
남 무엇보다도, 대학원 수업의 진도는 학부보다 훨씬 빠른데 학부생들이 수업을 들으면 수업 스케줄이 지연될지도 몰라. 그리고 학부생들이 같은 대학에서 대학원 수업을 들으면 다른 대학원의 새로운 사람들을 만날 기회를 잃게 될 수도 있어.

Speaking

The man expresses his opinion of the university's plan to allow undergraduate students to take graduate courses. State his opinion and explain the reasons he gives for holding that opinion.

Possible response

The man disagrees with the school's new policy to allow undergraduate students to take graduate courses. The first reason is that graduate students will not appreciate an undergrad taking the same class because the size of the class may get larger and prevent deep discussions. Also, the graduate program usually moves faster than that of the undergraduate school so undergraduate students might not be able to keep up with their studies. The second reason is that undergraduate students might lose an opportunity to meet new people in different graduate schools if

they go to grad school on the same campus. These are the reasons why the man strongly opposes the school's decision to allow undergraduate students to take graduate courses.

남자는 학부생들이 대학원 수업을 수강할 수 있도록 하는 학교의 새 정책에 반대한다. 첫 번째 이유는 학생수가 늘어나서 심도 있는 토론을 방해할 수 있기 때문에 대학원생들이 학부생들과 같은 수업을 듣는 것을 달가워하지 않을 것이기 때문이다. 또한 대학원 과정은 보통 학부보다 진도가 빠르기 때문에 학부생들이 교과 과정을 따라가지 못할 수도 있다. 두 번째 이유는 학부생들이 같은 학교의 대학원을 간다면 다른 학교 대학원에서 새로운 사람을 만날 기회를 잃게 될 수도 있기 때문이다. 이러한 이유로 남자는 학부생들에게 대학원 수업 수강을 허용하는 학교의 결정에 강력하게 반대한다.

4

Reading

Now read the passage about facial expression. You will have 45 seconds to read the passage. Begin reading now.

Facial Expression

Facial expressions play an important role in communication. When a person doesn't want to perform a certain act or task, their facial expression changes and people don't realize that 80% of communication is achieved not verbally but by body language and facial expression. The faces that we make let others know indirectly how we feel.

얼굴 표정은 의사 소통에서 중요한 역할을 한다. 어떤 일이나 과업을 하고 싶지 않을 때 사람들의 얼굴 표정이 변한다. 사람들은 의사 소통의 80%가 언어가 아닌 신체 언어나 얼굴 표정에 의해 이루어진다는 것을 깨닫지 못한다. 우리가 짓는 표정은 다른 사람들에게 우리의 감정을 간접적으로 알려 준다.

Listening

Now listen to part of a lecture in a psychology class. The professor talks about facial expression.

P Let's consider this common example; we observe a thirteen-year-old and his mother. The mother calls the boy and tells him to do the chores that he was supposed to do. When he is with his friends, he doesn't say yes like a good boy, but instead he says that is "uncool." If he were at home, he would have said yes. The important part is that he tells his mother, "Don't you think I am a little too old to be told what to do?" And when he gets home, he listens to his mother and does the chores, but his facial expression and his body tell his mother otherwise.

This body expression, trudging along, and his facial expression tell the mother he isn't happy about doing the chores. He feels that a mandatory task has all of a sudden become optional. He feels that the household chores are not his job anymore. He feels that he has more important things to do than doing household chores or there should be another designated person for that job. A lot is said without saying a word, just by the motion of his body or an expression on his face.

이 보편적인 예를 생각해 보죠. 13살 난 아이와 그의 엄마에 대해 살펴보겠어요. 엄마가 그 아이를 불러서 그가 해야 하는 집안일을 하라고 말합니다. 아이가 친구들과 같이 있을 때는 착한 아이처럼 알았다고 말하지 않고 대신 "불쾌한" 일이라고 말합니다. 아이가 집에 있었다면, 그는 알았다고 말했을 것입니다. 중요한 것은 아이가 엄마에게 "일을 시키기에는 제가 나이가 좀 많다고 생각하지 않으세요?"라고 말한다는 것입니다. 그리고 집에 돌아오면 그는 엄마의 말을 듣고 집안일을 하지만, 그의 얼굴 표정과 행동은 다르게 말하고 있습니다.

터벅터벅 걷는 것과 같은 신체적 표현과 얼굴 표정은 그가 집안일을 하고 싶지 않다는 것을 엄마에게 알려줍니다. 아이는 꼭 해야 한다고 생각했던 일이 갑자기 선택 사항이 된 것처럼 느낍니다. 그는 집안일이 더 이상 자신의 일이 아니라고 느낍니다. 집안일보다 해야 할 더 중요한 일이 있다고 느끼거나, 그 일을 할 다른 사람이 있어야 한다고 생각하는 것이죠. 한마디 말 없이도 그의 몸짓이나 얼굴 표정으로 많은 것을 전하게 됩니다.

Speaking

The professor talks about facial expression. Explain how the professor uses a 13-year-old boy to explain his views.

Possible response

The professor talks about how facial expressions are a form of body language that people commonly do not consider as nonverbal language. What I heard from this lecture is that a little boy, for example, shows this form of nonverbal language when his mother tells him to do a household chore. He's upset with his mother so he uses nonverbal communication to show dissatisfaction with his chores. His heavy breathing and unhappy face gives a signal to his mother. And he also points out that this observation of the boy is a prime example of actions and facial expressions.

교수는 사람들이 보통 비언어적 언어라고 생각하지 않는 얼굴 표정이 신체 언어의 한 형태라는 것에 대해 이야기하고 있다. 나는 이 강의로부터 예를 들어 엄마가 한 소년에게 집안일을 시켰을 때 소년이 비언어적 언어를 나타낸다는 것을 배웠다. 그 아이는 엄마에게 화가 나서 집안일을 하는 것에 대한 불만족을 나타내기 위해 비언어적 의사 소통 수단을 사용한다. 한숨을 쉬는 것과 불행해 보이는 얼굴은 엄마에게 신호를 보낸다. 또한 교수는 이러한 아이에 대한 관찰이 행동과 얼굴 표정의 주요한 예라고 지적한다.

5

Listening

Now listen to a conversation between two students.

W Hello, Sam. What's up today?

M Hey, Jody. I have a slight problem. My volunteer club was planning to take children to an exhibition in the city, but the school van broke down. I think the kids will be very disappointed.

W Well, being the captain of the club, I see you have a serious problem on your hands.

M Yeah, I don't know what to do. Do you have any suggestions?

W I guess you could borrow a car from your friend, Bob.

M I don't think he would lend me his car because it is brand new.

W How about using public transportation? Why don't you try that?

M That's a good idea, but it's not going to be easy to control the kids when we use public transportation. They are very active and always run around here and there, you know.

W Well, those are the only options I can think of.

M I guess I'll think about it a bit more.

여 안녕, Sam, 오늘 어때?

남 안녕, Jodie. 좀 문제가 있어. 자원 봉사 클럽에서 아이들을 시내 전시회에 데려가기로 했는데 학교 버스가 고장이 났어. 아이들이 매우 실망할 거야.

여 그래. 클럽의 회장으로서 문제가 심각하겠구나.

남 맞아, 어떻게 해야 할지 모르겠어. 뭐 좋은 생각이라도 있니?

여 네 친구 Bob에게 차를 빌리면 어떨까?

남 그의 차는 새 것이라서 빌려줄 것 같지 않아.

여 대중 교통을 이용하는 건 어때? 그렇게 해보지 그래?

남 좋은 생각이긴 하지만 대중 교통을 이용하면 아이들을 통제하기가 쉽지 않을 거야. 아이들은 매우 활동적이고 항상 여기 저기 뛰어다니잖아.

여 글쎄, 내가 생각나는 건 이게 다야.

남 조금 더 생각해 봐야겠어.

Speaking

The students discuss two possible solutions to the man's problem. Describe the problem. Then state which of the two solutions you prefer and explain why.

Possible response

The man's problem is that he is trying to find a way to take the kids to the exhibition in the city. But he finds out that the school bus broke down. The woman first suggests that he should borrow a car from his friend, but he thinks that since his friend's car is brand new, he probably won't lend it to him. I think the other alternative of using public transportation seems to be better because, although kids are very active and hard to control, he can educate them to follow his directions. Otherwise, the plan to go to the exhibition will be cancelled. Furthermore, he doesn't need to ask his friend to lend him a car. That's why I support trying using public transportation.

남자의 문제는 시내 전시회에 아이들을 데리고 갈 방법을 찾는 것이다. 그러나 그는 학교버스가 고장이 났다는 것을 발견한다. 여자는 일단 그의 친구로부터 차를 빌리라고 제안하지만 그는 친구의 차가 새 것이기 때문에 빌려주지 않을 것이라고 생각한다. 나는 비록 아이들이 매우 활동적이고 다루기 힘들더라도 지시에 따르도록 가르칠 수 있기 때문에 대중 교통을 이용하는 다른 대안책이 더 낫다고 생각한다. 그렇지 않으면, 전시회에 가는 계획은 취소될 것이다. 게다가, 그의 친구에게 차를 빌려달라고 물어볼 필요도 없다. 이것이 내가 대중 교통을 사용하는 방안을 지지하는 이유이다.

6

Listening

Now listen to part of a talk in a biology class.

P There are two theories behind the extinction of dinosaurs. The first theory supporting their extinction is related to the destruction of the food chain due to a meteor crash on the Earth. A meteor that crashed into the Earth created a dust ball so great that it blocked out the sunlight and destroyed all the plants. This caused the herbivores to die, and a decrease in herbivores meant no food for the carnivores. Due to such a disturbance in the food chain, dinosaurs ended up eating each other.

The second theory supporting the extinction of dinosaurs is the change in weather. When the meteor crashed into the Earth, it created a pile of dust that created carbon monoxide and polluted the air. The carbon monoxide created a massive greenhouse effect and global warming started to heat the Earth to great degrees. This change in weather due to the meteor crash caused the dinosaurs to become extinct because the Earth was uninhabitable. More specifically, the meteor crash caused a sudden increase in temperature that trapped air on the Earth and affected the dinosaur eggs. The increase in temperature caused the dinosaur eggs to hatch predominantly male. As a result, there was a lack of female dinosaurs for the males to mate with. These two theories generally state how the dinosaurs became extinct from Earth.

공룡의 멸종에 대한 두 가지 이론이 있습니다. 멸종을 뒷받침하는 첫 번째 이론은 운석이 지구와 충돌해서 먹이 사슬이 파괴된 것과 관련이 있습니다. 지구와 충돌한 운석은 거대한 먼지 덩어리를 생성했는데, 그 크기가 너무 거대해서 햇빛을 가리고 모든 식물들을 파괴했습니다. 이로 인해 초식 동물들이 죽게 되었고, 초식 동물의 감소는 육식 동물의 먹이가 없다는 것을 의미했습니다. 이와 같은 먹이 사슬의 파괴로 인해 공룡들은 결국 서로를 잡아먹게 되었습니다.
공룡의 멸종을 뒷받침하는 두 번째 이론은 날씨의 변화입니다. 운석이 지구와 충돌했을 때, 이산화탄소를 야기하는 거대한 먼지 덩어리를 만들었고 공기를 오염시켰습니다. 이산화탄소는 거대한 온실 효과를 초래했고, 지구 온난화는 지구를 엄청난 정도로 달구기 시작했습니다. 운석의 충돌로 인한 기후의 변화로 지구가 살 수 없게 되어 버렸기 때문에 공룡이 멸종되었습니다. 보다 자세히 말하자면, 운석의 충돌로 인해 지구를 감싸고 있던 공기의 온도가 갑작스럽게 상승해서 공룡 알에 영향을 미쳤습니다. 온도의 상승은 공룡의 알을 주로 수컷만 태어나게 했습니다. 그 결과, 수컷 공룡이 짝짓기 할 암컷 공룡이 부족하게 되었습니다. 일반적으로 이 두 가지 이론이 공룡이 지구상에서 멸종하게 된 이유를 말해줍니다.

Speaking

Using points and examples from the talk, explain the two different theories of how dinosaurs became extinct.

Possible response

The main topic of the lecture is the theory behind the extinction of the dinosaurs. The professor tells the students that there are two main factors which caused their extinction. The first factor is the lack of food due to the meteor crash which caused all the plants on the Earth to die, eventually killing off the dinosaurs. The second factor is intense heat and global warming due to air pollution from the meteor crash, which annihilated the living things on the Earth. The meteor crash trapped air on the Earth and caused an increase in temperature. As a result, dinosaur eggs were affected and primarily hatched male babies. As a result, dinosaurs had difficulty reproducing and eventually went extinct. The extinction of the dinosaurs is a good example of how species are destroyed by severe natural environments.

강의의 주제는 공룡의 멸종에 대한 이론이다. 교수는 학생들에게 공룡의 멸종을 야기한 두 가지 주요한 요인들에 대해서 말하고 있다. 첫 번째 요인은 운석이 지구에 충돌해서 모든 식물을 죽게 함으로써 먹이를 부족하게 해 결국 공룡을 죽게 한 것이다. 두 번째 요인은 운석의 충돌이 야기한 대기 오염으로, 강한 열과 지구 온난화를 일으켜 지구상의 생물들이 전멸한 것이다. 운석의 충돌은 지구의 대기에 공기를 가두고 온도 상승을 초래했다. 그 결과, 공룡의 알이 영향을 받아서 대부분 수컷 공룡을 부화하게 했다. 결과적으로, 공룡은 대를 잇지 못하고 결국 멸종하게 되었다. 공룡의 멸종은 생물의 종이 가혹한 자연 환경에 의해서 어떻게 파괴될 수 있는지를 보여주는 좋은 예이다.

Set 2

1 Which do you prefer to read — a novel, a magazine, or a poem in your spare time and why? Include specific details and examples to support your answer.

Possible response

I prefer reading a magazine during my free time for the following reasons. The first reason is that it is very rare that I have any free time and, when I do, it is only for a short time. I do not like to begin reading a novel that I know I'm not going to be able to finish. The second reason is that I follow sports regularly, and magazines help me stay up-to-date with all the stories in sports, such as soccer, volleyball, baseball, and basketball. These are the reasons I prefer reading magazines.

나는 다음과 같은 이유 때문에 여가 시간에 잡지를 읽는 것을 선호한다. 첫 번째 이유는 내가 여가 시간이 거의 없고, 있다 해도 짧기 때문이다. 나는 다 읽을 수 없을 것이라는 것을 아는 소설을 읽기 시작하는 것은 좋아하지 않는다. 두 번째 이유는 나는 정기적으로 스포츠 소식을 접하는데, 잡지를 통해서 축구, 배구, 야구, 농구와 같은 스포츠에 대한 모든 최신 정보를 얻을 수 있기 때문이다. 이와 같은 이유들로 나는 잡지를 읽는 것을 선호한다.

2 Some people like to eat their evening meal late, while others like to eat their evening meal early. Which do you think is better and why? Include specific details and examples to support your answer.

Possible response

Although some people enjoy having their evening meal late for some reasons, I think it is healthier for the body to eat the evening meal early. First, it is a good habit to get used to an early light dinner for healthy everyday life. If you eat late at night, you tend to sleep before your dinner has had a chance to be digested. Also, eating an early dinner could provide more free time to spend with one's family, and you can watch TV or talk about your day over tea together. So, I believe that eating an early dinner is a great way to be healthier and to have more time to bond with the family.

어떤 사람들은 몇 가지 이유로 저녁을 늦게 먹는 것을 좋아하지만, 나는 저녁을 일찍 먹는 것이 몸에 더 좋다고 생각한다. 우선, 건강한 일상을 위해 저녁을 일찍 먹는 것에 익숙해 지는 것이 좋은 습관이다. 밤 늦게 밥을 먹으면, 먹은 것이 소화되기 전에 잠자리에 들게 된다. 또한 저녁을 일찍 먹는 것은 가족과 함께 할 수 있는 더 많은 시간을 제공하며 함께 차를 마시면서 TV를 보거나 하루에 대해 이야기를 할 수 있다. 그래서 나는 저녁을 일찍 먹는 것

이 건강을 유지하고, 가족간의 유대를 돈독히 할 수 있는 시간을 가질 수 있는 좋은 방법이라고 생각한다.

3

Reading

A student wrote a letter to the editor of the school newspaper regarding the school's decision to take away the television screen in the student center rest area. Read the letter about taking away the television screen. You will have 45 seconds to read the letter. Begin reading now.

Disturbance in the Rest Area

I would like to make a statement about the rest area in the student center. The rest area has turned into a loud and crowded place to visit in-between class. I'd like to request that the school administration remove the big screen located in the rest area. The big television screen is becoming a disturbance for the students who would like to study between classes and have a quiet study time to themselves. By removing the big screen television, we would be able to control the noise level and the overcrowding in the rest area.

저는 학생 회관에 있는 휴게실에 관하여 언급하고자 합니다. 그 휴게실은 쉬는 시간에 매우 소란스럽고 붐비는 장소로 변했습니다. 저는 휴게실에 있는 대형 TV를 없애달라고 학교 당국에 요구하고자 합니다. 쉬는 시간에 공부하고, 혼자 조용히 공부할 시간을 갖길 원하는 학생들에게 대형 TV가 방해가 되고 있습니다. 대형 TV를 없애면 휴게실의 소란스러움과 혼잡함을 통제할 수 있을 것입니다.

Listening

Now listen to two students as they discuss the letter.

M I don't agree with this letter from the student. I feel that the rest area in the student center should have some entertainment for the students; after all, it is the rest area.

W Really? I've been to the rest area, and it was packed with students watching the highlights of last night's football game. It was just too noisy.

M Yeah, I understand what you're saying, but to get rid of the big screen television just because someone can't study in the rest area is unfair. Those students can go study in the library where it's quiet; students should be more responsible when it comes to issues like these.

W Well, I could hear them while I was approaching the rest area from the back entrance. That means people are too loud.

M You have a point there, but getting rid of the

television will only benefit those who study in the rest area. The rest area not only helps students rest, but it also unites students. The reason the rest area is so loud is because students are cheering for their school's sports teams.

W Now, I agree with you. Studying should be done in the library and resting should be done in the student center rest area.

M Absolutely!

남 난 이 학생의 편지에 동의하지 않아. 학생 회관에 있는 휴게실에 학생들을 위한 오락 시설이 있어야 한다고 생각해. 결국, 쉬는 공간이잖아.

여 정말? 나도 휴게실에 가 본 적이 있는데 지난 밤 미식축구 경기의 하이라이트를 보는 학생들로 꽉 차있었어. 너무 시끄러웠어.

남 그래. 무슨 말인지 알겠는데 누군가 휴게실에서 공부를 할 수 없다는 이유 때문에TV를 없애는 것은 공정하지 않다고 생각해. 그런 학생들은 조용한 도서관에서 공부할 수 있잖아. 이런 문제들에 대해서는 학생들이 좀 더 책임감이 있었으면 좋겠어.

여 글쎄, 뒷문을 통해서 휴게실 쪽으로 갈 때 사람들 소리를 들을 수 있었어. 학생들이 너무 시끄럽단 뜻이지.

남 네 말도 일리가 있지만 TV를 없애는 건 휴게실에서 공부하는 학생들에게만 이득이 될 거야. 휴게실은 단지 학생들이 휴식을 취하는 곳일 뿐만 아니라 학생들을 한데 뭉치게 하는 곳이야. 휴게실이 그렇게 시끄러운 이유는 학생들이 학교 스포츠팀을 응원하기 때문이야.

여 이제 너와 동감이야. 공부는 도서관에서 하고 휴식은 학생 회관의 휴게실에서 하면 되겠구나.

남 당연하지!

Speaking

The man expresses his opinion of the university's plan to take away the big screen television in the rest area. State his opinion and explain the reasons he gives for holding that opinion.

Possible response

The man is against the idea of the school taking the television screen out of the rest area. The first reason he disagrees with it is that the rest area is for resting, and some students prefer to watch television. If the students wanted to study, he feels that the library would be a more suitable environment. The second reason is that one of the purposes of the rest area is to provide a place for students to unite. By watching the big screen TV in the rest area, students can cheer for the school's sports teams together. These are the reasons he thinks that it is not a good idea to remove the television screen from the rest area.

남자는 학교가 휴게실에서 TV를 없애야 한다는 의견에 반대한다. 그가 반대하는 첫 번째 이유는 휴게실은 휴식을 위한 곳이고 일부 학생들은 TV를 보길 원하기 때문이다. 그는 만약 학생들이 공부를 하고 싶다면 도서관이 더 적당한 곳이라고 생각한다. 두 번째 이유는 휴게실의 목적 중 한 가지가 학생들을 단합하게 해주는 장소를 제공하는 것이기 때문이다. 휴게실에서 TV를 보면서 학생들은 함께 학교 스포츠팀을 응원할 수 있다. 이러한 이유로 그는 휴게실에서 TV를 없애는 것이 좋은 생각이라고 생각하지 않는다.

 4

Reading

Now read the passage about credibility. You will have 45 seconds to read the passage. Begin reading now.

Credibility

When people make a speech, there are certain ways to build credibility. In a public speech, the speaker must be knowledgeable about the topic he or she is talking about. Also, the speaker must have confidence in the topic and exude this to the audience. If a speaker has vast knowledge about a subject, but does not come off as confident, the speaker appears like he or she does not know much about the topic at hand. And of course, it doesn't hurt for the speaker to be charismatic.

사람들이 연설을 할 때, 신뢰를 형성할 수 있는 특정한 방법들이 있다. 대중 연설에서는 연설자는 자신이 말하는 주제에 대한 지식이 풍부해야 한다. 또한 연설자는 주제에 대한 확신을 갖고 이것을 청중에게 발산해야 한다. 만약 연설자가 그 주제에 대하여 많은 지식을 갖고 있지만 확신이 없게 비춰진다면 다루고 있는 주제에 대해 잘 알지 못하는 것처럼 보인다. 또한 연설자에게 카리스마가 있어서 나쁠 것은 없다.

Listening

Now listen to part of a lecture in a public speaking class. The professor talks about credibility.

P OK, so we said when somebody makes a public speech, credibility is very important. Which professions can you think of that involves a lot of public announcements or speeches and where trust is very important? How about politics! Credibility can make all the difference in the world of politics. Voters want to vote for the best candidate who builds rapport with them. Voters also want to be able to trust the promises that politicians make. For example, a lady named Sarah Marx ran for mayor. She was a financial manager of a company so she knew a lot about finances. At the time, the city was facing a huge financial problem. Sarah had a wealth of knowledge about finance, and was well suited to handle financial problems due to her knowledge and expertise. But, she did not exude confidence in her public speaking. Later, Sarah looked at her speech video and realized she looked down while she was speaking. She realized that this small thing could make the difference in building credibility with her audience. Sarah started looking at the eyes of her audience in her following speeches and the result was positive. In the end, Sarah won the election.

자, 누군가가 대중에게 연설을 할 때 신뢰성은 매우 중요하다고 언급했었죠. 대중 공지나 연설을 많이 하고 신뢰가 중요하게 여겨지는 직업으로 어떤 것이 생각나나요? 정치는 어떤가요! 정치의 세계에서는 신뢰성이 큰 영향을 미칠 수 있어요. 유권자들은 그들과 교감을 이루는 후보자를 투표하고 싶어해요. 유권자들은 또한 정치가들이 하는 약속들을 믿을 수 있길 원하죠. 예를 들어, Sarah Marx라는 여성이 시장 선거에 출마했어요. 그녀는 회사의 경리 부장이었기 때문에 재정에 대해 잘 알고 있었어요. 그 당시 도시는 큰 재정적 문제를 직면하고 있었어요. Sarah는 재정에 대한 지식이 많았고, 자신의 지식과 전문성 때문에 재정 문제를 해결할 적임자로 여겨졌죠. 그러나 그녀는 대중 연설에서 자신감을 보여주지 못했어요. 후에 그녀는 비디오로 자신이 연설하는 모습을 보고 자신이 연설을 하면서 아래를 내려다 본다는 것을 알게 되었어요. 그녀는 이처럼 사소한 것이 청중에게 신뢰감을 주는데 영향을 미칠 수 있다는 것을 깨닫게 되었죠. Sarah는 이어지는 연설에서 청중을 바라보기 시작했고, 결과는 긍정적이었어요. 결국 그녀는 선거에서 당선되었어요.

Speaking

Using points and examples from the lecture, explain how politics is related to credibility.

Possible response

The professor discusses ways in which politics and credibility are related. Credibility plays an important role in public speaking, especially in politics because voters vote for candidates whom they feel they can trust; therefore, building up their rapport and credibility with the voters can make all the difference in the world. The professor explains their relationship through the example of Sarah Marx. As qualified as she was for mayor, she did not have a lot of credibility with the public because she would look down when she gave speeches, and thus, showed a lack of confidence. She started looking into the eyes of the audience during her speeches and eventually won the election. The professor explains how politics is related to credibility through this example.

교수는 정치와 신뢰성이 어떻게 연관되는지에 대해 이야기하고 있다. 신뢰성은 대중 연설특히 정치에서 중요한 역할을 한다. 유권자들이 그들이 믿을 수 있다고 생각하는 후보에게 투표하기 때문이다. 따라서 유권자와 교감을 이루고 신뢰를 쌓는 것은 큰 영향을 미칠 수 있다. 교수는 이러한 관계를 Sarah Marx의 예를 통해 이야기한다. 그녀는 시장으로서의 자격이 있었지만, 연설을 할 때 고개를 숙여 바닥을 보았기 때문에 자신감을 보여주지 못했다. 이로 인해 그녀는 대중으로부터 많은 신뢰를 쌓지 못했다. 그녀는 연설하는 동안 관중과 눈을 맞추기 시작했으며 마침내 선거에서 당선되었다. 교수는 이 예를 통해 정치와 신뢰성간의 관계에 대해 설명한다.

5

Listening

Now listen to a conversation between two students.

W Hey, Thomas, how are you?

M I'm pretty good. How about you?

W I'm OK, but I've been stressed out recently.

M Why, what happened?

W It's just this internship we're doing. It takes up a lot of hours but doesn't pay too much. I am struggling to pay for tuition.

M Yeah, I know what you're saying. But it is an internship... we're lucky to be getting paid at all.

W Yeah, I know, but I'm barely able to make ends meet right now, and that's just with eating twice a day.

M I understand. Why don't you ask the manager for an increase in pay? I know I sure could use some extra money myself.

W Ha, ha, I know you could. But you're right, we're lucky to be getting paid at all and I don't want to look unappreciative. This internship is in very high demand; we were lucky to get this position in the first place.

M That's true. Have you thought about getting a part-time job on the side?

W Yeah I have, but with this internship and my studies, I barely have enough time as is. Well, that's life, I guess. I'll have to figure out what I'm going to do.

여 안녕, Thomas, 어떻게 지내니?
남 잘 지내. 너는?
여 별일은 없는데, 최근에 스트레스를 많이 받고 있어.
남 왜, 무슨 일이야?
여 우리가 하고 있는 인턴쉽 때문이야. 근무 시간은 긴데 월급이 많지 않잖아. 학비를 내기가 힘들어.
남 그래, 무슨 말인지 알겠어. 하지만 이건 인턴쉽이잖아... 돈을 조금이라도 받을 수 있다는 게 다행이야.
여 그래. 나도 알지만 지금 근근히 생활하고 있거든. 하루에 겨우 두 끼를 먹는데도 그래.
남 이해해. 매니저에게 월급을 올려달라고 해보는 건 어때? 나도 돈을 좀 더 받으면 유용할 것 같거든.
여 하하, 그렇겠지. 하지만 네 말이 맞아. 돈을 조금이라도 받아서 다행이고, 감사할 줄 모르는 사람으로 보이긴 싫어. 이 인턴쉽은 경쟁이 치열해서 들어오게 된 것만 해도 행운이니까.
남 맞아. 부업으로 아르바이트를 구하는 건 생각해봤니?
여 응, 하지만 인턴쉽과 공부만으로도 시간이 거의 없어. 그게 인생이겠지. 어떻게 해야 할지 생각해봐야 겠어.

Speaking

The students discuss two possible solutions to the woman's problem. Describe the problem. Then state which of the two solutions you prefer and explain why.

Possible response

The woman's problem is that she is not making enough money from the internship. The man first suggests that she try and ask for an increase in salary. But the woman does not want to look unappreciative and lose her job because it is in very high demand. It is especially true because many people wanted to get the position. I think that the idea of getting a second job is better than asking for a raise for the internship because an internship is more about job experience rather than money. The importance of an internship is learning practical knowledge and using the experience for the future. So, I support getting a second job to get the money she needs for school and living expenses.

여자의 문제는 그녀가 인턴쉽으로부터 돈을 충분히 벌지 못한다는 것이다. 남자는 먼저 임금 인상을 요구하라고 제안한다. 하지만 여자는 인턴쉽의 경쟁이 치열하기 때문에 감사할 줄 모르는 사람으로 보여서 직장을 잃기를 원하지 않는다. 많은 사람들이 이 직장을 원했기 때문이다. 나는 인턴쉽의 월급 인상을 요구하는 것보다 부업을 구하는 것이 낫다고 생각한다. 인턴쉽은 돈을 위한 것이기 보다는 직장 경험을 위한 것이기 때문이다. 인턴쉽의 중요성은 실질적인 지식을 얻어서 미래에 그 경험을 이용하는 것이다. 그래서 나는 학비와 생활비를 위해 다른 아르바이트를 더 하나 구하는 것이 낫다고 생각한다.

6

Listening

Now listen to part of a talk in a biology class.

P We've been talking about instinctive animal behavior. Today, I'd like to talk about the animal imprinting on baby geese and kittens. Konrad Lorenz, an Austrian zoologist and animal psychologist who studied instinctive behavior in animals, stated that cats and geese have a special period in development when they are first born. Lorenz observed that the young of birds, such as geese, spontaneously followed their mothers from almost the first day after they were hatched. He called this process imprinting. According to Lorenz, imprinting is a fast and natural process that occurs early in specie's life.

On the other hand, he observed helplessness in cats in their young stage. The newborn infant is wholly dependent on its parents. Since mammals are dependent on their mothers for nourishment, guidance and protection, it is important that the infant not lose their mothers. This phenomenon of imprinting that Lorenz has explored ensures that, in normal circumstances, the infant forms an attachment to its mother and never moves too far away. Baby kittens cling onto their mothers for food and for protection against predators.

동물의 본능적 행동에 대해서 논의하고 있었는데, 오늘은 새끼 거위와 고양이의 각인 현상에 대해서 이야기 해 보겠습니다. 동물의 본능적 행동을 연구해온 오스트리아 출신 동물학자이자 동물 심리학자인

Konrad Lorenz는 고양이와 거위가 처음 태어났을 때 발달 과정에 있어서 특별한 기간이 있다고 언급했습니다. Lorenz는 거위와 같은 새끼 새들이 부화한 첫날부터 어미를 따른다는 것을 관찰했습니다. 그는 이런 과정을 각인이라고 불렀습니다. Lorenz에 따르면 각인 현상은 생물체의 생애 초기에 일어나는 빠르고 자연스러운 과정이라고 합니다.

반면에 어린 고양이들에게서는 무력함을 관찰했습니다. 새로 태어난 고양이는 부모에게 전적으로 의존합니다. 포유류는 먹이를 얻고, 안내를 받고, 보호를 받기 위해 어미에게 의지하기 때문에 새끼가 어미를 잃지 않는 것이 중요합니다. Lorenz가 각인에 대해서 경험한 이러한 현상은 정상적인 환경에서 새끼가 어미에게 애정을 형성하고 결코 멀리 떨어지지 않는다는 사실을 확인해 주었습니다. 새끼 고양이는 먹이를 얻고 포식자들로부터 자신을 보호하기 위해 어미로부터 떨어지지 않습니다.

Speaking

Using points and examples from the talk, explain the two different examples of imprinting in the geese and the cat.

Possible response

The main topic of the lecture is imprinting in baby cats and geese. What I gathered from this lecture is that baby geese are born with the ability to follow the thing that it sees first when it is born. It imprints the first animal it sees and thinks it is its mother. For example, geese instinctively followed their mothers from the first day after they are hatched. He also pointed out that baby cats have a great deal of attachment to their mothers because they are dependent as infants. And this form of imprinting is seen in cats until they grow older. These are some of the important points stated by the professor regarding the imprinting of animals.

강의의 주제는 새끼 고양이와 거위의 각인 현상이다. 이 강의로부터 내가 배운 것은 새끼 거위가 태어났을 때 처음으로 본 것을 따라가는 능력을 가지고 태어난다는 것이다. 그것은 처음 보는 동물을 각인하고 어미라고 생각한다. 예를 들어, 거위는 본능적으로 부화한 바로 다음날부터 그들의 어미를 따라다녔다. 교수는 또한 새끼 고양이는 어릴 때 의존적이기 때문에 어미에게 강한 애착을 갖는다고 지적했다. 또한 이러한 형태의 각인은 고양이가 자랄 때까지 보여진다. 이것이 교수가 동물의 각인 현상에 대해서 언급한 중요한 요점들이다.

MEMO

MEMO